THE GREATER EAST ASIA
CO-PROSPERITY SPHERE

Studies of the Weatherhead East Asian Institute, Columbia University

The Studies of the Weatherhead East Asian Institute of Columbia University were inaugurated in 1962 to bring to a wider public the results of significant new research on modern and contemporary East Asia.

THE GREATER EAST ASIA CO-PROSPERITY SPHERE

When Total Empire Met Total War

Jeremy A. Yellen

CORNELL UNIVERSITY PRESS   ITHACA AND LONDON

First published 2019 by Cornell University Press

Library of Congress Cataloging-in-Publication Data

Names: Yellen, Jeremy A., 1977– author.
Title: The Greater East Asia Co-Prosperity Sphere : when total
    empire met total war / Jeremy A. Yellen.
Description: Ithaca [New York] : Cornell University Press, 2019. |
    Series: Studies of the Weatherhead East Asian Institute,
    Columbia University | Includes bibliographical references and index.
Identifiers: LCCN 2018047982 (print) | LCCN 2018052346 (ebook) |
    ISBN 9781501735554 (e-book pdf) | ISBN 9781501735561 (e-book epub/mobi) |
    ISBN 9781501735547 | ISBN 9781501735547 (hardcover)
Subjects: LCSH: Greater East Asia Co-prosperity Sphere—History. | Japan—
    Relations—East Asia. | East Asia—Relations—Japan. | Japan—Relations—
    Philippines. | Philippines—Relations—Japan. | Japan—Relations—Burma. |
    Burma—Relations—Japan. | Japan—History—20th century.
Classification: LCC DS889.5 (ebook) | LCC DS889.5 .Y45 2019 (print) |
    DDC 940.53/5—dc23
LC record available at https://lccn.loc.gov/2018047982

Contents

Acknowledgments

This book has been a labor of love, and at times extreme frustration. As a transnational study of Japan's wartime empire, it relied on help from a transnational group of scholars, archivists, librarians, and friends and family to whom my deepest thanks are owed. First and foremost, my deepest thanks to my family. My parents and grandparents always encouraged my inquisitive nature, even if it took me in directions they could not imagine. Most importantly, this work would never have come to fruition without the constant support of my partner, Sasha, who never stopped making fun of my insane mission to write a book on Japan's wartime empire. Tsumugi, our son, injected much-needed levity into the process and provided a wonderful distraction from the writing process. Without the two of you, writing this book would not have been such a rewarding experience.

I owe a great intellectual debt to the mentors and friends who helped me grow as a historian, and whose concerns shaped this project over the years. I owe my biggest intellectual debt to Andrew Gordon, who guided this project with a light hand but never failed to pose incisive questions and to provide extensive comments that helped me develop my ideas. Further, I would not be a historian of Japan were it not for Kenneth Pyle and the late Jim Palais, both of whom inspired me to think historically and to continue my graduate studies at the doctoral level. I would also like to thank Mickey Adolphson, Fred Dickinson, Niall Ferguson, Tom Havens, Erez Manela, Peter Mauch, Ian Miller, Janis Mimura, Dick Samuels, and Franziska Seraphim for reading and providing valuable advice on earlier versions of this study.

Equally importantly, I also benefited greatly from a group of scholars across Asia. Nojima (Katō) Yōko took me in as a research student and introduced me to primary documents as well as important secondary sources. The most unexpected form of support came from Mori Shigeki, who answered numerous questions I had on Japanese political history. In fact, he came to our first meeting at a café armed with a three-page list of all the books and articles I needed to read in order to understand the Greater East Asia Co-Prosperity Sphere. This was a kindness I still appreciate today. Iokibe Kaoru gave me an institutional home in the Institute of Social Science at the University of Tokyo, offered opportunities to present my work, and generously helped me secure a grant to continue research in Tokyo. Suzuki Tamon and Kokubu Kōji both introduced me to new sources and helped me navigate the world of Japanese academe. The late Lydia Yu-Jose provided an affiliation at Ateneo de Manila University and helped me gain access to a variety of archives in metro Manila. Finally, I want to thank Adachi Hiroaki and Kawanishi Kōsuke for sharing their own excellent work on Japan's Co-Prosperity Sphere with me at a critical stage of my writing process.

I would also like to thank the archivists and librarians who made this research less daunting and more enjoyable than I could have ever hoped. This project was born at Harvard and took me on a journey across Asia. In the process, I relied on the tireless assistance from archivists in Cambridge, Tokyo, Washington, London, Manila, Yangon, Kolkata, and Hong Kong. In particular, I would like to express my most sincere appreciation for the archivists and librarians at the Harvard-Yenching Library, the National Diet Library, the Ministry of Foreign Affairs Diplomatic Records Office, the National Institute for Defense Studies, the British Library, the National Archives of the United Kingdom, the José P. Laurel Memorial Library, the National Library of the Philippines, the Library of Congress, the National Archives Department (Yangon), and the University Library at the Chinese University of Hong Kong, where many of my best ideas emerged.

I have been fortunate to be among a fantastic group of fellow travelers and writers who often had a preternatural ability to distract me from my studies. While at Harvard, Javier Cha, Nick Kapur, Konrad Lawson, John Lee, Stefan Link, Shi-Lin Loh, Johan Mathew, Motokazu Matsutani, Sreemati Mitter, Sean O'Reilly, Danny Orbach, Julie Stephens, and Heidi and Michael Tworek often pulled me away from my desk to more pleasurable pursuits. A special thank-you goes to Tariq Ali, who always knew how to keep me inspired while at Harvard. Finally, the Department of Japanese Studies at the Chinese University of Hong Kong has offered a wonderful scholarly home and a place to finish this project. I am particularly thankful for research assistance from Ann Lui and Hanako Negishi as I completed revisions.

This book took its final form thanks to the tireless efforts of Emily Andrew and the staff at Cornell University Press. I appreciate Emily's continued belief in this project and her willingness to read chapters even before I submitted the manuscript for review. Emily also put me in touch with cartographer Mike Bechthold, who produced the wonderful map of Greater East Asia. Moreover, the blind review process was a fantastic experience. The three anonymous reviewers gave excellent constructive criticisms and pointed out important weaknesses in my arguments. Moreover, one anonymous reviewer went above and beyond the call of duty, pointing out simple ways to reframe my arguments in a more persuasive manner. Any faults or errors that remain, however, are exclusively my responsibility.

Finally, I would like to thank the academic foundations and groups that provided generous financial support for this project. This project took off owing to support from the Edwin O. Reischauer Institute of Japanese Studies, the Asia Center, the South Asia Initiative, and the History Department at Harvard University, which sent me across the world in search of documents. My dissertation research was supported by the Fulbright Institute of International Education (IIE) as well as the Japan Society for the Promotion of Science. Since coming to Hong Kong, book revisions and additional research were supported in part by a direct grant from the Chinese University of Hong Kong and a generous grant from the Research Grants Council of the Hong Kong Special Administrative Region, China (Project No. CUHK 24610615). The publication of this book was aided through a generous publication subvention fund from the Chinese University of Hong Kong.

A Note on Names, Transliterations, and Translations

When writing Japanese names, this book follows the Japanese practice of placing the surname first, followed by the given name. Exceptions to this convention are made only when Japanese authors of publications in English have put their names in Western order. This book transliterates Japanese-language words using the modified Hepburn system. The only exceptions to this are with widely recognized names like Tokyo, Kyoto, and Osaka. Finally, the translations from Japanese and Spanish are all mine unless otherwise indicated.

MAP. Japan's wartime empire, 1942

THE GREATER EAST ASIA
CO-PROSPERITY SPHERE

Introduction

WHEN TOTAL EMPIRE MET
TOTAL WAR

Rarely has a minor skirmish had such far-reaching consequences. Late at night on July 7, 1937, the Imperial Japanese Army, while holding training maneuvers, clashed with Chinese forces near the Marco Polo Bridge on the outskirts of Beiping (present-day Beijing).[1] Exactly what happened is unclear. At some point in the pitch-black night, mysterious shots were fired on the Japanese forces. A subsequent roll call revealed one soldier to be missing. The absent soldier soon returned, but Japanese commanders mistakenly presumed that the soldier had been captured by the Chinese and demanded the right to search the nearby town of Wanping. The Chinese side refused. The following day, fighting broke out between the two sides. What might otherwise have remained a localized conflict spiraled out of control. Chiang Kai-shek ordered a full-scale mobilization of the Nationalist regime in August 1937. Japan responded by rushing fresh equipment and troops to the mainland in the hopes of overwhelming both Nationalist and Communist forces. But such hopes were soon dashed. By early 1938, after the brutal seizures of both Shanghai and Nanjing, it became clear that Chinese forces were committed to the battle against Japan. Thus began the Second Sino-Japanese War (the China Incident, as Tokyo labeled it), an undesired and undeclared total war that inspired subsequent Japanese efforts to create a new order in Greater East Asia.

This was the true beginning of World War II in Asia. Before 1937, it may have been possible for Japan to avoid a total war for regional ascendancy. But each successive step taken from that fateful moment in July 1937—most taken to end

1

the China war—brought Japan closer to an all-out war with the Allied powers. On the domestic front, hard-liners in the military, the foreign ministry, and the political parties played more vocal roles in the policy arena, bringing about an authoritarian political system and a command economy to meet the needs of total war. Military officers further encroached in governmental life, occupying many key positions previously held by civilian elites. And policy making became geared toward the increasingly onerous burden of wartime mobilization. The creation of the imperial general headquarters–government liaison conferences in November 1937 ensured that top-level policy making centered on war-related issues.[2] These liaison conferences served as the stage for fights among army and navy elites for policy influence, where displays of bluster and strength and hot-headed war cries oftentimes overrode caution and prudence.

Developments on the foreign front, too, tilted toward global war. Prime Minister Konoe Fumimaro's refusal from January 1938 to deal with China's Nationalist regime and his venomous call for the regime's annihilation destroyed any remaining hopes of ending the war in China. His November 1938 declaration of a New Order in East Asia signaled a decisive break with the system of cooperative relations in East Asia and generated suspicions in Washington, London, and Moscow. By the summer of 1940, the Nazi juggernaut in Europe offered Japan a unique opportunity to advance south into the resource-rich territories of Southeast Asia. Advancing south and extending Japan's new order to Greater East Asia was seen as a win-win scenario: it would close off routes of aid to the Chiang regime while also providing critical materiel for Japan's war in China. From this point on, the logic of expansion trumped more moderate concerns. In September 1940 Japan joined Germany and Italy in the Tripartite Pact. Now allied to the hegemonic power in Europe, Tokyo pushed for ascendancy in Southeast Asia and the resources needed to end its war in China. Each subsequent move, from aggressive negotiations to the occupation of French Indochina, pressed Japan ever closer to global war. The descent into war was consummated on December 8, 1941 (December 7 in the United States), with surprise attacks on Pearl Harbor and across Southeast Asia. Although there was no direct path from the Marco Polo Bridge to Pearl Harbor, the incident in China set off a chain of events that led to war for hegemony in the Asia-Pacific.

The war in China also became the stepping-stone for grander visions of international order. Although Greek philosopher Heraclitus perhaps exaggerated when he called war "the father of all and the king of all," war has often fathered new visions for global politics.[3] The Napoleonic Wars and World War I, for instance, led to the reordering of international relations. World War I provided the stage for U.S. president Woodrow Wilson's dramatic entrance into world politics in 1918. Preaching a new, moral diplomacy, Wilson repudiated the imperialist order and sought to fashion a political system that would prevent future conflicts. In East Asia, this took shape in the 1920s as the Versailles-Washington system. Less than two decades later, Japanese leaders engaged in a similar process. Drunk on hard-fought victories and rapid expansion, they attempted to use the turning point of the China Incident to cast off what they saw as the inequities within global politics. The Versailles-Washington system, many argued, used lofty-sounding principles to preserve a status quo that benefited established empires over rising powers such as Japan. With war in China in full swing, a revolt against the old order was imminent. This revolt culminated in the creation of the Greater East Asia Co-Prosperity Sphere, the subject of this book.

Chaos in Europe gave Konoe confidence in Japan's revolt. With Nazi Germany ascendant in Europe, Japan's prime minister decided to make an announcement of his own. Konoe took to the airwaves on July 23, 1940, the day after his second cabinet assumed office, to reveal a bold new posture in foreign affairs. "In the realm of foreign policy," he thundered, "[Japan] must wholeheartedly maintain the Empire's own standpoint and walk the Empire's own path. Walking our own path by no means implies a passive, independent foreign policy. It does not mean simply responding to global changes. Instead, we must be resolved to lead these global changes and to use our power to create the world's new order. Consequently, foreign policy should not be swayed by developments right before our eyes. We must always consider ten to twenty—even fifty—years into the future."[4]

This desire to lead global changes reflected a radical shift in Japanese history. Since Japan's modern revolution in 1868, Japanese leaders worked to transform their nation into an equal with the "civilized" nations of the West. The pursuit of empire after 1868 in part emerged out of this desire to join the ranks of the other great powers. Only in possessing a colonial empire would Japan become a "first-class nation," the equal of Great Britain and the United States. Japanese leaders thus became model players in the Game of Empires, and they retooled their country's domestic institutions to best compete in international politics.[5] So successful were they that by the early twentieth century, Japan had defeated imperial Russia in a major war. By 1905, Japan had emerged as a regional power and had taken its first steps toward great power status.

By the late 1930s, however, the situation had dramatically changed. The West appeared to be in decline, with U.S. and British dominance in political-economic affairs in jeopardy. The global economic crash of 1929 hinted at the failure of liberal capitalism, and successive international crises offered evidence for the crumbling of Anglo-American power. The old order of the Versailles-Washington system appeared to be at a turning point, where it would be supplanted by a new vanguard coalition of fascist powers. At this point, Japan's imperial dreams remanifested as dreams for centrality in international affairs. Political figures, intellectual leaders, and the mass media spoke of a "great turning point" (*dai tenkanki*) in world history. Japan could finally shape its own destiny through the creation of a "new order" (*shinchitsujo*), a regional political-economic bloc over which Japan reigned supreme. Engaging in such a project, many thought, had world-historical significance. Imagining a new order wrapping across Asia represented not only the peak of Japan's imperial dreams but also the desire to bring Japan to the center of global history.

Japanese dreams for a new order took their final shape as the Greater East Asia Co-Prosperity Sphere. Foreign minister Matsuoka Yōsuke declared the Sphere in an August 1940 radio address that was intended to explain Japan's foreign policy. As he explained in a book published in May 1941, establishing this new order necessitated "the liberation of the peoples of the Orient from the shackles of Western Europe" and ridding the region of "the white race bloc." Only with the West ousted from Asia could Japan spread its family-state norms throughout the region and sow the seeds of Asian prosperity.[6] By July 1941, the Co-Prosperity Sphere had become the central goal of national policy, a goal that dominated discourse until the war's end in 1945.

Matsuoka declared the Co-Prosperity Sphere with all the fanfare and theatricality he could muster, but it initially amounted to little more than an abstract slogan. It was only after the Pacific War had begun in December 1941 that the Sphere began to take on new life. On December 10, 1941, two days after the Pearl Harbor attack, a liaison conference decided to name the conflict the Greater East Asia War. This new name reflected the fact that Japan was waging "a war that aims to construct a New Order in Greater East Asia."[7] It further legitimized the Greater East Asia Co-Prosperity Sphere as Japan's national policy and central war aim. Prime Minister Tōjō Hideki stated it best in a speech made before the House of Peers on January 21, 1942. "The Empire at present, with might and main . . . is pushing forward with the grand undertaking of establishing the Greater East Asia Co-Prosperity Sphere." This "order of co-existence and co-prosperity," he further noted, "will let all the nations and peoples of Greater East Asia take their proper place."[8]

Strikingly, however, even after making the Co-Prosperity Sphere the end goal of Japan's war, leading policy makers were still unclear as to what the term implied. At a liaison conference on February 28, 1942, none other than Prime Minister Tōjō—the man tasked with the responsibility for constructing the Co-Prosperity Sphere—felt it necessary to ask, "What's the difference between the national defense sphere (*kokubōken*) and the co-prosperity sphere (*kyōeiken*)?" What is even more astonishing than the question was the lack of any real response. Cabinet planning board president Suzuki Teiichi and army ministry Bureau of Military Affairs director Mutō Akira could not give Tōjō a clear answer.[9] Suzuki confused the issue even further when he replied that a resource sphere (*shigenken*) was "approximately the same thing as a co-prosperity sphere." The liaison conference members agreed to resolve this through further study of natural resources.[10] In this sense, Japan's new order resembled Hitler's. Both states did not enter the war with clearly defined ideas for economic order. In fact, Reich minister of propaganda Joseph Goebbels bluntly dismissed Nazi Germany's poverty of thought on the future European economic zone. "When the time comes," he told newspapermen on April 5, 1940, "we will know very well what we want."[11]

But necessity bred imagination. The raging war in the Asia-Pacific forced Japan to breathe new life into the Co-Prosperity Sphere. As the military advanced across Asia, intellectuals and policy makers imagined what would happen in the war's aftermath. Visions of order followed the Rising Sun battle flag. By mid-1942, as the Japanese Empire swelled in size, political intellectuals imagined the Co-Prosperity Sphere as stretching across the polities now dominated by Japan. They envisioned a new type of political-economic order, one that reached from the cold northern woods of Sakhalin to the southern tropics of the Netherlands Indies, from the Philippine archipelago to the jungles and deltas of Burma. The Sphere, many argued, was a project of "historical necessity" (*rekishiteki hitsuzensei*) that would bring Japan to the center of global history. Yet these dreams for centrality in global affairs withered and died as swiftly as they rose. By 1945, the deteriorating war situation and an enfeebled military had killed any chance of Japan surviving the war with its newfound empire intact.

This book explores the Greater East Asia Co-Prosperity Sphere, Japan's ambitious attempt to create a new order in East and Southeast Asia. The story of the Co-Prosperity Sphere is transnational and multifaceted, in many ways as sprawling as the empire it sought to encompass. But behind that expansive story there is a kind of order, and that order is my concern. The Co-Prosperity Sphere must be understood as more than a simple economic bloc, a slogan for Japanese imperialism and regional control, or the ultimate expression of a virulent Pan-Asian ideology. It was also a reaction to the challenges of diplomacy and empire in the post–World War I era, and a sincere attempt to envision a new type of political and economic order for the region during a time of global crisis. It epitomized Japan's revolt against the old order and attempt to build Asia anew—to establish centrality in regional affairs and world history. Further, although it was highly oppressive and domineering, the Co-Prosperity Sphere also featured active cooperation of nationalist elites across the region. To understand the Sphere, it is thus necessary to locate it in its proper transnational context and to pair stories of Japanese high policy with its reception in the periphery of Japan's wartime empire.

The Greater East Asia Co-Prosperity Sphere is best understood as a contested, negotiated process of envisioning the future during a time of total war. Moreover, this process occurred both in Japan and across Asia. For Japan, the story of the Greater East Asia Co-Prosperity Sphere is the story of imagining centrality within a pan-regional empire that was to take shape after the war's end. But since it depended on success in a war Japan had little chance of winning, the Sphere never consolidated into a true ideology—a consistent way of looking at the world or of ordering public affairs and private lives. It was constantly in flux. When Japan's wartime fortunes were on the rise, its principles were hazy and vague or subject to debates among core agencies, thinkers, and policy makers. Policy makers only agreed on central goals for the Sphere from 1943, by which time the specter of defeat loomed on the horizon. Even so, those goals were only partially implemented, and they were optimistically used by non-Japanese leaders for their own national ends. For Japan, then, the Sphere was a failed process of representing the future.

This book also focuses on the responses of Southeast Asian elites in the colonial capitals of two "independent" dependencies of Japan's wartime empire: Burma and the Philippines. Japanese wartime rule was brutal, oppressive, and domineering. But for elites in Rangoon and Manila, too, the Greater East Asia Co-Prosperity Sphere also brought opportunity. The Sphere provided the backdrop against which they imagined national futures of decolonization and independence after the war. Burmese and Philippine elites in the colonial capitals thus collaborated as caretaker for newly independent regimes. They pursued statebuilding efforts and gained broader experience in national governance, and in the process they strove to co-opt Japan's wartime empire for anticolonial ends.

Unequal Partners

Why Burma and the Philippines? Despite their vast historical and cultural differences, both Southeast Asian countries share much from which a comparative historian can draw. Their shared experiences of colonialism and similar position within Japan's wartime empire make them perfect lenses through which to study the Co-Prosperity Sphere.

First, both countries had a similar colonial past. The initial wars of conquest by the British and Americans inflicted misery and atrocities comparable to other colonial regimes. But Burma and the Philippines were both lucky in one sense: they were colonized by liberal empires that granted a degree of political autonomy. Great Britain, Burma's colonial master since 1885, allowed for popular participation in government beginning with the Morley-Minto reforms in 1909 and the diarchy system of tutelary democracy in 1923. The United States had done much the same toward the Philippines. The Jones Law, passed in 1916, ensured Philippine control over the legislative branch, composed of a senate and a house of representatives. By the mid-1930s, both colonies were granted further constitutional advances. The Tydings-McDuffie Act of 1934 gave the Philippines a cabinet government and set a 1946 deadline for independence. And the Government of Burma Act of 1935 provided for cabinet government and a bicameral legislature. By November 1939 the governor of Burma, Sir Archibald Douglas Cochrane, signaled that the endpoint of Burmese governmental progress was dominion status, the complete self-rule given primarily to Britain's white colonies.[12] Burma's British overlords were vague about when they would grant full self-rule, but there were clear trends toward a further constitutional advance.

This similarity in status was not lost on contemporaries. According to former governor-general of Burma Sir Reginald Dorman-Smith, one U.S. observer, Col. John Christian, wrote that with the single exception of the Philippines, "no tropical appendage of any great power enjoyed a greater degree of autonomy than did Burma." Dorman-Smith reacted to this statement in his unpublished memoirs: "Personally, I am not so sure that this was not an understatement." To the contrary, he insisted that "when all the window-dressings had been taken away, Burma did in fact enjoy greater autonomy than the Philippines."[13] Whatever we make of their debate, one point is crystal clear. Viewed from the late 1930s, both Burma and the Philippines appeared to competent observers as on similar trajectories toward self-rule.

Second, both countries maintained similar positions of independence within Japan's Co-Prosperity Sphere. Imperial policy makers in Tokyo saw no long-term benefit to direct colonial control. In seizing the Philippines, imperial general staff and cabinet members alike sought to oust U.S. power from East Asia. The attack on Burma, however, was initially seen as a way to prevent British and American aid from propping up the Chiang Kai-shek regime in Chongqing. Once occupied, however, both regimes were not important enough to retain as colonies—their real importance was symbolic. As the tides of war turned against Japan in 1943, Japanese policy makers turned both regimes into symbols of Japan's good intentions. Seeking to rally Asia behind the war and striving to end the conflict on favorable terms, Japan granted nominal independence to Burma on August 1 and to the Philippines on October 14, 1943.

The independence they received was nominal at best. Granting "full independence" to both countries, as Hatano Sumio writes, "was inconceivable."[14] Instead, Japan enacted independence in a way that preserved Japanese leadership and control while providing the flexibility to wage war across Asia.[15] On the very same day it bequeathed independence, Japan forced both countries to sign secret military agreements that gave the Japanese military freedom to act with impunity. The military could control anything deemed necessary for military action—from factories to labor, airfields to ports, and communication facilities to police affairs. Foreign observers were thus correct in spirit when they referred to the "independent" states in Japan's Co-Prosperity Sphere as "puppet governments."

Third, both regimes reacted to Japanese occupation and nation building in remarkably similar ways. Granted, the Philippines and Burma met their occupations with varying degrees of enthusiasm. Philippine leaders for the most part feared the Japanese arrival and served as a caretaker government to preserve longer-term independence. Moreover, the Philippine archipelago witnessed the fiercest and most sweeping anti-Japanese guerrilla resistance movement in Southeast Asia. Burmese nationalist and Thakin leaders, on the other hand, embraced Japan to oust their British colonial masters. In the initial phases of the war, the Burmese guerrillas were more pro- than anti-Japanese. Despite these differences, the realities on the ground led nationalist elites in the colonial capitals to collaborate in similar ways. Leaders in both Manila and Rangoon, some more willingly than others, received the Japanese occupation with open arms. But they did so with their eyes to the future, hoping to achieve or preserve longer-term political freedom. Once they gained nominal independence, each regime pushed forward state-building projects that focused on making independence a reality after war's end.

To highlight these interactions with Japan's new order, this study centers on political elites in the colonial capitals of Manila and Rangoon. Telling the story in this manner unfortunately leaves out developments outside of the colonial capitals, and at times leaves underexplored the excesses, the brutality, and the exploitative tendencies of Japan's wartime empire in both colonies. Moreover, it leaves out other areas of Japan's wartime empire, from Indonesia to British Malaya and French Indochina. But doing so highlights trends of collaboration with Japan's new order present across Southeast Asia. Moreover, it allows me to tell a transnational story, one that both crosses national borders and places the Pacific War and the Co-Prosperity Sphere in their proper regional contexts.

Imperial Dreams, Anticolonial Realities

Scholarship on the Co-Prosperity Sphere roughly divides into four schools of thought. The first, the orthodox school, views the Co-Prosperity Sphere as a euphemism for (largely economic) imperialism and attempts at political domination in Asia. This view was first and perhaps best laid out by Japanese historian

Kobayashi Hideo. Kobayashi understood the Sphere as the culmination of a longer process that began in 1931 with the Manchurian Incident. From that point on, Japan sought to mobilize the wealth and resources of occupied territories in the service of the Japanese Empire. Kobayashi and others in the orthodox school pay specific attention to attempts to industrialize the region and build true self-sufficiency: from the mobilization of colonial labor across the empire to the development of industry in occupied areas to meet the demands of total war, attempts at monetary unification through military currencies, and even investment and financial policy within the region. In all, they see it as an effort to mobilize wealth and resources to support Japan's war effort.[16] Scholars of East Asian and Southeast Asian history share similar understandings, and they highlight the way in which Japan sought to exploit the region.[17] Whatever the case, all these scholars would agree with Kobayashi that the Sphere constituted little more than "Japanese imperialistic expansion of colonial rule during the 'Fifteen Years War.'"[18]

A second approach is best termed the historical revisionist school. Largely popular outside of academic and intellectual circles, it includes those who interpret Japan's war in an uncritical and congratulatory light. Revisionists in general take wartime rhetoric and propaganda at face value. They view the Greater East Asia Co-Prosperity Sphere as the zenith of Japan's "holy war" and a sincere effort to liberate Asia. Moreover, they contend that Japan made a glorious sacrifice to bring about the end of empire in Asia. In effect, the revisionists use the incidental by-product of war (the end of empire) to beautify and justify the war itself. Granted, some revisionists are quite thoughtful. Take, for instance, Hayashi Fusao. Hayashi viewed the Pacific War as the final battle of a hundred-year struggle between two visions for order in Asia. The U.S. ideal, he argued, was the realization of a "White Pacific," whereas Japan strove to construct the Co-Prosperity Sphere. But Hayashi, who was writing in the 1960s, was also using World War II to offer a critique of the Cold War, which he saw as the continuation of Western colonialism. The Cold War, in his words, constituted the struggle for mastery between "Democracy Imperialism" and "Communism Imperialism."[19] Whatever its merits, this is not taken seriously in academic circles. Progressive historians since the 1960s have beaten back views of Japan's war as a war of liberation. Perhaps Ienaga Saburō best stated the problems with the revisionist view of history. "To call Japan's disgraceful and bloody rampage a crusade for liberation," he declared, "is to stand truth and history on their heads."[20]

Still, the historical revisionist school has propagated a historical view so alluring that it refuses to die. This selective view of history continues to resonate through the ever-present textbook debate and ill-timed statements by government officials. It has also reached a greater audience through the emergence in the 1990s of a so-called liberal historical view (*jiyūshugi shikan*), a right-wing effort among pundits, officials, and academics to build a sense of pride in Japan's past. The most representative work of these modern revisionists is Kobayashi Yoshinori's wildly successful manga, *Sensōron* (On War). *Sensōron* soon became a national best seller, and hardcover sales alone have thus far surpassed nine hundred thousand copies. Moreover, a vocal minority still embraces the war as an attempt to create a just order and true freedom in Asia. As recently as August 2014, Japan's former chief of staff of the Air Self-Defense Forces, Tamogami Toshio, caused a stir when he took to Twitter to insist that "the Greater East Asia War was a holy war. It brought about a world of racial equality."[21] Although political leaders remain more circumspect in their comments, Prime Minister Abe Shinzō generated howls of protest from China and Korea in December 2013 when he questioned whether Japan had actually committed "aggression" during World War II.[22] This sentiment is noticeable even to a foreign observer. Taking a quick stroll through local bookstores in Tokyo, one can find numerous books on the "truth" of the Greater East Asia War that question whether Japan waged a war of aggression or liberation.

The third perspective, the ideology school, views the Co-Prosperity Sphere as the culmination of broader intellectual or ideological trends reaching back to the turn of the twentieth century. Many in this school highlight the central role of Pan-Asianism. Some, like Matsu'ura Masataka and Eri Hotta, convincingly show that Pan-Asianism was not simply the aim but also the cause of Japan's war for Greater East Asia. Pan-Asian ideology provided the central justification for Japan to wage a colonial war of aggression while declaring the conflict a holy war for the liberation of Asia. In this context, they see the Co-Prosperity Sphere as the ultimate political form of Pan-Asian ideology, one that recasts imperialism as an ideological mission.[23]

Others in this school of thought believe the Sphere constituted a synthesis of diverse ideologies. Eizawa Kōji argues that the Sphere featured an eclectic mix of fascist, Japanist, neo-Confucian, and Pan-Asianist components. These joined into a "'holy war ideology' that both beautified and justified the Pacific War."[24] And Akazawa Shirō contends that the culture of wartime Japan was a mix of two competing ideologies: Japanism (*Nipponshugi*) and the total war system (*sōryokusen taisei*). On the one hand, Japanist ideologues attacked Western ideas from Marxism to liberalism as incompatible with the traditional Japanese state. But Japanist ideology, in focusing on the somewhat nebulous *kokutai* (national polity), lacked a positive program to build a new political or economic system. Total war system thought made up for this, calling for a parallel restructuring of

Japan's economy and society along Nazi German lines. The conjoining of Japanism and total war system ideology, Akazawa argues, created the hegemonic ideology of wartime Japan, one that informed not only wartime culture but also the realities of the Co-Prosperity Sphere.[25]

The final major school of thought emphasizes the Co-Prosperity Sphere as an abortive vision for the future. Scholars in this vision school largely agree that the Sphere was a political dream for a Pan-Asian order, one that allowed Japan to assert regional political-economic domination and deny it at the same time. Various dreams for a new order were advanced by people across the political system, from intellectuals to technocrats, businessmen to reformist bureaucrats, and military men to diplomats. These dreams covered the gamut of affairs, including regional economic structures, new political systems, innovative forms of international law, transportation networks, and even education systems.[26] The most interesting research in this vision school highlights how those "dreams" changed during wartime, when Japan's ultimate defeat began to loom on the horizon. On the one hand, Adachi Hiroaki has shown how technocrats, reformist bureaucrats, and business leaders refocused their attention on securing much-needed raw materials for the war effort.[27] On the other hand, Akira Iriye and Hatano Sumio show how the foreign ministry redefined Japan's war aims as part of an effort to end the war.[28]

Each of these perspectives provides important insights into the Co-Prosperity Sphere. But Japan's new order remains surprisingly understudied. First, despite the attention to World War II–era Japan, there are no book-length monographs in English that explore the Co-Prosperity Sphere from the perspective of Japanese high policy.[29] English-language literature on the Sphere often focuses on the initial stages of the Pacific War, thus only telling part of a broader story of visions for the future that both reached across Asia and shifted with the geopolitics of war. Second, the existing scholarship does not pay sufficient attention to *how* the new order highlights Japan's response to the challenges of empire and diplomacy in the post–World War I world. Finally, much of the best scholarship still centers on either the metropole or on individual colonies. By taking a transnational and comparative approach, and in placing the stories of the imperial center and of two independent peripheries in dialogue, this book offers a nuanced and transnational window into Japan's wartime empire. It shows how the Co-Prosperity Sphere was a contested, negotiated process, one that bound Japan's imperial dreams with anticolonial aspirations of nationalist leaders in Burma and the Philippines. In the process, this book sheds light on a unique period in world history—a period when Japan's total empire met total war, to dramatic effect across East and Southeast Asia.

To tell the story of the Co-Prosperity Sphere, however, it is necessary to start with the dislocations following World War I.

When Total Empire Met Total War

World War I was transformative in global history. The so-called Great War pitted empires against each other in a fight for survival or expansion. It transformed the way wars had been fought, mobilizing state and society to an unprecedented extent. The Great War has come to be seen as the world's first total war, a conflict that could only be successfully fought by mobilizing entire populations and economic resources. Moreover, it was a global war, with hostilities even extending across Asia. Japan used the war to expand its imperial interests in China and the South Pacific, as well as to stage an extensive occupation of Siberia until 1922. In the process, Japan was for the first time recognized as a world power. But it was in Europe that the war took the greatest toll; by 1918 much of Europe had been devastated. The Great War delivered the death blow to four major dynastic empires—the Ottoman, Habsburg, Romanov, and Hohenzollern Empires.

One of the most important impacts of World War I was the rise of total war thought. Staff officers stationed in Europe during World War I sent back reports that revolutionized Japanese thinking about modern warfare. The relentless trench warfare and efforts among belligerents to achieve wartime autarky led military strategists to see warfare as dependent on self-reliance in resources and production. Those belligerents who were not self-reliant would lose in future wars. This new understanding of warfare led military strategists to treat the control of richer territories such as China and Manchuria as a national imperative. As early as 1918, Ugaki Kazushige, then a section chief in the general staff office, wrote in his diary that a major lesson of World War I was the necessity for "self-sufficiency" (jikyū jisoku). "There is a need," he argued, "for a self-sufficient economic sphere that extends to the continent and in particular to China. It is imperative to make China and Japan into a single economic unit."[30] Further army studies throughout the 1920s reinforced the notion that Japan lacked the resources to meet the needs of modern warfare, turning the attention of the general staff and the Kwantung Army to the resource-rich areas of Manchuria, Mongolia, and China proper.[31]

But perhaps the biggest initial impact of the Great War was the ideological blow it delivered to the prevailing logic of international relations. Imperial expansion—facilitated through conflict, displays of force, and secretive alliance diplomacy—now appeared irrational and retrograde.[32] Perhaps nothing symbolized the winds of change more than the emerging contest of visions between

Bolshevik leader Vladimir Lenin and U.S. president Woodrow Wilson. Lenin preached a socialist internationalism that rejected all forms of foreign and colonial domination and called for class struggle as the preeminent global concern. Wilson, conversely, championed a strain of liberal internationalism that emphasized free trade, disarmament, collective security, and conference diplomacy as the keys to a liberal, democratic peace. Yet despite their different points of origin, Lenin and Wilson shared much in their understandings of global trends. They both saw themselves as revolutionaries who held messianic and universalist visions for world politics. By 1918, both called for a new moral program to undermine imperialism. Both saw national self-determination as an inherent rejection of empire, although Wilson remained more cautious and less consistent in his advocacy for empire's end. Moreover, both Bolshevism and Wilsonianism repudiated secret alliances. They advocated a new world order that rejected secretive and imperial diplomacy in favor of peaceful relations.

It was Wilson's vision that set the tone for international politics in the 1920s. Through the Versailles peace conference of 1919 and the Washington conference of 1921–22, in particular, the United States led a dramatic new enterprise of order making that enshrined Wilsonian principles into the international system. The new order in East Asia in the 1920s is best thought of as part of the Versailles-Washington system. It heralded the retreat of empire in favor of multilateralism and conference diplomacy. Henceforth, peace was to be secured through free economic intercourse, arms limitation, democratic governance, an end to secret alliances, and the establishment of collective security institutions such as the League of Nations (which, ironically, the United States did not join). The Versailles-Washington system was further reinforced by a series of international conventions, from the Treaty of Versailles to the League of Nations Covenant, the Five-Power Treaty, the Four-Power Treaty, the Nine-Power Treaty, the Kellogg-Briand Pact, and the London Naval Treaty. These conventions advanced the Wilsonian mission to refashion international relations in support of peace, multilateralism, and conference diplomacy.

For Japan, this signaled a new trajectory in foreign affairs and brought new challenges for diplomacy and empire. Before 1919, Japan had been a model player in the Game of Empires in Asia, using military might, secret alliances, and territorial expansion to secure national goals of wealth and strength. But the Versailles-Washington system changed the rules of the game. By the 1920s, imperialism no longer fit the global standard of "civilization," the norms of international relations that prevailing powers used to justify their hegemony. To participate in this new order Japan gave up many of the fruits of its participation in the global war. In 1922 Japan withdrew its troops from the Shandong concession in China and recalled all troops involved in the Siberian Intervention. Moreover, a series of agreements committed Japan to limiting naval armaments, abandoning the Anglo-Japanese Alliance in order to participate in multilateral diplomacy, promising a policy of nonintervention in Chinese affairs, and making peaceful, economic expansionism the hallmark of its foreign policy. Cooperation, multilateralism, and free economic intercourse were to replace balance-of-power diplomacy and military competition in international affairs.

Most scholarship understandably highlights the skepticism with which Japanese leaders met the new Wilsonian order. The naval disarmament treaties in Washington (1922) and London (1930) generated a fierce debate within the Japanese navy and led to the rise of a generation of "hot-blooded young officers" who sought to rebel against the disarmament treaties.[33] Many officers in the army, too, scorned the Versailles-Washington system as little more than imperialism, American style.[34] After all, for all the high-minded discourse in the 1920s, no imperialist power actually liberated their colonies. Scholars of diplomatic history thus often focus on the early critiques of a young Konoe Fumimaro, then a fledgling member of the House of Peers. On the eve of the Paris peace conference, Konoe wrote a scathing critique that rejected Wilsonian ideals as sugarcoating the maintenance of an unfair status quo that perpetuated Anglo-American dominance. Konoe saw the world as divided into "haves" and "have-nots." "Have countries" (*moteru kuni*) such as Britain and the United States held an expansive network of colonies, territories, or resources that far surpassed "have-not countries" (*motazaru kuni*) such as Germany and Japan. He argued that the aggressive promotion of democracy, justice, and humanism represented a cynical attempt to preserve the unjust global division of land and resources. Prophetically, Konoe argued that unequal access to markets and resources might "compel Japan to attempt to overthrow the status quo as Germany did before the war."[35]

More recent works, however, have begun to emphasize the strengths of Japan's engagement with the new order. Frederick R. Dickinson argues that Japanese state and society saw the early interwar era as a remarkable opportunity to build a "New Japan," a polity and society that exemplified the liberal internationalist trends of the day. He highlights considerable excitement in Japan for democracy, conference diplomacy, multilateralism, disarmament, and peace throughout the 1920s. Even Konoe offered his grudging support of the internationalist trends of the time as a key to international status. Konoe and others, Dickinson argues, recognized and even supported Wilsonian internationalism as "*the* standard of 'civilization' in Tokyo after 1919."[36]

Whether guarded or excited, continued support for this new standard of "civilization" rested on assumptions of stability, economic gain, and international status. Participation in the Washington-Versailles system, on the one hand, would make Japan an important player in the major decision-making bodies of the day. Japanese power in international affairs would be less dependent on continental and maritime expansion than on global trade and multilateral engagement. Moreover, free trade would ensure growth and prosperity, despite Japan's relative lack of territory or resources.

Nonetheless, by 1930 a convergence of domestic and foreign crises threatened the very foundations of the old order. On the domestic front, a bitter political battle between the Hamaguchi Osachi cabinet and the armed forces over arms limitation in the wake of the London Naval Treaty of 1930 convinced hotheaded officers that the government took national security far too lightly. Young, rebellious officers began to argue that weakness on defense and empire represented a failure of the political system, a sense compounded by the rural crisis and deepening recession at home. Some groups within the army thus viewed political change at home and expanded empire in Manchuria as two sides of the same coin, and they pressed for both through systematic campaigns of violence that began to undermine the commitment to peace.[37] On the foreign front, the global economic crisis in 1929 undermined the economic interdependence on which the Versailles-Washington system was based. Japan's cooperation in the world system of "free trade" had stemmed from assumptions of vast economic gains. As the major powers undermined free trade, forming protectionist economic blocs to counter the Depression, concerns and dissatisfactions with the order increased in size and scope. Such concerns were exacerbated by a revitalized Chinese nationalist movement, which threatened Japan's long-standing "special interests" in Manchuria and Mongolia.[38]

The combination of political and economic crises gave renewed cogency to empire as a means of solving Japan's problems. It was at this point that the total war theorists in the military took matters into their own hands. Staff officers in the Kwantung Army led by Lt. Col. Ishiwara Kanji and Col. Itagaki Seishirō exploited the situation in September 1931, initiating what came to be known as the Manchurian Incident, a full-scale invasion of Manchuria in direct defiance of official orders. The general staff sent daily orders telling the conspirators to stop, only to receive mocking replies. This insubordination paid vast dividends. Tokyo remained unable to quell the Kwantung Army without admitting to the world that Japan had lost control of its army. By early 1932, policy makers in Tokyo accepted the seizure of Manchuria as a fait accompli. In September 1932, one year after the Manchurian Incident had begun, Japan formally recognized the new, "independent" satellite regime of Manchukuo.

The Manchurian Incident did not initially represent an abrupt break in East Asian international relations. Japan may have followed up by withdrawing from the League of Nations in 1933 and abandoning the London Naval Treaty's arms limitations in 1936, but the crisis in Manchuria did not overturn the post–World

War I settlement. A commitment to internationalism in Japan's foreign policy establishment continued unabated even after Japan left the League of Nations. More importantly, the very creation of an independent satellite regime such as Manchukuo highlights the power that national self-determination continued to hold in post–World War I international politics. Even bold new moves toward empire were justified in the language of independence and self-determination. As Prasenjit Duara has argued, Japan served as the vanguard of a "new imperialism," which recast colonial intent in the language of self-determination by creating "independent" or legally sovereign nation-states.[39] Even Ishiwara, the planner of the Manchurian Incident, spoke of Manchurian and Mongolian independence in the language of self-determination. "Those who speak of ethnic self-determination," Ishiwara argued as early as 1929, "must recognize that Manchuria and Mongolia are [territory of] the Manchurian and Mongolian peoples."[40] As will be shown in this study, this new imperialism reached its peak during the Pacific War. By late 1943, Thailand, the Chinese Nanjing regime, the Philippines, and Burma had joined Manchukuo as independent regimes within the Greater East Asia Co-Prosperity Sphere. These regimes (aside from Thailand) received what Hatano Sumio has scorned as the "Manchukuo model of 'independence,'" a façade that afforded Japan a high degree of intervention into their internal affairs.[41]

Over the course of the 1930s, Manchukuo emerged into what Louise Young calls Japan's "total empire." Empire building in Manchukuo, she shows, entailed a mass and multidimensional mobilization of Japanese state and society, transforming Japan in enduring and irrevocable ways. Total empire contributed to a culture of war fever and changed the mass media into a vehicle of support for imperial expansion. It led to the emergence of "imperial interest groups" that called for military expansion abroad and confrontation with Japan's great power rivals. Total empire led to the creation of new state apparatuses and greater state intervention in the economy, polity, and society. And Manchukuo served as a testing ground for revolutionary new ideas, providing intellectuals and bureaucrats with a vast laboratory for enacting social and economic reforms.[42] Disillusioned with liberal capitalism in Japan, intellectuals, radical officers, and military technocrats saw Manchukuo as a new way forward. Following German precedents, they strove to create a "totalist" managerial state, one through which intelligent organization of economy, state, and society would allow "have-nots" such as Japan to compete with the global "haves."[43] Moreover, they saw Manchukuo as critical in liberating the peoples of the world from capitalist and communist domination, and in creating a base for Asian revivalism. The "total empire" of Manchukuo incubated ideas that gained relevance once Japan broke away from the old order.

It was the China war, however, that ultimately impelled this decisive break. The Marco Polo Bridge Incident in 1937 set Japan on a collision course with the old order. Moreover, Japan's rapid military and political advance into China fed into a sense of destiny of regional leadership. By 1938 Shōwa Kenkyūkai intellectuals Miki Kiyoshi and Rōyama Masamichi had begun advocating that Japan take advantage of its "holy war" in China to construct an "East Asian Cooperative Community" (Tōa kyōdōtai). Prime Minister Konoe followed up with similar initiatives. On November 3, 1938—the anniversary of Emperor Meiji's birthday—Konoe announced the establishment of a "New Order in East Asia." This new order, he argued, centered on an all-embracing partnership between Japan, Manchukuo, and China. Together, they would build a new future for the region, one that would ensure a sense of fairness in international politics and "guarantee permanent stability in East Asia." Moreover, Konoe hinted that even China's Nationalist regime had a role to play in the new order if it "abandons traditional policies" of resistance to Japan.[44] In all, the declaration served as Japan's official rejection of the Versailles-Washington system.[45] Foreign minister Arita Hachirō followed up in late November 1938 by informing the United States that Japan would no longer protect the principle of the Open Door and the commitment to equal opportunity in China.[46] Thus began Japan's project of imagining the future Asian order, a project that would be consummated with the establishment of the Greater East Asia Co-Prosperity Sphere.

Japan thus embarked on a dramatic new enterprise of empire and order building at the very moment it plunged into total war in China. This convergence of total empire and total war affected all aspects of Japan's new order. First, at the most basic level, it impelled policy makers and political intellectuals to imagine in earnest what Asia would look like under Japanese leadership, and to return to a regime of secretive diplomacy to bring that about. Perhaps no one was more important in this early process than foreign minister Matsuoka, who announced the creation of the Greater East Asia Co-Prosperity Sphere in August 1940. As will be shown in chapters 1 and 2, Matsuoka aimed to return to a system of secret alliances that would help Japan carve out a pan-region in Asia. Matsuoka further hoped this pan-region would be recognized by both world powers and regional elites alike. In this context, he sought to forge pacts or alliances with Germany, Italy, the Soviet Union, and the United States. After the outbreak of the Pacific War in December 1941, however, this attempt to imagine a new Asia was taken up by other leaders of Japan's foreign policy establishment: from intellectuals to political and military leaders, from bureaucrats to captains of industry. Through 1945, political intellectuals and policy makers engaged in a sophisticated debate about the future Asia that Japan would help fashion.

Second, the fact that Japan built its new order as it plunged into total war meant that Japan needed to exploit Asia, to forge a regional autarky for its national survival. Simply put, without exploiting the vast resources of its colonial partners,

TABLE 1. Percentage of trade with the metropole

COLONY	METROPOLE	IMPORTS			EXPORTS		
		1937	1938	1939	1937	1938	1939
India	Britain	39.0	31.5	31.4	33.2	32.3	33.7
Malaya	Britain	15.1	15.7	18.4	8.8	11.1	14.2
Neth. Indies	Netherlands	16.7	19.1	22.2	23.6	20.1	20.4
Indochina	France	53.4	53.5	53.1	55.2	46.1	47.3
Philippines	United States	60.8	58.0	68.1	80.4	81.7	77.2
Taiwan	Japan	83.3	86.3	89.4	92.5	93.2	92.0
Korea	Japan	85.0	82.2	87.3	87.4	83.5	80.8
Manchukuo	Japan	52.8	75.1	78.9	47.4	50.0	57.5

Taken from Hori Kazuo, *Higashi Ajia shihonshugi shiron*, vol. 1 (Minerva Shobō: 2009), 217.

Japan would be unable to bring about its aim of order creation. Economic historian Hori Kazuo has shown Japan's high level of dependence on colonial Asia in the late 1930s, once the China war had ramped up.[47] As can be seen in table 1, Japan dominated trade with its colonies. In 1937, 83.3 percent of Taiwan's total imports came from Japan, and 92.5 percent of the colony's exports went to Japan. Likewise, in the same year 85 percent of Korean imports were from Japan, and 87.4 percent of its total exports went to Japan.[48] As Hori has shown, these figures remained remarkably consistent throughout the early years of Japan's war in China.

So necessary was it that Japan exploit its Asian colonies that the value of Japanese exports to its own colonies or occupied territories surpassed that of Great Britain and France in absolute terms. By the time total war began, Japan had become more reliant on its colonial partners for economic growth than any other imperialist power in Asia, and it had "deeply subsumed its peripheral societies into the Japanese economy."[49]

This pressure to exploit Asia expanded dramatically as the war years progressed; technocrats hoped to institutionalize exploitation into the political economy of their new Asian empire. This desire owed to longer-term trends. In the years after the Great Depression, intellectuals and policy makers became convinced of the collapse of liberal capitalism. Western capitalist countries, after all, had reacted in ways that exacerbated the global economic crisis. They abandoned free trade for protectionism and managed currencies, and they ushered in a deep depression that battered much of the world. Japan, which relied heavily on foreign trade to offset its limited resource base, keenly felt the shock of this abandonment of free trade. Faced with the global crisis, 1930s Japan turned to German notions of industrial policy and bloc economics while working toward regional autarky. Accordingly, the government began to play a broader role in mobilization, setting economic plans not just for the nation but for the region as well. By the early 1940s, policy makers and intellectuals alike viewed hierarchically structured regional bloc economies—led by a strong state—as necessary for economic growth. This was what many wartime planners hoped to see with the Greater East Asia Co-Prosperity Sphere.

Intellectuals envisioned that the Co-Prosperity Sphere would attain self-sufficiency through a regional hierarchy of production. Japan would account for the highest skill and most capital-intensive production. Lesser-developed nations or peoples, on the other hand, would focus on a descending range of economic activities, from lower-skill, labor-intensive production to natural resource extraction. Even those who called for pluralism within the Sphere, wherein component areas should independently supply and plan themselves, remained convinced of the necessity of Japanese leadership. Asia would thus exist as an appendage of the broader Japanese economy, to be exploited for the region's benefit. In this sense, Asia's economic potential was always imagined in the context of Japan's national survival. It was only from late 1943, as defeat loomed on the horizon, that intellectuals and policy makers began to tone down their dreams of regional autarky.

Third, the convergence of total empire and total war led policy makers to envision expansion into Southeast Asia through a hierarchy of political arrangements. On the one hand, the Greater East Asia Co-Prosperity Sphere witnessed the dramatic rise of the new imperialism, or the Manchukuo model of nominally independent satellite regimes. These defensive satellite regimes included Manchukuo, the Chinese Nanjing regime, Thailand, the Philippines, and Burma. The rhetorical focus on Asian liberation as well as the establishment of these "independent" regimes have led some scholars to speak of the Sphere as "imperialism without colonies."[50] But the truth is more complex. Japan's new, "anti-imperial" imperialism only applied to select regimes. The old imperialism of direct colonial rule never died out. Korea and Taiwan received no gestures toward independence—they were to be incorporated into Japan proper, as part of its inner territories (naichi). By 1945 this imperialism became more inclusive, with Japan planning to offer a greater stake to Koreans and Taiwanese in the politics of Japan proper.[51] Policy makers, however, never sought to grant even nominal independence to Japan's two long-standing colonies. And Malaya, Singapore, French Indochina, the Netherlands Indies, and other outer territories (gaichi) were to remain as dependent parts of the empire as directly controlled territories. This was so widely understood that on the festivities in Singapore surrounding the emperor's birthday in April 1942, General Yamashita Tomoyuki, a Southern Expeditionary Army commander often referred to as the Tiger of Malaya, stated that the peoples of Malaya and Sumatra had become "subjects of the Japanese Empire."[52]

This division of the Co-Prosperity Sphere into colonial regimes and nominally independent states continued throughout the war. In this sense, Japanese policy makers and intellectuals saw the new order as *both* colonial and anticolonial at the same time. The Sphere championed a new imperialism that harnessed the logic and sentiment of anticolonial nationalism, but it never abandoned old imperialism outright. In this sense, Japanese policy makers perhaps unconsciously mimicked aspects of the British imperial mandate system that emerged after World War I.[53]

Fourth, the convergence of total empire and total war provided the background in which transnational elites in Burma and the Philippines joined hands with Japan. As noted earlier, politicos in both countries collaborated with the Japanese Empire and received nominal independence within the Co-Prosperity Sphere. But mere puppets they were not. As I will argue in chapter 4, leaders of satellite regimes in Burma and the Philippines decided to work with the Japanese for patriotic ends. Burmese nationalists in Rangoon entered Japan's imperial embrace to seize independence from Great Britain, which had refused to give assurances of either independence or dominion status. Philippine governmental elites in Manila also went over en masse and served as a caretaker regime. Granted, there were a wide variety of reasons behind the decisions to collaborate: from efforts to preserve the social order, to opportunism, and perhaps a degree of compulsion. But patriotism was foremost among them. Many nationalist elites in the colonial capitals worked with Japan out of a desire to promote or preserve independence in whatever form they could achieve. Nationalist elites, in this sense, sought to use the Japanese Empire for anticolonial ends. They are best thought of as what I call patriotic collaborators.

Collaboration: that simple term meaning "to work together" that has come to imply high treason. Patriotism and collaboration thus appear to present-day observers as incompatible as day and night. Collaborators are seen as those who enrich themselves or secure individual, family, or group goals at the expense of the integrity or independence of the nation.[54] But at the level of elite politics, patriotism and collaboration with a foreign power are not mutually exclusive. Those collaborators working for political freedom, for independence, to alleviate human misery, or to remake their societies should not be dismissed as mere traitors. Far from it, they can also be considered patriots. In the European context, one could argue that French collaborators Marshal Philippe Pétain, Pierre Laval, and Admiral François Darlan were, in their own way, patriots. Far from being a mere shield against the Germans, they saw defeat and occupation as a unique opportunity to carry out a veritable revolution in institutions and values.[55] German domination, in other words, was the price they had to pay to restore French greatness. Denmark also provides a strong example of patriotic collaboration.

The Danish government saw resistance to Hitler as futile and negotiated an agreement that allowed for formal independence and relatively mild German oversight. In the process, Denmark carved out a comfortable niche in Hitler's empire, at least until 1943.[56] In the Chinese context, a perfect example of patriotic collaboration is that of Yu Chonghan, the first head of the Control Yuan of Manchukuo. He worked with the Kwantung Army in Manchuria to bring an end to warlord politics, improve life, and develop self-governing institutions.[57]

Patriotic collaboration applies even more strongly to wartime Southeast Asia. Political elites in the colonial capitals found themselves caught between two empires—the invading Japanese and their former colonial masters. For some, they found much to gain by temporary cooperation with the Japanese. Many across the region met Japanese decisions with mixed emotions, from hopeful cooperation to passive resistance. Some nationalist elites struggled to make the most out of the situation, to ensure that wartime occupation could have positive legacies in the postwar era. This is why—unlike in Europe—many wartime collaborators in Southeast Asia are now considered national heroes.

This study shows how collaborationist leaders from both the Philippines and Burma *actively used* the Co-Prosperity Sphere for national ends. In chapter 6, I show how both colonies engaged in state-building projects, in some cases creating new governmental institutions their countries had lacked under colonial rule. Philippine and Burmese leaders gained hands-on training in these institutions. With the creation of limited foreign policy, economic, and defense establishments and through gaining firsthand experience in governmental affairs, local leaders sought to preserve their nations during the war and prepare (to the extent possible) for the responsibilities of independence after war's end. An irony was thus embedded in Japan's wartime imperial project. Although Japanese leaders imagined constructing a regional imperium, they helped build institutions that nationalist leaders hoped would facilitate the transition to postwar independence.

The story of Japan's Greater East Asia Co-Prosperity Sphere will unfold through two overarching but interlocking narratives. One storyline narrates Japanese high policy and shows how the policy establishment viewed Asia's future between 1940 and 1945. This narrative (recounted in chapters 1–3 and parts of chapter 5) explores visions for the Co-Prosperity Sphere and shows how those visions developed and changed with the tides of Japan's war in Asia. Ultimately, it is a history of failure. The Sphere, after all, was the stillborn intellectual child of Japan's revolt against the old order. Yet studying these dreams offers insights into a history of what might have been, an empire that may have been forged had Japan survived the war with empire intact. The other storyline (chapters 4–6) highlights the Co-Prosperity Sphere as a contested process in the Philippines and Burma. It shows why "patriotic collaborators" in Manila and Rangoon chose to embrace their new Japanese overlords, and it narrates how they understood, contested, and co-opted parts of Japan's imperial project. If the first storyline is a history of a failed idea, this second storyline shows how imperialism is ever a negotiated process, even during war. It is a story about harsh imperial control co-opted to further national goals. It is to these two stories that we now turn.

Part I
THE IMAGINED
SPHERE

INTO THE TIGER'S DEN

The Tripartite Pact, which was signed to great fanfare in Berlin on September 27, 1940, shook the foundations of global politics. Unsurprisingly, both U.S. ambassador to Japan Joseph C. Grew and Japanese ambassador to Great Britain Shigemitsu Mamoru could not contain their shock and dismay. Grew had believed that war with Japan could be avoided until Japan signed the Axis alliance. "I saw the constructive work of eight years swept away," Grew bemoaned to a fellow Foreign Service officer in February 1941, "as if by a typhoon, earthquake, and tidal wave combined."[1] Shigemitsu, too, thought the decision to join the alliance "passed human understanding." He wrote after the war, "I felt that the alliance placed Japan in an international position from which it could not be saved, and I could not express the depths of despair into which I plunged."[2] This dismay was understandable. The Tripartite Pact constituted a major turning point in foreign policy and hinted at a further estrangement between Japan and the United States. It alerted American public opinion to a looming catastrophe in the Pacific and created the atmosphere in which U.S. president Franklin D. Roosevelt aligned more closely with the British.[3] And it provided the context in which Japan seized an expanded empire in Southeast Asia by force of arms. Moves that would have been impossible without the Tripartite Pact ultimately embroiled Japan in a war for the Asia-Pacific, a war Japan had little chance of winning.

Despite its importance in the road to Pearl Harbor and the Pacific War, the diplomatic history surrounding the Tripartite Pact remains understudied.[4] The pact is largely understood as Japan's trump card against the United States, a means of scaring U.S. leaders away from a confrontation that might lead to a two-ocean war. But a surprising undercurrent in the diplomatic history of 1940 hints at another reason for the Axis Pact: *fears* of German designs on Asia also influenced Japanese leaders to join the Axis powers.

This may appear puzzling. After all, a cursory reading of the Japanese newspapers, the media, or the intellectual discourse of the 1930s shows that public opinion was highly pro-German. The broader Japanese public admired Hitler and saw in him the symbol of a shared resistance to the Anglo-American international order. Moreover, German intellectuals such as Karl Haushofer, Carl Schmitt, Werner Sombart, and lesser-known theorist Friedrich von Gottl-Ottlilienfeld exercised a decisive influence on the thinking of Japan's reform bureaucrats, the planners of Japan's wartime empire.[5] And perhaps most importantly, Japan and Germany shared a virulent anti-communism that led the two rising powers into a diplomatic and political-strategic embrace. Both nations joined together in the Anti-Comintern Pact in 1936, which Roosevelt found worrisome enough to issue his famous "quarantine" speech the following year. At first glance, then, the creation of a full-blown Axis alliance in 1940 appears little more than the denouement of a longer process of German-Japanese engagement and cooperation.

Such an interpretation is indeed correct. But there is more to the story. For a brief moment in the summer of 1940, pro-German sympathies were tempered by a strong undercurrent of suspicion and doubt. This chapter sheds light on the impact that fears of imagined German designs on Asia had on the Japanese decision to join the Tripartite Pact. This is not to say that fears of Germany were the primary driver of politics in the late 1930s and early 1940s. Far from it; concerns about Soviet and U.S. intentions toward Asia were more deeply entrenched in the minds of policy makers. Instead, I will show fears that emerged and dissipated in a single historical moment—that of German ascendancy of Europe. In one of history's little ironies, Japanese distrust of German motives helped bring the Axis alliance to fruition. As Germany gained ascendancy over much of Europe, many within Japan's foreign policy establishment began to fear that Berlin would seek to control French and Dutch colonies in East Asia. These fears, of course, were not based on any broad understanding of Germany policy. But they nonetheless convinced Japanese leaders to extend their new order to Greater East Asia. In the process, foreign minister Matsuoka declared Japan's willingness to enter the tiger's den of an alliance with Germany to capture the prize of expanded influence in Southeast Asia.

In this context, the journey into the tiger's den of a German alliance also sheds light on the birth of the Greater East Asia Co-Prosperity Sphere. Although it is unclear whether he came up with the slogan, foreign minister Matsuoka Yōsuke first used it less than two months before concluding the Tripartite Pact. Historian

Akira Iriye thus perceptively points to this as a major contradiction in Japanese policy making. At the moment Japan championed the anti-Westernism of the Co-Prosperity Sphere, it was also entering into the Axis alliance with Germany and Italy.[6] At first glance, Iriye has hit on one major puzzle of Japan's new order. Why ally with two Western powers as part of a broader revolt against the West?

This chapter deals with this puzzle. It was the broadening of Japanese interests to "Greater" Asia that led Matsuoka to announce the creation of the Greater East Asia Co-Prosperity Sphere in August 1940. Scholars have done excellent research on the long-term trajectory that led to the birth of the Co-Prosperity Sphere, and the ways in which Japan's Pan-Asian ideology was oriented at building legitimacy in the region. But focusing on the longer-term trends obscures a shorter-term goal of Japan's new order. The Co-Prosperity Sphere indeed constituted propaganda, but not only toward Asia. The timing of the declaration—at the height of concerns over German motives toward the region—suggests that the Co-Prosperity Sphere also constituted propaganda aimed at Berlin. In broadening the scope of its sphere of interest to "Greater" Asia, Japanese leaders sought to deny Germany a hegemonic position in Japan's backyard. Japanese preeminence in East and Southeast Asia served as the precondition for joining the Axis Pact. In this context, the Co-Prosperity Sphere propaganda was utilized to oust competitor colonial regimes from Asia, which was to remain under the aegis of imperial Japan.

Facing West, Eyeing the South

By the late 1930s, expanded German-Japanese political cooperation appeared inevitable. Japan and Germany joined in the Anti-Comintern Pact in November 1936, owing in no small part to the efforts of the military attaché to Berlin, Ōshima Hiroshi. To many across the Japanese political establishment, the German-Japanese pact represented more than mere resistance to Soviet communism. Most competent observers alike also saw it as a first step toward a shared resistance to the existing Anglo-American–led world order. The Anti-Comintern Pact appeared to herald the birth of a Berlin-Tokyo axis and to initiate a new era of partnership between the two powers.

But the honeymoon was short-lived. Despite the existence of pro-Axis voices across the political establishment, and despite the fact that many saw Japan as creating a new world order with Germany, Japanese leaders sought to avoid any action that risked antagonizing the United States, Great Britain, and France. Accordingly, since early 1939 Japan dragged its feet in negotiations for an all-embracing military pact with Germany and Italy. Foreign minister Arita Hachirō, in particular, was wary of Nazi Germany, and he advanced a "middle-of-the-road diplomacy" (*chūdō gaikō*) that refused to involve Japan too deeply with Europe's rising powers.[7] In this Arita found support from both Prime Minister Hiranuma Kiichirō and Navy Minister Yonai Mitsumasa. The only alliance they were willing to sign was one directed solely against the Soviet Union. This attitude frustrated Italian foreign minister Galeazzo Ciano, who from March 1939 noted his skepticism "about the possibility of an effective collaboration between the phlegmatic and slow Japanese and the dynamic Fascists and Nazis."[8] Japan's continued hesitation led Hitler and Mussolini to seek an alternative solution: they abandoned the notion of cooperation with Tokyo and established a bilateral alliance, the Pact of Steel, in May 1939.

Japanese policy makers soon worried about the ramifications of their foot dragging, and they sensed that their desire to avoid antagonizing the Western democracies was leading to a growing estrangement with Berlin. This perceived estrangement began on August 23, 1939, when Hitler broke with the Anti-Comintern Pact against the Soviet Union and signed the German-Soviet Non-aggression Pact. Japanese leaders had been warned that this might happen, yet the move still shocked Tokyo. Hitler, after all, signed the pact while Soviet Corps commander Georgy Zhukov's tanks overran Japanese positions at Nomonhan on the border of Mongolia and Manchuria. Grand Chamberlain Hata Shunroku thus recorded the German-Soviet pact in his diary as a "bolt from the blue," and Konoe Fumimaro later labeled it one of the two German betrayals that undermined the Axis alliance. Further, the Hiranuma cabinet saw Berlin's move as a "breach of faith." Hiranuma publicly decried the situation in Europe as "baffling" and promptly resigned.[9]

This distrust increased as the German Blitzkrieg began. An internal foreign ministry document completed in late April 1940, as the Third Reich expanded into Norway and Denmark, noted the nonaggression pact as a sign that Germany no longer sought to bind its fate to that of Japan. Strikingly, the report worried that Tokyo "can no longer hope for German sympathy with our New Order in East Asia" and recommended a policy of cooperation to prevent estrangement with Berlin and Rome.[10] Foreign ministry suspicions remained unabated in the following months. A May 1940 internal report warned, "If German antagonism toward Japan strengthens, do not be caught off guard and do not allow Germany to take policy that spurs the Soviet Union to attempt to restrain Japan."[11]

Germany's lightning-fast successes only intensified this anxiety. The war soon spread to the Low Countries and France, with the Wehrmacht seizing victory wherever it went. By June 25, 1940, Germany controlled much of Western Europe, and many in Japan judged that it was only a matter of time before Britain fell as well.[12] With Germany's sudden ascent, Japanese policy makers worried not only over a possible estrangement but also over the fate of Dutch and French colonies in Asia. Berlin, after all, could seek to exercise control over both French Indochina and the Netherlands Indies—the very core of Japan's envisioned empire in East Asia. Thus from mid-May 1940, after the defeat of the Netherlands, the Yonai cabinet began seeking assurances that Germany would respect the status quo in the Netherlands Indies. From late June, after the fall of France, they sought similar guarantees toward French Indochina.[13] Even important officials in the army began to fear that if Japan is not careful, then "the Netherlands Indies will fall into Hitler's hands."[14] On May 17, foreign minister Arita instructed the ambassador to Germany, Kurusu Saburō, to acquire confirmation that Germany's invasion would not affect Japan's interests in the Netherlands Indies.[15] And on June 21, Kurusu met with German secretary of state Ernst von Weizsäcker to discuss measures toward French Indochina. "Japan," Kurusu told Weizsäcker, "cannot remain uninterested in Indochina."[16]

Much to the chagrin of Japan's diplomatic establishment, Berlin remained largely silent concerning Southeast Asia. German foreign minister Joachim von Ribbentrop did in fact renounce German claims on the Netherlands Indies on May 20, 1940.[17] But he made this statement against the fierce opposition of his ministry, and the German foreign ministry never officially reaffirmed the Third Reich's intentions to stay out of the region.

Japanese diplomats thus kept seeking reassurance. Special ambassador to Italy Satō Naotake cabled Tokyo that at his July 8 talks in Berlin, Ribbentrop "took an evasive attitude toward Japan's colonial demands."[18] Ambassador Kurusu also questioned his German counterparts from mid-May but did not find them forthcoming. On July 10, Kurusu sent a telegram to foreign minister Arita lamenting his lack of success. "Germany," the telegram reads, "does not seem to have a clear attitude regarding [the fate of] the Netherlands East Indies and French Indochina. We cannot secure a definite promise or a pledge—it is very regrettable that Germany seems to be trying to avoid giving a promise on these issues."[19]

Why were Japanese leaders so fixated on Southeast Asia? Germany's extraordinary successes generated fears that Japan was missing a rare opportunity to advance south. Expansion into Southeast Asia was partly viewed as an end unto itself. Expansionist aims into Southeast Asia had increased in size and scope from the end of World War I, with Pan-Asianists such as Ōkawa Shūmei drawing attention to the moral imperative of Japan's regional leadership.[20] By the outbreak of World War II in Europe, a critical mass had been reached that helped translate the more aggressive notion of Pan-Asianism into policy. It was at this point that the phrase "Don't miss the bus!" became popular among the government and populace alike. Many believed Japan had a window of opportunity to advance its interests in the region and to extend the reach of Japan's new order into Southeast Asia as well.

From early May 1940, internal reports began to stress the "South Seas" (*Nanyō*) and the "South" (*Nanpō*), terms for modern-day Southeast Asia, Oceania, and the Indian subcontinent, as integral parts of Japan's new order. This culminated in a top-secret report from May 31 that underscored the necessity of expanding into Southeast Asia. Economically, the South Seas area constituted a resource treasure trove that would help Japanese industry deal with the repercussions of a hardened U.S. attitude. Politically, Japan would expel U.S. influence from Southeast Asia and would forge "relations of co-existence and co-prosperity" with the region.[21] Accordingly, from early June, the imperial headquarters sent military planners and spies to the Philippines, Malaya, French Indochina, Thailand, Sumatra, Java, and New Guinea to start planning for military operations against Southeast Asia (a rather ironic measure, as two months earlier the military had planned to start withdrawing troops from China in 1941). And on June 22, Iwakuro Hideo, a section chief in the army ministry's Bureau of Military Affairs, astounded the army general staff by calling for an immediate surprise attack on Singapore.[22]

Iwakuro's call to seize Singapore reflected popular anxieties that Japan might miss out on its golden chance to expand south. In late June 1940 the *Mainichi shinbun* reported the newfound focus on Southeast Asia, noting, "Calls for a complete change to foreign policy have been elevated to the status of national belief."[23] Without a stronger attitude toward the European war, many feared that Japan might lose out in any redistribution of colonies at war's end. Minseitō Party president Machida Chūji rode this wave of popular enthusiasm, declaring that Japan must "overhaul its foreign policy" to take advantage of the world's great turning point. Such an overhaul required Japan "to secure a powerful foothold" in Asia and create its "living space" through "a political-economic union centered on Japan, Manchukuo, and China, but also including Asia and the South Seas." And the nationalistic Socialist Masses Party (*Shakai Taishūtō*) on June 20 called for "a revolutionary change to the diplomacy of obeying England and America."[24]

Such overwhelming support and fears of "missing the bus" generated more authoritative statements of Japan's regional leadership. The first of these came with foreign minister Arita's radio address of June 29, 1940, titled "The International Situation and Japan's Position." Arita maintained that East Asia and the South Seas constituted a natural region with a shared geography, history, and economic and racial makeup. It fell on Japan, as an Asian nation, "to maintain the coexistence, co-prosperity, and security" of the region. At the same time, he reasserted the government's intention to maintain its neutrality toward the European war, and in turn he expected "that Western countries will not disturb the peace and stability of East Asia."[25] Historian Hatano Sumio argues that through this speech, Arita and the Yonai cabinet sought to restrain the public clamoring for an alliance with Nazi Germany and to prevent an aggressive expansion south. Indeed, one of the points of Arita's radio address was to ensure that any expansionism would be peaceful in nature.[26] Nonetheless, pressures to move south could not be staved off for long. Further, Arita's statement gave greater credence to the notion of Japan as the sole East Asian stabilizer, able to act unilaterally in the service of regional interests.

Now looking south, the foreign ministry began to imagine how far Japan's new order would extend. One of the more zealous top-secret draft plans, completed on July 9, 1940, argued that the new order would bind such disparate territories as French Indochina, Thailand, the outer South Seas area, Burma, Far Eastern Siberia, outer Mongolia, Australia, and New Zealand into a relationship of close economic reliance. Similar to Arita's statement, the policy plan argued for Japan as the sole force guaranteeing the region's security and development. Under Japan, it maintained, "the whole of the Orient will become a strong Co-Prosperity Sphere."[27]

Expansion into Southeast Asia also had a practical side as well—it went hand in glove with resolving the China quagmire. Advancing into Southeast Asia, army leaders believed, would cut off the British and French aid that was helping keep afloat the Chiang Kai-shek regime, leaving Chiang no hope but to surrender. And seizing leadership over Southeast Asia would ensure access to natural resources for Japan's war effort in China. Japanese historians have thus persuasively argued that army planners believed expanding south would "allow them to end the China war in a favorable manner."[28] Of course, such expansion did not necessitate the use of military force. Policy documents generally highlighted the necessity of using diplomatic measures to procure natural resources from the Netherlands Indies and to create sympathy across the region for Japan's war aims.

To summarize, by mid-1940—when Hitler's empire stood ascendant in Europe—Japanese leaders had begun to see expanding into Southeast Asia as an imperative in the creation of Japan's new order. And the foreign policy establishment worried that Germany's seizure of the Netherlands and France meant that Hitler could seek political control over Dutch and French colonies in Asia. Although in May 1940 Ribbentrop promised that Germany would not intervene in Southeast Asian affairs, he never repeated this promise, even after continued questioning from Japanese diplomats. This, of course, did not imply a German desire to control French Indochina and the Netherlands Indies. But it heightened Japanese concerns.

The foreign ministry's Bureau of Eurasian Affairs took these concerns to heart. Satō's cable of his July 8 talks with Ribbentrop convinced section chief Andō Yoshirō and others in the Bureau that Germany intended to seize French and Dutch colonies in Asia. As a countermeasure, Andō produced a draft plan for strengthened relations with the Axis powers. Andō's plan claimed that Germany would soon defeat Britain and achieve hegemony over Europe and Africa. It was only a matter of time before Berlin turned its eyes to Southeast Asia. Japan thus had a window of opportunity to force Germany to recognize Japanese interests in and leadership over the region. To this end, Andō was willing to forge "the highest level partnership, short of entering the war."[29] By July 1940, mid-level bureaucrats in the foreign ministry were willing to ally with Germany to ensure Japanese preeminence in Asia.

Discussions of Andō's draft plan, which took place at a mid-level bureaucratic meeting on July 16, confirmed that such fears reached across the foreign policy establishment. Present at the meeting were three section chiefs from the foreign ministry's Bureau of Eurasian Affairs, one foreign ministry secretary, and representatives from the army ministry, the army general staff, and the navy ministry.[30] An excerpt of the conversation reveals shared understandings between army general staff and foreign ministry officials of possible German designs on the region.

Andō Yoshirō (foreign ministry Bureau of Eurasian Affairs, section 1 chief):	The greatest difficulty with strengthening relations [with Germany and Italy] is as follows. Ambassador Satō's telegrams give off the vague sense that Germany will seize the reins of power in the Netherlands East Indies and French Indochina, and only aims to provide Japan with economic benefits. Namely, it seems that Germany will not recognize Japanese political leadership [over the region].
Lt. Col. Takayama Hikoichi (army ministry):	I also think so. To the extent possible, we need to act forcefully to make Germany recognize [Japanese] leadership over French Indochina and the Netherlands East Indies.
Andō:	. . . Looking at the telegrams sent the other day by Consul General Yamaji, it seems that Germany plans to offer the territory to the east of the Netherlands East Indies to Japan. Stated differently, this means that Germany plans on taking Java and Sumatra.

Takayama:	Regarding the future of the Netherlands East Indies and French Indochina, the attitude Germany takes toward Japan greatly depends on the attitude Germany plans to take toward the Soviet Union in the postwar era. For Germany, the postwar era is not far off. So if Germany plans to deal harshly with the Soviet Union, then it might unexpectedly entrust us with French Indochina and the Netherlands East Indies. But if they immediately commence with the creation of the new order in Europe, then the French Indochina and Netherlands East Indies issue might become quite problematic. However, for now Japan should consider that Germany intends to take over French Indochina and the Netherlands East Indies, and must take measures to deal with this. We need to be thoroughly prepared for this.
Andō:	I agree. We should fiercely oppose German efforts to take political leadership over the region.
Ishizawa Yutaka (foreign ministry Bureau of Eurasian Affairs, section 3 chief):	I also agree.[31]

No doubt owing to these fears, the meeting pushed through Andō's draft plan of partnering with Germany with only minor revisions. As historians Hatano Sumio and Kawanishi Kōsuke have noted, such fears spurred on a desire within the army and the foreign ministry to ally with Germany.[32]

These concerns even reached the ears of Shigemitsu Mamoru, then Japan's ambassador to Great Britain. "Many on the Japanese side," Shigemitsu recalled in his memoirs, "were seized with panic about what would happen to British colonies in Asia, and feared what would become of the Japanese Empire once Dutch and French colonies were occupied by Germany." If Germany gained political control over the European colonies in Asia, they feared, then Japan would be far worse off than before the war. So wrapped up were their minds around Germany's ultimate victory that most "would not lend an ear to dissenting opinions." They could have no peace of mind without an immediate alliance with Germany that delineated each power's sphere of influence. Japanese leaders, Shigemitsu realized, worried that Japan might "miss the bus."[33]

Strikingly, Japan's foreign ministry experts were scared of a phantasm. No evidence or intelligence showed German intentions to claim the Southeast Asian colonies. Surprisingly, the Bureau of Eurasian Affairs remained almost wholly reliant on predictions of German successes in Europe and meetings with top German officials. The Nazi regime seemed destined to defeat Britain and gain hegemony in Europe and Africa. Berlin's evasive and tight-lipped attitude was taken as proof that the Nazi regime had designs on Asia. This intelligence failure no doubt had much to do with longer-term changes in the foreign ministry. In the wake of the Manchurian Incident of 1931, the foreign ministry underwent radical personnel and structural changes that undermined the diplomatic establishment's ability and prestige.[34] Moreover, this was also an interministerial intelligence failure. Had those in the foreign ministry engaged in discussions with the army, they might have learned of German ambassador Eugen Ott's statement to Lt. General Mutō Akira and General Koiso Kuniaki on June 24, 1940, which reaffirmed Germany's statement of disinterest in the Netherlands Indies (and French Indochina).[35] At the very point when broader intelligence could have painted a clearer picture, Japan found itself in the dark, worrying over phantom German aims.

These phantom concerns reached the highest levels of Japan's policy elite and began to affect policy in late July 1940. But they ran into a roadblock with the cabinet of Prime Minister Yonai Mitsumasa. Yonai, a navy man, opposed a more robust foreign policy, favoring friendlier nations with the Western maritime powers.[36] He had objected to the Anti-Comintern Pact and close relations with Nazi Germany. Instead, Yonai pursued a middle-of-the-road strategy, seeking friendly relations both with the Axis and with Britain and the United States. Further, his president of the cabinet planning board, Takeuchi Kakichi, rejected the army and reformist bureaucrat plans for a new domestic order and a centrally planned economy. This was anathema to the army, which not only sought far-reaching domestic reforms but also called for a more activist leadership. The army wanted a leader committed to the German alliance, one who could capitalize on the dramatic events in Europe. They hoped to find such leadership in Konoe Fumimaro, the very person who (during his first stint as premier) declared the new order in East Asia. With the next suitable premier in mind, the army overthrew the Yonai cabinet. On July 16, army minister Hata Shunroku resigned. The army refused to nominate a successor, and the Yonai government collapsed.[37] Konoe—the army favorite—succeeded Yonai as premier.

The decision to bring back Konoe as premier put Japan on the path to the southern advance. In preparation for his premiership, Konoe ordered the so-called Ogikubo conference on July 19, 1940. Attended at Konoe's residence

in Ogikubo by soon-to-be Prime Minister Konoe, foreign minister Matsuoka
Yōsuke, army minister Tōjō Hideki, and navy minister Yoshida Zengo, the conference sought to align understandings of national policy. But even the participants
remained divided or unclear on the conference's impact.[38] Still, the conference
laid the groundwork for a German alliance and expansion to the south. The ministers agreed to "take proactive measures to bring British, French, Dutch, and
Portuguese colonies in East Asia into the New Order in East Asia." Moreover,
they determined to bring about Japanese hegemony in Asia by strengthening the
"Japan-Germany-Italy axis."[39]

Konoe continued this process after forming his second cabinet on July 22,
1940. Two days later, Konoe held a four-minister conference on national policy,
attended by Konoe, foreign minister Matsuoka, army minister Tōjō, and navy
minister Yoshida. They reaffirmed that Southeast Asia lay within Japan's "living space" (*seikatsuken*), which would eventually reach as far as India, Burma,
Australia, and New Zealand. Initially, however, Japan would focus on incorporating China, Manchukuo, French Indochina, the Dutch East Indies, and the South
Seas. And the ministers asserted the necessity of Germany and Italy "consenting
to Japan's political leadership over and cooperation with the region."[40] Later that
day, a draft letter of orders to ambassador to Germany Kurusu Saburō reaffirmed
the necessity of keeping Germany from infringing on Japan's sphere or exercising
indirect control over French or Dutch colonies. The letter included concerns over
German policy toward Southeast Asia:

> It is possible that Germany intends to use France and Holland to place
> in their own hands political leadership over French Indochina and the
> Netherlands East Indies, and will only provide limited economic rights
> to Japan. But these areas are indispensable for the Empire's construction
> of its new order, and the Empire absolutely needs to obtain political
> control over the region. Accordingly, if Germany's attitude is [such to
> control French Indochina and the Netherlands East Indies], be prepared
> for considerable friction with Germany, and be resolved to make the
> Empire's aims come to pass.[41]

The Konoe cabinet immediately codified this desire to expand south. The new
administration's very first liaison conference—held on July 22, 1940—adopted
a policy document, "Outline for Dealing with the World Situation," which noted
the two imperatives of ending the so-called China Incident and expanding into
Southeast Asia.[42] Strikingly, the "Outline" noted that if the chance arose, Japan
was "to seize advantageous conditions and take military action" to advance
south.[43] Such action against the European colonial powers remarkably did not
hinge on the successful resolution of the war in China. Japan could commit to

both at the same time. Should the China war remain unresolved, Tokyo would merely strive to avoid opening hostilities with any third power in the region. But if leaders sensed favorable conditions, then they could call for a military advance into Southeast Asia despite the continuing campaigns in China. In the case that war broke out, however, Japan would limit hostilities to Britain's Asian colonies and would do its utmost to avoid any conflict with the United States. Yet wishful thinking never prevented wars, so thorough preparations were to be made in case Tokyo found itself at war with Washington. The "Outline" laid bare the fact that Japanese leaders understood that expansion would lead to confrontation with Britain and the United States, even though Tokyo sought to limit the scope of those conflicts.

The policy elite rarely questioned this expansionist logic. Granted, Emperor Hirohito looked with disquiet on Japan's desire to move south without first ending the war in China. Hirohito told Lord Keeper of the Privy Seal Kido Kōichi on July 30, 1940 that the government "is turning toward the South owing to the people's dissatisfactions with the failed China Incident."[44] Nonetheless, the emperor was either unwilling or unable to change policy—no doubt owing to the importance wartime elites attached to expansion into Southeast Asia. After all, Japan could hardly continue its extensive operations throughout China without relying on the region's abundance of natural resources. Worsening relations with the United States and Great Britain made expanding the nation's influence even more critical. Hence the plan emphasized *military expansion*. And strikingly, its adoption points to a shared understanding between previously antagonistic army and navy elites of the necessity of initiating hostilities (such a consensus was a prerequisite for ensuring that policy was carried out). Although the "Outline" sought to use diplomatic means when available, one can almost read into the plan the inevitable failure of such diplomacy. It placed greater emphasis on the use of force once diplomatic endeavors proved fruitless.

On July 26, 1940, the Konoe cabinet adopted "The Main Principles of National Policy," which declared that Japan would construct a "New Order in Greater East Asia" centered on Japan, China, and Manchukuo.[45] This was the first official policy document noting the term "Greater East Asia," with "Greater" implying the inclusion of Southeast Asia, Oceania, and the Indian subcontinent.

Thus, the southern advance became national policy at precisely the moment when the ruling elite wondered about the future of Japanese rule over Southeast Asia. The brilliant but explosive foreign minister Matsuoka Yōsuke took to the radio waves on August 1, 1940, to explain this new national policy. "The essence of our country's foreign policy," Matsuoka argued, "must focus on the establishment of a Greater East Asia Co-Prosperity Sphere that centers on Japan, Manchukuo, and China." This notion of a Co-Prosperity Sphere—a regional political bloc of Asian nations led by Japan—would replace Japan's New Order in East Asia as the fundamental vision for the future. In this context, it fit firmly into a long-standing

Pan-Asian discourse and rejected the political settlements that emerged in the wake of World War I. But the timing of the declaration and the language used also suggest that this Co-Prosperity Sphere slogan might have also had a short-term aim: recognition from Germany of Japan's preeminent position in Southeast Asia. After all, Matsuoka made abundantly clear the position Southeast Asia held in Japan's foreign policy designs. "It goes without saying," Matsuoka declared, "that the South Seas are also included in the establishment of the Greater East Asia Co-Prosperity Sphere." Moreover, Matsuoka stressed that Japan would be willing to cooperate with any country "that understands the new state of affairs in East Asia and voluntarily pushes forward in the creation of a new world."[46] In making this statement, was Matsuoka not also declaring Japan's sphere of interest in Southeast Asia to potential allies such as Germany?

There is good reason to believe that Matsuoka in part oriented his Greater East Asia Co-Prosperity Sphere speech toward Germany. After all, in the summer of 1940, Matsuoka was no doubt as wary of German motives as other members of the foreign policy elite were. This may appear surprising, for Matsuoka in 1937 had seen a partnership with Germany as natural and inevitable. He celebrated the signing of the Anti-Comintern Pact as joining together the fates of the two rising powers.[47] But both direct and circumstantial evidence points to Matsuoka's growing distrust of Germany. If we are to believe Matsuoka's personal aide, Saitō Yoshie, Matsuoka had felt wary of Germany since his childhood days, and even after becoming foreign minister he still professed, "There are no less trustworthy people than the Germans."[48] Moreover, Matsuoka himself wrote in 1941 of his dislike for the "White man's bloc" in Asia. He further argued that in creating the new order in East Asia, Japan "is determined to shatter the White man's mastery [hakujin seiha] over all of the Orient."[49]

This point is of critical import. After all, from the moment Matsuoka took office in July 1940, he began to reformulate the Kasumigaseki bureaucracy, dismissing many former ambassadors and ministers and filling key positions with zealous supporters of his leadership and the Axis alliance. In the process, Matsuoka recalled no fewer than thirty-nine diplomats from posts abroad. Though professional diplomats such as Shigemitsu saw him as destroying Japan's diplomatic establishment in a "bloodbath," Matsuoka merely ensured a foreign ministry supportive of his foreign policy making.[50] Matsuoka is critical to understanding the Tripartite Pact. After all, it was Matsuoka, more than anyone else in the Japanese government (outside of the army), who from July 1940 pushed for the alliance with Germany and Italy.[51]

On August 1, the same day he announced the Co-Prosperity Sphere, Matsuoka invited German ambassador Eugen Ott to his home in Sendagaya, where they drank tea and discussed (among other things) the fate of Southeast Asia. "Japan," Matsuoka explained to Ott, "is currently trying to establish a new order in East

Asia—with Japan, Manchuria, and China as its core—that also includes the South Seas. We aim to liberate and free the Sphere's peoples and ethnicities, and plan coexistence and co-prosperity where all peoples and ethnicities jointly prosper."[52] But with Germany newly ascendant in France and the Low Countries, Matsuoka worried about Berlin's Southeast Asia policy. He questioned Ott on Germany's attitude toward the South Seas. Ott, however, gave a noncommittal answer and refused to take any position on Greater East Asia until Japan presented a concrete plan outlining the advantages to Germany.[53] In fact, most of Ott's replies conveyed to Matsuoka a sense of apathy toward improved relations. Ott even noted his personal dissatisfaction with what he considered Tokyo's insulting treatment, and he complained that Satō Naotake was sent to Rome and Berlin as part of an effort "to estrange Japan from Germany and Italy." As later accounts show, Germany's cold reception "no doubt gave Matsuoka a feeling of inner unease."[54]

Such questioning highlights the anxiety with imagined German expansion in Asia. Matsuoka did all he could to avoid drawing ire from Berlin. When Ott asked Matsuoka what he meant by the "South Seas," Matsuoka left vague the extent of Japan's new order. Instead, he merely gave the cautious reply that it includes Thailand, but may be expanded in the future. This reply, however, ran counter to the consensus held among the Konoe cabinet that French Indochina and the Netherlands Indies were to form the core of Japan's new regional order. And it even contradicts Matsuoka's own statements. He asserted at an August 2 press conference, "It is obvious that French Indochina and the Netherlands East Indies are included in the Greater East Asia Co-Prosperity Sphere."[55] Ott thus found Matsuoka's assertion odd and noted his confusion in an August 29 meeting with Lt. General Ōshima, Japan's former ambassador to Berlin. "Foreign minister Matsuoka," Ott observed, "stated that the Greater East Asia Co-Prosperity Sphere region only goes as far as Thailand; it is strange that it does not include the Netherlands East Indies."[56] It seems logical, then, to conclude that Matsuoka deliberately obscured the scope of Japan's regional designs to avoid antagonizing the nation with whom Japan sought to create a new world order. Matsuoka himself hinted at this on August 27, when he told Ōshima, "Germany will take a great loss from Japan's advance into the South Seas."[57] This lack of forthright communication epitomized the mistrust that was endemic to the Axis partnership.

Into the Tiger's Den

Despite this distrust, Matsuoka championed a closer working relationship with Germany. On July 23, 1940, the day after taking office, Matsuoka called on the Bureau of Eurasian Affairs to discuss section chief Andō's draft plan for the Axis alliance. Matsuoka refused to accept Andō's draft plan, which called for "the highest level partnership, short of entering the war." "This is no good," he told Andō, stressing that an alliance was meaningless without the risk of war. Matsuoka even wrote the proverb "One cannot capture a tiger cub without venturing into the tiger's den" into the page margin of Andō's draft plan.[58] The German alliance, in short, was too important to miss out on. Matsuoka was willing to venture into the tiger's den of a stronger alliance with Germany to capture the prize of expanded influence in Southeast Asia.

On July 30, Matsuoka's close aide drafted a new plan, "On Strengthening Cooperation among Japan, Germany, and Italy," which reflected Matsuoka's hopes for the alliance. Approved by the foreign, army, and navy ministries on August 6 after only minor revisions, this plan reflected shared policy aims within the Japanese government, and it became the cornerstone of the Konoe cabinet's efforts to join the Axis alliance. The new plan called not only for stronger cooperation but also for a basic understanding of each nation's respective interests. This included the respect for each power's sphere of influence: Germany and Italy would have their "living space" (*seikatsuken*) in Europe and Africa, whereas Japan would control East Asia and the "South Seas." The policy paper also called for a deeper economic and political partnership, for peaceful relations with the Soviet Union, and for limited cooperation in their respective wars. Notably, it also emphasized the widest scope of Japan's "living space" (*seizonken*). Japan's new order would center on Japan, Manchukuo, and China, but it would reach as far as the old German mandate islands, French Indochina, English Malaya and Borneo, the Netherlands Indies, Burma, Australia, New Zealand, and India.[59]

By late August, the changing war situation in Europe made German leaders more interested in an alliance with Japan. The difficulties the Luftwaffe faced achieving air superiority over Britain convinced Berlin to delay indefinitely Operation Sea Lion, the planned invasion of the British Isles. Sensing a protracted war on the horizon and worrying that the United States would join the war in support of Britain, the Nazi leadership now viewed Japan as a potential ally. Japan would serve as the cork to bottle up American might; U.S. power would be effectively neutralized if war against Germany also meant risking war in the Asia-Pacific. Ribbentrop indicated Berlin's now-favorable view toward Japan in an August 23 cable to Ambassador Kurusu, revealing that Germany would soon send Special Envoy Heinrich Georg Stahmer to negotiate the pact.

Meanwhile, Japanese initiatives for the alliance proceeded apace. A four-minister conference of September 6, 1940, affirmed the goals of the August policy paper. The ministers foresaw the world as splitting up into four blocs: East Asia, the Soviet Union, Europe, and the United States. To ensure the nation's ability to create its East Asian order, the four ministers agreed with the recommendation to negotiate an alliance with Germany and Italy.[60] They started the process through a series of talks beginning on September 9 with Stahmer, mostly at Matsuoka's home in Sendagaya. Stahmer stated in plain language Germany's designs: the alliance with Japan would help restrain the United States from intervening in Europe. Stahmer spoke of the necessity for a "strong, determined, and clear attitude" from the Axis powers, one that would serve as a "powerful and effective threat" against the United States. In return, he made clear Germany's intention to "respect Japan as political leader of Greater East Asia."[61] Japan had finally received the assurance it sought.

In the wake of the Stahmer talks, Matsuoka sold the idea of allying with Germany at a September 14 four-minister conference and a liaison conference. One of the tactics he chose stressed the freedom Japan would gain to enact its designs on Southeast Asia. Matsuoka stated, "Shall we immediately sign an alliance with Germany and Italy, or shall we turn down the Axis and stand alongside England and America? We have reached a point where Japan must make a decisive decision." Matsuoka continued, considering worst-case scenarios. He wondered aloud what would happen if Tokyo continued to treat discussions for an Axis pact in an ambiguous manner. This could have drastic ramifications. Matsuoka argued that if Germany defeats Great Britain, they might reach a compromise with the United States. In the worst-case scenario, he argued that Germany might "not allow Japan to have a hand in British, Dutch, and European [Southeast Asian] colonies." On the other hand, things did not look any better should Japan tilt toward the United States. Doing so, he argued, would force Japan to "give up on our dreams for a new order in East Asia, and spend at least a half century bowing our heads to Britain and America." Matsuoka concluded that Japan cannot consider an alliance with the United States. "The only path left to us," he said, "is an alliance with Germany and Italy."[62]

The September 19 imperial conference and September 26 Privy Council discussions further committed Japan to the Tripartite Pact, after some revisions from the continuing discussions with Berlin. Much of the deliberations focused on the Axis pact as a military alliance directed against the United States. Matsuoka himself argued that the alliance with Germany would help prevent a Japanese-American clash in the Pacific.[63] But strikingly, an undercurrent of doubt penetrated the Privy Council discussions. Ishii Kikujirō, a Japanese diplomat who had been foreign minister during the World War I era, voiced strong misgivings with the proposed pact. Hitler, Ishii argued, would prove a dangerous ally. The German leader, after all, had publicly spoken of alliances as little more than temporary expedients. Further, Ishii argued that Hitler would work to prevent Japan from emerging as a great power. Germany under Hitler was thus no friend to Japan. In fact, Germany throughout its modern era brought about disaster or misfortune to its allies. "Bismarck once said," Ishii thundered, "that in international alliances one horseman and one donkey are required, and that Germany must always be the horseman." For all his skepticism, Ishii still supported the proposed alliance, but he warned that Japan must take great care in any dealings with Berlin.[64]

The following day, on September 27, 1940, Japanese ambassador Kurusu, German foreign minister Ribbentrop, and Italian foreign minister Ciano signed the Tripartite Pact in Berlin to great fanfare. The Tripartite Pact provided the basic working relationship between the three nations for the rest of the war. Japan agreed to recognize the leadership of Germany and Italy in Europe. In turn, Germany and Italy would respect Japanese control of Greater East Asia. All member nations agreed to support each other if attacked by a power (outside of the Soviet Union) not currently involved in the wars in Europe and East Asia. Thus the Axis powers were born.

But Matsuoka weakened the pact on the very day of its signing through a secret understanding with Ambassador Ott. This secret understanding—produced through a flurry of letters between the two diplomats—stressed that, in the event of an attack by a third power, the signatories would declare war *only* *after* consultation and an agreement that an "attack" had actually taken place. This altered the Tripartite Pact in an important way: it gave Japan an escape route from its *automatic* treaty obligations to come to Germany's military aid. Ott confirmed this fact in a letter to Matsuoka. "Needless to say," he wrote, "the question, whether an attack within the meaning of article 3 of the Pact has taken place, must be determined through the joint consultation of the three contracting parties."[65] The inclusion of this secret release owed to pressure from the Japanese navy—it was the condition on which they assented to the pact. Moreover, the secret understanding highlights the high-handedness of German diplomats in Tokyo; Ott entered into the agreement without foreign minister Ribbentrop's authorization or knowledge.[66] Thus Ott conferred on Japan a significant diplomatic advantage, effectively ensuring a lopsided alliance almost wholly in Japan's favor. The amended alliance both confirmed Japanese leadership over Southeast Asia and provided a one-sided guarantee of military aid to Japan.

Still, not all in Tokyo agreed with the decision to bind their fate with Berlin and Rome. Many in the Shōwa Kenkyūkai opposed the pact. The navy, too, had fiercely disagreed with signing the Tripartite Pact since 1939. Navy minister Yoshida publicly argued against the pact, which he thought "would turn both [England and the United States] into enemies."[67] The navy ultimately assented after Yoshida collapsed and entered the hospital on September 3, 1940—no doubt this had much to do with the favorable secret understanding Matsuoka signed with Ott.[68] But as Michael Barnhart and Mori Shigeki have argued, Yonai's successor, the weak-willed Oikawa Koshirō, also assented to the alliance to obtain for the navy higher materials allocations and a primary role in Japan's advance to the south.[69] Cabinet information board head Itō Nobufumi also decried the idea of working closely with Germany. He argued that the alliance would have a harmful economic impact, inhibiting Japan from attaining the self-sufficiency needed to fight future total wars. Further, he just did not trust Germany. "When push comes to shove," he argued, "you don't know what Germany will do. Consequently, we ought not rely even a little on other countries."[70]

With such widespread distrust of Berlin, why did Japan become a willing party to the Tripartite Pact? The most convincing existing scholarship views the Axis alliance as aimed at the United States. Konoe himself argued that one big aim of the pact was "the prevention of the U.S. entry into the war."[71] Matsuoka, too, made a similar argument. At the September 19 imperial conference and again at the September 26 Privy Council discussions, he argued that the German alliance was instrumental "to avoid war" with the United States in the short term and to reconcile with Washington in the longer term.[72] It should be clear, however, that this represents only one side of the story. *Fears* of German motives toward Asia also drove Japan into a German embrace.

U.S. ambassador Grew had caught wind of these fears in August 1940. "There are indications," he recorded in his diary, "that irritation with Germany is growing in official Japanese circles. Many believe that Germany still wishes Chiang Kai-shek to win and that a German victory in Europe would result in the establishment of German interests in China. Possible German designs on the Netherlands East Indies in such an event are also causing anxiety." Grew furthermore noted increasing frustrations in Japan with German efforts to embroil Japan in an anti–Anglo-American alliance. "Clearly," he wrote, "the Germans are overplaying their hand." Within a few months, however, Grew had changed his tune. "It is painful," Grew wrote in October 1940, "now to see that even as late as August I wrote that the Japanese Government was getting fed up with the Germans in their efforts to embroil Japan with the United States." A month after his August diary entry, after all, Japan had joined an alliance Grew believed was aimed at bringing about war with the United States.[73]

But Grew had been closer to the truth than he realized. Japanese leaders shouldered great fears that Germany would seek to acquire and control French and Dutch colonies in East Asia. Granted, Japanese decision makers were well aware that Nazi Germany lacked a strong navy necessary to seize those colonies. But even claiming those colonies (and asking for Japanese help in seizing them) would have drastically limited the scope of Japan's new order. This was anathema to those who saw their nation as the leader of an expanded international order encompassing Southeast Asia. The alliance with Berlin and Rome effectively served to thwart imagined German ambitions in Asia. It is thus best understood as being directed at *both* Germany and the United States.

Strikingly, this context of fear of imagined German motives in Asia—fears that emerged and dissipated in a single historical moment—helps us view in fascinating new light Japan's Greater East Asia Co-Prosperity Sphere. Viewed from a longer perspective, the Co-Prosperity Sphere declaration represented the culmination of a Pan-Asian vision for Japanese hegemony over East Asia, a vision that had its deepest roots in the breakdown of the Versailles-Washington system. Other scholars have noted that the Co-Prosperity Sphere epitomized a propagandistic means to secure loyalties in the region for Japan's imperial project or to win over the United States.[74]

But viewing the birth of the Co-Prosperity Sphere through a shorter-term lens leads to a different perspective. The timing of its establishment—in the summer of 1940, at the height of concerns about German motives toward Asia—suggests that the Co-Prosperity Sphere was in equal measure part and parcel of a propaganda campaign aimed at Berlin. As Japanese historian Kawanishi Kōsuke has most forcefully argued, fears that Germany might claim territories essential to Japan's order led leaders in the foreign ministry to call for extending their sphere of influence into Greater East Asia and to consider leadership of this expanded area the sine qua non for closer relations with Berlin. This explains why Matsuoka argued in his August 1 speech that Japan would "take active measures to cooperate" with any nation that understands "the new state of affairs in East Asia."[75] The implied target was no doubt Germany, with whom the Konoe cabinet had already decided to forge an alliance. The Greater East Asia Co-Prosperity Sphere, then, served in part as propaganda to make Japanese preeminence in Southeast Asia the precondition for signing the Tripartite Pact.[76]

The Berlin foreign policy establishment understood Japanese intentions. On August 7, 1940, Ambassador Kurusu sought to defend the Co-Prosperity Sphere idea in a meeting with foreign minister Ribbentrop and state secretary Weizsäcker, of which Weizsäcker left a detailed report. Kurusu maintained that this Co-Prosperity Sphere would include "Greater East Asia, including the South Pacific, on a broad basis." Yet it was clear that discussions related primarily to Japanese interests in Southeast Asia, as Kurusu used the Co-Prosperity Sphere announcement to seek Berlin's approval of a Japan-dominated Greater East Asia. "Kurusu," Weizsäcker wrote, "did not mention the statement of our disinterestedness regarding these overseas problems, which we had made to the Japanese in May of this year, but it was plain to see what he was aiming at, and he was obviously acting upon instructions from Tokyo in this matter."[77] And Kurusu would continue to use the notion of "Greater East Asia" to emphasize Japanese primacy over Southeast Asia. He met with German foreign ministry Commercial

Policy Bureau director Emil Weihl on August 22 to inform Weihl that Germany would henceforth have only economic—not political or military—interests in the Netherlands Indies.[78] The Co-Prosperity Sphere propaganda was in part an attempt to keep Germany out of Japan's own backyard. Only *after* the Tripartite Pact was signed would Japanese policy makers start to imagine what the Sphere implied for the region.

The mistrust surrounding the formation of the Axis alliance had longer-standing impacts and perhaps reveals why the Axis would fail to cooperate throughout the war. Adolf Hitler's megalomania and well-known disdain of Japan certainly served as an important factor. Hitler held all non-Europeans in contempt; he would have rather allied with Great Britain, whose global policies and far-flung empire he admired and respected. In fact, the Japanese humiliation of the British Empire at Singapore in February 1942 appears to have caused Hitler considerable personal distress. Moreover, by March 1942 Ribbentrop's press bureau spoke in bitter terms over Japanese victories, because they belonged to the "yellow race" and came "at the expense of the white race."[79] In an amusing twist of fate, Japanese military victories begot the very estrangement Japan had feared in 1939 and 1940.

But the process and structure of the Tripartite Pact played a role as well in the failure of the Axis. The Tripartite Pact was, at its core, an older style of alliance, one that the major powers had rejected in favor of multilateralism and confer-ence diplomacy in the wake of World War I. The pact stipulated that participants were to recognize each other's sphere of influence and aid each other if attacked by a third power (excluding the Soviet Union). Most importantly, from Tokyo's perspective, the pact kept Germany out of Japan's East Asian domain. This was a weak foundation from which to build a close-knit alliance or to prosecute a global war. The January 18, 1942, "Tripartite Military Pact" between Germany, Italy, and Japan further institutionalized the sphere-of-influence nature of Axis relations.[80] The pact simply divided operational areas between the Axis powers at 70 degrees east longitude, giving Germany and Italy responsibility for the Near East, Middle East, and European theaters and Japan control over the Pacific and East Asian theaters. Even though policy makers such as diplomat and foreign minister Shigemitsu Mamoru pushed for greater diplomatic and military coop-eration, such efforts came to naught. As one Finnish representative in Tokyo bit-terly complained after the war, "all the cooperation in the Axis you could put in a small handbag."[81] The Greater East Asia Co-Prosperity Sphere may have been a campaign to oust the West from Asia, but it created an alliance that served Japan poorly during the Pacific War.

Japan's new order thus encompassed the two conflicting trends of anti-Westernism and anti–Anglo-Americanism. Anti-Western, Pan-Asian sentiments sat alongside a desire to work with other "have-not countries," Germany and Italy. In joining other "have-nots," Japan would help topple the old order and create a "fair" and "just" new order—one in which rising powers would have equal access to markets, resources, and living space. Both sentiments meant roughly the same thing to policy makers and pundits alike: the creation of a Japan-led order in East Asia. Tensions between anti-Western and anti–old order sentiments remained unresolved during the war, with an important impact on relations with the Axis Powers. As Reto Hofmann has shown, from the Japanese perspective, the very fact that Germany and Italy were part of the West limited the potential for intensive collaboration in their shared efforts to overthrow the old order.[82]

Both Konoe and Matsuoka lived to be conscience-stricken over the decision to ally with Germany. With the signing of the Tripartite Pact, Tokyo continued tumbling down the slippery slope to war with the United States and Great Britain. Berlin's failure to consult Tokyo over important policies engendered further difficulties. Konoe viewed the German decision to invade the Soviet Union without consulting Japan as Berlin's "second betrayal," one that contributed to the fall of both empires.[83] The invasion, Konoe no doubt realized, placed the Soviet Union firmly in the Allied camp and removed any restraints from the full exercise of American and British power in Asia. By this time, Konoe would no doubt have agreed with Italian foreign minister Ciano, who complained in his diary that the Germans were "possessed by the demon of destruction."[84] The irascible Matsuoka, too, came to regret the pact with the same vigor and emotional power with which he hailed its signing. In May 1941 he had lauded the Tripartite Pact as "one success of my diplomacy."[85] But seven months later, he looked on his diplomacy with new eyes. On December 8, 1941, when Tokyo announced the attack on Pearl Harbor, Matsuoka lamented it from his sick bed at his home in Sendagaya. As tears welled up in his eyes, Matsuoka bewailed, "I am now painfully aware that the signing of the Tripartite Pact was the biggest mistake of my lifetime. . . . When I think of this, it will bother me even after I die."[86]

2

ORDER BEGETS WAR

The alliance with Nazi Germany and the birth of the Greater East Asia Co-Prosperity Sphere served as the first major steps toward establishing Japan as Asia's leading power. But Matsuoka was just warming up. In the wake of the Axis Pact, Japan's volatile foreign minister began an all-out diplomatic offensive to construct the Sphere. Aiming partly at the great powers and partly at Asia, Matsuoka used what is best thought of as sphere-of-influence diplomacy to achieve Japanese hegemony. He believed peaceful but hard-nosed diplomacy would convince Asian countries and the Great Powers alike to recognize Japan as the head of an Asian family of nations. The Co-Prosperity Sphere ideal represented the linchpin of his grand strategy to remake Asia under Japan. Yet the centrality of the Sphere to Matsuoka, surprisingly, is rarely mentioned in English-language studies on Matsuoka's foreign policy.[1]

This chapter focuses on the rise and fall of Matsuoka's sphere-of-influence diplomacy. He pursued this diplomacy in two major ways. First, Matsuoka saw peaceful negotiations in Asia as key to building legitimacy of Japanese leadership and to gaining acceptance of the new order. To this end, he played a central role in the mediation of a border crisis between Thailand and French Indochina, and he supported economic talks with French Indochina and the Netherlands Indies. Intelligent diplomacy, he believed, served imperial ends. Only through agreements with Southeast Asian nations could Matsuoka turn his vision for a Greater East Asia Co-Prosperity Sphere into reality. Second, and more importantly, Matsuoka hoped to use negotiations with the United States and the Soviet

Union, in particular, to gain acceptance of the Co-Prosperity Sphere and respect for Japanese hegemony in Greater East Asia. Believing the age of Wilsonian internationalism had ended, he responded to the challenges of diplomacy and empire by returning to the imperialist diplomacy of the nineteenth century, modified to meet the needs of the new era. He called for a cooperative imperialism, one in which great powers recognized and respected each other's spheres of influence and interest. Matsuoka hoped this strategy would not only secure Japan's position as a stabilizing force in East Asia but also promote peaceful relations with other regional blocs.

Matsuoka's vision blended great imagination with great naïveté, and realism with artlessness. He thought of the movement toward pan-regions in global and universal terms, and thus he overlooked how other great powers might react to Japanese moves. A foreign policy daydreamer, Matsuoka sought to secure Japan's future on a diplomatic house of cards: any failure, and his whole diplomatic edifice would come tumbling down. Nonetheless, he alone crafted a deep and consistent foreign policy vision for the Greater East Asia Co-Prosperity Sphere in the early years of Japan's war, and in the process he popularized and normalized the Sphere as the end goal of Japanese policy. Other policy elites ultimately accepted and drew on his visions, but for their own ends. Many across the foreign policy establishment no doubt saw the Co-Prosperity Sphere as a useful slogan for propaganda that was otherwise lacking in substance. Stated differently, to other elites the Sphere was so vacuous and vague as to mean nothing, and it was thus something into which they could inject their own ideas.

By the time of Matsuoka's dramatic fall from power in July 1941, his vision for the Co-Prosperity Sphere laid in tatters. With the failure to improve relations with the United States and the outbreak of the German-Soviet war, his diplomacy appeared to be an abject failure. By that time, however, the Sphere had taken on a life of its own as the central goal of Japanese policy. In the hands of military leaders, the Sphere became a call for self-existence and self-sufficiency in global affairs. And it only worsened relations with the so-called ABCD powers: America, Britain, China, and the Dutch. Herein lies a major irony of Japan's Co-Prosperity Sphere ideal. Although Matsuoka used it for the purposes of peace and order, his time as foreign minister propelled Japan down the path toward total war in the Asia-Pacific.

Stargazing Diplomacy

Matsuoka's sphere-of-influence diplomacy emerged from his reading of the trends of the times. Like many of his counterparts, Matsuoka believed the world would break up into a series of blocs led by strong states. He thus felt a keen need for his diplomacy to garner the great powers' recognition of Japan's position in Asia. Matsuoka, in fact, hinted at his ideas for diplomacy in May 1940, two months before he became foreign minister. Writing for the journal *The Pacific Ocean* (*Taiheiyō*), Matsuoka noted that the future of the Pacific would be decided by Japan and the United States. Conflict was not inevitable, however, as "reasonable men" could find a way to avoid war. The means to do so rested in each great power "possessing its own sphere of influence." Any incursion into another power's sphere would invite significant tensions at best, and war at worst. Matsuoka signaled that the recognition and respect of these spheres of influence represented the primary means to keep the peace in the Pacific.[2]

Matsuoka advanced this sphere-of-influence diplomacy on assuming the foreign ministry portfolio. As discussed in chapter 1, he pushed for the Axis Pact in part to gain diplomatic recognition of Japan's preeminent position in Asia. In return, Japan recognized German and Italian supremacy in Europe and North Africa. Matsuoka pressed ahead the following day, September 28, 1940, drafting "The Main Points of the Empire's Diplomatic Policy."[3] This little-known policy document, which was brought to light by Japanese historian Kawanishi Kōsuke in 2016, epitomizes Matsuoka's sphere-of-influence diplomacy and provides a clear window into the world the volatile foreign minister sought to build. This document, as Kawanishi argues, shows how important the Greater East Asia Co-Prosperity Sphere was to Matsuoka's diplomatic strategy.[4] Overall, Matsuoka's strategy in the "Main Points" was simple: Japan must extend its new order to Southeast Asia and convince the great powers to respect Japan's regional hegemony.

On the one hand, the "Main Points" called for the construction of the Greater East Asia Co-Prosperity Sphere, which would encompass not only the core region of Japan, Manchukuo, and China but also French Indochina, the Netherlands Indies, British Malaya, Thailand, the Philippines, British Borneo, and Burma. In the short term, Matsuoka argued that relations with these member countries would be forged via broad-based bilateral agreements. Japan would strengthen economic, political, and military relations with Thailand and gain Thai support for the Co-Prosperity Sphere. Moreover, Japan would sign economic accords with French Indochina and the Netherlands Indies and would "plan for a political partnership" that provided for "independence and mutual aid."

More importantly, the "Main Points" sought diplomatic recognition of the Co-Prosperity Sphere from the Soviet Union, Great Britain, and the United States. The linchpin to this strategy was the Soviet Union, which Matsuoka's rivals in the army general staff had long marked as Japan's traditional and hypothetical enemy. Japan had fought with the Soviet Union in a series of disastrous engagements that have come to be known as the Nomonhan Incident. From May through mid-September 1939, the Kwantung Army clashed with the Red Army at Nomonhan, a quiet Mongolian village near the Manchukuo border. Initiated by the Kwantung Army without direct approval from Tokyo, this conflict added tensions to the already fraught relations between the two Asian powers over Japan's position in Sakhalin/Karafuto.[5] Even after a new border agreement formally ended the Nomonhan Incident in June 1940, Moscow kept committing forces to the region. By July 1, more than one-fifth of land forces and one-third of Soviet tanks were deployed in Northeast Asia.[6] Such forces massed on the border to Manchukuo constituted an ever-present worry for elite policy makers. Matsuoka thus called for a formal rapprochement.[7]

The "Main Points" highlights the centrality of Matsuoka's sphere-of-influence diplomacy in bringing about such an understanding. He believed Japan could sign a treaty or nonaggression pact that would not only solve tensions over Sakhalin/Karafuto but also delineate each power's sphere of influence. The "Main Points" thus called on both powers to "outline living space from the Near East to the Asian continent (including China)." Matsuoka, in short, even wanted to partition China into Japanese and Soviet spheres. Japan would recognize Soviet supremacy over Xinjiang and Tibet in return for Soviet respect for Japan's special position in Mengjiang (Mongol Border Land) and Outer Mongolia.

Once this deal with the Soviet Union had been achieved, Matsuoka would shift focus to Britain and the United States. First, the "Main Points" called for fresh measures to gain British "recognition and cooperation with the establishment of our East Asian Great Co-Prosperity Sphere." In return, Japan could broker a peace deal between Germany and Britain, offer open economic relations, and provide a security guarantee for the British dominions of Australia and New Zealand. Second, the "Main Points" called for aggressive negotiations with the United States for both a new commercial treaty and for a nonaggression pact that would "divide the Pacific Ocean into East and West" and be based on each side "accepting the other's spheres of influence." To bring about such a pact, the only real bargaining chip Matsuoka could think up was that Japan would respect the independence of the Philippines. Matsuoka believed this multifaceted diplomacy would convince the Anglo-American powers to recognize Japan's dominant position in Asia.

This approach was by no means unique or novel—it harked back to late nineteenth-century European visions of informal empire. "Spheres of influence" had gained official recognition at the Berlin conference of 1884–85, which formalized Europe's infamous Scramble for Africa. The conference's final act noted that a state might exercise "influence" instead of "protection" or "sovereignty" over another territory.[8] In effect, it sanctioned boundary marking or territorial expansion through agreements among imperialist powers, and in doing so obviated open conflict for new territories. The expansion of European empires into Africa and Asia in the late nineteenth century made great use of such spheres of influence. Matsuoka was cut from this older diplomatic cloth, and his approach resembled nineteenth-century imperialist politics, but with one modification. Whereas earlier spheres of influence were concluded through negotiations among imperialist nations coupled with force of arms in the periphery, he sought to assert its influence via negotiations with both the great powers *and* with individual Asian countries on the periphery.

Matsuoka referred to himself as "either a genius or a madman," and this document unmistakably shows elements of both.[9] As farsighted as it was unrealistic, the foreign minister's sphere-of-influence pipe dream highlighted Japan's future as poised on a knife edge. In pursuing his sphere-of-influence diplomacy, Matsuoka strove to build a new world order that would emerge after war's end.[10] This new world order, however, depended on a string of improbable foreign policy successes that brooked no failure. Granted, Matsuoka found a mildly receptive partner in Soviet leader Joseph Stalin. But, as will be discussed in greater detail below, he offered little to win over policy makers in either Washington or London, and he provided no real means of generating excitement from Southeast Asian colonial elites. Moreover, his hard-nosed vision overestimated Japanese power, and he failed to grasp the difficulties Japan would have negotiating this vision with the United States, the true world power of the day. Matsuoka may have had a global vision, but this vision was as impractical as it was naïve.

Building the Co-Prosperity Sphere

The first major aspect of Matsuoka's diplomatic strategy was to build the Greater East Asia Co-Prosperity Sphere. He thus worked to establish Japanese leadership over the "South." The fall of the Netherlands and France by June 1940 provided a favorable opportunity to do so, offering the context by which Japan could forge Asia anew. It was within this crisis of empire in Asia that Matsuoka worked for a peaceful economic advance south, seeking to bring French Indochina, Thailand, and the Netherlands Indies into Japan's political-economic orbit. To this end, he mediated a border dispute between Thailand and French Indochina, and he lent his support to economic negotiations with both French Indochina and the Netherlands Indies. David J. Lu is correct to note that in many senses, such policy constituted reactions to emerging situations rather than a coherent strategy.[11] But Matsuoka, as seen in the "Main Points," did have a general policy direction. Although Matsuoka did not always take center stage, it is reasonable to assume that he understood these negotiations as essential parts of his mission to pull Southeast Asia into the Greater East Asia Co-Prosperity Sphere.

The diplomatic stage had been set in the summer of 1940, well before Matsuoka drafted his "Main Points" and when his Southeast Asian policy was still in its infancy. Taking advantage of French weakness after the Nazi Blitzkrieg, Japan strong-armed the Vichy regime into a series of concessions. An August 30, 1940, agreement between Matsuoka and French ambassador Charles Arsène-Henry forced Vichy to recognize Japan's "preponderance of interest in the Far East" and to "guarantee the superior status" of Japanese subjects over those of any third power. Moreover, the Japanese army would be granted the right of passage and the authority to station troops, transport war material, and make use of airfields in northern Indochina. In return, Japan would acknowledge French primacy in Indochina.[12] The military settlement initially derailed in negotiations in Hanoi but would be resolved by a well-timed Japanese ultimatum. Governor-General Jean Decoux ultimately capitulated to Japanese demands and allowed the Japanese military to use three airfields and to station six thousand troops in northern Indochina. Japan's occupation of northern Indochina began on September 22, 1940.

French weakness emboldened Thai irredentist nationalism and triggered a border dispute. Between 1893 and 1907, France had seized large tracts of territory from the former kingdom of Siam. Over the following three decades Thai leaders found their country bound to an uneasy status quo, with irredentist designs remaining little more than a dormant sentiment.[13] But the drive to reclaim "lost territories" became more pronounced by 1938, with the ascendance of nationalist premier and virtual military dictator Field Marshal Plaek Pibulsongkram (known as Phibun). The Phibun regime indicated expansionist designs when it changed the country's name to Thailand on June 24, 1939. By replacing a foreign-imposed name with the Thai language equivalent, Phibun sought a homeland for all ethnic Thais and strengthened claims over territories ceded to France. From June 1940, Phibun began a diplomatic (and ultimately military) offensive aimed at reclaiming the "lost territories," especially Luang Prabang and Pakse, from French Indochina.[14] The ensuing border dispute constituted the first test for Matsuoka's Asian diplomacy and for Japanese dreams of regional leadership.

Most in Japan did not initially welcome the dispute. By November 1940, however, Matsuoka began to express interest in mediating a mutually beneficial outcome. As his biographer notes, Matsuoka turned a November 5 four-minister conference into a classroom on the "dos and don'ts of diplomacy," wherein he instructed his fellow ministers of the great gains waiting to be made under his guidance and mediation.[15] On November 20, he had the Japanese legation in

Bangkok notify Phibun of Tokyo's desire to arbitrate. The following day, Matsuoka gained support from Prime Minister Konoe, army minister Tōjō Hideki, and navy minister Oikawa Koshirō to "act swiftly to mediate the dispute." Arbitration did not imply altruistic intentions. Instead, it served as an opportunistic means to advance Japanese interests in Southeast Asia. By mediating the conflict Japan could expand its influence within Thailand and French Indochina and "establish the Empire's leadership position in Greater East Asia."[16]

Whatever the case, the decision to arbitrate spawned a political contest between the foreign ministry and the army general staff over Southeast Asia policy. Both sides worked toward the same end goal: the construction of a new order and Japanese leadership in the region. The point of conflict was instead over the best means to achieve these ends. For his part, Matsuoka saw skillful diplomacy and peaceful expansion as more effective in securing Japanese interests, and he worked to use the border dispute as a springboard to establishing leadership within the Co-Prosperity Sphere. But Matsuoka found himself at odds with firebrands in the military who criticized the foreign ministry's "lukewarm diplomacy" as impeding Japanese interests. Instead, they saw the border dispute as a unique opportunity to establish a dominant position in the region, as well as a steppingstone toward a *military* advance south.[17] But debates even raged within the army. It was the sign of the chaotic times of "inferiors dominating superiors" that a colonel was seen angrily giving orders to a general on policy toward Indochina.[18] Hard-liners in the army general staff argued that Japan should seize French Indochina and Thailand, and one even called for a sneak attack on the Netherlands Indies.[19] In the end, the more moderate views of Col. Doi Akio prevailed within army circles. Doi emphasized the importance of establishing military bases throughout French Indochina and Thailand; his ideas informed a December 23 general staff intelligence plan and later became important military demands.[20]

Imperial general staff chief Sugiyama Hajime emerged as the mouthpiece of these demands and Matsuoka's biggest rival. Intelligent but not the most gifted of Japanese wartime leaders, Sugiyama was meticulous and had a head for detail.[21] Yet his physical appearance belied his intellectual abilities. He was a powerfully built man, but his solid chin and wide shoulders were offset by a noticeably smaller right eye and mismatched eyebrows, giving him the impression of someone out of touch with the world. Younger officers derided him as "halfwit Hajime" (*boke Hajime*). Senior officers spoke of him as "the toilet door" because his opinions swung whichever way they were last pushed.[22] Even so, Sugiyama saw himself as engaging in the critical role of "bugler of the entire military," the mouthpiece of military demands. He remained willing to play the role of the "emperor's whipping boy" and to bear the brunt of the emperor's displeasure to fulfill such ends.[23] In the debates over policy toward French Indochina and Thailand, Sugiyama served as the voice of the more hardline elements within the general staff, arguing for a military advance into Southeast Asia and a military alliance with Thailand. In the process, he frequently clashed with Matsuoka.

Matsuoka defended himself from Sugiyama's attacks with a fascinating mixture of brash, hard-line statements, conflicting views, and non sequiturs. At times Matsuoka championed policy so hard-line that it bewildered Sugiyama and the general staff; other times he stressed caution, calmness, and conciliation. From late December 1940, Matsuoka continually deflected Sugiyama's calls for a military advance by outdoing him in expansionist rhetoric, even calling for sneak attacks on British territory and the "seizure of Singapore." At other liaison conferences, he took the opposite tack. On January 19, 1941, he argued against doing anything that would hinder the negotiations, and on January 30, Matsuoka even questioned, "Wouldn't it be inconvenient for the military if we antagonized Britain and America?" Other times, he would "rattle on about complex diplomatic stratagems."[24] Matsuoka was willing to resort to any means to keep diplomacy in the realm of the foreign ministry. This was especially pertinent owing to Japan's headless political system, one in which the high command (*tōsuibu*) answered directly to the emperor. To keep firm hold on the reins of foreign policy, Matsuoka needed to show what one historian calls a perplexing mix of "un-Japanese candor, an aptitude for histrionics, an amazing loquacity and a stubborn urge to have the upper hand."[25] He had a knack for knocking his opponents off balance.

Phibun initially rebuffed Japan's desire to arbitrate. But a heated-up conflict ultimately forced Japan's hand and provided the impetus for a softening of Phibun's views. On January 6, 1941, Thailand launched a military offensive against Indochina. The Thai side at first made quick gains in Laos, but a surprise French naval strike on January 17 dramatically changed the conflict and threatened to derail the Thai offensive. A ragtag French collection of available warships and cruisers sunk two Thai torpedo boats and disabled a gunship before steaming away. The French ships ran out of gas and barely made it back to port. But the Thai side remained unaware of this, and Phibun afterward indicated his willingness to accept foreign mediation. The situation became even more chaotic when the British governor-general of Singapore, Shenton Thomas, engaged in a clumsy attempt to arbitrate.

At this point, Japan stepped in to mediate the conflict. Nonetheless, debates still raged between Matsuoka and the general staff about how arbitration would serve Japanese interests. The culmination of the debates came on January 19, at a customary Sunday breakfast that turned into an impromptu liaison conference. The general staff, as usual, urged strong intervention, pressing for a military alliance with Thailand and coercive measures to browbeat Indochina into accepting Japanese mediation. Matsuoka, however, cautioned the general staff against any action that might provoke Britain and the United States, or any action that could impede the ongoing economic negotiations in both the Netherlands Indies and French Indochina. Owing to Matsuoka's continued resistance, cooler heads prevailed and the liaison conference decided against seeking a military pact with Thailand and a military advance farther into Indochina.[26]

The general staff, however, continued to argue for the necessity of a Thai military alliance and measures to advance military interests in Indochina. Sugiyama even appealed directly to the emperor, advocating a military pact with Thailand. But Sugiyama was rebuffed. Matsuoka, in fact, had preempted Sugiyama and secretly convinced the emperor to refuse the general staff's requests. "I've thought about it," Hirohito told the army and navy chiefs of staff on January 24. "Because there is a large pro-British faction in Thailand, this [military] agreement is too dangerous to submit. There is also the important issue of rice with French Indochina, so keep in contact with the government and don't make any slipups." Sugiyama left the meeting red-faced, embarrassed, and in a state of shock—and he lost his temper for the only time in his distinguished career.[27] Matsuoka had publicly humiliated Sugiyama.[28] This was a big victory for the foreign minister, who in the process cemented foreign ministry predominance in policy toward Southeast Asia. Diplomacy would trump military matters, at least for a time.

By late January, Japan secured both Thai and French approval to mediate the conflict, and the foreign policy establishment sought to use the negotiations as a solid foundation on which to build the Co-Prosperity Sphere. Japan's aims for the negotiations are instructive in this regard. Drafted by the foreign ministry's South Seas Bureau and adopted at a February 5, 1941, liaison conference, the aims were decidedly political in nature. In return for mediating the dispute, the plan stipulated that neither Thailand nor French Indochina could make military or political agreements with any third country, and that both would recognize Japan's "leadership position in the East Asia Co-Prosperity Sphere."[29] Those aims were largely met. Matsuoka and his aide, Special Ambassador Matsumiya Jun, drove hard negotiations. By March 10, after cajoling both sides and even threatening military intervention into Indochina, they contrived a middle-of-the-road solution. The agreement provided for the return of Luang Prabang, Pakse, and parts of northwestern Cambodia to Thailand. The agreement also demarcated the deep-water center of the Mekong River as the new borderline. In return, Thailand would demilitarize the newly ceded territories and provide equal rights and treatment to French citizens residing therein. Moreover, although they did not receive a declaration of Japan's leadership position in the Co-Prosperity Sphere,

Japan did secure a clause forbidding both French Indochina and Thailand from entering an agreement detrimental to Japanese interests.[30]

The formal signing on March 11 was met with great fanfare. The *Asahi shinbun* celebrated the accord as "a historic victory for our diplomacy" and as symbolic of "the establishment of our leadership" in the region.[31] Even the army general staff gave grudging respect to Matsuoka's power politics. Firebrand section chief Tanaka Shin'ichi, one of the three most influential staff officers in the military, saw the arbitration as "the first step to the establishment of Japan's leadership position in Thailand and French Indochina."[32] Japan had used power and prestige to resolve a thorny conflict. In the process, it had pulled French Indochina and Thailand further into Japan's orbit and prevented any extension of British influence in Asia. The Japanese government could boast, as it did in a series of statements released on March 11, 1941, that it stood for "the maintenance of peace in Greater East Asia" as well as closer relations with its two partners.[33] The border crisis thus confirmed Japan as continental Southeast Asia's hegemonic power. This was a great victory for Matsuoka and an encouraging first step toward realizing his dream of a Greater East Asia Co-Prosperity Sphere.

Matsuoka's Asian diplomacy also took shape through economic talks with both the Netherlands Indies and French Indochina. Unlike the border dispute, Matsuoka did not take center stage in these talks. Far from it, the desire to secure such much-needed resources and economic privileges reflected a wide consensus among the policy elite. Active resource acquisition and economic development, after all, would help Japan meet its mobilization goals and secure resources for the war in China. Even hard-liners in the army agreed that Japan needed to pursue resource acquisition peacefully, if only at first. Nonetheless, it is still necessary to discuss both sets of economic negotiations in the context of Matsuoka diplomacy. Both talks aligned with Matsuoka's strategy to assert Japanese leadership over Southeast Asia. Through the peaceful talks, that is, Japan would not only forge close economic relations; it would also pull French Indochina and the Netherland Indies within the political orbit of the Greater East Asia Co-Prosperity Sphere.

The strategy for negotiations was first described in the "Outline of Economic Policy for the South," a policy document adopted by the Konoe cabinet on August 16, 1940. With this document, the Konoe cabinet called for "the completion of the economic Greater East Asian Sphere." Japan would divide Greater East Asia into an "inner sphere" composed of French Indochina, Thailand, Burma, the Netherlands Indies, the Philippines, and British Malaya, and an "outer sphere" of British India, Australia, and New Zealand, and it would use both spheres not only to secure military resource needs but also to "implant the Empire's political power" across Asia. To these ends, the "Outline" called for a host of measures including removing impediments to trade and to Japanese economic activities, eliminating restrictions on the movement of Japanese enterprises and people, acquiring guarantees for exports, and "securing Japan's leading position in [regional] trade."[34]

The "Outline," in fact, served as a springboard for expanded economic talks with both French Indochina and the Netherlands Indies. On September 3, the Konoe cabinet adopted a plan for economic expansion in French Indochina, and they followed up on October 25 by approving a parallel plan for the Netherlands Indies. Featuring similar language and ideas, both plans called for close economic relations and making both territories "see the reality that [they are] part of the Greater East Asia Co-Prosperity Sphere." They aimed to help Japan create "resource independence" through joint development and the supply of strategic resources. Moreover, both plans called for repeals to existing restrictions on Japanese economic activities and for the employment of Japanese advisers to guide economic development.[35] But the focus on building the economic sphere belied decidedly political aims. In fact, on July 22, 1940, foreign ministry Bureau of Eurasian Affairs section chief Ishizawa Yutaka had penned a draft report that laid bare the political implications of Japan's economic advance into the Netherlands Indies. Ishizawa's report noted that whereas the negotiations would be primarily economic, they would aim at "securing political leadership in the South Seas."[36] What is clear here is the extent to which the wartime ruling elite saw trade and economic interests as tied to political interests and supportive of Japanese regional hegemony. This sense that the flag would follow trade was no doubt widely shared throughout the foreign policy establishment.

Japan conducted negotiations with both territories through mid-1941. On the one hand, Japan pursued economic negotiations with French Indochina. Matsumiya Jun headed a preliminary mission to Hanoi from October 18 to November 28, 1940, and from December 1940 the talks moved to Tokyo. What is notable about these talks is the absence of any Japanese stress on leadership within Indochina. This, no doubt, owed to the fact that Japan by September 1940 already occupied northern Indochina and had additionally secured recognition from Vichy France of Japan's "preponderance of interest" in East Asia. Whatever the case, the talks did significantly advance Japanese interests. On May 6, 1941, Vichy gave in to Japanese demands and signed agreements providing Japan preferential amounts of rice, coal, tin, raw rubber, manganese, and other mineral products. Japan also received a host of other privileges in Indochina, from equality of treatment to an agreement to allow Japanese nationals access to many professions prohibited to foreigners.

Whereas the negotiations with the French were a resounding success, economic talks in the Netherlands Indies were thornier and harder fought. Japan sent two economic missions there. Successful businessman turned commerce and industry minister Kobayashi Ichizō headed the first mission to Batavia from September 12 to October 21, 1940. Following Kobayashi's failure to secure Japanese demands, Matsuoka turned to House of Peers member and former foreign minister Yoshizawa Kenkichi. Cosmopolitan, a skilled diplomat, and highly confident in English, Yoshizawa was renowned for the tenacious, slow-moving negotiations he had used as a minister to China, and he was seen as a more suitable diplomat for difficult talks. Yoshizawa, however, fared no better than his predecessor. After arriving in Batavia on December 28, 1940, Yoshizawa found himself hard pressed to secure the crude oil, aviation gasoline, rubber, tin, and other resources Japan desired. Perhaps more importantly, the Dutch ignored or rejected other demands that would have given Japan a special position in the economy of the Netherlands Indies.

The talks would have taxed Japanese diplomatic abilities even in the best of times; but Matsuoka's gaffe-prone nature only made them more difficult. In an inopportune speech before the Diet on January 21, 1941, Matsuoka called the Netherlands Indies an integral "part of the Greater East Asia Co-Prosperity Sphere" and argued that the colony "should have close, inseparable relations with Japan."[37] He followed up with yet another bungle on January 29, when he complained of groundless suspicions of Japan's new order. Matsuoka dismissed those suspicions, arguing that based on the traditional values of *hakkō ichiu*, "There cannot be anything wrong with our resolution to lead Greater East Asia."[38] These gaffes antagonized the Netherlands and reinforced their desire to stonewall the negotiations. On January 31, the ambassador to Tokyo, J. C. Pabst, responded by noting that the Dutch government "rejects the idea of incorporating the Netherlands East Indies in any new order in East Asia under the leadership of any nation."[39]

From this point, the Netherlands rebuffed any and all Japanese demands, refusing on the grounds that Japan might re-export strategic goods to Germany. On June 6, 1941, the Netherlands gave their final response: they refused to provide the resources Japan desired, ignored or rejected other demands, and denied Japan any special position in the Netherlands Indies' economy. U.S. ambassador to Japan Joseph C. Grew recognized the implication. "The Dutch reply," he wrote, "intimated without so saying that the Netherlands East Indies could not be regarded as falling within any co-prosperity sphere under Japanese leadership."[40] Faced with this intransigence, the Japanese government folded. Tokyo recalled the Yoshizawa delegation and suspended the negotiations to prevent a formal rupture of relations and "to leave room for future discussions."[41] Yoshizawa left

Batavia on June 27, 1941. Negotiating political-economic leadership over the Netherlands Indies thus proved a frustrating prospect. Japan failed to produce any semblance of a diplomatic victory—the Dutch had resisted efforts to expand Japanese economic as well as political control over the Netherlands Indies. From this point on, only war or threats of force could bring the colony into Japan's new order.

Matsuoka's initial attempts to construct a Japanese sphere of influence in Asia thus met with mixed results. On the one hand, he took the first big steps toward the construction of the Greater East Asia Co-Prosperity Sphere. Matsuoka's negotiation of the Thai-Indochina border dispute expanded Japanese influence and cemented Japan's status as the primary guarantor of stability in continental Southeast Asia, at least for a time. Moreover, the Japanese negotiators browbeat the French delegation by May 1941 into accepting Japanese economic demands. On the other hand, diplomacy with the Netherlands Indies ended in utter failure. Japan proved unable not only to advance political and economic leadership over Indonesia but also to procure sufficient oil and other resources for mobilization campaigns. The collapse of the Netherlands Indies negotiations was by no means Matsuoka's sole fault. But the failure nonetheless increased discontent in government with Matsuoka's role as the primary arbiter of Japan's foreign policy. Matsuoka's peaceful strategy to build the Co-Prosperity Sphere still had a chance to succeed. But success or failure depended on Matsuoka's main calling: sphere-of-influence diplomacy with the United States and the Soviet Union. Stated differently, the life or death of Matsuoka's vision for the Greater East Asia Co-Prosperity Sphere depended on whether Japan's bombastic foreign minister could reach an accord with the great powers of the day. It was great power politics that would decide the fate of Southeast Asia.

Matsuoka's Grand Design

Matsuoka's Asian diplomacy thus played second fiddle to his primary aim: reaching a grand bargain with the great powers. That is, he hoped that sphere-of-influence negotiations with both the United States and the Soviet Union would help create a sense of sympathy for or understanding of Japan's new order. First, the foreign minister laid the groundwork for negotiations with the United States. In this, he faced a Herculean task. By 1941 Washington argued that Japan's adherence to the Tripartite Pact, its war in China as well as its support of the collaborationist Wang Jingwei regime in Nanjing, its disavowal of the Open Door policy, and its efforts to build a "new order" or "co-prosperity sphere" made Japan almost as dangerous for Asia as Hitler's new order was for Europe. Matsuoka set out to gain U.S. acceptance of the Co-Prosperity Sphere and the new reality of Japan as the stabilizing power in Asia.

Among the first things he did was to initiate cordial discussions with U.S. ambassador Grew. On October 5, 1940, Matsuoka invited Grew for tea to discuss the problems in U.S.-Japan relations. During this meeting, he worked to mollify U.S. suspicions about Japan's decision to join the Axis. Matsuoka disingenuously dismissed the Axis Pact as "not aimed at any particular country," and he spoke of it as part of Japan's peaceful attempts to construct a new order in Greater East Asia. Moreover, he hinted that the rights and interests of the powers in China would be protected in the aftermath of Japan's "unfortunate" war in China, and he stated that he welcomed the cooperation of all nations in developing the new order. Most importantly, however, Matsuoka's statement sought a broader understanding of Japan's interests in Asia. "If the United States understands . . . Japan's intentions with regard to the establishment of a new order in East Asia, there will be no change whatever in the relationship between Japan and the United States following the conclusion of this treaty."[42] As historian Mori Shigeki notes, Matsuoka no doubt saw this conversation as the opening salvo of his diplomatic fight for U.S. recognition of Japan's leading position in East Asia.[43]

Meanwhile, Matsuoka sought to select someone to help pursue his sphere-of-influence diplomacy in the now-vacant ambassadorship in Washington, a vacancy caused by none other than Matsuoka himself. The luckless former ambassador, Horinouchi Kensuke, had been purged in the so-called Matsuoka cyclone, a series of dismissals that Matsuoka used to bring the Kasumigaseki bureaucracy under his personal control. Matsuoka first asked Matsumoto Shigeharu, a young, high-caliber journalist from the Dōmei News Agency, to assume the post. After Matsumoto refused, Matsuoka turned in late August 1940 to his second and final choice: Admiral Nomura Kichisaburō.

History has been unkind to Nomura; most historians believe he had no business playing at ambassador. But Matsuoka did not make his selection carelessly. Nomura, in fact, was the navy's foremost expert on the United States, having sustained contacts there reaching back to his World War I–era tour of Washington. Moreover, Nomura had been a strong proponent of the Washington Treaty System of naval arms limitation through the 1930s, and he even tried to avert a looming crisis with the United States during his short stint as foreign minister in late 1939. But as Peter Mauch notes, Matsuoka had subtler, Machiavellian designs in selecting the "sailor diplomat" as his ambassador. Matsuoka sought someone so far removed from policy circles that he would exert no influence over the policy process. "Compensating for his lack of influence, Matsuoka's envisioned emissary would command a high level of personal prestige in both Japan and the United States."[44] Matsuoka, in short, saw Nomura as a convenient mouthpiece for his sphere-of-influence diplomacy.

Nomura twice refused Matsuoka's advances but finally relented on November 8, 1940, after the navy indicated its desire that he go to Washington. The following month, on December 19, Matsuoka introduced the new ambassador at an America-Japan Society luncheon convened in Nomura's honor. The audience of three hundred guests at the Imperial Hotel in Tokyo was, according to the *Japan Times and Advertiser*, "the most distinguished gathering of Americans and Japanese held in Tokyo in recent years."[45]

True to form, Matsuoka hijacked Nomura's introduction with a pompous display of political grandstanding and one-upmanship, celebrating his "victory" in his "three-months' siege and attack" over the old admiral. But what is notable about his performance was the heart of the speech. Matsuoka laid out, in plain terms, the essence of his sphere-of-influence diplomacy and his vision for the new order. The "fundamental cause" of the U.S.-Japan rift, Matsuoka argued, "is American misapprehension of Japan's aims and aspirations." Japan was waging neither "an imperialist war of greed an aggression in China" nor a "war of conquest." Instead, Matsuoka argued, his country was engaged in a moral crusade. The China war was a vehicle of construction, one that would bring "peace and unlimited prosperity" to Greater East Asia. Moreover, Japan welcomed help in this great mission. "We shut the door nowhere and to none," Matsuoka contended. "Any nation that desires to take a hand in this great task is welcome. But mind you, there shall be 'no conquest, no oppression, no exploitation' under the new order which we conceive!" Matsuoka continued:

> Japan's ideal . . . is to enable all nations to take their proper place in the world. It is my humble opinion that the world should be reorganized and reformed in a more rational way as, for instance, crystals are formed according to the law of nature. Minerals of different nature agree between themselves as to which of them shall give way to the other at their junction, and take their permitted shapes and allotted shares of space, yielding or being yielded to, as they build up a perfect crystal. When international society is crystallized in a similar manner, in accordance with the spirit of justice and equity, then and only then will genuine and lasting peace prevail throughout the world. The new order we envisage is a realization of such an international society, which we intend to begin by setting up in this part of the world under our leadership. The Pact of Alliance recently concluded by Japan, Germany and Italy points to the same goal.[46]

In sum, Japan would not change course. Matsuoka wanted his American colleagues to realize that their frustrations or fears would in no way sway Japanese policy. Japan would continue its crusade in China, would build the new order in Greater East Asia, and would remain loyal to the Tripartite Pact.

What a performance this was! Matsuoka insisted that any blame for deteriorating relations sat squarely on U.S. shoulders. The U.S.-Japan estrangement was, at its core, an American failure of imagination. If only Americans removed the veil covering their eyes and understood Japan's moral crusade, they would realize that Japan desired a world of true peace and justice. Failing to do so, he warned, might invite a clash that "may prove fatal to all Humanity," an "Armageddon that would end in the total destruction of our culture and civilization." After this jolt to his distinguished audience, Matsuoka urged common sense, compromise, and time to solve their problems. "Half a century is but a passing moment," he pleaded. "Let us all have a bit of patience. This is my appeal."[47]

The foreign minister's thunderous remarks owed much to his understanding of the American character. Matsuoka had spent his formative years in Oregon in the 1890s, and his experiences as a boy and young man colored his understanding of his adoptive homeland. He perceived the United States as the Wild West, the land of cowboys and ruffians. To Matsuoka, a calculated show of strength was necessary to gain an American's respect and friendship. Surprisingly, this view remained untempered by his years in Washington. In August 1945, in fact, reporters asked Matsuoka a simple question: "What are Americans like?" His response is telling:

> Now assuming that you are walking on a small path in a field, which is so narrow that only one person can pass through, and an American comes from the opposite direction. You are facing each other, and neither side is willing to yield his right of way. Soon becoming impatient, the American will clench his fist and sock you in the jaw. Taken by surprise, you may lower your head and let him pass by. Next time when you meet him at the same path, he will simply raise his fist. He considers that the best solution.
>
> On the other hand, if you do not retreat the first time, and you engage in a counterattack, the American will be shocked and take another look at you. "Well, this fellow knows what he is doing," so recognizing, he will become your best friend.[48]

Thus, his tough stance. Matsuoka believed that although they might preach pacifism and good relations, Americans responded to bravado and swagger. Talk tough, and Americans would come to terms with his sphere-of-influence diplomacy in Asia. This fundamental misinterpretation clouded Matsuoka's vision and would sound the death knell of his grand design before it got off the ground.

On January 22, 1941, the day before Nomura set sail from Yokohama, Matsuoka gave the ambassador secret orders for his tenure in Washington. For the most part, the orders reflected the points outlined in Matsuoka's America-Japan Society speech the month prior. Matsuoka instructed Nomura to stay the course. Tokyo would remain faithful to the Tripartite Pact and continue its moral crusade in China. Moreover, Nomura was tasked with bringing about a mutual understanding of Japan's Co-Prosperity Sphere. The orders noted:

> My *motto* for the establishment of the Greater East Asia Co-Prosperity Sphere, and indeed for the great principle of *hakkō ichiu* on which it is based, is no conquest, no oppression, no exploitation. In a word, we will create, starting with Greater East Asia, a realm of international neighborly cooperation, and thus will seek to set an example for the world.
>
> Putting aside this ideal for the moment, our country is compelled by the very real need to lay a path to self-sufficiency in the Greater East Asia Sphere. Should America, which reigns over the Western hemisphere and also extends from the Atlantic to the Pacific, label Japan's ideals and ambitions as unjust? Can America not consent to Japan's aims? What our country is considering is by no means an exclusive [economic zone]. America should come and cooperate in the development of the Greater East Asia Sphere; those fears that we will cut off the supply to their much-needed rubber and tin are laughable.[49]

This was Matsuoka's sphere-of-influence diplomacy incarnate. He called on Nomura to secure U.S. recognition of the Greater East Asia Co-Prosperity Sphere. The United States reigned over the Western Hemisphere with its Monroe Doctrine, so it would be hypocritical to criticize Japanese aims in Greater East Asia as unjust. Matsuoka, in short, viewed a quid pro quo acceptance of each other's regional ascendancy as the prerequisite to peaceful and positive relations.

Matsuoka followed up with further instructions on February 7, 1941, four days before Nomura arrived in Washington. The foreign minister again criticized the U.S. hard-line stance and its failure "to understand Japan's true intentions." He called on Nomura to break the impasse but again gave very little room for negotiation and simply told the ambassador to maintain a defiant posture. Nomura was to stress the absurdity of war, which would bring "not only ruin to both countries, but also the collapse of world civilization." In fact, a

Japanese-American war would be to the benefit of the Soviet Union alone. The Soviets, Matsuoka argued, would not miss the golden opportunity to expand in China and "bolshevize much of Asia." Aside from this, the only negotiating tactic the foreign minister offered was to stress Japan's "unshakable resolve to press ahead with its established national policy, even risking [the future of] the League of Nations." Matsuoka called for cooperation, not opposition. The key to such cooperation, however, was recognition of Japan's new order. "America," Matsuoka wrote, "should not interfere without permission in other great powers' living space [*seikatsuken*]."[50]

This negotiating strategy suffered from a fundamental misunderstanding of U.S. policy. Since the 1930s, the U.S. Department of State rejected sphere-of-influence politics and argued that any international leadership must be moral in nature, reflective of a spirit of justice and fair play.[51] In this context, Washington refused to recognize leadership as something that could be gained by declaration or unilateral action. On February 14, 1941, Joseph W. Ballantine, the assistant chief of the U.S. State Department's Division of Far Eastern Affairs, communicated this to Hashimoto Tetsuma, the director of the right-wing Japanese organization Shiunsō, during the latter's visit to Washington. Ballantine's oral statement argued against any recognition of "superiority" in international affairs. Such a recognition "would be inconsistent with the fundamental conception which we hold that all nations are equal under international law." Likewise, the statement emphasized that Washington had abandoned its Monroe Doctrine and any pretensions of asserting U.S. superiority within the Western Hemisphere.[52] Hashimoto reported his findings on March 19, 1941, to Lord Keeper of the Privy Seal Kido Kōichi and other members of the ruling elite.[53] But by that time, Matsuoka had left Tokyo for his whirlwind tour of Europe, so it is unlikely that Hashimoto's report reached Matsuoka's ears. Whatever the case, this pointed to the vast diplomatic chasm that separated Matsuoka from his adversaries in Washington.

Nomura thus faced an unenviable task. Although he went to Washington at the navy's behest, he nonetheless served as an agent of Matsuoka's sphere-of-influence diplomacy, tasked with gaining U.S. sympathy for Japan's aims in Asia. But Matsuoka only armed Nomura with a vague promise of recognizing the U.S. sphere of influence in the Western Hemisphere. This was something in which the Roosevelt administration had no interest. Otherwise, he provided no wiggle room or sound negotiating strategy. Indeed, he sent Nomura armed solely with implicit threats and warnings of Japan's "unshakable resolve." Like it or not, Japan would continue the war in China, build its Co-Prosperity Sphere, and remain faithful to the Axis alliance. Ever the optimist, Matsuoka still hoped for a positive outcome. This was a tall order, one even a smooth-talking professional diplomat would have found impossible to fill. And Nomura was no smooth talker.[54]

Leaving Nomura to this challenging task, Matsuoka moved to the next major piece of his global project: a whirlwind tour of Berlin, Rome, and Moscow. Matsuoka saw a stronger relationship with the major powers in Europe as an important part of his grand design. The traditional view holds that Matsuoka sought to forge a "four-power entente." That said, some Japanese historians now question whether the historical record truly supports this interpretation. Some have found no historical evidence or documentation about the possibilities of a "four-power entente." Others argue that Matsuoka was by no means naïve and state that well before his European trip he realized that German-Soviet relations had deteriorated beyond a point to where Moscow could join the Axis.[55] Whatever we make of this debate, it is nonetheless clear that Matsuoka saw his European diplomacy as connected to the emerging world order. What, then, was Matsuoka trying to accomplish?

The answer to this question, too, lies in Matsuoka's sphere-of-influence diplomacy. Whether the foreign minister truly aimed at a four-power entente is not as important as what he hoped to gain from engaging in discussions. Matsuoka sought from Moscow similar terms to those he sought from Berlin and Washington: recognition of each power's respective sphere of interest. And he believed that an accord with Moscow would be a powerful diplomatic lever to be used against Washington. As Matsuoka explained to his secretary before departing to Europe: "To shake hands with Germany is a temporary excuse to shake hands with the Soviet Union. But that hand shaking with the Soviet Union is also nothing more than an excuse to shake hands with the United States."[56] So it is likely that Matsuoka may have envisioned a four-power entente not as an end unto itself but as a means to completing his pan-region sphere-of-influence diplomacy. As Kawanishi astutely notes, Matsuoka hoped his negotiations would result in a world where the great powers would "respect each other's co-prosperity spheres."[57]

The purpose behind Japan's "hand shaking" with Moscow was explicated in "Outline for Negotiations with Germany, Italy, and the Soviet Union," a policy document prepared by the foreign ministry on January 6, 1941. The "Outline" articulated Matsuoka's hopes for negotiations and voiced Matsuoka's global vision in stark terms. It called for a world "composed of four large spheres: the Greater East Asia Sphere, the European Sphere (including Africa), the American Sphere, and the Soviet Sphere (including India and Iran). (Britain will retain Australia and New Zealand, and will on the whole be treated like Holland.)"

Japan would serve as political and economic leader of the Greater East Asia Co-Prosperity Sphere. In this context, Japan would "assume responsibility for maintaining order" in the region. Most importantly, however, the policy paper pressed for mutual recognition of each other's spheres of influence. "The [Japanese] Empire," it noted, "will consent to the Soviet position in Xinjiang and Outer Mongolia; the Soviet Union will consent to the Empire's position in North China and Mengjiang."[58] This was sphere-of-influence diplomacy writ large.

By January 18, 1941, after only minor revisions, the general staff recorded its "unanimous agreement in regard to foreign minister Matsuoka's trip to Europe."[59] A February 3 liaison conference further adopted Matsuoka's negotiation plans and decided that Matsuoka would leave in early March and return in mid-April. Matsuoka visited the emperor on February 10 to inform him of the negotiation plans. During the meeting, which lasted for one hour and forty-five minutes, Matsuoka emphasized that the world was breaking up into four great blocs and hinted that the negotiations would serve Japan's interests as political leader of the Greater East Asia Co-Prosperity Sphere.[60] The stage now set, Matsuoka left for Europe in high spirits on March 12, 1941.

In Berlin, the foreign minister met three times with his counterpart, Joachim von Ribbentrop, and once with Hitler between March 27 and 29. Matsuoka, naturally, was most interested in pressing for the active engagement of Soviet Russia. But he encountered a nation with very different aims. Far from pushing for a Eurasian Axis, the German side proclaimed that the Japanese should attack Singapore. Foreign minister Ribbentrop argued that such an attack "would be a very decisive factor in the speedy overthrow of England." Moreover, it would immobilize the United States, which could not risk sending its fleet into Asia. Ribbentrop concluded that the conquest of Singapore "would amount to cutting the Gordian knot in East Asia." Hitler echoed this view, noting that the time was ripe for Japan to attack. Britain had already lost the war, he argued, so Japan had much to gain by taking a bold gamble with Singapore. "Such a moment will never return," Hitler claimed. "It is unique in history."[61] Matsuoka evaded any firm commitment but noted that he would discuss the idea on his return to Tokyo.

Matsuoka brought up his central aim the following day. In his meeting with Ribbentrop on May 28, he questioned "whether the Führer had ever considered the possibility of a Russian-Japanese-German alliance." Ribbentrop, however, refused to entertain such an idea, calling closer collaboration with the Soviets an "absolute impossibility." In truth, this hard-line attitude owed to Operation Barbarossa, the plan to attack the Soviet Union. But since Hitler distrusted the Japanese, he had ordered Ribbentrop to keep the attack secret. Whatever the case, Matsuoka followed up by asking whether he should stay in Moscow on his return trip to negotiate a nonaggression pact or a treaty of neutrality. The following day, Ribbentrop responded that Japan need not worry about the Soviet Union. If Russia should attack Japan, Ribbentrop argued, "Germany would strike immediately." Ribbentrop further emphasized that Russia was Germany's concern; Japan simply should "push southward toward Singapore without fear of any complications with Russia."[62]

In a perceptive analysis, Akira Iriye argued that neither side gained much from Matsuoka's trip to Nazi Germany. The German side failed to gain assurances of Japan's attack on Singapore, and Matsuoka could not forge his "quadri-partite scheme."[63] Nonetheless, it is possible that Matsuoka saw equal value in the realm of media politics. Matsuoka, after all, was the first "media" foreign minister and a public relations genius. He was a man who "knew the power of the press" and was "determined to utilize it to its fullest extent."[64] It is reasonable to assume that he also hoped the reporting on the pomp and splendor of his Axis trip would make both Stalin and Roosevelt more receptive to negotiations.

Whatever the case, it was the German Blitzkrieg against Belgrade that paid the biggest dividends with Soviet Russia. On April 6, as Matsuoka's train headed toward Moscow, German troops began the so-called April War against Yugoslavia. This move shocked Stalin, who had concluded a treaty of friendship with Yugoslavia the previous day, and epitomized the deteriorating relations between Berlin and Moscow. Once he heard the news, Matsuoka believed that he would find more willing partners in Joseph Stalin and foreign minister Vyacheslav Molotov. Reflecting as his train sped east, Matsuoka said with complete confidence, "Now my Moscow negotiations will be successful."[65]

Stalin and Molotov indeed hurried to compromise with Japan, but Matsuoka still found negotiations hard-fought. In the end, Matsuoka secured a five-year treaty of neutrality at the expense of Japan's concessions in North Sakhalin. The pact, drawn up on April 13, promised "peaceful and friendly relations" between Japan and Soviet Russia, and neutrality should either country open hostilities against a third power. Strikingly, Matsuoka even received an official statement confirming both nations' spheres of influence. The Soviet Union pledged to "respect the territorial integrity and inviolability of Manchukuo," whereas Japan in turn promised to do the same for the Mongolian People's Republic.[66]

This was hardly the sphere of influence that Matsuoka imagined when he first concocted his grand strategy. But this was not for lack of effort. On April 9, Matsuoka had pressed Molotov for a secret accord "that would recognize North China and Inner Mongolia as Japan's sphere of influence, and Outer Mongolia and Xinjiang as the Soviet sphere of influence." Molotov, however, showed little interest. He responded that such negotiations would "take time" and requested that they be "postponed to a later date."[67] On his return to Japan, Matsuoka told

FIGURE 1. Foreign minister Matsuoka signs the Soviet-Japan neutrality pact while Soviet leader Joseph Stalin (second from right) watches. The pact was signed at the Kremlin on April 13, 1941, in Moscow. Photo courtesy of Getty Images.

a liaison conference that he followed up with this sphere-of-influence strategy in his talks with Stalin. At one point, he recalled, Stalin laid a map on the table and spoke of purchasing Karafuto (South Sakhalin) from Japan. Stalin insisted that Japan's colonial holding "has us by the throat" in the area from "Kamchatka in the east to the Maritime Province (Primorskaya) in the west." But Matsuoka refused to bite. He retorted, "You have to look at the map on a grander scale. Wouldn't it be nice for India and Iran to go to the Soviet Union? Japan would turn a blind eye to this."[68] Nothing concrete, however, came of this far-reaching discussion with Stalin. But even retelling this story at a liaison conference on April 22 highlighted the stress Matsuoka placed on his sphere-of-influence diplomacy.

Although the negotiations did not result in a secret accord, Matsuoka had every right to be excited. The neutrality pact and the accompanying pledge to respect the territorial integrity and inviolability of Manchukuo and the Mongolian People's Republic validated Matsuoka's sphere-of-influence diplomacy. After the signing of the pact on April 13, Matsuoka toasted his victories, repeatedly. First at the Kremlin, then later at the Japanese embassy, and finally at Moscow station as he was boarding the Trans-Siberian Railway, he downed round after round of champagne, vodka, and *sake*. A separate but related victory came when Stalin unexpectedly came to Moscow station to bid farewell to the Japanese foreign minister. "I, too, am Asian," Stalin reportedly said. "We must work together!"[69] Such a show of friendship was out of the ordinary, wrote Molotov in his postwar memoirs, "because Stalin never met or saw any one off," even foreign dignitaries. "The Japanese, even the Germans, were startled." The train was delayed for an hour, and Stalin's entourage "all but had to carry" the inebriated Matsuoka into his carriage.[70]

The foreign minister luckily had a long trans-Siberian trip to recover, and to refocus and redouble his efforts. Now that he had made deals with Berlin and Moscow, Matsuoka could turn his full attention to Washington, confident that his vision was within his grasp.

Matsuoka's Fall

Matsuoka's foreign policy victories, however, were short-lived. Less than three months after his return to Japan, Matsuoka was removed from his post. His fall in large part owed to developments in U.S.-Japan relations. Matsuoka had used his Moscow trip to lay the groundwork for negotiations with Washington. He visited the U.S. ambassador to the USSR, Laurence Steinhardt, to discuss his visions for an amicable settlement, in the hopes that his discussions would reach President Roosevelt's ear.[71] It was from those discussions that Matsuoka hoped to begin negotiations. But when Matsuoka arrived at Dairen on April 21, 1941, he was shocked to learn that Japan had already opened exploratory talks with Washington. Over the next few days, he learned that the talks already featured a "proposal for understanding" drafted by the so-called John Doe Associates.[72] Adding insult to injury, the proposal was tantamount to a complete reversal of Matsuoka's strategy. Most egregiously to the foreign minister, the proposal would have weakened Japan's commitment to the Tripartite Pact. It also included provisions to end the war and withdraw from China, and it promised peaceful expansion in Southeast Asia in return for U.S. help in acquiring essential resources. So committed was Japan to opening these exploratory conversations that Lord Keeper of the Privy Seal Kido, in an April 19 audience with the emperor, said that in negotiations Japan would neither betray Germany and Italy nor infringe on "our national policy of constructing the new order, the Greater East Asia Co-Prosperity Sphere."[73] Whatever the case, these new events severely handicapped Matsuoka's sphere-of-influence diplomacy.

It is beyond the scope of this study to deal with the Washington conversations in detail. Suffice it to stress that they had little chance of success. Whatever the case, Matsuoka chose the worst possible way to respond to the machinations of the John Doe Associates. Instead of co-opting their activities, Matsuoka worked to quash them. Matsuoka hoped to negotiate with Washington from a position of strength. On May 12, he released a revision to the "proposal for understanding" that, among other things, reaffirmed Japan's commitment to the Axis Pact and eliminated any language of a Japanese withdrawal from China. In this sense, he simply reasserted his own sphere of influence strategy. As the U.S. Department of State noted, Matsuoka's May 12 plan advocated "joint overlordship by Japan and the United States of the Pacific area, with apparently little thought for the rights and interests of countries other than Japan and the United States."[74]

Matsuoka followed up by taking every opportunity to emphasize Japan's stalwart support of the Tripartite Pact, especially in the event of an American entry into the European war. This only increased U.S. disillusionment with Japanese policy making, and with Matsuoka in particular. On June 24, the U.S. secretary of state, Cordell Hull, released to Nomura an oral statement that obliquely criticized the foreign minister. The statement noted Japanese leaders' "frequent calls for support of Nazi Germany and its policies of conquest" and questioned, "is it not illusory to expect that adoption of a proposal such as the one under consideration offers a basis for achieving substantial results along the desired lines?"[75] From this point on, Matsuoka insisted that Japan should suspend Washington conversations. His unwillingness to press forward with negotiations became the most immediate cause of his downfall. Given the importance the Konoe cabinet placed on reaching an accord with Washington, it was from this point that the cabinet turned against Matsuoka.

The German invasion of the Soviet Union on June 22, 1941, created an additional setback, destroying Matsuoka's vision of a world divided into four blocs. Coming just two months after the neutrality pact with Soviet Russia, it undermined the public support and broad popular adulation for Matsuoka. Moreover, it led to turmoil within the Konoe cabinet. Although the German Blitzkrieg did not catch Tokyo completely by surprise, it led to fierce debates about Japan's best course of action. For his part, on June 23 Matsuoka argued that Japan should abandon its neutrality pact and launch an immediate offensive into the Soviet Union. This generated some interest, especially among mid-echelon military officers. Over the following week, liaison conferences discussed the options— either move north and attack the Soviet Union, or move into southern Indochina. Matsuoka continually argued for an advance north against the Soviet Union and warned against any advance into Indochina. "Going south," he argued on June 28, "is akin to playing with fire, so if we go south we will likely go to war against Britain, America, and the Soviet Union."[76] He even reasoned that a move south would make impossible Japanese efforts to acquire strategic resources and foodstuffs.

This time, Matsuoka's magic failed him. He remained unable to convince Japanese leaders to abandon the southern advance and attack the Soviet Union.

Unable to decide, the Konoe cabinet went with both strategies. An imperial conference on July 2 ratified policies for the move south and north. It called for preparations to be made against the Soviet Union, although any such move would be delayed until the advent of more favorable conditions. More importantly, it committed Japan to occupying the whole of Indochina, regardless of the risk of war with the United States and Great Britain.[77] This decision to move south owed to a combination of stalled negotiations in Washington and Japan's failure in the Netherlands Indies. Staff officers in both branches of the military believed that expansion would help Japan acquire critical strategic resources such as rice, rubber, and tin. Moreover, they believed the threat of further expansion would strike fear into the hearts of Dutch leaders and make it easier for Japan to demand greater privileges and raw materials allotments from the Netherlands Indies.[78] Some hotheaded mid-echelon officers even saw deep-water ports, airfields, and military bases in southern Indochina as of critical significance in the coming war for East Asia. Pressures had built up to abandon Matsuoka diplomacy and to forge "co-prosperity" through a show of force.

By this time, Matsuoka's ouster was only a matter of time. His acerbic personality, his failure to improve relations with Washington, and fears of the popularity with which his calls to attack Soviet Russia garnered among unruly mid-level army staff officers deepened suspicions about his suitability as foreign minister. In the end, the Konoe cabinet secretly decided to oust Matsuoka the only way it could: by resigning en masse. On July 16 the cabinet resigned, and the following day Konoe formed his third cabinet. The members were largely the same; the lone change was that Vice Admiral Toyoda Teijirō replaced Matsuoka as foreign minister. With this, Matsuoka's hard-nosed sphere-of-influence diplomacy, and his vision for the Co-Prosperity Sphere, had come to a crashing close.

Order Begets War

As this chapter has shown, Matsuoka had a broad vision for the future of global politics, one in which the Greater East Asia Co-Prosperity Sphere would take center stage. This vision was in important ways a product of the past. Matsuoka diplomacy pushed for a return to the imperialist "sphere of influence" (or Monroe Doctrine) diplomacy of the nineteenth century. Of course, this was "sphere of influence" diplomacy for the new era. Matsuoka, like others in the policy elite, saw the world as breaking up into four major blocs, with each bloc led by a strong state. The foreign minister's grand strategy thus focused on achieving ascendancy in Southeast Asia through a series of economic and political agreements, and gaining recognition of this preeminent position through bilateral talks with the United States and the Soviet Union. Even in the best of circumstances, it is highly unlikely that he would have succeeded in bringing to fruition such an ambitious but improbable vision for world politics. But his acerbic personality, his unwillingness to compromise, and his misunderstanding of global norms further ensured that the new order he imagined would not come to fruition. Nonetheless, in the process Matsuoka helped popularize and normalize the Greater East Asia Co-Prosperity Sphere concept within the lexicon of elite politics. The concept gained wide approval: it was abstract enough to fit any policy group's purpose.

Thus the Sphere ideal not only survived Matsuoka's fall but thrived. By July 1941 it had taken on a life of its own as the *central goal* of Japanese policy. This new centrality can be found in the policy plan adopted at an imperial conference on July 2, little more than two weeks before Matsuoka's ouster. "However the world situation may change," the plan noted, "the Empire will hold fast to its aim to construct the Greater East Asia Co-Prosperity Sphere and thereby to contribute to the establishment of world peace." From this point forward, advancing into Southeast Asia and constructing the Sphere served the aims of Japan's "self-existence and self-defense" (*jison jiei*). This represented a fundamental change. No longer was the Co-Prosperity Sphere the simple expression of a Monroe Doctrine for Asia, something to be secured through diplomacy with both Asia and the great powers. By the time of Matsuoka's fall, it had become tied to Japan's very existence. Moreover, policy elites recognized that both Britain and the United States stood in the way of Japan's aims. Thus, although the plan advocated continued diplomatic means of advancing Japanese interests in Southeast Asia, it also called on Japan to be prepared for war against Britain and the United States.[79]

This new conception of the Sphere—a resource network to ensure Japan's "self-existence and self-defense"—was the brainchild of the military. From late January 1941, the Twentieth Group of the army staff office (the War Guidance Group) began to tackle what they referred to as the "southern problem." By February 7, the group had penned a draft plan that called for the construction of a "self-existence and self-defense economy" in Southeast Asia alongside measures to weaken British power. The War Guidance Group, however, cautioned against fighting both Britain and the United States, seeking instead to split the latter from its British partner (*Ei-Bei bunri*) and to localize hostilities against Britain and the Netherlands. The plan never reached a liaison conference, but it gained the general acceptance of elites in the army and navy policy communities in the following months. The biggest change came at the behest of the navy, which argued on February 10 that Britain and the United States were "inseparable" and that any show of force would mean war with the Americans.[80] In the lead-up to the July 2 imperial conference, the military thus came to a consensus that Japan should forge deeper links with French Indochina, Thailand, and the Netherlands Indies to serve Japan's "self-existence and self-defense." Moreover, Japan should not hesitate to use force, even against the United States, in the service of those interests.

Any aggressive move to build the Co-Prosperity Sphere could now be justified in the context of "self-existence" and "self-defense." Naval general staff chief Nagano Osami, for instance, championed the occupation of southern Indochina under the assumption that it would create "self-sufficiency within the Greater East Asia Co-Prosperity Sphere."[81] And he cared little what such a move would do to U.S.-Japan relations. As he approved the occupation, Nagano reportedly muttered, "This means war with America."[82] Japanese troops began their "peaceful" entry into southern Indochina on July 28, 1941.

The die had been cast. From this point, the United States and Japan began a quick descent to war. The United States had given explicit warnings against any further occupation of Indochina. U.S. policy makers believed that doing so would constitute a real and imminent threat to the Netherlands Indies and Singapore. On July 26, U.S. president Franklin D. Roosevelt followed up by freezing all of Japan's American assets. On August 1, the United States banned exports to Japan of high-grade gasoline and reduced shipments of other types to "normal amounts." Moreover, since Assistant Secretary of State Dean Acheson refused to release funds to allow Japan to purchase oil, this partial embargo became a de facto total oil embargo.[83] The British and Dutch governments promptly followed suit. Not only did Japan lose access to 88 percent of its oil supply; it also lost three-quarters of its foreign trade. Moreover, with the release by Roosevelt and Winston Churchill of the Atlantic Charter on August 14, Japan found itself challenged to return to an earlier framework of cooperation or suffer isolation from the world outside the Axis powers.[84] At this point the Japanese media reached a "war-fevered" pitch, complaining of an "ABCD encirclement." Japan, they argued, was fenced in by America, Britain, China, and the Dutch.[85]

Japan responded to economic strangulation and perceived encirclement in a way that surprised the world. Instead of backing down, Japan became even more bellicose and confrontational. Faced with the loss of international influence and possible return to third-power status, Japanese leaders called for war. An imperial conference on September 6, 1941 committed Japan "to resolve on war against the United States (Great Britain and the Netherlands) if there are no prospects for our demands to be met by early October."[86] This policy was further confirmed, albeit delayed, after Tōjō Hideki became premier in mid-October. The descent to war had begun, and it was consummated with a surprise attack on Pearl Harbor and other British and American holdings on December 8, 1941.

This war was a bold gamble at best, irrational at worst. Japan, after all, struck from a position of great weakness. Perhaps no one understood this better than Iwakuro Hideo, a section chief in the army ministry's Bureau of Military Affairs who took part in the first round of informal negotiations in Washington. In August 1941, while traveling back to Japan aboard the *Ryūta Maru*, Iwakuro drew up a graph that highlights the depth of Japan's materiel deficiencies.

Iwakuro argued that Japan maintained only one-tenth the productive capacity of the United States—not a promising figure. But many fire-eating officers in the general staff believed that Japan had a window of opportunity to attack with at least some chance of success. Moreover, pundits, media outlets, and military men emphasized that material deficiencies could be counterbalanced by *Yamato damashi*, or Japanese spirit. It was spirit, not materiel or technology, that led to triumph in war. This argument had been used during the Russo-Japanese War of 1904–5 and was used again in the lead-up to the Pacific War. According to Iwakuro, this belief that spirit trumps technology led decision makers into a "war that Japan had no prospects of winning."[87]

It was a war most Japanese leaders decided on nonetheless. The road to war has been well trodden by historians, and it is beyond the scope of this study to retell in detail. Suffice it to state that the problems in U.S.-Japan relations, many of which have been discussed above, played a major role. The pressures for war by unruly mid-echelon officers in both the army and navy and the lack of strong-willed, moderate leadership only added fuel to the fire. An often-overlooked factor leading to war was the very structure of the Japanese state. The emperor occupied an ambiguous position in the center of Japanese political life, appearing as one who

TABLE 2. Productive capacity: United States and Japan

AREA	U.S. PRODUCTION	RATIO: JAPAN/US
Steel manufacturing	95 million tons	1/20
Oil production	110 million tons	1/100
Coal production	500 million tons	1/10
Electric power	1800 kW	1/6
Aluminum	600 thousand tons	1/6
Aircraft production	120 thousand	1/5
Automobile production	6.2 million	1/50
Ships	10 million tons	1/2
Industrial workers	34 million people	1/5

Taken from Iwakuro Hideo, *Sensō rikugun bōryaku hishi* (Tokyo: Nihon Keizai Shinbun Shuppansha, 2015), 329.

could wield decisive power. But traditions of the emperor intervening in politics largely in informal ways created a power vacuum at the heart of government by the 1930s. This power vacuum led to endemic bureaucratic infighting and made difficult any compromise that might sacrifice Japanese interests. The Meiji Constitution had further included the "cancer" of the right of supreme command, which made the military unaccountable to civilian authority. By November 1941, it would have taken a figure of enormous influence, courage of conviction, and political clout to reign in the military and impose his will on unruly subordinates. Sadly, no such leader existed in Tokyo.

Strikingly, the Greater East Asia Co-Prosperity Sphere played an important role in the lead-up to war. As noted above, by July 1941 the Sphere was used to justify Japan's aggressive advance south into Indochina. Equally importantly, the Sphere also drove a wedge between the United States and Japan. Exhortations of the new order served as a constant reminder of Japan's ties to its Axis partner, Nazi Germany. Moreover, the Co-Prosperity Sphere ideal broadcast the desire to create an economic bloc in which Japan reigned supreme, which meant that Japan would no longer honor U.S. rights, privileges, and business interests in China. The Sphere, that is, epitomized Japan's rejection of the Open Door policy, and the old order more broadly.[88] However ill defined and ill understood the Sphere was, it had become a major impediment to reaching an understanding with the United States.

The U.S. foreign policy establishment was not blind to this situation. U.S. leaders condemned the Sphere as the epitome of Japanese imperial ambitions. In late October 1941, Ambassador Nomura cabled foreign minister Tōgō Shigenori about U.S. distrust of the Co-Prosperity Sphere "as something that aims to use force to enlarge [Japan's] exclusive sphere of influence."[89] Nomura accurately read the U.S. mood. Moderates such as Ambassador Grew heaped scorn on the "high-sounding" slogan as a smokescreen that even lulled Japanese into believing their acts are wholly moral and righteous.[90] Secretary of State Cordell Hull similarly disparaged the Sphere. On November 17, 1941, Hull told Japan's special envoy, Kurusu Saburō, and Ambassador Nomura that the United States believed "that the Japanese formula of a 'new order in greater East Asia' is but another name for a program to dominate all of the Pacific area politically, economically, socially, and otherwise, by military force." Three days later, he repeated to Nomura that slogans such as the "new order in East Asia" and the "co-prosperity sphere" only served to convince the American public "that there was a partnership between Hitler and Japan aimed at enabling Hitler to take charge of one-half of the world and Japan of the other half."[91] Hull frequently mentioned that there was little that was peaceful about Japan's "new order" or "co-prosperity sphere." "Hitler is using similar terms," he told Nomura, "as synonyms for purposes of conquest."[92] Even on the eve of Pearl Harbor, U.S. officials spoke of the Co-Prosperity Sphere as inimical with a Pacific settlement.[93]

Likewise, Japan complained of efforts to block the Co-Prosperity Sphere. Vice Foreign Minister Amō Eiji protested in an October 13, 1941, position paper that the "rupture of economic relations" and pressure from the United States, Britain, and the Netherlands "is making it more and more difficult to establish the Greater East Asia Co-Prosperity Sphere."[94] Amō's view, in fact, represented the norm within the foreign ministry. At a December 1 imperial conference, foreign minister Tōgō Shigenori also insisted that U.S. policy "has consistently been to thwart our immutable policy of constructing the New Order in East Asia."[95] This notion of the United States blocking the new order was even cited in the December 7, 1941, memorandum breaking off negotiations with the United States. The memorandum, handed by Nomura to Hull one hour after the Pearl Harbor attack had begun, criticized U.S. demands as calculated to destroy Japan's leading position in Asia. Moreover, it complained of U.S. intentions "to obstruct Japan's efforts toward the establishment of peace through the creation of a new order in East Asia."[96]

By this time, war had begun. At 1:30 a.m. on December 8, the military launched a successful surprise attack on Pearl Harbor, alongside concurrent attacks in Guam, the Philippines, Hong Kong, and Malaya. The Japanese government followed up the same day, releasing an imperial rescript declaring war against the United States and the British Empire in the name of "self-existence and self-defense." From this point forward, Japan would build its new order by force of arms. Two days after war began, on December 10, a liaison conference named the conflict the Greater East Asia War.[97] The new name, which was broadcast across Japan on December 12, stated in clear terms what had become Japan's primary goal: "the construction of the New Order in Greater East Asia."[98] The following day, at a rally in Hibiya Park attended by tens of thousands of joyous onlookers, Prime Minister Tōjō restated this in clear and vivid terms. "The victory of Japan," he thundered, "will be the victory of the East Asia Co-Prosperity Sphere, as well as the victory of the creation of the new world order."[99] Diplomacy had failed. From this point on, Japan's sphere of influence in Asia would be forged through the fires of global war.

3

IMAGINING CO-PROSPERITY

For the first six months of the Pacific War, the Japanese military ran wild. As of May 1942, the Japanese war machine had overrun Asia without suffering any significant setbacks. Hong Kong and Singapore fell on December 25, 1941, and February 15, 1942, respectively, followed by successes in the Netherlands Indies, Burma, and the Philippines. The rapid advance led to unbridled optimism and a sense of destiny within the Japanese military, as demonstrated in Japan's Malayan campaigns. After the fall of Kuala Lumpur, Mustapha Hussain, the nationalist Young Malay Union's vice president, demanded Japanese support for Malayan independence. "After all," he later noted in his memoirs, "was the Japanese slogan not 'Asia for the Asians'? Was Malaya not for the Malays?" But the Japanese commander with whom he spoke brushed aside Hussain's wishes and gave an unambiguous view of Japan's new empire. "Let the Japanese be the father. Malays, Chinese and Indians live like a family. However, if the Malay child is thin, and needs more milk, we will give him more milk."[1] This description paints a clear picture of how some commanders on the ground may have seen Japan's new order. Much to the dismay of independence activists, it appeared that Japan would build an extended empire, one in which Japan served as the imperial father of a family of Asian nations.

What is truly striking, however, is just how unprepared political leaders in Tokyo were for building an extended empire in East Asia. By 1941, even after four years of war in China, the occupation of French Indochina, and efforts to exert economic and political leadership over Southeast Asia, the Japanese state had given scarcely any thought to the burdens of creating a new international system. For all that policy makers trumpeted the Greater East Asia Co-Prosperity Sphere, they had done little to imagine what the slogan implied for the region. Even when the Co-Prosperity Sphere became national policy in July 1941, policy makers understood it merely in the service of *national* ends of self-existence and self-defense. What would happen after Japanese forces ousted the European colonial powers from Asia? What type of political, economic, and legal order would Japan create? How would it function? In short, what would Japan's Greater East Asia Co-Prosperity Sphere look like? Policy makers rarely grappled with these questions before the attacks of December 8, 1941.

The Pacific War changed everything. The realities of the global conflict necessitated concrete war aims. Political leaders and intellectuals alike recognized the need for detailed understandings of how to govern occupied regions and how to build a legitimate postwar order. The total war thus generated in Japan a total whirlwind of intellectual activity. This chapter explores this whirlwind of public and private efforts to imagine the Greater East Asia Co-Prosperity Sphere in the first year of the Pacific War. As Japan reached the zenith of its imperial expansion, policy makers and intellectuals began in earnest to imagine the Co-Prosperity Sphere and to outline its nature and workings. The Tōjō administration hoped to lead this process and called for new visions, plans, and state organs to build the new Greater East Asia. Nonetheless, no dominant vision emerged for the Sphere in the first year of the Pacific War. Visions for the future and attempts to institutionalize order in Greater East Asia followed the Rising Sun battle flag, not vice versa. Although most early visions were never adopted into policy, they still show the utmost extent of Japanese dreams for the region, dreams that may have been put into practice had Japan survived the Pacific War with empire intact.

Exploring this intellectual whirlwind also provides a useful corrective about the Pacific War. The dominant historical scholarship still understands the war as a "clash of visions" between the United States and Japan. On the one hand, the United States fought for an open East Asia, one committed to the Open Door, the principle of national self-determination, and an Asia not dominated by a single power. On the other hand, Japan fought for a closed East Asia: it sought to free the region from Western imperialism only to integrate it into the Greater East Asia Co-Prosperity Sphere.[2] Certainly, it is true that the war was fought over which power would dominate Asia, and Japanese elites rejected the Anglo-American vision for Asia's future. But this does not mean that Japanese leaders shared a common understanding about the postwar order. Indeed, they initiated war with abstract notions of what would come after, and they were deeply divided about how to implement Japan's new imperium. It was only *after* war had begun that Japan began a serious effort to envision Asia's future. The outbreak of war thus did not represent a clash of visions, at least initially. Instead, early wartime successes impelled leaders to think more clearly about how Japan would reshape the region.

Unclear War Aims

Despite its role in leading to war, on the eve of Pearl Harbor the Co-Prosperity Sphere constituted little more than a vague expression of Japan's regional leadership. Intellectuals in particular were unimpressed with the slogan. They recognized that Japan was attempting to build the region anew, but they remained confounded about the specifics. An October 7, 1941, diplomacy round table at the navy ministry's brain trust, the Naval Intelligence Division (*Kaigunshō Chōsaka*), highlights this general confusion. Its intellectuals, the *crème de la crème* of Japanese thinkers, saw the Co-Prosperity Sphere as "too unrealistic" or in dire need of clarification. "I have tried to read much about it," stated Chūō University professor Tamura Kōsaku, "but it is filled with contradictions and I could not grasp it." Others, including legal scholar Matsushita Masatoshi, foreign policy commentator Inahara Katsuji, and Meiji University professor Saegusa Shigetomo, argued that the slogan itself made little sense. "The reality," they declared, "is that Japanese occupation brings not 'prosperity' but 'poverty.' It would be better to parade the slogan of Lebensraum." Matsushita even stated that the Co-Prosperity Sphere ideal had little value on the domestic front. He argued: "It can be said that the 'Greater East Asia Co-Prosperity Sphere' [slogan] has not been successful. It is banal and overly unrealistic. For instance, the general populace and women are much more interested in the everyday rice problem than they are in the issue of the New Order in East Asia. If we do not advance a realistic slogan that Japan must work for the defense of the homeland, we will be unable to lead our people."[3]

This confusion was not limited to the navy brain trust. Dōshisha University law professor Tamura Tokuji, writing for the *Diplomatic Review* (*Gaikō jihō*) in August 1941, valiantly described the Co-Prosperity Sphere as a new type of political union of states, but he could not come to any conclusions on the specifics.[4] Perhaps most damningly, Shōwa Kenkyūkai intellectual Rōyama Masamichi, the preeminent thinker behind the new order in East Asia who in 1938 had called for an "East Asian community" (*Tōa kyōdōtai*), voiced concerns about the Co-Prosperity Sphere. "One cannot avoid the impression," he wrote in April 1941, "that explanations of the Co-Prosperity Sphere's scope and contents are extremely abstract and vague." Despite his own attempt to develop an understanding of Japan's new order, Rōyama could not give his blessing to its newest form. He thought it overly complicated and geopolitically unrealistic. "Thus," he argued, "the specific regional concept of the Greater East Asia Co-Prosperity Sphere will not come into being, nor is there room for it to appear."[5] Intellectuals, in short, saw the Sphere as neither a powerful slogan nor a convincing statement of war aims.[6]

Governmental elites faced similar difficulties, even after launching the Pacific War. In the introduction, I noted how Prime Minister Tōjō Hideki, cabinet planning board president Suzuki Teiichi, and army ministry Bureau of Military Affairs director Mutō Akira had difficulties articulating the difference between Japan's national defense sphere and its co-prosperity sphere. This shocking lack of understanding was all too common. At a liaison conference on February 26, 1942, chief of the general staff Sugiyama Hajime felt it necessary to ask Prime Minister Tōjō, "What is the extent of the Greater East Asia Co-Prosperity Sphere?"[7] Moreover, at an official Greater East Asia Construction Council meeting on March 11, 1942, Ōtani Kōzui, a committeeman tasked with drafting population policies, could not contain his dismay. "From the start, the government has not given a clear definition of the Greater East Asia Co-Prosperity Sphere," he complained. If the government could not provide a convincing vision, how could he? Ōtani continued: "I find it extremely troubling that I am asked to state my views on it. I don't know where it is. Interpreting from a narrow sense, the Co-Prosperity Sphere is [composed of] Manchuria and China. But before we knew it, it had become a Co-Prosperity Sphere in Greater East Asia. I have absolutely no understanding of what Greater East Asia is."[8] Deeper thinking was sorely needed.

The army general staff was perhaps the only policy-making group that gave serious thought to the aftermath of war before the Pacific War began. In March 1941 the general staff published a top-secret study that outlined practical strategic considerations for an occupation of Southeast Asia. This study, written under the direction of Col. Obata Nobuyoshi, was drafted by a group that had little knowledge, experience, or familiarity with Southeast Asia. Nevertheless, it still offered the first (and perhaps most important) plan for the region.[9] The study called on Japanese forces "to restore law and order, making it easier for Japan to acquire natural resources" from the occupied territories. Resource acquisition constituted the most important goal of occupation: without resources, Japan would be unable to compete in the global, total war. This focus on raw material acquisition led the planners to emphasize stability and continuity of government over all else. Japan thus should avoid any unnecessary changes to governmental apparatuses and should impede any push by local populations for political autonomy. Instead, Japan was to rule through existing governmental organs, making use of local (nonwhite) personnel to administer the territories. The overall aim was clear: Japan was to replace the European colonial powers as Asia's hegemon without being bogged down in administrative affairs. This would obviate the nuisances of governance and would allow Japan to focus on its central goal of securing natural resources.[10]

The study spent eight months collecting dust on a general staff bookshelf, but the drift to war gave it a second life. By November 1941, the impending failure of Japan's informal conversations with the United States led leaders to take another, more detailed look at the army policy plan. A November 15 liaison conference endorsed its main ideas.[11] A follow-up liaison conference on November 20 adopted its recommendation to rule occupied regions through military administrations that would "make use of existing organs of government." The aims of this military occupation would be the "speedy procurement of raw materials" necessary for national defense and the establishment of an economic system that served Japan's military needs. Policy makers recognized that this would put an undue burden on local peoples, so the policy plan stressed the necessity of fostering trust in the military government. In this context, military administrations were to "rescind any policies that cause opposition." But independence was out of the question, and the plan warned against "prematurely bringing about independence movements."[12]

Not all were happy with the army plan. Col. Watanabe Wataru, an elite planner in the prime minister's Total War Research Institute (*Sōryokusen Kenkyūjo*) who was later dispatched to the Malay Peninsula with the Japanese Twenty-Fifth Army, harshly criticized the general staff's occupation policies. In his memoirs, written not six months after the outbreak of the Pacific War, Watanabe denounced occupation policies as "extremely superficial" at best and "materialistic" at worst. He believed they were not undergirded with any guiding spirit or ideology that would win hearts and minds across Southeast Asia. Without any meaningful ideology to guide Japanese actions, he believed the occupation would devolve into little more than "the nature of a thief. When hungry, grab and eat whatever is there, and take home the rest." Watanabe, a veteran of state affairs, thought little of general staff planners as well. "The brilliant group," as he sarcastically described them, "lack common sense and have little life experience. From my perspective, they appear childish."[13]

Private criticisms notwithstanding, the realities of the Pacific War brought about a deepened commitment to the general staff study. As Japanese forces ran wild across Asia, Tokyo moved to ensure control over the region in ways that aligned with the ideas of the general staff. Shortly after Pearl Harbor, a liaison conference adopted a cabinet paper, "Outline of Economic Policies for the South," which spoke of Japanese control emerging through a "Greater East Asia Co-Prosperity Sphere autarkic system."[14] Occupied territories would provide Japan with natural resources and export markets for finished goods. The Philippines, Borneo, the Netherlands Indies, and Malaya would be developed for such vital resources as petroleum, nickel, copper, bauxite, manganese, and chrome. Thailand and Indochina would serve as sources of foodstuffs for Japan. Trade within the empire would be subject to Japanese controls. Japan would allow free trade but would prioritize the export of Japanese products to enterprises producing goods for export to Japan.[15] A March 1942 navy ministry report, which provided guidelines for the administration of navy-occupied areas, spelled out what Japanese rule meant in even more candid detail. Building off the "Outline," the navy report also dealt with the extent of control over occupied territories. Politically, Japan would seek their "permanent retention" and would strive for "the organic integration of the entire region into the Japanese Empire." The region would also be brought under a Japanese economic umbrella. To keep Southeast Asia as a supplier of raw materials, Japan would discourage the creation of new manufacturing industries. Moreover, Tokyo would tightly hold the reins of finance. "As our financial institutions are established and strengthened," the report wrote, "they shall gradually assume the financial hegemony hitherto held by the enemy institutions."[16]

Although the studies spoke in terms of permanence, in reality they constituted temporary wartime policies. Before Pearl Harbor, little thought had been paid to how Japan's extended empire would operate in the postwar era. The general staff and navy ministry policy papers spoke little of war aims or end goals. They gave little sense of how Japan's new empire would function throughout the region. Moreover, policy makers had neither worked out an understanding of how Japan's empire differed from its European counterparts nor pondered how local peoples would receive or understand the new order. "There was little attempt," writes historian Akira Iriye, "to distinguish Japanese policy from those of the Western colonial powers. The only difference was that Japanese, rather than Westerners, would be the rulers."[17] This continuity is telling. In the end, policy makers merely sought for Japan the positions of power and influence vacated by the West.

Imagining Co-Prosperity

The requirements of global war, however, changed priorities. No longer would an occupation plan that lacked a guiding spirit be fit to guide national policy. From early 1942, a broad discussion had begun to articulate different possibilities for Japan's Greater East Asia Co-Prosperity Sphere. In this sense, Pearl Harbor and the subsequent attacks forced policy makers and intellectuals to contemplate what they hoped to achieve with the new order. A wide variety of groups took part in this discussion; some of the most notable included the Total War Research Institute, the Naval Intelligence Division, and the National Policy Research Association (*Kokusaku Kenkyūkai*). These groups published widely to give meaning to the Co-Prosperity Sphere, and each drew together some of the best minds of wartime Japan.

The Total War Research Institute was created in late September 1940 to conduct policy reports on matters pertaining to Japan's "national defense," broadly defined. The institute encouraged research on what might happen if Japan found itself embroiled in a total war. To this end, it was staffed by elite bureaucrats from each of Japan's major ministries and headed by cabinet planning board president Hoshino Naoki.[18] From April 1941, each ministry sent its top young candidates as "research students" to be affiliated with the institute for a period of one year. In all, they represented the crème de la crème of Japan's elite civil servants. The first class of students—thirty-six in all—was drawn primarily from the civilian bureaucracy (only four students were taken from the military).[19] And it was these young civil servants, plus a smattering of people from outside government, who helped articulate a vision for the future Japan would build for the region. This vision took the shape of a January 27, 1942, secret policy document titled "Draft Plan to Establish the Greater East Asia Co-Prosperity Sphere."[20]

Another important vision was created by the Naval Intelligence Division. Created in 1939 by Rear Admiral Takagi Sōkichi to serve as a counterweight to the army's growing influence in Japanese politics, the Intelligence Division soon secured the cooperation of some of the era's most important political intellectuals. Its list of members reads like a veritable who's who of wartime Japanese intellectual life and compares favorably to that of the more famous Shōwa Kenkyūkai.[21] The research group that collaborated on envisioning regional order centered on Yabe Teiji, a political scientist, international affairs pundit, and professor at Tokyo Imperial University. Yabe was neatly poised to take part in this endeavor. He had been a member of the Shōwa Kenkyūkai and had participated in its discussions in 1938 to build a new China. From January 9, 1942, Yabe began political meetings to articulate war aims and the nature of the Co-Prosperity Sphere. Yabe was joined in this effort by Matsushita Masatoshi, Tokyo Imperial University assistant professor Ōkōchi Kazuo, Keiō University professor Nagata Kiyoshi, and Kyoto School philosopher Kōyama Iwao.[22] Together, this group developed a blueprint for the political, intellectual, economic, and legal foundations of the new order, which took shape in a September 1, 1942, secret policy document, "On the Greater East Asia Co-Prosperity Sphere."[23]

Finally, some of the most voluminous work on the new order in Greater East Asia was produced by the National Policy Research Association.[24] This was a conservative, private research organization that produced policy papers on matters of national interest. First formed by Yatsugi Kazuo in October 1933 under a different name, the research group briefly disbanded before Yatsugi reorganized it in

1937. Yatsugi viewed the group as an important means to bring together leading intellectuals, military officers, and bureaucrats to draft national policy and to influence the policy process, and he succeeded in building an organization with wide membership. The association grew from having 476 members in 1937 to more than two thousand in 1940—most of whom were scholars, government officials, politicians, and people in the financial and business worlds.[25]

In February 1942, the Research Association established a Greater East Asia Problem Investigative Committee (*Dai Tōa Mondai Chōsakai*) to develop a ten-year plan for Greater East Asia.[26] Some of the committee's influential members included intellectual Takahashi Kamekichi, vice foreign minister Amō Eiji, former ambassador to the United States Horinouchi Kensuke, political science scholar Ōiwa Makoto, former director-general of the Cabinet Legislation Bureau Kanamori Tokujirō, and National Policy Research Association founder Yatsugi Kazuo. The group wrote policy papers and published a widely circulated weekly bulletin that dealt with all aspects of the Greater East Asia Co-Prosperity Sphere. The association's most important visions were outlined in two documents, both of which were written in 1942: "Basic Plan for the Political Structure of the Greater East Asia Co-Prosperity Sphere" and "Basic Plan for the Economic Structure of the Greater East Asia Co-Prosperity Sphere."[27]

These organizations played a part in a broader debate about the nature and workings of the Sphere.[28] This debate covered the gamut of issues from economic and political structures to legal institutions, ideology, education, and culture. It led to the production of secret documents circulated in government that were meant to serve as a practical guide for policy makers. None were ever adopted as official policy, but they provide a yardstick for the extent of dreams for Asia's future. Reading them together, a number of themes emerge.

Politically, all visions saw the world as dividing into four or five blocs—or pan-regions—led by powerful states. Japan's "historic mission" was thus to use the Greater East Asia Co-Prosperity Sphere ideal to forge Asia anew under Japanese leadership. Of course, leaders and intellectuals alike did not always agree on how far the Co-Prosperity Sphere extended (some included India, Australia, New Zealand, and eastern Siberia; others did not). But they were clear on its overall intentions: Japan would create a new form of interstate relations, one that rejected liberal internationalist visions of equality of nations. In fact, intellectuals argued that such notions of equality constituted mere "mechanical equality" (*kikaiteki byōdō*), a deceit that allowed the West to maintain the status quo of world rule and colonial mastery. The Co-Prosperity Sphere, however, was different. It constituted neither a means to colonial rule nor an international order supporting Westphalian notions of sovereignty. As one group put it, "We cannot possibly treat [the peoples of Greater East Asia] with across-the-board equality."[29]

Instead, the Co-Prosperity Sphere would create a new "moral order," an organic hierarchy where all countries or territories would occupy subordinate positions under Japan. This sense of subordination was highlighted by the oft-quoted phrase that Japan would enable "each to its proper place" (*ono ono sono tokoro o eshimeru*) in the new order. In this context, "proper place" meant serving as cogs in Japan's imperial machinery, taking on subordinate roles for the good of the region. Stated differently, "proper place" is best understood through Yabe Teiji's notion of "relations of organic difference" (*yūkiteki sai kankei*).[30] The region's leading ethnic group would serve as the natural leader. Weaker peoples would offer their trust and join the leading ethnicity in creating a regional community, serving in roles that best suited their intellect, culture, and standards of living. This idea recognized an inherent inequality that existed among peoples throughout the world. But it was not meant to be colonial or harshly domineering. Far from it: "organic difference" would lead to natural harmony—the harmony found in familial organization, where every member had its own function or role to fill. It sought to impose functionalist, corporatist, and family-state norms on the international sphere.

The Japanese Empire would stand at the apex of the international system, as "head" (*koshu*) of this new "familial community" (*kazokuteki kyōdōtai*) of nations.[31] This role as the region's familial head, most argued, was a "historical necessity." As the only power capable of resisting Western imperialism and the only Asian nation to industrialize within the span of a generation, only Japan could bring its colonized Asian brethren into a single, united family of nations. As family head, Japan would maintain the basic leadership roles of safeguarding regional autonomy, providing for defense, promoting policies of prosperity, and mediating any disputes among component countries and territories.

Other territories would occupy positions in a political hierarchy under Japan—from independent states to protectorates and directly controlled territories. In this sense, independence was not assured in Japan's new empire. Moreover, although the Sphere would permit the existence of "independent countries," this did not imply freedom from Japanese control. Most visions recognized that independence would be circumscribed. For instance, the Total War Research Institute's study made clear that independent countries (Manchukuo, China, Thailand, and the Philippines) would only have independence within the context of Japan's new order. "This is different," the report asserted, "from an independence based on the ideas of liberalism and national self-determination."[32] This refusal to grant full independence was common among all studies, which recognized the propagandistic value of liberation but wanted to ensure Japanese control.[33] As Kawanishi Kōsuke correctly notes, the Japanese stress on "liberating Asia" only meant "liberation" from Europe; it never implied the former colonies would be free from Japanese control.[34]

The Sphere would also include protectorates and directly controlled territories. There was little agreement as to which territories would become protectorates and which would be directly controlled by Japan. But the most important plans discussed these territories in similar ways. Protectorates were areas deemed unready for immediate independence owing to their "civilizational level." For instance, the Total War Research Institute report noted that Burma "has had a strong anti-British independence movement and, moreover, is historically and culturally suitable for independence." But the report still argued against granting full independence, owing to Burma's lower level of civilization. Countries such as Burma would occupy a space in Japan's empire similar to mandate-rule colonial territories such as Egypt or Palestine. And Japanese planners justified protectorates in the same way the colonial powers justified League of Nations mandates: they would help countries such as Burma prepare for future independence.[35] Finally, most agreed that strategic territories and resource "treasure troves" such as the Netherlands Indies, Malaya, Singapore, and island chains in the Pacific should be directly controlled by Japan.[36]

The more detailed studies even delved into relations within the Sphere. On the one hand, the National Policy Research Association noted that member nations would be free to interact with each other to meet their national interests.[37] The Naval Intelligence Division, on the other hand, called for tighter controls. Direct relations or alliances would not be permitted, and member countries would have little contact with one another. Instead, each state would be bound solely to Japan, which would secure cooperation for regional goals. The navy planners thus hoped to stave off antagonistic, competitive relations in which multiple states jockeyed for position or influence within the Sphere. But more importantly, through this measure the navy brain trust sought to secure Japan's position as the leading nation. The plan even refused to tolerate the existence of powerful regional agencies outside of Tokyo that might threaten Japanese leadership. Japan would allow discourse in the form of joint conferences. But the sole purpose of such conferences would be to promote the *image*, not the *reality*, of regional cooperation. "We should prevent the conferences from wrongly putting pressure on the empire," the navy report maintained. "Therefore, the organization's bills shall at first have mainly propagandistic value. Over time, [the conference's reach] shall extend to real bills. We need skillful measures [to manage] this."[38]

This focus on interstate relations highlighted the necessity for a new system of international law, one that transcended the central focus placed on the nation-state. Japanese intellectuals made powerful critiques of the contradictions inherent to Western international law. They saw self-determination, the equality of nations, and a state's right to exist as high-sounding principles with little applicability to real life. As international law scholar Matsushita Masa-toshi (one of the authors of the navy study) argued, the notion of a right to exist "was little more than an abstract concept, or more specifically an empty idea."[39] After all, what meaning could it have in a world where powerful states so frequently denied self-determination to weaker peoples, or where global powers could invade weaker states, with full knowledge that any illegal occupation or violation of territorial sovereignty would be permitted by international society? What meaning was there to international law when powers routinely *de facto* permitted acts that were *de jure* illegal? Nonetheless, although intellectuals made powerful critiques of Western international law, they failed to develop new legal norms for a world led by regional spheres. Intellectuals simply argued that Japan should do its utmost to forge a new international law that best fits the complexities of the new world order as well as Japan's hierarchical international system.[40] This was hardly a positive first step toward institutionalizing Asia under Japanese leadership.

Whatever the case, the political future envisioned in these plans was far more sophisticated than the mere slogan of "imperialism without colonies." Even in 1942, political intellectuals and bureaucrats alike saw the Co-Prosperity Sphere as a hybrid of old imperialism of colonial and territorial rule and a new imperialism of "independent" satellite regimes that were informally controlled by Japan.[41] Rapid military advances abroad in this sense engendered a sense of optimism and navel gazing. Political intellectuals naïvely assumed that Japan could impose on Asia a new imperial system, one that bound a hierarchy of polities in a dependent and subservient relationship, without first winning the hearts and minds of occupied territories.[42]

Even greater intellectual energy was spent on the economic nature of the Co-Prosperity Sphere. Intellectuals, expecting the world to break up into pan-regions, agreed that Japan's best course was to create its own economic "pan-region."[43] They crafted many names for this new economic vision: a "pan-regional economy" (*kōiki keizai*), an "organic economy" (*yūkiteki keizai*), an "independent economy" (*jiritsu keizai*), a "self-sufficient economy" (*jikyū keizai* or *jikyū jisoku keizai*), an "autonomous national defense economy" (*jiritsuteki kokubō keizai*), a "high-level controlled economy" (*kōdo tōsei keizai*), and a "high-level autarkic economic sphere" (*kōdo jikyū keizai ken*). The names implied a dual aspect to the Greater East Asia Co-Prosperity Sphere economic structure. On the one hand, it would serve as a defense economy to help Japan meet its resource and military needs as it engaged in global war. In this context, intellectuals called on Japan to promote self-sufficiency in critical resources and in defense industries. On the other hand, the regional economy was viewed as one part of the *Pax Nipponica* that would greet war's end: a functionalist economy and yen zone that would bring self-sufficiency and prosperity to the region.

Whether in wartime or peacetime, however, the Co-Prosperity Sphere was conceived as an "organic," "hierarchical" bloc economy that tied Japan to dependent territories. All studies emphasized the Sphere as tying together a diverse set of economies from the industrialized core region of North China, Manchukuo, and Japan to the plantation economies of Southeast Asia. And all saw Japan as playing the leading role in guiding the region toward self-sufficiency. But there was less agreement over how it would do so. Some called for a centralized structure locating all important industries in Japan, whereas others called for a pluralistic and confederated economic structure. Whatever the case, most agreed that the Asian economy would be linked through a yen standard, where price values would be based on the yen equivalent; comprehensive pricing policies; common financial institutions; new transportation networks; and common economic and trade policies.[44] And most agreed that since self-sufficiency was unachievable, the Co-Prosperity Sphere would avoid becoming an exclusive economic zone. Instead, it would maintain trade relations with other co-prosperity spheres throughout the world.[45]

Economic ties within the Sphere would be based on two main principles. First, all natural resources, industry, and production would be used to create a system of defense for East Asia. In this context, the "South" would, at first, serve as a supply base for military needs and foodstuffs.[46] Japan would seek military resources such as petroleum, rubber, siderite, tin, nickel, and bauxite; fibrous resources such as cotton, wool, hemp, and lumber; and rice, flour, and sugar to meet domestic needs for food. So vast were these resources throughout Southeast Asia that one man likened Japan's acquisition of them to "a cat being given a whale."[47] Japan could use this overabundance of resources to help "reinforce the frailties of the Japanese economy" and to ensure the region's security.[48]

Second, the Greater East Asia Co-Prosperity Sphere would not be a simple, exploitative structure. Instead, it would be a planned economy that would bring wealth and development to the region. As the National Policy Research Association study noted, only a planned economy could meet the needs of a region as diverse as Asia. Greater East Asia, that is, was beset by "considerable differences" among its component territories, whether in "standards of living and cultural level, political power, [or] level of economic development."[49] Only a control economy could best manage these differences and pursue distinct measures for the entire region's benefit. Nor was this to be a traditional imperial or colonial relationship, one designed to ensure Japan's permanent supremacy. In fact, most called for wiping out the "colonial economic character" of the region as the first step toward East Asia's revival. Many studies even hinted at evening out developmental levels, at least to a certain extent. For instance, the navy study called on Japan to avoid "ideas that permanently treat the regional economic sphere as a resource supply area and a dumping ground for finished goods."[50] Japan had a responsibility not only to facilitate economic development within the region but also to guide and nurture the region's ethnic capital and production capabilities. In the process, Japan would help overcome Asian poverty.

These tensions between exploitation and development owed to the fact that Japan launched its dramatic enterprise of empire building while engaged in total war. Thus exploitation and the promise of development took on wholly new meanings. Japan could not merely mimic the colonial policies of "imperialist" powers and use the region as a resource supply post. Doing so was not only unsustainable; it would also convince Asians that Japan was no different from its imperial predecessors. Nor could Japan gravitate toward a simple humanist sentiment of uplifting the region. A balance had to be struck between the two. Japan would not be able to create the Co-Prosperity Sphere without ensuring resource self-sufficiency and a dramatic expansion in defense production necessary to fight a total war. A productive use (exploitation) of Southeast Asian resources would help meet this need. Yet most also argued that Japan's new managed economy should also uplift the region, developing the region's ethnic capital and production capabilities, even the expense of nonstrategic industries in Japan. In a sense, intellectuals called for a benevolent empire of exploitative development— one that would serve Japanese needs but would also modernize Greater East Asia and bind it into a harmonious whole.

This push for a managed economy that would both exploit and develop the region had deep roots in the 1930s. The global depression that battered most Western economies had convinced Japanese planners and political intellectuals alike that the liberal-capitalist world order was on the brink of collapse. In response, they turned to German ideas of state planning and regional economic blocs (*Grossraumwirtschaft*) as the swiftest route to national power.[51] With the outbreak of the Pacific War, regional economic planning had become all the more essential. A "have-not" nation that lacked the resource base of the British Empire or continent-sized powers like the United States and the Soviet Union, Japan could hardly fight a global, total war and plan for the postwar peace without mobilizing the region in the service of Japanese aims. Moreover, intellectuals argued that Japan was the most natural leader for the region. Japan would replace Western capitalist "exploitation" with a system of exploitative development that would bring true "co-prosperity" to the region. Exploitative development would help secure an Asia independent from Western control and Japan's position as father of an Asian family of nations.

Conflicts over Co-Prosperity

Still, these visions remained mere dreams, in the realm of what-could-be. They no doubt informed policy makers' views about the Sphere, but they never generated sufficient interest to reach cabinet or liaison conference discussions. In the first year, only two measures intended to shape Asia's future reached the highest level of decision-making, and both were led by the Tōjō cabinet. On the one hand, the prime minister launched the Greater East Asia Construction Council to forge a new vision for Asia after war's end. On the other hand, Tōjō created the Greater East Asia Ministry, amid great opposition, to help implement and oversee the construction of the new order.

The Greater East Asia Construction Council was launched in February 1942 to discuss Asia's future. This council brought together political leaders, governmental offices and ministries, captains of industry, and directors of industry control associations to transform the Greater East Asia Co-Prosperity Sphere into something more concrete. Prime Minister Tōjō best stated the council's aims in his opening address on February 27, 1942. He argued that the war constituted a "global revolution." To deal with this revolution, Tōjō called on the council "to study and deliberate on important matters pertaining to the establishment of the empire's hundred-year plan and the construction of the Greater East Asia Co-Prosperity Sphere."[52] Of course, council members recognized that a hundred-year plan was more fantasy than reality. Instead, they discussed the gamut of regional affairs, from education to population measures, economic affairs, mining, electricity, fisheries, trade, and transportation, and they sought to forge a consensus on policies over the next fifteen years. In this sense, the Greater East Asia Construction Council was tasked with the creation of a definitive plan for the region's future.

The most important areas of discussion revolved around regional economic policy. Nonetheless, as the meticulous research by Japanese historian Adachi Hiroaki reveals, the council was beset by divisions over the policy that best served Japan's new empire. All parties agreed that Japan should serve as the leader of an expanded autarkic bloc to be created over the next fifteen years. But differences emerged over the means to this end. The vigorous debates that ensued revolved around two main issues: (1) where state-of-the-art industry and production should be located; and (2) what groups should control regional planning.

The cabinet planning board argued that Japan should avoid the risk of centralizing production of critical industries in Japan. In this approach, they borrowed the ideas of economist Hinoshita Tōgō, who rejected a vertical hierarchy tying the region to Japan as an "anachronism." Hinoshita believed that Japan should instead spearhead a "pluralist autarkic sphere" (tagenteki jikyūken) in which each component region could plan and supply itself. Taking his arguments as a point of departure, the cabinet planning board called for the creation of a "core region" of Japan–Manchukuo–North China throughout which Japan would disperse key industries and production networks. This "core region," they hoped, would free up necessary space and farmland within the "inner territories" (naichi) to allow the Japanese people, the "leading ethnicity," to expand its population and to secure self-sufficiency in foodstuffs. Readily available food and free space would also ensure Japan's continued population increase and vitality to remain the leading force behind the Co-Prosperity Sphere.[53] The cabinet planning board found strong support from the army, which hoped to create self-sufficiency by transferring important industries to North China, a critical area for Japan's autarkic plans.[54] Moreover, the army opposed any unidimensional plans for economic development.

On the other side of the clash stood the ministry of commerce and industry. Its members stressed the sustained leadership of Japan proper. In this context, they insisted on centralizing critical industries within Japan's "inner territories" and establishing strict controls over regional production. The ministry of commerce and industry vision borrowed much from businessman Yoshida Hideo, who argued that concentrating industry in Japan would create "the economic foundation of Japan's leadership over East Asia." Yoshida did note that Japan may be forced to shed labor-intensive production, but he insisted that "leadership within the Co-Prosperity Sphere" necessitated a firm grip over the machinery, metal, and chemical industries. Bureaucrats in the ministry of commerce and industry built off Yoshida's ideas, maintaining that Japan could centralize production but still direct region-wide industrial plans.[55] They would accomplish this task by strengthening the industry control associations, the groups that oversaw war production and served as the most important organizational link between government and business.[56] Forging the control associations into a "unified central organization," they argued, would streamline the process of controlling industry throughout Greater East Asia. This use of the control associations was a naïve decision. The control associations, after all, would have gained a conflicting mandate as defenders of the vested zaibatsu business interests and as organs to implement national economic policy. Directors of major control associations quickly jumped on the ministry of commerce and industry bandwagon, happy with a chance at a central role in planning for the region.

The conflict, however, was never resolved to either side's satisfaction. On April 17, 1942, the Greater East Asia Construction Council finalized a plan titled "Fundamental Policy for Constructing the Economy of Greater East Asia." But the "Fundamental Policy" never reconciled the views of the cabinet planning board, the military, and the ministry of commerce and industry. Instead of hashing out a compromise, the drafters simply decided to give every group what they desired, at the expense of clarity and focus. The final plan, which was approved with no changes on May 4, 1942, notes:

> The distribution of industry in Greater East Asia will take as preconditions the demands of national defense as well as the position of the Japanese people [*Yamato Minzoku*]. Plans to construct the Japan-Manchukuo-China economy will correspond to military gains made in the Greater East Asia War. The location of all industries will be considered with the aim of ensuring suitable sites for suitable industries [*tekichi-tekigyō*]. Necessary revisions to established plans will be made to show peak efficiency, and with this we resolve to construct a comprehensive economy across Greater East Asia.[57]

This was an ambiguous statement that jammed together the wishes of all concerned parties. In calling for a "core region" in Japan–Manchukuo–North China and for "suitable sites for suitable industries," and in hinting at a unified and centralized regional economy, the "Fundamental Policy" failed to reconcile the conflicting ideas of the cabinet planning board and the ministry of commerce and industry. Moreover, the policy makes no mention of the control associations, which the commerce ministry hoped would play a pivotal role in centralized planning. As Adachi concludes, "this wording is extremely difficult to understand, and it is unclear where the focal point is located."[58] Despite trying to set in motion plans for East Asia's future, the council created little more than an abstract, vague policy statement. In the process, the council muddied the waters of regional economic planning, creating a situation in which no group got what it wanted.

Even so, the "Fundamental Policy" still had a fleeting chance at becoming national policy. On May 8, 1942, the Tōjō cabinet approved the plan and submitted it for review at a May 19 liaison conference. But opposition from the high command sounded the death knell for the now-muddied and vague policy statement. The liaison conference proposed further study and deliberation, and decided that the plan "is no more than something to be used for future reference."[59] Later efforts by the Greater East Asia Construction Council to clarify economic policy became even more difficult to implement.[60] The attempt to hash out a grand, fifteen-year plan for the regional economy thus ended up producing little more than "reference material" and interministerial animosity.

While the Greater East Asia Council was holding its discussions, the Tōjō government began a parallel effort to create a formidable institution to guide Greater

East Asia policy. These efforts culminated in what would become known as the Greater East Asia ministry. Historian Baba Akira has argued that the ministry was created as part of an attempt by the military to dispossess the foreign ministry of policy-making influence.[61] Indeed, the military was more than happy to see yet another downtick in foreign ministry power. But for Tōjō, the consummate bureaucrat, the new ministry constituted part of a sincere (yet failed) attempt to centralize and rationalize policy for the Greater East Asia Co-Prosperity Sphere. Consolidating policymaking power in a single governmental agency, Tōjō believed, would better prepare Japan to wage a global war and to build the region anew after the war's end.

The initial impetus to create the Greater East Asia ministry came from the East Asia Development Board (*Kōain*) and the cabinet planning board. Both agencies championed the creation of an agency that could streamline foreign policy and help construct the new Greater East Asia. Working in tandem with the army and navy, they called for a new state organ that would cooperate with the military administrations to develop Asia and govern the polities within the Sphere. These efforts received Prime Minister Tōjō's blessing, and from July 1942 the cabinet planning board began to draft policy plans for the Greater East Asia ministry's creation.

The final plan to establish the ministry was brought before a cabinet meeting on September 1, 1942. It called for a powerful new state organ that would exercise jurisdiction over Greater East Asia (excluding Japan's inner territories [*naichi*], Korea, Taiwan, and Karafuto). The plan saw this new ministry as administering the region's political, economic, and cultural affairs, and engaging in all aspects of governance outside of "pure diplomacy," which would remain the exclusive realm of the foreign ministry. The ministry would also engage in a wide range of other affairs, from developing business and colonial undertakings to creating new laws, promoting culture, and dealing with the movements of people throughout the Sphere. Most importantly, it would "work hand in glove" (*sakuō kyōryoku*) with the high command to support the network of military administrations across Greater East Asia. To create the new Greater East Asia Ministry, the plan called for the amalgamation of a variety of governmental agencies. It was to be composed of the Manchurian Affairs Bureau, the East Asia Development Board, the foreign ministry's East Asia Bureau and South Seas Bureau, and the ministry of colonial affairs.[62]

The plan became the source of bitter opposition between the Tōjō cabinet and the ministry of foreign affairs. Foreign minister Tōgō Shigenori was livid; his fury was palpable at a September 1 cabinet meeting that discussed the draft plan. He complained of the whole effort to create a new ministry as a colossal waste of time and effort. On the one hand, Tōgō protested that since the new ministry would take over foreign ministry activities across Asia, it would damage the prestige of Japan's diplomatic establishment. Tōgō also insisted that, in crafting policy on behalf of occupied Asia, the proposed Greater East Asia Ministry laid bare Japan's colonial intent. The lack of respect for independence would generate suspicions of the new ministry as little more than a "colonial ministry" and would alienate the peoples of occupied Asia. Prime Minister Tōjō, however, dismissed these objections. The premier instead stressed that the new ministry's primary role lay not only in building Greater East Asia but also in meeting the spiritual and mobilization needs of Japan's total war. For three hours straight, Tōgō and Tōjō locked horns with such vehemence that the other cabinet members found it difficult to get a word in edgewise.[63]

With no consensus reached, the embattled foreign minister made his final gambit: Tōgō threatened to withhold support from the plan, while at the same time refusing to relinquish his position as foreign minister. This was an act of desperation—Tōgō's continued intransigence and refusal to resign his post threatened to bring down the Tōjō cabinet at the high point of Japan's imperial expansion, when cabinet members needed to present an image of unity.[64] At this point, the emperor informally intervened in the political process. In a meeting with navy minister Shimada Shigetarō in the imperial study, the emperor stated his desire that the situation "be straightened out without a mass [cabinet] resignation." Afterward, the emperor summoned Lord Keeper of the Privy Seal Kido Kōichi to the imperial chamber to inform him of the decision. With the emperor's desire made clear, Tōgō's gambit had failed. The foreign minister had no recourse but to resign. That same evening, Prime Minister Tōjō was officially named foreign minister in Tōgō's place, and after his instatement ceremony the cabinet officially voted to establish the Greater East Asia ministry.[65] The new ministry began official operations two months later, on November 1, 1942.

Tōjō's hopes for the ministry, however, were soon dashed. Like most early visions for the Sphere, the new institution was handicapped by the very war effort it was supposed to aid. Although born amid great conflict and among fantasies of potential, the Greater East Asia Ministry ended up primarily as an agent of cultural diplomacy. The ministry never grew into a powerful policy engine to build Asia anew, and it never gained relevance in Japan's political life. It simply did not have the time. By April 1943, five months after its founding, the war situation was so dire that Tōjō turned to Shigemitsu Mamoru and the foreign ministry to help reenvision Japanese policy as well as the nature of the Greater East Asia Co-Prosperity Sphere. From 1944, the Greater East Asia Ministry had become so enfeebled that its activities were run concurrently by the foreign minister. It never became more than a paper creation, remaining another dream of what could have been had Japan solidified its wartime gains.

FIGURE 2. The newly formed Greater East Asia Ministry, 1942. Photo courtesy of *Mainichi shinbun* and Aflo.

Hakkō Ichiu: Recasting Japanism as Internationalism

These difficulties in crafting compelling visions or meaningful institutions were matched by even greater struggles to articulate a persuasive ideology. Most government pronouncements reflected a triumphalist sense of Japan's wartime victories but offered little to justify Japanese stewardship over the region. Prime Minister Tōjō, for instance, celebrated the historic fall of Singapore in a speech made to the House of Peers on February 16, 1942. Reveling in this epoch-making victory, the premier spoke of a broader set of aims for the global war. Japan, he asserted, was fighting "to have all the nations and peoples of Greater East Asia take their proper place" and to create "a new order of coexistence and co-prosperity based on moral principles." But Tōjō did not expound on his ideas—he only made the cryptic comment that the new order would have "a completely different nature" than that of Anglo-American imperialism.[66]

What "ideals" or "moral principles" would form the basis of the new order? How would Japan justify its new empire? To answer this, officials and intellectuals alike generally turned to the Japanist notion of *hakkō ichiu*. Often translated by the government as "universal brotherhood," this political slogan is better understood to mean "the whole world [more literally, the eight corners of the world] under one roof." So commonly cited was *hakkō ichiu* that it even appeared in the founding statement of national policy the Konoe cabinet had adopted on August 1, 1940.[67] By 1942, *hakkō ichiu* represented the fundamental ideal behind the new order. Whereas the Anglo-American powers trumpeted a postwar order of liberalism and democracy (which by the 1940s were both well-understood terms), Japanese leaders argued that this abstract, Japanist notion represented a better way forward.

Although the phrase had already been in use, its popularization owed in no small part to the efforts of former foreign minister Matsuoka Yōsuke. From October 1940, Matsuoka argued that Japan's foreign policy was based on "*hakkō ichiu*, or spreading morality to the world, and allowing all its people to take their proper place." He further popularized the phrase in the media, and before long many news reports and governmental weeklies spoke of Japan's new order through the lens of *hakkō ichiu*. Matsuoka likely made use of this "old-fashioned and vague" Japanist term to highlight Japan's role in building a new world order, one dominated by "spheres of influence." It was only after Matsuoka was ousted from government that Japanese leaders began to see *hakkō ichiu* in opposition to the U.S. ideology of democracy.[68]

Efforts to celebrate *hakkō ichiu* and other Japanist concepts abroad, however, fell on deaf ears. Japanism never had wide appeal outside Japan. Intellectuals thus recognized Japan's great difficulties in articulating a persuasive ideology that could win the hearts and minds of occupied regions. A September 30, 1941, ideology round table at the Naval Intelligence Division highlighted these difficulties. Hōsei University professor Tanikawa Tetsuzō noted that the slogan meant little in China, and that the Chiang Kai-shek regime "slanders [*hakkō ichiu*] as something that contains imperialistic ambitions." Political journalist Sekiguchi Tai further dismissed the slogan as lacking "the substance necessary to lead the people. Is not *hakkō ichiu* little more than an excuse aimed both at home and abroad?" The biggest incrimination, however, came from Fujita Tsuguo, a legal scholar and member of the Japan Colonization Society (*Nihon Takushoku Kyōkai*). "In America," he stated, "people will counter by questioning the relationship Japan's *hakkō ichiu* has with their own assertions of the Open Door and equal opportunity. It would be nice if *hakkō ichiu* contained ideas that could break down those assertions. Sadly, it does not." Fujita rejected the slogan as vague at best and believed it lacked true guiding principles at worst. "I have no clue," he argued, "what this slogan is made for."[69]

Not much changed after the outbreak of the Pacific War. One year later, the Naval Intelligence Division called attention to equally vexing problems with Japan's ideology. Tokyo Imperial University professor and diplomatic historian Kamikawa Hikomatsu lamented these struggles in a September 1942 diplomacy round table. "Our country," he bemoaned, "is the winner in military warfare but the loser in ideological warfare." He criticized both Japanese and German efforts at justifying their wars, and he regretted the fact that neither had produced an ideology that could "overcome Anglo-American thought." Kamikawa also derided liberal internationalist ideology as "a clichéd principle," but he admitted that it had "international and universal [implications]" and generated wide appeal. In contrast, he saw Japanese thought as "crude" and "unskillful." Japan had an in-group ideology; its most basic concepts, such as the *kokutai* (Japan's emperor-centered national polity), the Kingly Way (*ōdō*), the Way of the Gods (*kannagara no michi*), and *hakkō ichiu* were impenetrable to those outside Japan's cultural sphere and "cannot be understood by people who are not already believers." Kamikawa thus asserted Japan's need for an international and universal ideology that could stand counter to liberal internationalism and "Anglo-American thought."[70]

Kamikawa looked with hopeful eyes to Dōshisha University law professor and noted neo-Kantian Tamura Tokuji to create such an ideology.[71] In many ways, Tamura was a perfect choice. An expert in law, government, and politics, he became one of the most prolific writers on the norms, ideals, and structure of Japan's Co-Prosperity Sphere. Since 1939, Tamura had championed a "new internationalism" to unite countries in harmony and cooperative relations.[72] His new internationalism was premised on the inevitable overthrow of Wilsonian liberal international order. The Wilsonian order, Tamura argued, had been a breeding ground for international conflict. War was a struggle for survival: it was born out of clashes over natural resources or over outlets for surplus population. The only way to obviate war in international life, then, was through guaranteeing resource security and outlets for population growth. Fortunately, Tamura believed that world trends toward the emergence of "contiguous large territorial states" would solve the problem of war in international life.[73] The consolidation of large states would generate a peaceful global society committed to a new internationalism, one defined by friendly relations and the renunciation of aggression.

With the establishment of Japan's Greater East Asia Co-Prosperity Sphere, Tamura retooled and refined his new internationalism. Now he saw the future as being led by "contiguous regional power spheres," each headed by a powerful state. Japan's sphere, he argued, would overcome the arbitrary liberalism status quo powers used to coerce and oppress. In its place, Japan would help form a "just society," one that stressed harmony and service. And Japan's uniqueness would pave the way for these changes. The China Incident and the Greater East Asia War, he argued, awakened people to the distinctive aspects of Japanese thought. Tamura asserted that the Imperial Way, the Way of the Gods, the *kokutai*, the National Founding Spirit, and the ideal of *hakkō ichiu* formed what might be thought of as Japanism. This Japanism would provide a new way forward in international life.

The defining component of his Japanism was *hakkō ichiu*. To Tamura, this world of *hakkō ichiu* implied a concerted effort to inculcate familial norms into international society. "The ideal of *hakkō ichiu*," he argued, "is to create throughout all humankind an affection found in families, to spread the spirit of the family in foreign countries and in societies across the world, and to create in those societies a family-like structure." Familial groups in the Japanese context operated in a broader hierarchy dominated by a single patriarch. Tamura stressed the benefits of extending this type of system to the international order. First, with status came social responsibility: the patriarch had great power, but he could only use it benevolently to serve the family's needs. Second, this strict familial hierarchy—one in which everyone knew their "proper place" within the pecking order—would remove friction and allow groups to focus on mutual aid. To Tamura, the centrality of the family was the true benefit of *hakkō ichiu* thought, as only family spirit could bring true morality and harmony to international politics.[74] Nonetheless, the implications of *hakkō ichiu* thought were clear to outsiders. Extending the family structure to the international system threatened to disavow Westphalian notions of sovereignty and replace them with the authority of an international patriarch. In Asia, this international patriarch would be none other than the Japanese emperor—the head of Japan's family state.

Tamura recognized that *hakkō ichiu* and other components of Japanism remained abstract and vague, but he still argued for their global relevance. Japanist ideals, he argued, "are not simply unique Japanese principles; they are in fact global principles."[75] Tamura thus believed the biggest issue was how to articulate better the global relevance of Japanese thought. In part this new understanding would emerge as intellectuals clarified the meanings of Japanism. But to an equal degree, Japan had to improve its *branding*. Japanism, Tamura insisted, is an unwieldy term and "unhelpful in generating understanding, trust, and sympathy among people in foreign lands."[76] But Japan's very future depended on winning the thought war with the Allied powers. Whereas military defeat would be no more than a temporary setback, ideological defeat would lead to complete ruin. With a sense of urgency Tamura came up with a host of -isms to help brand Japanese thought as universal, all while remaining true to the central ideal of *hakkō ichiu*.[77]

Tamura thus sought to tackle Japan's crisis of legitimacy by articulating Japanism as a distinct type of internationalism. He took elements that ideologues used to stress Japanese uniqueness—from the family-state structure to ideas of harmony and Japan's national polity—and advertised them as global in relevance. And Tamura was by no means alone in doing so. He participated in a broader trend in the intellectual life of the 1940s, where Japan's best and brightest minds sought to draw attention to the global relevance of Japanese thought. All major policy initiatives dealing with the Greater East Asia Co-Prosperity Sphere looked to *hakkō ichiu* as the defining principle behind Japan's new order.[78] And some even argued that the *hakkō ichiu* ideal was powerful enough to unite the peoples of Asia, despite their different religious, ethnic, cultural, and climatic backgrounds.[79]

The focus on *hakkō ichiu* epitomized the desire to overcome the bane of individualism, liberalism, modernity, and Western thought. But it highlighted a surprising parochialism. No matter how beautiful a brand Tamura and others sought to create, the wine was old, and so was the bottle. Japanism, however branded, remained more than likely to draw the ill will of dependent territories. Calls for family, benevolence, service, and cooperativism ring hollow when used to justify binding states or peoples into subordinate positions. People from Southeast Asia who had well-established religious or cultural traditions found themselves hardpressed to understand even the most basic premises.

This was understood by men such as Lt. Col. Ōtsuki Akira who were sent to the periphery of Japan's wartime empire. A staff officer in the Southern Expeditionary Army who dealt with propaganda and strategy, Ōtsuki was transferred to the Philippines in August 1942 to take part in the Japanese military administration. After the war, he recalled being flabbergasted by efforts to use worthless ideas such as *hakkō ichiu* in occupied territories. Before Ōtsuki was sent to the Philippines, a politician in Japan's mass party, the Imperial Rule Assistance Association, visited military headquarters to discuss creating a propaganda section in Manila to proselytize "the spirit of *hakkō ichiu*." But in Ōtsuki's words, the explanation of *hakkō ichiu* in the politician's brochure was "rambling and pointless." Ōtsuki admitted that Japanese might understand if they listened patiently, but the same could not be said for the Filipinos, especially owing to their long-standing Christian beliefs. He recalled: "What I found most grueling was how to explain our official war aims. How is one to translate into English the phrase, bring the eight corners [of the world] into one household [*hakkō o ōite ie to nasu*]? I carried this worry from the time I first went to the Philippines. So, I said this before sending him away: 'It's one thing if you are confident you can make them understand, but if you can't, then go home! You'll be inviting nothing but confusion to the military administration.'"[80]

This underscores a disconnect between the dreams in the capital and the realities on the ground. The narrow focus on the familial nature of *hakkō ichiu* and the global relevance of Japanese thought created a significant blind spot for intellectuals and policy makers, and for wartime Pan-Asianism more broadly. They failed to consider *how* Japan could gain legitimacy while instituting its regional hegemony. In the process, they provided little with which to win the hearts and minds of people across the region.

Between Britain and Rome

The months following December 8, 1941, witnessed a flood of dreams for Asia's future. These dreams were a new development: it was only after the Japanese military began its dramatic expansion across Asia that political intellectuals and policy makers began serious efforts to imagine the Greater East Asia Co-Prosperity Sphere. The East Asian conflict only began to turn into a clash of visions after the Pacific War had already begun. The broader public and private debates that emerged in 1942 concerning how Japan would reorder the world and build Asia anew may have informed officials about possibilities for the Sphere's future, but they had little impact on governmental policy. The only dream the Tōjō government was able to bring to fruition was the creation of a new Greater East Asia ministry to oversee Asian affairs. In some ways, this new ministry reflected the broad consensus that Japan would dominate the Co-Prosperity Sphere, just as Japan had dominated Manchukuo since 1932. But even this dream was soon rendered meaningless by the realities of total war. In a sense, then, Japanese visions, ideologies, and efforts at institution building in 1942 constituted little more than works in progress. The first year of co-prosperity featured a government groping in the dark, trying to forge a new way forward.

Nonetheless, there were still shared understandings of the nature of the Sphere. All major policy initiatives and visions pointed to the Sphere as more than imperialism without colonies. Intellectuals saw the Sphere as featuring a flexible mixture of imperial arrangements. Japan would pursue formal colonialism when necessary and informal "anticolonial" control when desirable. Most visions also pointed to the Sphere as a system of exploitative development. Japanese economic planning would extract capital and resources to guarantee Asian security, but in the process it would also develop and "uplift" the region. Finally, many saw the Sphere as an opportunity to introduce Japanist, familial values of *hakkō ichiu* into the international system. Doing so would free Asia from the hypocrisy of Westphalian norms of sovereignty (which were frequently honored in the breach) and allow the region to reorganize as an organic, familial community. Policy makers and intellectuals alike agreed about Japan's most basic purpose: Japan would forge a new system that exercised control over a broader pan-region. The future they sought to build was shaped by the realities of total war.

The prevalence of visions offers a stark contrast with Japan's partner, Nazi Germany. At the height of its power, leaders of the Third Reich remained reluctant to articulate a detailed political vision for Europe's future. Goebbels and Hitler may have stressed the Third Reich's European mission, but they had little to say about what Europe would look like after war's end. As historian Mark Mazower argues, in truth they likely did not have one. Hitler prioritized the conquest of Europe and the Soviet Union over detailed planning for the region's future.[81] Whereas both Japan and Germany articulated desires for a new order, Japanese leaders and political intellectuals were less willing to wait until after the war had ended to define more fully what that meant.

Strikingly, some even argued that Japan would be best served by learning from the two greatest empires in human history: Rome and Great Britain. The most detailed such argument was written by Yabe Teiji and appeared in the Naval Intelligence Division study.[82] Yabe's focus was on Roman and British styles of leadership and rule, and their lessons for Japan. On the one hand, Yabe argued that Rome was deeply embedded in its own empire and thus provided the model for "immanent" status. Rome allowed all the peoples of its empire to acquire Roman citizenship. This allowed subjugated peoples to contribute to the empire, but it caused the original Romans to lose their individuality. As Roman culture permeated the empire, the Romans lost their original individuality. On the other hand, the British Empire (excluding the dominions) provided a model for a "transcendent" position. Britain always remained apart from the conquered. The British were the quintessential colonial masters, cut off from the locals in all aspects of life: from race to character, religion to language. This allowed the British to maintain their individuality, but it also fed into a willingness to discriminate and exploit. British rule thus never gave rise to a sense of English pride in its dependencies or crown colonies. Rather, it brought about antipathy and resistance.

Yabe believed these relationships between ruler and ruled in past empires offered important lessons for the Co-Prosperity Sphere. First, Japan must not operate like Britain, an oppressive and dominating "transcendent" power.

Instead, Japanese leaders should heed the example of the Roman Empire, which created a system that mobilized the hearts and minds of the ruled. "Like Rome," he argued, "Japan must build a relationship where Japanese pride is the pride of the peoples of Greater East Asia, and the prosperity of the peoples of Greater East Asia is Japan's prosperity." But the important task was to rule like Rome without getting absorbed into its own empire—to be both inherent to and apart from the empire at the same time. Japan, in short, must forge an identity as an integral part of the region while also maintaining its *kokutai*, the mystical source of Japanese uniqueness. And Yabe refused to admit any antagonistic relationship between these two positions. This owed to the "special characteristics of Oriental thought," which refuses to see life as a choice between two opposing alternatives. Thus Yabe called for a Sphere in which Japan was "immanent while transcendent, transcendent while immanent."[83]

Yabe, in short, wanted to have his cake and eat it, too. In the process, his argument veered more into the realm of philosophy than practical politics, and he disregarded how the Sphere would be received by its various localities. This was the problem not only with Yabe's thought but also with that of most intellectuals and policy makers across the political spectrum. They failed to consider *how* Japan could gain legitimacy of leadership while promoting Japanese dominion. Many argued that Japan's natural leadership abilities and "moral energy" would convince Asia to accept Japanese leadership with open arms. Furthermore, the very fact that Yabe and others looked to Rome and Great Britain—two great empires—for models points to the *imperial* nature of the Sphere. Intellectuals hoped Japan would dominate its Sphere in a similar manner to how Rome and Great Britain had dominated their empires. And if Japan heeded the lessons of Great Britain and Rome, it would be the successor to the greatest empires in human history.

Of course, just how Japan would be able to secure such an empire remained unclear. The very men who were sent to the war's front lines recalled being shocked by the technological prowess of the colonial empires. Nogi Harumichi, an officer sent by the navy to the Celebes in Indonesia, was one such man. He sailed abroad with a mental image taken from Shimada Keizō's popular comic strip, *The Adventures of Dankichi*. Nogi expected small desert islands populated "with black natives under palm trees." He was stunned by what he saw, from running hot water to refrigerators, ceiling fans to Western toilets. Nogi noted after the war that the occupied areas taught him just how developed Europe was. "Grand refrigerators were manufactured in Europe, while in Japan we still used iceboxes. Here the Japanese military was full of people who'd come directly from farming villages, never even been to Tokyo. Many didn't even know how to urinate in a Western toilet. A lot of them stood on top and blasted away. A distant anxiety grew in me: 'Can Japan win?'"[84] Whereas intellectuals dreamed of forging a new regional empire, men on the front lines such as Nogi worried whether Japan would be able to accomplish much.

Nogi's doubts were spot-on. By 1943 the tides of war had shifted, and Japan found that acquiring resources to fight the global war had become far more important than constructing a new Greater East Asia. Japan lacked the wherewithal to sustain a meaningful comparison with either the Roman or British Empire. As will be discussed in chapter 5, to keep intact its empire and regional influence, Japan shifted toward a more cooperative and liberal internationalist vision for the region's future. Herein lies a major irony of Japan's quest to imagine a Greater East Asia Co-Prosperity Sphere: groups in control of the state only committed Japan to the principles undergirding the new order after it looked next to impossible to implement. In this sense, December 8, 1941, initiated an imperial moment that Japan was unable to consummate. This imperial moment, however, had important impacts on the periphery of Japan's wartime empire. It is to the periphery that we now turn.

Part II
THE CONTESTED SPHERE

4

THE PATRIOTIC COLLABORATORS

In late December 1941, two nationalist leaders waited in anticipation. As Japanese forces rushed toward Manila, Mayor Jorge B. Vargas stood waiting at the Manila port, watching Philippine president Manuel L. Quezon's speedboat evacuate toward the temporary U.S. military headquarters on the island of Corregidor. Slowly walking back up the gangway to the shore, Vargas remembered Quezon's impassioned plea for leaders to collaborate with the Japanese. "Well, some of us have to stay," Vargas noted, not a little bitterly. "I've got more to do now than I know how."[1] While Vargas shuddered at the impending occupation of Manila, Burmese nationalist Thakin Aung San was in Bangkok, awaiting the Japanese invasion of Burma with hopeful expectancy. Together with his comrades in the Japan-sponsored Burma Independence Army, Aung San participated in the *thwe thauk* blood-drinking ceremony. Each slit open a finger, dripped a little blood into a silver goblet filled with liquor, and drank the mixture while pledging their loyalty and willingness to die for the cause of independence.[2] The following month, Aung San's group accompanied Japanese forces in the invasion of Burma.

Both Vargas and Aung San played important roles for the expanding Japanese Empire. Imperial expansion—no matter how swift, overwhelming, or complete—requires active support from groups in subordinated territories. Without the political collaboration of elites between the edge of empire and the imperial center, empires would have a weak grasp over their peripheries. Japanese planners recognized this fact. A November 20, 1941, liaison conference decision thus called for the establishment of collaborationist regimes and promised to govern with as light a hand as possible.[3] As Japanese forces stormed across Asia, they sought out willing partners to help maintain peace and order. Vargas and Aung San were by no means the only ones called on to collaborate. In the Philippines, almost the entire existing leadership ultimately worked with the Japanese military government. In Burma, too, revolutionary groups and political elites aided the invading Japanese forces in fighting the British and establishing a new regime.

This chapter shifts focus to the incorporation of the Philippines and Burma into Japan's wartime empire. It explores why nationalist elites and revolutionary leaders in the Philippines and Burma chose to collaborate with Japan. What led leaders to make such choices, and what did they hope to achieve? A rich tradition of scholarship has grappled with these questions from both the Philippine and Burmese perspectives.[4] Yet most narratives examine each country's decision to collaborate in isolation, exploring collaboration through a national instead of a regional or comparative lens.[5] This chapter considers the histories of Philippine and Burmese collaboration side by side, highlighting a striking similarity of purpose behind each regime's willingness to work with Japan.

This chapter explores why nationalist elites in Manila and Rangoon decided to work with Japan. Leaders from both countries received Japanese forces with varying degrees of enthusiasm, and they ultimately engaged in relations that were partly antagonistic and partly collaborative. Nonetheless, Philippine and Burmese leaders evinced a striking similarity of purpose. Whether to preserve the existing order, bridge the gap toward a more hopeful era of postwar independence, or bring about an immediate national liberation, top-level leaders in the colonial capitals often collaborated to safeguard or advance their country's interests. This chapter thus suggests that nationalist elites in the Philippines and Burma are best thought of as patriotic collaborators. Caught between two empires, they did what they could amid a global war to ensure their postwar ambitions. The Burmese actively accommodated Japanese forces to ensure liberation from the British Empire. The Philippines, however, served in what is best thought of as a caretaker regime, cooperating to secure gains under Japan or to await an American return. It was these patriotic collaborators who thrust their countries forward as showcases of the new imperialism of Japan's Co-Prosperity Sphere. To tell the story of the patriotic collaborators, however, we must first turn to the longer histories of both colonies.

America's Philippines

War with Spain in 1898 brought about the emergence of the United States as a global power and a colonial ruler over the Philippines. Taking advantage of Spain's weak position in the Pacific, U.S. president William McKinley dispatched Commodore George Dewey's fleet to Manila. In a battle on April 30 that lasted a mere six hours, Dewey's fleet laid waste to the Spanish fleet, sinking three warships and disabling seven. It is unclear whether the United States had intended to seize the Philippine archipelago, but by July McKinley had begun to champion "the general principle of holding on to what we get." In October, McKinley insisted that "duty requires we should take the archipelago."[6] Ultimately, on December 10, 1898, Spain acceded to U.S. demands for control over the Philippines. Less than three years later, the United States had put down Emilio Aguinaldo's nationalist rebellion and confirmed itself as the regime's new colonial master. Thus began four decades of what has come to be known as "Hollywood" in the Philippines.

U.S. colonial rule limited the scope of political divisions in the Philippines. The realm of Philippine politics had but one salient political issue: *independence*. Independence was the axis around which colonial Philippine politics revolved— the source of political capital and the primary sustenance for nationalist politicians. Thus Philippine oligarchs steadily worked toward, and fought over, the sponsorship of a new independent regime. Moreover, independence was almost always the sole domain of the Nacionalista Party, which dominated Philippine politics until the Japanese invasion in 1942. Although Nacionalista politicians regularly trumpeted such slogans as "social justice" and reducing peasant poverty, those issues were always relegated to the back burner. Owing to the pervasive power of Philippine nationalism, Nacionalista politicians could only ignore the independence issue at their own peril. Leaders such as Manuel L. Quezon and Sergio Osmeña gained their popularity through the ability to articulate the nationalist desires for independence.[7] Perhaps Quezon best voiced these desires: he frequently claimed to "prefer a government run like hell by Filipinos to one run like heaven by Americans."[8]

The U.S. government gradually facilitated political autonomy in the Philippines. By 1916, with the passage in Washington of the Jones Law, the Philippines took control of the legislative branch. The existing national assembly and commission were replaced with a senate and a house of representatives. But the question of independence remained unsettled. The Jones Law solidified a commitment to independence "as soon as a stable government can be established," but it provided no fixed date.[9] Yet independence had been promised. Manuel L. Quezon—the charismatic and slippery nationalist politician who had lobbied at critical times for its passage—claimed much of the credit for the Jones Law. He returned to Manila a national hero and became the president of the Senate.

But as historian Theodore Friend contends, Philippine leaders preferred the political popularity gained from criticizing their foreign masters to the responsibilities of *actually governing* an independent nation. In fact, Quezon and Osmeña privately feared premature independence. Quezon was so upset in 1916 over the proposal of the Clarke Amendment, which would have granted complete independence within four years, that he took to bed sick. Osmeña, too, reportedly trembled with fear.[10] Both Quezon and Osmeña thus breathed a sigh of relief when Congress passed the Jones Law but omitted the Clarke Amendment. For this reason, Americans complained about Philippine politicians as being two-faced and inscrutable. "They tell you in private that they don't want independence," one observer noted, "then they'll go to Congress and work for an independence bill."[11] But publicity was the point. It reflected positively on politicians at home. In this context, nationalist politicians at times even wished they had a more repressive colonial master. "Damn the Americans," Quezon cried out. "Why don't they tyrannize us more?"[12] A domineering United States, after all, would ensure that Quezon's star would burn bright within Philippine politics.

From 1918 to 1934, Philippine politicians led commissions to Washington to press for immediate and complete independence. These independence missions, however, were also the stage on which elite battles raged. Personality or factional politics at times trumped commitments to a free Philippines. Quezon, for instance, did not merely seek independence. He also wanted personal credit for it, so he was more than willing to sabotage the efforts of other elites. From December 1931, Senate president pro tempore Sergio Osmeña and Speaker Manuel A. Roxas led a mission to the United States. This mission occurred when the United States was embroiled in economic crisis. Lobbyists and pressure groups pushed Washington to get rid of its Philippine possessions both to prevent competition in the cane sugar and coconut oil markets and to restrict the immigration of Philippine workers. These domestic pressures helped Osmeña and Roxas secure the passage of the Hare-Hawes-Cutting Act of 1933—the first act to set a timetable for Philippine independence. But this spurred Quezon to action. He roused the Philippine Senate to reject the act, citing concerns that the United States would retain military bases and that U.S. borders would be closed to Philippine exports and immigrants. But the primary reason behind his opposition was because the act was the brainchild of Osmeña and Roxas. "It is even doubtful," writes Friend, "whether he would have supported a better act, as long as Osmeña and Roxas were its sponsors."[13]

The rejection of the Hare-Hawes-Cutting Act was a great gamble but also a personal triumph for Quezon. Hard on the heels of his victory, Quezon went on an independence mission of his own, meeting with Millard Tydings and other leaders to strike a new independence agreement. The result of his efforts was the Tydings-McDuffie Act, which established the Commonwealth of the Philippines and set a timetable for independence. President Roosevelt signed the

Tydings-McDuffie Act on March 24, 1934, and the Philippine legislature unanimously ratified it on May 1. With this, Quezon had his own independence law, which he sought to distinguish from its predecessor. The distinction between the Tydings-McDuffie Act and the Hare-Hawes-Cutting Act, however, was not as great as Quezon claimed. Both called for the creation of a commonwealth government with primary responsibility for domestic affairs. Each plan promised independence after ten years. The only difference was that the Tydings-McDuffie Act did not guarantee U.S. army bases after independence. But this small difference obfuscated what was obvious to contemporary viewers: Quezon killed the Osmeña-Roxas independence initiative to replace it with his own.

Quezon's game of political theater had ended, and independence was just over the horizon. The Commonwealth of the Philippines inaugurated a period of quasi-sovereignty that lasted from 1935 until the scheduled independence day of July 4, 1946. A Philippine convention drafted the fledgling government's constitution, which remained in force until 1973 (minus the wartime years, 1943–45). The constitution called for a separation of powers and direct elections for a unicameral legislature (later amended to a bicameral legislature) and the commonwealth president. Quezon and Osmeña served as the first president and vice president, respectively. With the advent of the commonwealth, the day-to-day tasks of governance were largely left in Philippine hands. Nonetheless, the United States remained close at hand. Washington retained control over foreign affairs and defense, appointing a high commissioner to manage the colony's transition to full independence.

Less than four decades after Dewey's fleet helped subjugate Manila, then, the United States had already promised to relinquish control over the Philippines. This was not out of altruism or enlightened rule. More than any local desire for independence, it was U.S. pressure groups and economic lobbyists that pushed Washington to liberate the Philippines. But this mattered little to Philippine activists. Nationalist ambitions satisfied, Philippine leaders inaugurated the commonwealth government and prepared themselves for a new, independent regime. And this new independent regime was led by none other than Quezon, who had by 1940 centralized power and turned the executive branch into "a de facto dictatorship."[14]

With independence assured, only a few unabashed Filipinos looked to Japan for leadership. One such man was Pio Duran, an associate professor of law at the University of the Philippines whose brand of nationalism was notable for its open and zealous Japanophilia. In 1935 he called on Filipinos to join forces with their Asian brothers and form a "Monroe Doctrine for the Orient." This view was influenced by his own negative contacts with Americans, whom he thought were two-faced, racist, and contemptuous of Filipinos. It further resulted from his reading of international politics. Only the colonial West, Duran thought, could advance high-sounding ideals such as "equal opportunity for all" but apply them solely to white men. Only the colonial West could forge a far-flung empire in Asia and then condemn the Japanese for doing the same thing in Manchuria. In calling on Filipinos to join with Japan, Duran was trying to restore a sense of racial and ethnic pride and promote a racial awakening. In this spirit, Duran wrote that Filipinos should accept Japanese leadership for no other reason "than to terminate the unjustified and arrogant fiction of the 'white man's burden.'"[15]

Some radical nationalists such as the charismatic Benigno Ramos also looked to Japan as a potential benefactor. An able poet, politician, and orator, Ramos had a meteoric rise in government until he broke with Quezon's Nacionalista Party in 1930. He created an anti-establishment weekly newspaper called *Sakdal* (Accusation), which he used to advance his populist ideas of social reform, reduced taxation, wealth redistribution, and independence as a panacea for the nation's ills. *Sakdal* condemned the Tydings-McDuffie Act as a smokescreen for U.S. colonialism, and Ramos called for "immediate and complete independence." Ramos went to Japan from December 1934 to August 1938, where he promoted the belief that Japan would help the Philippines gain true independence. His propaganda helped incite a peasant rebellion in May 1935. In this Sakdal Uprising, mobs of more than sixty thousand Sakdalista seized municipal buildings in fourteen towns in the central Philippine island of Luzon. The mobs expected armed support from Japan, but such support never came. The uprising was promptly crushed. Despite this defeat, Ramos never lost faith in Japan, which he considered "the true friend of Philippine independence."[16]

But Ramos and Duran were in the minority. People in the Philippines counted themselves as the most Westernized people in the region and had strong pro-American leanings. Thus, when storm clouds brewed in the Pacific in the late 1930s, most educated Filipinos viewed Japan with wary eyes. Suspicions of Japan only increased with Japan's undeclared total war in China. Eufronio M. Alip, a professor at Santo Tomas University, noted in 1938 that the middle class feared a "Japanese political and military invasion" after gaining independence, despite the lack of any supporting evidence.[17] Journalists and pundits noted this disquiet in a more flamboyant manner, speaking of a "yellow peril" and an imminent "Japanese menace" from which the Philippines needed longer-term protection. One pundit even noted that had Commodore Dewey not seized the Philippines, "the flag of the Rising Sun would be flying over the archipelago now."[18]

Perhaps influenced by these fears, in the summer of 1938 Quezon made a private, three-week trip to Japan. Consul General Uchiyama Kiyoshi imagined that the trip was made to begin negotiations for a neutrality pact.[19] The American press argued that Quezon sought a pledge to respect Philippine independence. Both were likely true, in addition to Quezon's hope to gauge actual conditions in wartime Japan and to present an offer of friendship. The trip, after all, came at a point when well-informed Filipinos had begun to worry about a Japanese invasion after the Philippines attained independence. Whatever the case, Quezon had public and private meetings with Premier Konoe Fumimaro, foreign minister Ugaki Kazushige, Matsuoka Yōsuke, and others, but he only received a statement from Ugaki that the Philippines "need have no fear" of Japan.[20] On returning to Manila, Quezon played down the political nature of his trip, stating that he "went to Japan without political or official purpose."[21]

What is truly striking, however, is the lessons Quezon took from his trip. Talking off the record to the press corps on August 3, 1938, Quezon mentioned a newfound admiration for Japan, from which he believed the Philippines had much to learn. This admiration had little to do with military affairs or notions of Japanese power. He called the Japanese military "insignificant" and noted that its current influence in the political system was an "abnormal situation which is bound to pass." Instead, he stated that Japan's true strength came from the work ethic of the average farmer and worker, who were more productive, industrious, and orderly than any other people. "It is not the navy of Japan that impresses me," Quezon noted; "it is the fellow in the factory and the field." A stony-faced Quezon even expressed a desire to put hardworking Japanese families on public display in government-owned model farms and rice fields. "Of course, I can not do that," he admitted. "For if I do, there will be howls. I wish I could do that. Marvelous, those fellows!" By copying the Japanese work ethic, the Philippines "would be the greatest country on earth."[22] Quezon later stood in front of forty thousand students at the Rizal Memorial Stadium, calling for the adoption of Japanese discipline and the Bushido spirit. The fascinating desire for self-colonization—changing the nation by imitating Japan—provides a stark contrast to Quezon's more consistent, long-term push to remove U.S. colonial influence from the Philippines.

By 1940, however, Quezon changed his tune. Concerns about war with Japan had by this time become a common theme in the Philippine press. Thus Quezon was no longer dismissive of the Japanese military. In fact, on August 3, 1940— two days after Japan declared the Co-Prosperity Sphere—Quezon bemoaned the pessimistic outlook for national defense. The Philippine army, formed in 1935, was undermanned, underfunded, and undertrained, used outdated equipment, and had drawn up woefully inadequate defense plans. Noting this, he regretted his earlier optimism about security once his nation became independent and argued, "the horizon is a little dark."[23] The situation looked even bleaker by April 1941, when U.S. high commissioner Francis B. Sayre reported "considerable uneasiness here over a possible Japanese invasion."[24] With American attention fixated on Europe, Philippine leaders no doubt wondered over the U.S. commitment should the global storm of World War II strike the shores of the archipelago.[25]

But Quezon could remain confident in united popular support against any external threat. "Should the United States enter the war," Quezon publicly trumpeted, "the Philippines would follow her and fight by her side." High Commissioner Sayre echoed this view, writing in June 1941 of "a growing sentiment here in the Philippines of loyalty to the United States."[26] This sentiment of loyalty even included leftist groups and intellectuals. They viewed independence with equal fervor to Quezon's conservative Nacionalista leadership, and they remained similarly suspicious of Japanese motives in East Asia. While militarily unprepared for a future in the shark-infested waters of the Pacific, Philippine elites remained optimistic that public sentiment rested clearly behind the commonwealth and the United States.

Britain's Burma

Like the Philippines, colonialism in Burma was relatively liberal in nature. The British had won control over the kingdom of Burma in a series of wars between 1824 and 1885, annexing Burma as a province within the British Indian Empire in 1886. Over time, they fostered the rise of an active civil society and a middle class. This urbanized middle class evolved as a direct result of opportunities provided by the colonial order: economic opportunities, improved education, and new careers in law, business, and the lower and middle echelons of colonial administration. Britain established a firm rule of law, through which the growing middle class participated as litigators and barristers. The new legal profession in Burma, in fact, served as natural training and recruiting grounds for the political elite. By the 1930s, the small and financially insecure (and largely ethnic Burmese) middle class, which saw itself as besieged by Indian immigration and its dependence on Indian capital, championed a new political nationalism and movement for independence.

Over time Britain extended to Burma a degree of political participation, which was actively taken up by the new middle class. At first, this constitutional advance occurred within the context of Britain's Indian Empire. With both the Morley-Minto reforms of 1909 and the extension of the diarchy system of tutelary democracy in 1923, Burma received limited popular participation as a province of India. But with the Government of Burma Act of 1935, which detached

Burma from India, Burma became a curious entity within the British Empire. Neither part of the Indian Empire nor a crown colony, Burma operated in the space between colony and dominion (the autonomous, largely white polities within Britain's empire that received the benefits of independence without the drawbacks of having to pay for their own defense). The Government of Burma Act provided for cabinet government and a bicameral legislature, of which the 132-seat House of Representatives was wholly elected. Thus from 1937, when the act went into effect, local politicians and bureaucrats could involve themselves in the business of running the state. Whereas in 1900 all 132 officers in the higher civil service were of European descent, by 1940 Burmese accounted for 62 of its 162 members. Burmese likewise made up 99 percent of lower civil service officers.[27]

The extension of greater self-government led a more vibrant albeit tumultuous political world. As in most young democracies, Burma's politics in the 1930s were ripe with turmoil, uncertainty, and threats of violence. Riots, brawls, bribery, and profanity marked politics in the wake of the separation from India. Meetings of the legislature overflowed with insults or slurs, with new legislators bellowing "You are descendants of dragons!" or "May your bodies be eaten by crocodiles in the Irrawaddy!"[28] And British intelligence reports constantly complained about the tangled webs of "plots and intrigues for place and power" within Burmese politics.[29]

Though Burma's British masters may have viewed their regime as enlightened or developmental, they refused to divest control over important governmental affairs. Even after the separation from India in 1937, only noncritical areas of government were transferred to the Burmese. Britain withheld control over defense, foreign affairs, and monetary policy. The British governor of Burma still exercised direct rule over the Frontier Areas (also known as the Scheduled Areas, the Excluded Areas, or Upper Burma), the hilly jungled regions of Burma that were home to minority ethnic groups such as the Karen, the Shan, the Kachin, and the Chin. Moreover, the governor of Burma still sat atop Burmese politics as the ultimate arbiter of the political system. He had the last word in all matters of state, and he could place restrictions on any legislation affecting his "special responsibilities" or "discretionary powers."

Owing to this state of affairs, the British colonial project received a mixed response from local peoples. Minority groups such as the Karen embraced their British overlords. The Karen occupied a special position in colonial Burma, providing manpower for the military and police and receiving, in turn, protection and special consideration from the British. The Burma Rifles, the military force used to maintain order, was populated largely by Karen, Kachin, and Chin peoples. This led Burman nationalists to associate the Karen, Burma's largest minority group, with the more authoritarian aspects of British rule and contributed to mutual strife that exploded during the Japanese occupation era.[30]

Ethnic Burmans, conversely, regarded the British coolly. Particularly in the wake of World War I, a vocal minority spurred on an emergent nationalist movement, one that grew to be more national than cultural in character. In the cities, this political awakening was reflected in the rise of nationalistic political groupings such as the General Council of Burmese Associations (GCBA), which opposed any type of cooperation with the British and pushed for immediate dominion status. But it faced fierce internal divisions over the means and timing of the home rule campaign, which hampered its effectiveness as a political organization.[31]

In the villages in Lower Burma, the *pongyi* (Buddhist priests) and rural leaders harangued the vices of British rule. Dissatisfactions were exacerbated by a growing agrarian crisis that followed the 1930 depression in rice prices. This crisis culminated in the great Hsaya San Rebellion of 1930–32, which Britain crushed with blunt and brutal force. Hsaya San was a former monk, physician, and district GCBA leader who railed against the failure of elite politicians to alleviate the agrarian crisis and the plight of the peasantry. He rode the wave of peasant discontent as the Galon King, the leader of a vast peasant rebellion that broke out in December 1930 after acting Burmese governor Sir J. A. Maung Gyi refused to reduce the usurious taxes on the peasantry. More than eight thousand governmental troops were deployed throughout Burma to suppress the various uprisings. By the end of 1932, more than 1,300 rebels had been killed and a further 9,000 had been captured or had surrendered.[32]

By the late 1930s, political nationalism had taken a fierce hold in the colonial capital of Rangoon. This nationalism was reflected in an extended political duel between the most important politicians of prewar Burma—U Saw and Dr. Ba Maw. U Saw was a "big, jovial, but ruthless man" who was the most important political leader in the 1930s.[33] Ba Maw, Burma's first premier from 1937 to 1939, was the princely narcissist among narcissists, a "handsome, brilliant and debonair" man who led with his "magnetic personality" and silver tongue.[34] The similarities between Ba Maw and Saw are striking. Both were barristers who had gained a degree of prominence for the trial defense of the Hsaya San peasant rebels (though Ba Maw far outshone Saw, who was only a low-level pleader). Both leaders strove to outdo each other in anti-British sentiment, whether as an appeal for greater self-government or in a play for popular support. Both leaders sought restrictions on Indian immigration. More strikingly, both U Saw and Ba Maw, no doubt influenced by Mussolini's Blackshirts, had their own private armies and reportedly had ambitions for becoming dictator.[35] And both leaders commanded two of the most important nationalist parties in

Burmese politics: Saw headed up the Patriot's (Myochit) Party while Ba Maw led the Poor Man's (Sinyetha) Party. Perhaps their biggest difference rested in visions for Burma's constitutional future. Whereas Saw expressed a desire for dominion status, Ba Maw rejected independence within any political framework under British leadership.

The political nationalism of Ba Maw and U Saw was also reflected in the rise of another movement: the Thakins, a radical group of anticolonial and anti-British youths. These young, middle-class students and intellectuals were highly influenced by Marxist ideas. They appropriated the title Thakin, or master, which traditionally had been used as a sign of reverence for the British. In doing so, they announced themselves as the true masters of Burma, making a powerful political statement of equal status with the white colonial elites. Moreover, the Thakins paired this anti-British sentiment with a uniquely "Burman" nationalism, which stressed the supremacy of Burmese culture and civilization over the ethnic minority groupings. Most importantly, the Thakins sought the destruction of the Government of Burma Act of 1935 and the framing of a new Burmese constitution. To this end, they organized demonstrations and anticolonial strikes that reached out to the largely unpoliticized segments of society: the students, peasants, and workers.[36]

The Thakins organized a political vanguard movement, the Dobama Asiayone (We Burmans), to advance their more radical brand of Burmese nationalism. Formed in May 1930 by students at Rangoon University, the Dobama Asiayone emphasized Burma's anticolonial struggle, calling for nothing less than complete independence from Britain. The movement rose to national prominence in 1938 and, after bringing about the collapse of Ba Maw's government, emerged as a primary competitor to U Saw's Patriot's Party. The conflict between the Patriots and the Thakins was, in many senses, a struggle between rival generations of the political elite. Both groups had the same end goal of independence, but favored different means to that end. Whereas U Saw sought to gain it through cooperation and negotiation, the Thakins favored subversion or even revolutionary struggle.

The Thakins, nationalist youth, and some political leaders found inspiration in Japan. This stands as a stark contrast to the Philippines, where most of the educated middle class regarded Japan as a "yellow peril." Many Thakins and middle-class students held naïve hopes that a benevolent (and fellow Asian) Japan would liberate Burma from foreign rule. According to one of the organizers of the Rangoon University strike of 1936, the nationalistic youth "took pride in the glory and prowess of Japan." "We hoped," he continued, "that one day there would be a showdown between Japan and the Colonial West in which Japan would emerge victorious, of course, and that under the aegis of the great gap, we of the downtrodden East would be freed from European Colonial bondage!"[37] But such views were still in the minority—and would not come to the fore until the outbreak of World War II.

By the late 1930s, then, there existed broad support for independence among Burma's middle-class elite. Nationalists, of course, remained divided over the best course of action. Whereas some sought to collaborate with London in return for dominion status or home rule, others would stop at nothing less than a full British withdrawal from Burma. All sides, however, saw the outbreak of World War II in Europe as a godsend, a rare opportunity to press for the elusive goal of national independence. It was in the context of world war and the perception of a declining British Empire that Burmese nationalists—the Thakins, U Saw, and Ba Maw—all ultimately courted the embrace of imperial Japan.

The "Magna Carta of Treason"

On December 8, 1941, Japanese forces attacked the Philippine archipelago. Two days later, the Japanese Fourteenth Army, headed by Lt. General Honma Masaharu, launched its ground offensive against the Philippine island of Luzon. "The Japanese," U.S. general Douglas MacArthur noted in his memoirs, "knew where to strike," hitting all areas of strategic importance.[38] Despite a desperate defense waged by the undermanned and underequipped forces, the Philippine-American military could do little but stall the inevitable. The Bataan Peninsula fell to Japanese forces on April 9, 1942. Nearly one month later, on May 6, Lt. Gen. Jonathan A. Wainwright surrendered to General Honma.

Japan did not attack with visions of long-term colonization. Army planners did not see the colony as worth the hassle. They dismissed the Philippines as economically unimportant for the new order, at least in the long term, and rejected resource acquisition as a major goal for the occupation. Even the March 1941 general staff study argued that the Philippines' major exports—sugar, copra, coconut oil, and tobacco—would be "difficult for the East Asian Co-Prosperity Sphere to consume." Instead, the main purpose of the attack was geopolitical in nature. The general staff study argued that the attack would bring about the "destruction of the U.S. Armed Forces' strongholds in the Philippines" and would thereby expel Japan's main geopolitical rival from Asia. Once U.S. forces were expelled, Japan was to avoid the burdens of direct rule at all cost and was to limit its intervention in governmental affairs. The military was instead to seek out willing collaborators who would advance Japan's cause for the region.[39]

This desire to set up a collaborationist regime reflected an accurate assessment of the limits of Japanese power as well as the burdens of direct colonial rule. The decision to occupy much of Southeast Asia at the same time meant that any Japanese occupation force would be relatively small. Setting up indirect systems of rule through existing organs of government and gaining the active cooperation of local leaders would thus ensure a smooth transition to informal Japanese control. More importantly, however, a legitimate government would have an easier time overseeing public services such as transportation, electricity, gas, water, and hospitals, services that the Japanese could use to their military and political advantage. Moreover, promptly restoring peace and order would allow military leaders to divert forces to more critical areas.

On January 2, 1942, Japanese forces reached the southern outskirts of the Philippine capital, Manila. To spare the city from bombing and the ravages of war, General MacArthur had declared Manila an open city one week earlier and had evacuated all military units. He further advised Quezon, Vice President Osmeña, Chief Justice José Abad Santos, and Philippine Army Chief of Staff Basilio J. Valdes to vacate Manila and transfer the seat of government to the island of Corregidor, an "impregnable" fortress located at the mouth of Manila Bay. On leaving, Quezon appointed his executive secretary, Jorge B. Vargas, as mayor of Manila to administer the city during its upcoming occupation. With no strong opposition, the Japanese army began its occupation of Manila.[40] Tanks and troop transports rolled in, followed by the infantry on the most unlikely but effective military transport vehicle of the Pacific War: bicycles. In one of the more unimpressive sights of military prowess, companies of soldiers in rows of three pedaled down the streets of Manila, parading Japan as the new occupying power. By January 3, Japanese forces formally established the Japanese Military Administration of the Philippines.

Japan wasted no time behind the scenes in searching for collaborators. On the afternoon of January 4, 1942, Lt. Gen. Maeda Masami, chief of staff to General Honma, summoned Senator Quintin Paredes to seek Philippine cooperation with the new military administration. In forming a collaborationist government, he suggested that Philippine elites could mitigate the impact of the war and help restore peace, order, and a semblance of normalcy to daily life. Paredes responded positively, assuring Maeda that "leaders and other Filipinos are willing to collaborate as much as possible." Maeda also met separately with Mayor Vargas, Senator Benigno S. Aquino, and Senator Claro Recto to push for "a Committee composed of prominent leaders" that would help restore normalcy and order to everyday life.[41]

Meanwhile, Philippine leaders deliberated on the best course of action. From January 5, 1942, Chief Justice of the Supreme Court José Yulo called an emergency meeting at his Peñafrancia Street residence in Manila to discuss whether to collaborate and "to adopt a plan of action." This meeting was limited in participation to Quintin Paredes, Jorge B. Vargas, Benigno S. Aquino, José P. Laurel, and Teofilo Sison. But it set the tone for discussions, which ran until January 12, among around thirty men that represented a microcosm of the Philippine political elite. The Peñafrancia Street meetings were recorded for posterity, no doubt to be used as evidence of patriotic intent in the postwar era. To this end, while giving "emphatic, repeated, and vehement protests of loyalty" to President Manuel L. Quezon, the members deliberated the worst-case scenario: whether to "swear allegiance to the Japanese Empire" and collaborate with Japan.[42]

These leaders were more than mere turncoats. Various accounts reveal that before evacuating to Corregidor, Quezon instructed those who stayed behind to cooperate. Although it is difficult to know what took place in the chaos before the Japanese arrival, it is highly likely that Quezon asked those remaining to minimize the sufferings of the civilian population.[43] Of course, it would also be remiss to argue that those who met at Yulo's house were merely good soldiers acting on presidential orders. As with all leaders facing military occupation, a complex tangle of emotions and responsibilities led to their willingness to collaborate. Fear of reprisals should they refuse, combined with a sense of responsibility to alleviate the struggles and tribulations caused by occupying forces, certainly played a part. They no doubt also worried over the social consequences of noncooperation. As a wealthy, landed ruling class, the Philippine oligarchs prioritized the preservation of law and order and the prevention of social revolutionary tendencies that might threaten their stewardship of the nation and the nation's future independence. Moreover, some may have worried that more unscrupulous collaborators might enrich themselves to the detriment of the nation. Whatever the case, the Philippine elite worked for Japan while hoping for an ultimate Allied victory.

Leaders at the Peñafrancia Street meetings also grappled with the question of *how* they would work with Japan. Three ideas were floated. First, Paredes proposed the establishment of a Philippine republic to work with the Japanese military administration. But Secretary Jorge Bocobo and Rafael Alunan both argued against this idea. Bocobo insisted that a new republic would serve Japanese propaganda and would be used to show that the Philippines had abandoned the United States. Alunan also dismissed the idea as little more than a "puppet government in the style of the Chinese Nanjing Regime." Second, Bocobo proposed limiting collaboration to a civil emergency administration. Third, José Yulo suggested that they propose the continuation of the commonwealth government.[44] Most agreed with Yulo and hoped to persuade Japan to recognize the commonwealth and hold elections for a provisional president and vice president.

The outcome, however, revealed the futility of these discussions. Lieutenant General Maeda made it clear that Japan would only consider Paredes's choice, the establishment of a collaborationist regime. Maeda held Japan's mailed fist in plain sight. He plainly stated that Japan could "force Filipino leaders to form a government, but would prefer" otherwise. Yet if the Philippine leaders closed off all other options, Japan would rule the Philippines directly through a "government of iron backed by military force."[45] In the end, the Philippine elites had little choice but to establish a provisional Philippine council of state and to "negotiate" later for an independent republic. Claro M. Recto stated that such cooperation was their obligation. They could not afford to let others rule for personal or for Japanese interests.[46] In the end, the only major decision Philippine leaders could make was the personal one of whether to cooperate with Japan's military administration.

In a move of high symbolic meaning, the Japanese accepted the official Philippine reply in a January 23, 1942 ceremony at the former residence of the U.S. high commissioner on Dewey Boulevard, which High Commissioner Francis B. Sayre had evacuated four weeks prior. This geography of power provided yet another reminder of Philippine weakness in the new *Pax Nipponica*. It was fitting that the Philippine delegation's official reply, which Recto later called the "Magna Carta of Treason," highlighted the unequal, subservient relationship with their new overlords.[47] Instead of "assisting" Japan, they would "obey . . . the orders issued by the Imperial Japanese Forces." And instead of pleading for "independence and freedom," the official reply merely highlighted the ideals of "freedom and happiness," ideals they feared would be in short supply in the time to come.[48]

After indicating his satisfaction with their reply, Maeda read Order No. 1 to Mayor Vargas and the Philippine contingent. Japan officially appointed Vargas as "Chairman of the Executive Commission," a position with power to govern under Japanese commands. Vargas headed the same governmental structure of six departments that existed under the commonwealth. But the center of power now rested squarely with the Japanese military administration. The Japanese could exercise jurisdiction over judicial courts, appoint "commissioners" for each department, and approve other governmental appointments. Furthermore, each department in the Executive Commission was subject to the influence of "a Japanese adviser and Japanese assistant advisers." Despite this change in power holding, the military administration sought to maintain continuity in personnel. Departments were headed and staffed by individuals who had held posts in the commonwealth, with many holdovers among lesser personnel.[49]

Formal ceremonies at an end, Maeda invited the members to the former U.S. high commissioner's dining room for a toast. Once everyone had arrived, he

TABLE 3.   Philippine Executive Commission, 1942

Chairman of the executive commission	Jorge B. Vargas
Commissioner of the interior	Benigno S. Aquino
Commissioner of finance	Antonio de las Alas
Commissioner of justice	José P. Laurel
Commissioner of agriculture and commerce	Rafael R. Alunan
Commissioner of education, health, and welfare	Claro M. Recto
Commissioner of public works and communications	Quintin Paredes
Chief justice of the Supreme Court	José Yulo
Auditor-general and budget director	Teofilo Sison

opened the champagne, raised his glass, and, together with all present, toasted to the prosperity of the Philippines and its cooperation with Japan. Mayor Vargas answered in turn, expressing many of the same desires. Shouting "Mabuhay" (Hurrah!), all welcomed—in varying degrees of enthusiasm—a new period of cooperation between Japan and the Philippines.[50] The official organization of the executive commission was soon to follow. Appointments were finalized on January 26, and the "Articles of Organization" were completed three days later. By the end of January, the Japan-sponsored government had taken shape, as shown in table 3.[51]

This group served until the Japanese bequeathed independence in October 1943. By March 1942, a wide-reaching network of appointments had been made to governmental offices and provisional governorships. Thus began what David Steinberg has called "dual government," in which the collaborationist Manila regime was set against Quezon's government in exile in Corregidor and, later, Washington.[52]

For Filipinos, however, there was little doubt where the real power and authority resided. The presence of occupying forces served as a constant reminder of the realities of the new East Asian order. Moreover, the Japanese military administration issued orders limiting Philippine control over their homeland. Order No. 3, issued to Vargas on February 20, 1942, made all executive commission statutes "subject to the approval of the Commander-in-Chief of the Imperial Japanese Forces in the Philippines." And Military Ordinance No. 2, issued on March 14, deleted all prohibitions or limitations on civil rights, benefits, and privileges of Japanese nationals residing in the Philippines. This ordinance effectively opened every inch of the Philippines to Japanese exploitation.[53]

Within four weeks of entering Manila, Japan had established a system of indirect rule that included most of the prewar Philippine political elite. In doing so, Japan overcame a primary hurdle facing occupying forces in imperial ventures: securing local cooperation. This political success is even more striking given the

FIGURE 3.   Lt. Gen. Honma Masaharu inspects Philippine and Japanese governmental officials. Those present include Teofilo Sison, Quintin Paredes, Rafael R. Alunan, José P. Laurel, Antonio de las Alas, Beningno S. Aquino, José Yulo, Jorge B. Vargas, Japanese consul Kihara, and other Japanese officials. Photo courtesy of Getty Images.

fact that Japan had yet to conquer the country. It remained engaged in bitterly contested battles with Philippine-American forces across the archipelago (most notably on Bataan). And the Philippines witnessed a more formidable and ferocious guerrilla resistance movement than any other country in the region. The most successful of these guerrilla armies, Luis Taruc's radical Hukbalahap (Anti-Japanese People's Army), claimed by 1943 to have as many as twenty thousand active soldiers in central Luzon.[54] This has led some writers to speak in harsh terms about Philippine collaboration. Writing immediately after the war, David Bernstein argued that the balance sheet of Philippine resistance is "marred only by the fact that too many prewar political leaders collaborated."[55] But it is hard to imagine how leaders could have acted differently. A sense of responsibility toward the nation and a combination of fear and restrained hope for the future played a role in convincing leaders to cooperate with Japan.

For his part, Quezon remained willing to support the collaborationist regime. On January 29, 1942, while still on Corregidor, he released a cautious statement supporting the Philippine executive commission. He stated that if such a commission exists, it "was evidently for the purpose of safeguarding the welfare of the civilian population and can, in no way, reflect the sentiments of the Filipino towards the enemy." Quezon even told MacArthur that the members of the executive commission were not traitors. "They are not Quislings," he insisted, but "virtual prisoners of the enemy" and "victims of the adverse fortunes of war."[56] This position irked U.S. High Commissioner Sayre, who scorned it as "non-committal" in its refusal to repudiate the Philippine executive commission.[57] But Quezon insisted that those who stayed behind were merely doing their duty.

At times it was not the collaborators but the United States at whom Quezon directed his anger. On hearing about the U.S. "Europe First" policy and the early 1942 decision to send large amounts of American supplies and planes to Europe instead of the Philippines, Quezon blew up. Sitting in his wheelchair, body wracked with incessant tuberculosis-induced coughing, Quezon vented at MacArthur's chief of intelligence, Col. Charles A. Willoughby. MacArthur writes of Quezon's "bewildered anger" at the United States as something he could never forget.[58] His physician and wife could not control his rage. "Listen to what the 'shameless' ones are saying in Washington," Quezon screamed. "For thirty years I have worked and hoped for my people. Now they burn and die for a flag that could not protect them. . . . Where are the planes this *sin verguenza* is boasting of? *Que demonio*—how typically American to writhe in anguish at the fate of a distant cousin while a daughter is being raped in the back room!"[59]

Quezon, however, soon got cold feet. In early February, he learned of Prime Minister Tōjō's January 21 statement to the imperial Diet offering possible future independence. "If the Filipino people understand the empire's true intentions and cooperate with the construction of the Greater East Asia Co-Prosperity Sphere," Tōjō asserted, "then the empire will gladly grant them the honor of independence."[60]Fearing the effect this might have on the Philippine people, "especially the less educated classes," Quezon wrote to President Roosevelt on February 10, 1942, asking the United States to recognize independence and to cooperate with Japan in neutralizing the Philippines.[61]

Quezon considered continuing this quest from Washington almost a year later. In late January 1943, once Tōjō restated Japan's commitment to granting independence, Quezon—now in Washington—drafted a policy memorandum intended for Roosevelt. "It would be both wise and proper," Quezon's memorandum noted, "to proclaim Philippine independence *now*, rather than to wait until 1946." At the very latest, he hoped that Roosevelt would advance Independence Day to April 9 (the anniversary of the fall of Bataan) or July 4, 1943. Doing so, he argued, would be a "shot heard 'round the world" that would give faith and courage to those in Japanese-occupied areas.[62] Quezon never sent this memorandum to the White House, but it calls attention to his continued concern about his country's loyalties. After all, why push the independence issue if not for worrying about shifting Philippine allegiances?

With Japanese-sponsored independence on the horizon, Quezon sent an agent to see whether the Philippines remained loyal. In May 1943 his personal doctor, Lt. Col. Emigdio Cruz, departed Washington to get firsthand information and to speak with leaders in Manila. The tale that Cruz spins, which was published in the *Philippines Free Press* in early 1948, ranges from fantastic to downright fanciful.[63] He describes multiple close calls with a Japanese military that actively sought his capture, giving the story an air of suspense that his real trip may not have had. In the end, Cruz claims to have made it to Manila, met with Roxas, Yulo, Alunan, and other leaders, and learned of their loyalty to the commonwealth. Roxas told him, "there is no doubt of the loyalty of the Filipinos, including those who are holding positions of government. It can be safely stated that 95% of the entire Filipino people are true and loyal to America and the leadership of President Quezon." Roxas even stated that Laurel, the soon-to-be president of the Japan-sponsored Philippine republic, was likely collaborating "for the best interests of the Filipino people."[64] Heartened by this news, Cruz left the Philippines in early November 1943 to report to MacArthur and Quezon.

While it at times seems to straddle the line between history and fiction, we should not wholly discount Cruz's story. The historical record suggests that Quezon did send someone to the Philippines to report on the loyalty and actions of leaders who collaborated with Japan. And he happily reported his relief on debriefing his agent. In a November 29, 1943 letter to Pilar H. Lim, Quezon noted that he sent an agent to Manila to secure "personal information about people and affairs, and he tells me that I can have absolute confidence in those whom I have trusted. If you should come this way again, I will tell you more about it. I am very happy over this news and I give you my heartfelt congratulations."[65]

Collaborating Philippine leaders, too, defended their actions. José P. Laurel, after becoming president of the Japan-sponsored Republic of the Philippines in 1943, often told Japanese liaison officer Hamamoto Masakatsu that he only became president to protect his country. According to Hamamoto, Laurel stated, "If I have to shoot you and all the other Japanese, I would do it so as to protect my country."[66] Claro M. Recto, who served as foreign minister under the Laurel regime, argued for collaboration as a form of public service. In an extemporaneous speech in October 1943, he stressed that it was service, not the "pomp of power," that truly mattered. "If the nation is lost, all is lost with it."[67] Strikingly, Sergio Osmeña offered an impassioned defense of the collaborators in a speech made shortly after he landed in Leyte with U.S. forces in October 1944. "Not all public officials," he argued, "could take to the hills to carry on the heroic struggle." He continued:

> Some had to remain in their posts to maintain a semblance of government, to protect the population from the oppressor to the extent possible by human ingenuity and to comfort the people in their misery. Had their services not been available, the Japanese would either have

themselves governed directly and completely or utilized unscrupulous Filipino followers capable of any treason to their people. The result would have been calamitous and the injury inflicted to our body politic beyond cure.[68]

Even visiting Japanese officials supported such claims. Takeuchi Tatsuji, who led a research commission to the Philippines from December 1942 to October 1943, noted in his diary on December 23, 1942, less than two weeks after his arrival:

We Japanese have every reason to suspect that the "cooperation" we are getting from the Filipino leaders—from Jorge Vargas down—is more apparent then genuine: they are merely biding their time till the end of the war. Their collaborative gestures seem prompted solely by their desire to keep to a minimum the sufferings and hardship which might be inflicted upon their people by occupying personnel. Difficult to tell just how many of these collaborating Filipino politicos are really interested in constructing a new Philippines under [the] guidance of Japan.[69]

In the end, the Philippines was a place of great contradiction. It was in the Philippines that Japan hailed its greatest political success and suffered its biggest military headaches. On the one hand, the Philippine leadership went over to the Japanese side en masse and participated in a collaborationist regime. On the other hand, the Philippines witnessed a widespread and intense guerrilla resistance. As Teodoro A. Agoncillo notes in his seminal work on the Japanese occupation, the official and unofficial accounts of the guerrilla units in the Philippines are "so staggering that it will take a lifetime to write even half of the history of that movement."[70] Granted, the history of collaboration and resistance was a complicated affair. Just as thugs, robbers, and sadists joined the resistance movements, some political elites may have collaborated for personal gain or group enrichment. But to the more high-minded individuals in Manila, the underlying motive behind both collaboration and resistance was one and the same. Political collaborator and military resister alike worked to create an independent Philippines in the wake of the global war.

"Britain's Difficulty Is Burma's Opportunity"

The outbreak of World War II in Europe in September 1939 weakened Great Britain's hold over its Asian empire. Eyes fixated securely on Berlin, British leaders in London devoted little time to Burmese affairs. At the same time, the war invigorated Burmese nationalists. "The Axis victories had changed the entire picture for us," Ba Maw recounted in his memoirs. "I was convinced that, however the war might eventually end, British power in Asia would never be the same again, and our liberation was nearer and surer than ever."[71] Ba Maw was not the only one to feel this way. By the time the war broke out, "Britain's difficulty is Burma's opportunity" had become an oft-spoken mantra.[72]

Taking advantage of this unique opportunity was the challenge of the day. Ba Maw did so in two ways. First, he courted Japan. Ba Maw anticipated that Japan would enter the war, and he hoped to use Tokyo to finance Burma's independence campaign. Ba Maw thus sent a mission to Tokyo in November 1939 led by his closest friend and president of the Burma-Japan Association, Dr. Thein Maung. Ostensibly a trip to sell rice, inspect schools, and sightsee, the mission's true intention was to secure support for a peaceful Burmese independence movement. Thein Maung stayed for a month, during which he hammered out a "firm assurance" for financial help from Japan. By the following year, Ba Maw had begun to see Japan's potential in more revolutionary terms. This owed to his talks with Thakin Aung San and the People's Revolutionary Party, a hardline faction of Thakin activists. In January 1940 Aung San contacted Ba Maw to ask for his help in igniting a Burmese revolution. Although he had not worked out the details, Aung San hinted that Ba Maw's Japanese contacts would prove important to their cause.[73] On reflection Ba Maw found the meeting inspiring. Now convinced that armed insurrection could ensure Burmese independence, Ba Maw contacted the Japanese consulate to ask for funds, military equipment, and instructors.

At the same time, Ba Maw also issued a clarion call for independence through his role as head of the Freedom Bloc. Formed in late 1939 as an amalgamation of Ba Maw's Poor Man's Party, the Dobama Asiayone, students, monks, and other nationalists, the Freedom Bloc fought tooth and claw to secure independence from Britain. During the February 1940 session of the legislature, the Freedom Bloc struggled to pass an amendment to have Britain recognize Burma "as an independent nation with the right to frame her own constitution." The House of Representatives rejected the amendment, siding instead with Prime Minister U Pu's policy of first supporting the war to prove that Burma is "fit for the full measure of responsible government."[74] From this point on, many in the Freedom Bloc shifted to overt antiwar propaganda. Their uncompromising stance gained steam once the German Blitzkrieg in Western Europe laid bare the limits of British power.

The activities of the Freedom Bloc brought a harsh reaction from Britain. Invoking the Defense of Burma Act, British authorities from May 1940 initiated a policy of mass arrests and severe repression. Thakin Nu, Thein Maung, and others were arrested for subversive statements by mid-July. In a dramatic move, Ba Maw resigned from the House of Representatives in late July. He then delivered scathing attacks on Burmese support for the war, and he was arrested for sedition on August 6. British officials in Burma viewed him as "the most dangerous 'Quisling' in this country" and arrested him to prevent subversive activities and to thwart "his pursuing intrigues with the Japanese."[75]

Britain, however, could no longer suppress pressures for a constitutional advance. The activities of the Freedom Bloc prompted U Saw, Ba Maw's rival who became prime minister in September 1940, to lobby for Burmese autonomy. Whereas the Freedom Bloc demanded complete independence, Saw sought dominion status. He took his cue from the governor of Burma, Sir Archibald Douglas Cochrane, who signaled in November 1939 that dominion status was the natural end point of Burmese governmental progress.[76] Throughout 1940 and 1941, Saw embarked on a quest for a clear, unequivocal statement from London that Burma would be granted dominion status by the end of the war.

The Atlantic Charter and changes in British wartime rhetoric emboldened U Saw. The charter, which was signed by both Winston Churchill and Franklin Roosevelt on August 14, 1941, made a sober call for peace by means of free trade, national self-determination, economic cooperation, disarmament, and collective security. The third clause committed Britain to assure "the right of all peoples to choose the form of government under which they will live" and to restore "sovereign rights and self government to those who have been forcibly deprived of them."[77] Although the British drafters never intended to restore self-government to its colonies, in practice the clause was seen as a promise for national self-determination. This explosive principle thus invigorated anti-imperialists across the British Empire. Arch-imperialist secretary of state for India and Burma Leo Amery was livid. In his diary on August 14, he grumbled that Burmese ministers had already approached the governor-general of Burma and demanded that Britain live up to its word. Amery wrote, "We shall no doubt pay dearly in the end for all this fluffy flapdoodle."[78]

Amery's fears were soon realized. Obsessed by the opportunity dangling before him, Saw visited London with his secretary, Tin Tut, in October and November 1941 to pry out a promise of political emancipation. Saw found a lukewarm ally in the governor-general of Burma, Sir Reginald Hugh Dorman-Smith, an Irishman who sympathized with Burmese aspirations for independence but wanted it to be a peaceful if drawn-out process. Although he did not think Saw would meet with success, Dorman-Smith believed that the trip might boost morale and ease tensions in Burmese politics.[79] Saw nonetheless remained hopeful. Britain, after all, was in a time of crisis and needed the full support of its empire. What better way could London gain global support than by living up to its promises? Saw cherished the idea of becoming the hero who pressured Burma's colonial master into offering the gift of dominion status, so he played up Burma's constitutional advance. "What Burma wants to know," he proclaimed, "is whether, in fighting with many other countries for the freedom of the world, she is also fighting for her own freedom. Does victory by the democracies, mean full self-government to Burma? The demand for complete self-government is a unanimous demand of the Burmese people, and it was made incessantly long before the Atlantic Charter."[80]

This was by no means the first time Burmese leaders took up the issue of a constitutional advance with London. Since 1929, Burma's British overlords issued statements asserting that the goal of political development was "the attainment of Dominion Status."[81] But this remained a distant dream before the outbreak of war in Europe. The war gave Burmese nationalists an opportunity to demand a greater level of self-government. On February 29, 1940, Senator U Kyaw Din moved a resolution calling on London to grant dominion status.[82] Hard on the heels of this resolution, on June 22 Prime Minister Maung Pu sent a letter asking for a constitution that would allow Burma to become a self-governing and fully equal member of the British Commonwealth.[83] London, however, deflected this call, sticking to its policy that dominion status would be considered in the future. The Atlantic Charter, however, gave Burma's demands further relevance and power. Saw was more than happy to use its principles to demand self-government.

U Saw found some sympathy, but Churchill and Amery were cool to the Burmese request. On September 9, 1941, Churchill had publicly repudiated the commitment to self-government, stating in the House of Commons that the Atlantic Charter referred only to "European nations now under the Nazi yoke."[84] Amery, too, refused to clarify Britain's policy. He insisted that it was "not the time to enter upon constitutional controversies" and issued ambiguous and cautious replies that dominion status would be attained "as a process of natural growth." Amery's clearest reply came in a letter to U Saw on November 3, 1941. Amery stated that only after "the war is brought to a victorious end" would London "be willing to discuss the problems to be solved in Burma."[85]

Such guarded statements failed to resonate with Saw. "I have not been able to get an assurance to take back to Burma," he lamented to the press on November 3. "I know that the Government and the British people are very busy at the moment with the war; I only want a definite assurance that Burma will be placed on the same level as other parts of the British Empire. There is no immediate prospect of that coming about." Saw even placed his complaints in the context of the Atlantic Charter and Britain's war aims of freedom and liberation. "My only request to the British Government and people is that before they free the countries under Hitler let them free the countries which are in the British Empire." But, he continued, the situation does not look promising for Burma.[86] In a last-ditch effort, Saw requested on November 11 that Burmese affairs be transferred to the dominion office. This, he argued, could be taken as a sign that Burma was on the road to self-government. But Churchill and Amery refused, insisting that it was "not practicable" to discuss independence or dominion status while still engaged in a global war.[87]

U Saw left London disappointed and in low spirits. He had not gone to London "simply to kiss Mr. Churchill."[88] But kissing Churchill is all he accomplished. Far from receiving dominion status, Saw had won the mere reiteration of a hazy old promise to consider self-government after war's end. This is unsurprising. As Christopher Bayly and Tim Harper have noted, Burma in 1941 "was so far down the list of political priorities as to be invisible."[89] And the Churchill government remained unwilling to consider granting independence within Britain's Asian empire. Disgruntled as Saw was, he still admitted to his commitment to working with Britain. Burma, he argued, "would rather trust the devil we know than the devil we don't."[90]

But his faith had been shaken. On leaving, Saw stated ominously, "I cannot foresee what the attitude of my people will be when I explain the response of the British Government to my request."[91] As it turned out, Saw did not make it back to Burma until after the war, and his tale remained untold. Unwilling to go home empty-handed, Saw spent several weeks in a failed attempt to drum up support in the United States. In Washington, he hoped to persuade President Roosevelt to intercede with Churchill to apply the Atlantic Charter to Burma. Roosevelt, however, brushed aside discussions with Saw on Burmese independence in a polite but cool manner. On his way back to Burma, however, opportunity knocked. Saw reached Hawaii on December 8, 1941, the day after the Japanese surprise attack on Pearl Harbor. Halted at Hawaii, he was forced to retrace his journey home via the United States and Europe. At Lisbon, Saw courted a Japanese embrace. He contacted the Japanese legation and offered Burmese support should the Japanese decide to invade.[92] Unfortunately for Saw, however, the British had cracked Japan's diplomatic and naval cypher messages and were aware of his overtures. The British police arrested U Saw on his arrival in Egypt on January 19, 1942, and kept him prisoner in Uganda for the following four years.[93]

Governor Dorman-Smith secretly rejoiced. He had been worried that on his return, Saw might rally public sentiment against Great Britain. In a letter to Amery in October 1944, he hinted that Japan's invasion of Burma had saved Britain from a political disaster. Had U Saw returned and told his side of the story, Dorman-Smith wrote, anti-British resentments and pressures would undoubtedly have intensified in size and scope. Dorman-Smith further emphasized this in his unpublished memoirs. "The lesson which I learnt arising out of the U Saw mission," he wrote, "was that it is possible to lose a country by haggling over a phrase."[94]

It was the nationalist Thakins who ultimately pushed Burma into Japan's rough embrace. They found a benefactor in Suzuki Keiji. An army colonel in the imperial general headquarters, Suzuki was a rough, forceful, and driven personality in the army intelligence community. He was a man of independent thought and action—a "swashbuckling, eccentric character," one who has been better described as Japan's Lawrence of Burma.[95] So forceful was he that one of his subordinates, Sugii Mitsuru, remembers him thus: "a ruffian with an extremely strong personality. An outlaw. If I use a derogatory term, a *yakuza*."[96]

In March 1940 Suzuki received unofficial orders to go to Burma and research how to close off the Burma Road, the Allied aid route to the Chiang Kai-shek regime. After giving the problem some thought, Suzuki decided the best course of action was to contact Thakin leaders and encourage a revolt against the British. In the wake of a successful revolt, his Burmese partners could then close off the Burma Road.[97] Taking the false name Minami Masuyo, Suzuki traveled to Rangoon in July 1940. He eventually linked up with Aung San to form what became the Burma Independence Army.

It was during his talks with the Thakins that his independence of thought shone through. Suzuki, a man of high purpose reminiscent of the *shishi* in Bakumatsu Japan, openly flouted his orders and instead sought to instill a spirit of independence in Burma. At his first meeting with Thakin Nu, he insisted that the Burmese should seize their own freedom. "Don't be worried about independence," he insisted. "Independence is not the kind of thing you can get through begging for it from other people. You should proclaim it yourselves. The Japanese refuse to give it? Very well, then; tell them you will cross over to some place like Twante and proclaim independence and set up your own government. What's the difficulty about that? If they start shooting, you just shoot back."[98] Suzuki never lacked for such sentiments. In 1942, when it appeared that the occupying Japanese forces would not grant independence, Suzuki even urged Aung San and his colleagues to rise against the Japanese.[99]

By the time Suzuki had fully settled in Rangoon, however, Aung San was nowhere to be found. Along with fellow Thakin Hla Myaing (Bo Yan Aung), Aung San slipped away from Burma on August 8, 1940, disguised as Chinese crewmen on a Norwegian boat bound for Amoy (present-day Xiamen Island) in China. He left to evade British authorities, which had issued a warrant for his arrest. But more importantly, Aung San hoped to contact communist forces near Chongqing and plead for weapons and support for Burmese independence.

It is unclear how he thought to traverse the 1,700 kilometers that separated Amoy from Chongqing. Aung San spoke of having to rely on his own wit and resourcefulness. As he later recalled, however, he simply "wandered the streets like a lost child" and despaired that his mission and boyhood dreams would end in failure.[100]

After a fruitless three months of "waiting and wandering" in the international settlement on Kulangsu Island, Major Kanda from the Japanese military police (*Kenpeitai*) located Aung San and invited him to Japan.[101] This offer owed to the machinations of Ba Maw's group. Dr. Thein Maung had entrusted to Suzuki a letter and a picture of Aung San and Thakin Hla Myaing. Suzuki forwarded the documents on to the military police. After locating Aung San, Major Kanda showed him the documents as proof of the sincerity of the Japanese offer. Minds at ease, Aung San and Hla Myaing agreed to travel to Japan. They finally met Suzuki (along with Sugii) at Haneda Airport in early November 1940.[102] Thus began the oft-told, heroic story of the Thirty Comrades, a group of Burmese that formed the core of a new military force for Burma's liberation from British rule.

The majority of their time in Japan, however, involved much waiting and brooding. The general staff thought (not for the last time) that Suzuki had overstepped his bounds in bringing the young Thakins to Japan, and they were initially reluctant to make use of them. After arriving in Tokyo in November 1940, Aung San thus endured three months of down time. He devoted some of that time to discussing the future of Burma with Suzuki, Sugii, and Higuchi Takeshi. The fruits of such discussions resulted in Aung San's "Blue Print for Burma," which Suzuki circulated among the Tokyo policy elite. Much of the remaining time he spent experiencing a daily life not wholly to his liking. A rather shy and soft-spoken young man of twenty-five, Aung San was not used to dealing with the opposite sex, and he got embarrassed when female Japanese students gave him eggs and milk. So one could imagine his shock and dismay when Suzuki offered to get him a prostitute in the licensed quarters, hoping that he would relax and have a little fun. Enjoying oneself in the women's quarters, Suzuki insisted, "is nothing, no more than taking a bath." Aung San was equally dismayed when he went to a local restaurant to find Suzuki treating a Korean patron with contempt.[103]

Aung San's trip to Japan proved pivotal for the Burmese independence movement. During his stay, Suzuki convinced the military of the utility of the Burmese nationalists. On February 1, 1941, nearly three months after Aung San's arrival, Japan's imperial general headquarters created the Minami Kikan, a secret, joint army-navy group committed to closing the Burma Road and aiding the Burmese independence movement. Suzuki was appointed its leader and, following common practice, the organization named itself after his alias, Minami Masuyo.

The Minami Kikan created the February Plan, which provided for the training of thirty Burmese patriots in military tactics and strategy in preparation for an armed uprising. Once trained, the Minami Kikan would help them reenter Burma and would continue to provide the funds, arms, ammunition, and training necessary to fight the British. All Japan asked in return was the closure of the Burma Road.[104] This was diplomacy on the cheap.

Aung San, disguised as a Chinese seaman in an outfit complete with false teeth, returned to Burma in February 1941 to convince fellow Thakins to join the cause. "We were eager for news and Aung San did not disappoint us," remembered Thakin Hla Pe (Bo Let Ya), one of the Thirty Comrades. And the Thakins were equally happy with the plans for military training. Hla Pe continued, "We accepted the plans; we had no choice, and we were all agreed that British power could only be ousted by force. It was a long night for us, and when we had finished talking, we fell into the deep sleep of the fulfilled."[105] In the following weeks and months, Aung San's Japanese contacts smuggled the group out of Burma.

By July 1941, the Thirty Comrades (in reality, only twenty-seven) had assembled in the deep forests of Hainan Island for military training. They were divided into three groups that were to focus on high command, regular combat duty, and guerrilla fighting. Under the greatest secrecy, they received a crash course in combat, command, guerrilla warfare, explosives, espionage, and other tactics. The training was so intense that it almost broke the Burmese youths. Within a few weeks most of them looked like scarecrows, ragged and gaunt. Moreover, they struggled in a different cultural context, having to communicate in an unfamiliar language and eat unfamiliar foods.[106] In a remarkable understatement, Hla Myaing called the training "rough going." Thakin Tun Ok noted that some of them became so desperate that they plotted to steal a boat to return to Burma.[107] Nonetheless, the Burmese patriots persevered. By October, the Thirty Comrades had completed their training and were transferred to Taiwan to await further orders.

Yet the decision to train the young Thakin nationalists did not imply that Japan had great plans for them. Indeed, army leaders had only vague notions of what to do with them. Plans drafted by the imperial general headquarters through September 1941 claimed any attack on Burma would "depend on the situation." Indeed, the imperial general headquarters decided in October to create the Fifteenth Army, the force that ultimately invaded Burma. Even in its creation the following month, however, the Fifteenth Army was meant as a rearguard force. It was to oversee a limited occupation of airfields in Moulmein to stabilize operations in the Malay Peninsula. The Fifteenth was not created with the intent of seizing Burma from the British. Strikingly, it was not until late December 1941 that Col. Hattori Takushirō, a section chief in the army general staff's operations section, had crafted more detailed (though still somewhat vague) plans for an invasion of Burma.

Suzuki took advantage of this ambiguity to seek out a broader role for the Burmese nationalists and to thrust the Minami Kikan into a position of value. In mid-October Colonel Suzuki, Aung San, and nine other "comrades" flew to Tokyo to participate in war games for an invasion of Burma. The war games confirmed the decision to send a mixed brigade of Japanese troops to occupy the vicinity around Moulmein. But the simulation also provided an opportunity for the Minami Kikan and the Burmese nationalists. Once this territory was taken, the Thirty Comrades would organize an independence army and invade Burma, receiving when necessary assistance from the Japanese brigade.[108] Furthermore, on October 15, Suzuki received orders to send Hla Pe, Ba Gyan, Hla Maung, and Tun Kin back to Burma to recruit guerrilla forces for an armed uprising.[109]

The resignation of the Konoe cabinet on October 16, 1941, and the appointment of Tōjō Hideki to the premiership the following day, however, threatened existing plans. It is unclear why. Perhaps Tōjō's efforts in October to launch a full-scale review of the September 6 decision for war threw into doubt the future of any armed uprising. Alternatively, it is also possible that the imperial general headquarters did not want trivial projects such as the Minami Kikan to imperil military plans for the region. Whatever the case, from October 25 the imperial general headquarters repeatedly ordered Suzuki to recall the four patriots back to Taiwan. But Suzuki cared little for these orders. He assumed that the drift to war warranted sending in the Thirty Comrades as soon as possible. He therefore disobeyed orders and stalled, giving the four Burmese a chance to begin their operations. At first Suzuki hid them in Bangkok, cabling Tokyo that they had escaped and were nowhere to be found. Two weeks later, on November 13, he ordered Hla Pe, Ba Gyan, Hla Maung, and Tun Kin to enter Burma.[110] Hla Pe and Ba Gyan were arrested at the Thai border, but Hla Maung and Tun Kin managed to cross into Burma.

The Thirty Comrades were finally called to action with the outbreak of the Pacific War. The Minami Kikan followed the Southern Expeditionary Army to Saigon and later to Bangkok. Suzuki reached Bangkok on December 12, and the remaining members of the Thirty Comrades arrived two weeks later. On December 23, the Fifteenth Army took over the direction of the Minami Kikan.[111] Suzuki immediately recruited two hundred more ethnic Burmese soldiers, holding their induction and swearing-in ceremonies for the new Burma Independence Army (BIA) on December 27 and 28. With this, the meager force had increased to around three hundred members, including seventy-three Japanese soldiers.

On New Year's Eve, Suzuki informally dissolved the Minami Kikan and in its place established the BIA.[112] Suzuki appointed himself as its commander with the rank of general. Aung San served as senior staff officer (with the rank of major general), and six other comrades held positions of either staff officer or group commander. This was cause for great celebration; the Burmese patriots honored the occasion by holding the symbolic *thwe thauk* blood-drinking ceremony described at the beginning of this chapter. Moreover, the Thirty Comrades and some Japanese members took new *noms de guerre*. Aung San took the name Bo Teza. Suzuki assumed the name Bo Mogyo (Commander Thunderbolt), making adroit use of the prophecy that Burma's British masters would be struck down by a thunderbolt.

When Japan's Fifteenth Army launched the invasion of Burma in January 1942, the BIA accompanied Japanese forces in mainly supporting roles. Despite many recruits' eagerness for battle, the ill-equipped and largely untrained units did little real fighting. Their primary tasks included generating local support for the war effort, gathering intelligence, and sabotaging British operations. Only a small group of BIA forces—commandos under Thakin Tun Shein (Bo Yan Naing)—took part in actual fighting at Shwedaung. Others took initiative to set up military centers at Pyinmana, Pegu, Kaiklat, and Rangoon to train young Burmese patriots in modern warfare, guerrilla tactics, and sabotage.[113]

Perhaps the BIA's greatest victory rested in its visibility. Their imaginations fired by stories of Aung San's army, some Burmese showed their spirit and commitment to the BIA by running wild. One group hoped to curry favor with Aung San by killing Chinese months in advance of the BIA's arrival.[114] In Tavoy and other towns in southern Burma, members of Burma's new army were greeted as heroes. Not surprisingly, once in Burma the BIA swelled in size. Japanese sources indicate that by the end of February 1942, the BIA had reached a total of 4,860 men.[115] In the following months, the BIA ballooned in size to between ten and thirty thousand strong, of which perhaps four thousand members engaged in actions against the British.[116] British intelligence noted that half of the BIA were "high-minded young Nationalist idealists" while the other half were "mere thugs out for what they could make."[117]

Although highly visible, the BIA was not always a fetching sight. Many members may have bustled with pride and patriotism, but the BIA for the most part was a tattered, unkempt, and sick young force. "They were magnificent in their raggedness and suffering," Hla Pe later noted. "Hundreds were blinded or crippled for life, thousands were yellow with fever. . . . Totally lacking in training and in experience . . . this army presented an amazing picture of noise and bustle, patriotism and pride, and inexperience and inefficiency." Hla Pe could hardly forget the sight of crippled, impoverished Burmese in their early teens who spoke of their suffering proudly and wisely.[118]

And the BIA, whose recruits came mainly from the commercialized regions of southern Burma, remained unpopular across Upper Burma. Many Karen soldiers, in fact, refused to retreat with the British army, joining forces with local Indians to wage a guerrilla war against the BIA and the Japanese. To punish Karen guerrillas for the death of a senior Japanese officer who was cut down during a Karen raid, Suzuki ordered the BIA to take reprisals against two large Karen villages. A bloodbath ensued. The worst incidents occurred in the Myaungmya district, southeast of Bassein, where Karen men, women, and children were brutally massacred. Members of the BIA even killed former Karen parliamentarian and cabinet minister Saw Pa Tha and his English wife during the turmoil. Such actions ignited a broader war between the Karen and Burman people before the Japanese army restored order. Within the span of a few months, BIA troops destroyed more than four hundred Karen villages and took the lives of nearly two thousand Karen people.

Meanwhile, Burmans were stunned at the rapidity of Japanese successes. Not one month after the Japanese invasion of Burma, locals were stunned by the rapid fall of the "impregnable" fortress of Singapore on February 15, 1942. U Ba U recalled being so dumbfounded by Singapore's fall that he woke up his friends to tell them the news. "Nobody," Ba U recounted, "expected Singapore to fall so quickly and easily . . . everybody in the East thought it was impregnable."[119] Britain's collapse in Burma was equally swift. Rangoon fell to Japanese forces on March 8, 1942. The Japanese advance then gained in speed. Confident, bold Japanese tacticians used the jungle for maneuver and surprise, astounding a British leadership that was more suited for desert than jungle warfare. Reinforced with troops transferred from Malaya and the Netherlands Indies, Japan in the following two months seized control over most of Burma. As Field Marshal Sir William Slim noted, the Allies had been "outmaneuvered, outfought, and outgeneraled."[120]

Ethnic Burmans initially rejoiced. "The Japanese army," former BIA soldier Maung Maung recalled in his memoirs, "had a strong propaganda appeal: Asian brothers were coming to set their Asian brothers free!"[121] Peasants and townsfolk, too, rejoiced at what they thought was the end of foreign rule. Even Thakin Nu, who was noted for his fierce anti-Japanese stance, wrote of how the Japanese arrival inspired the popular imagination. "Burmans," he noted, "had such faith in the Japanese that when the Japanese bombers came they would not take cover in the shelters. Some tore off their shirts and waved a welcome; they sang and danced and clapped their hands, and shouted and turned somersaults as if they did not care a curse what happened."[122] Nu was careful to argue that the "bad hats" and "old lags" were joined by committed nationalists in celebrating Japan's invasion. One wealthy Burmese woman was so enthusiastic that she prepared, at considerable cost, a dinner fit to feed more than one hundred Japanese soldiers and officers.[123]

Burmese nationalists had every reason for excitement. Suzuki's Minami Kikan continually emphasized that the sole purpose of their work was the immediate liberation of Burma. Tokyo also made similar, albeit guarded, promises. On January 21, 1942, Prime Minister Tōjō stated in the imperial Diet that Japan would gladly "grant the honor of independence" to both the Philippines and Burma if they cooperated as members of the Greater East Asia Co-Prosperity Sphere.[124] The following day, Japan broadcast another message from Tōjō in both Burmese and Hindi stating that Japan would not only stamp out British power in Asia, it would also strive "to liberate the Burmese people and to aid them in their ambitions for independence."[125]

Hopes for immediate independence, however, were left unrealized. Suzuki's plans met with fierce opposition from Southern Expeditionary Army planners. Senior staff officer Colonel Ishii Akiho worried that an uncooperative Burmese government in Rangoon might restrict Japanese access to Burma or hamper military operations. On February 6, 1942, Ishii submitted plans arguing that it was in Japan's interest to hamper the emergence of a true Burmese government. He maintained that the Burmese regime should have the "outward appearance of independence," but the true locus of authority should rest with the commander of the occupying forces. Genuine independence, he argued, should only be granted after war's end.[126] Despite receiving orders to bestow independence immediately after the occupation of Rangoon, Ishii continually resisted. He cabled Tokyo, arguing that "it is too early to consider Burmese independence," and persuaded the Fifteenth Army and the chief of staff of the Southern Expeditionary Army to delay independence.[127] On March 15 Japan instead established a military administration in Rangoon.

After securing control over Rangoon, Suzuki allowed Thakin leaders to create the collaborationist Burma Baho government under Thakin Tun Ok. From its inception, the Baho government aimed at bringing order and a semblance of normalcy to Rangoon and to war-torn areas of Lower Burma. On April 7, 1942, the Baho government issued its first order to rationalize its administration of Burma through villages, towns, townships, and districts. Nonetheless, the new government was handicapped by incompetence. Flooded with young Thakin nationalists inexperienced in administrative affairs, the government failed to establish its administrative authority. British intelligence sources derided governmental leaders as "pathetically inept" and surrounded by unprincipled, unscrupulous, and corrupt followers.[128] Adding insult to injury, the Baho government lacked adequate communication facilities and legitimacy as Burma's central ruling authority.[129]

Unsurprisingly, Japanese military authorities soon lost patience with the inept Baho government. By May 1942 the military administration began preparing for a new central administration, one led by seasoned administrators. The pro-Japanese Ba Maw—who had escaped from Mogok jail in April 1942—seemed the natural choice to head the new government. Ba Maw was happy to comply. On August 1, General Iida Shōjirō, commander of the Fifteenth Army, sanctioned the formation of a Burmese central executive administration that preserved the existing governmental bureaucracy. The new cabinet was led by Ba Maw and included the members as shown in table 4.

Ba Maw also advertised widely for experienced and trained civil servants to join his administration. They were told to report to Rangoon by September 1, but most did not return to duty until later that year. Ba Maw put all on a three-month probationary period, threatening to discharge any administrator whose work was found unsatisfactory.[130] By the end of 1942, Burma had a working political regime in Rangoon.

Meanwhile, Japan also reorganized the BIA into a smaller, more disciplined military force of five thousand men. The Southern Expeditionary Army ordered the official dissolution of the Minami Kikan on June 10, and on June 18 it decided to transfer Suzuki back to Japan. From there, reorganization proceeded apace. Aung San disbanded the BIA on July 8 and issued instructions for those who wished to join the new Burma Defense Army (BDA) to participate in an examination in Mandalay, Pegu, or Mingaladon.[131] General Iida inaugurated the BDA on July 28, 1942, appointing Aung San as commander and Aung Than as chief of staff.[132]

TABLE 4. Burmese Central Executive Administration, 1942

Prime minister and minister of interior	Dr. Ba Maw
Minister without portfolio	Thakin Mya
Finance minister	Dr. Thein Maung
Agriculture minister	Thakin Than Tun
Forestry minister	Thakin Tun Ok
Commerce and industry minister	U Hla Pe
Transportation and irrigation minister	Thakin Ba Sein
Education and health minister	U Ba Win
Justice minister	U Tun Aung
Public works recovery minister	Bandula U Sein

Although Burma had received a new government and military force, it was clear that true power rested in Japanese hands. Military Order No. 20, issued by General Iida on August 1, 1942 (the same day Ba Maw's government was formed), made clear that "absolute precedence" would be given to the demands of the Japanese army. In this spirit, Iida sat atop a new fiefdom of authority. He held the sole legislative power, could appoint and dismiss all major officials in the administration, and could supervise administrative, judicial, and prosecution affairs. Japanese advisers assisted each of the new departments, and the executive administration required Japanese approval for decisions on important affairs. Following British precedent, Japan took direct control over the Frontier Areas and other territories directly governed by Britain. And Iida, as commander of the military administration, could command Aung San's baby, the newly formed BDA.[133]

This was a sad twist of fate. Anti-British fervor and desires for national liberation tied Burmese nationalists to Japan, the only regional power with the wherewithal to oust Burma's British masters. As Khin Myo Chit noted in her memoirs, this did not result from any love for Japan. "No one loved the Japanese," she wrote. "But anti-British feeling had been roused to the pitch of driving us into the arms of whoever was against the British. . . . Whoever won the war, it seemed that our lot would be the same. Just a change of masters, just one yoke for another."[134] In the end, Burmese nationalists helped lop off their country's British head only to replace it with a Japanese one.

The Patriotic Collaborators

Both Philippine and Burmese national leaders in Manila and Rangoon are best thought of as patriotic collaborators. Although a complex array of motives no doubt influenced these leaders, their collaboration was not a simple expression of political opportunism or self-interest. They also collaborated out of a desire to promote national interests ahead of narrow personal, familial, or group goals. For the patriotic collaborators, short-term cooperation was a tactical move, done for the sake of achieving or preserving longer-term political freedom.[135]

Philippine and Burmese elites may have collaborated for patriotic ends, but as this chapter has shown, the backgrounds were quite different. The Philippines in some respects represented the country *least likely* to collaborate. Filipinos saw themselves as the most Westernized, cosmopolitan people in Asia owing to their longer history of colonialism. Filipinos often wryly noted that their country had spent "four hundred years in a convent" of Spanish colonialism, followed by "forty years in Hollywood." More importantly, Filipinos looked forward to independence from the U.S. empire, scheduled for 1946. These factors, combined with wartime atrocities and general cruelty, contributed to the birth of a larger, more formidable anti-Japanese guerrilla resistance than any other in Southeast Asia.

Patriotic collaboration with Japan, however, was possible because Philippine elites saw the Japanese imperial project as limited in time. They served as a caretaker regime, and resolved to endure as long as Japanese domination seemed unassailable. Ultimately, however, they believed the United States would prevail in war and make good on its promise of independence. Until then, Philippine leaders would collaborate to preserve law, order, and social stability. Laurel used such terms to explain his collaboration. Throughout the war, he wrote of his governmental leadership as not of choice but necessity. Laurel equated his service to the country in the same terms as soldiers who answered the call to arms out of courage and conviction of purpose.[136] "The real cake is coming," he told a noncollaborator on October 16, 1943 (two days after receiving nominal independence from Japan). "In the meantime, there is no harm in being satisfied with the cookies. When the Americans come back, I'll hand over the government to them."[137] Even Leon Ma. Guerrero, as a staff member of the wartime Philippine embassy in Japan, highlighted the challenges of patriotism in the wartime regime. In a letter to Teodoro E. Evangelista in 1944, Guerrero argued that he served to the best of his ability "under circumstances where the easier part of patriotism would be merely to stand aside and criticize or condemn."[138]

It is equally possible to view Philippine collaboration as a collective attempt to hedge their bets. After all, there was no guarantee of an Allied victory. Even without Quezon's instructions, Philippine leaders may have chosen collaboration as an alternative path to postwar independence. No doubt, such a choice would ultimately be rewarded in form, if not in substance. From January 1942, Japan made repeated offers of independence, conditional on active participation in the Greater East Asia Co-Prosperity Sphere. Although it remained uncertain whether such independence would be nominal or genuine, it made sense to work with Japan in the short run. They could always claim to have been playing a double game, enduring until MacArthur fulfilled his promise to return. For a national elite focused on independence, collaboration constituted a winning hand.

Granted, Philippine collaboration was not purely altruistic or other-regarding. As Tanigawa Yoshihiko has argued, the landowners and industrial tycoons that made up the Philippine political establishment in Manila also collaborated to prevent any outbreak of social revolution that might threaten their stewardship of the state.[139] Others did so from opportunism and, perhaps, a degree of compulsion. But it is difficult to disaggregate such aims for control within Philippine politics from their desires for national independence. Likely they saw both as connected. Safeguarding their own supremacy in Philippine political-economic life would help ensure a smooth transition to postwar liberation and strong relations with the Philippines' natural partner, the United States.

Of course, not all collaboration was patriotic. Alfred W. McCoy's seminal study of elite politics in the Philippines' Western Visayas offers insights into collaboration outside of the colonial capital. McCoy shows how the two major factional groups in wartime Iloilo collaborated with *both* the United States and Japan. Instead of reflecting patriotic motivations, both factions collaborated for group security and gain. They recognized that the war would not last long enough to use Japan to help crush their factional opponents. It thus made sense for each faction to keep a foot in both the U.S. and Japanese camps. In collaborating with both powers, they preserved patron-client relations and elite politics through the Pacific War.[140] This type of factional politics was undoubtedly prevalent in the fluid and highly contested provinces. It is less clear, however, whether McCoy's study can be generalized to politics in Manila. Nationalist elites in Manila held greater responsibilities than those in the provinces. They remained committed not only to their factional and sectional interests but also to the country as whole.

Moreover, the existence of patriotic collaboration does not imply that the whole populace welcomed Japan. Most, in fact, had little enthusiasm for Japan's cause. Their lack of enthusiasm was continually dampened by the brutality of Japan's new order, from the Bataan death march to the all-too-common instances of beating, slapping, interrogation, theft, and torture. Japanese officials thus recognized the silent hostility with which they were met. At the parade and festivities celebrating the first anniversary of the fall of Bataan, one over-eager Philippine lower-level official tried to court the friendship of a Japanese bureaucrat. He argued that the majority of Filipinos are pro-Japanese, and perhaps 90 percent of Filipinos understand Japan's true desire to unify Greater East Asia. But the Japanese official was not fooled. "You are mistaken," he reportedly replied. "I am afraid that forty-five per cent of the population continues to be pro-American, five per cent are pro-Japanese, while the remaining fifty per cent are comedians."[141]

Burma provides an even clearer case of patriotic collaboration. Unlike in the Philippines, the war in Burma presented nationalists with a golden opportunity to seize independence. This collaboration was more opportunistic in nature. Burma's Thakin leaders, in particular, did not expend much intellectual energy on the all-important question of who would win the war. Far more significant to them was immediate action to expel the British. The specifics would be worked out in the wake of a British retreat. This obsession with national liberation owed to numerous factors—from natural desire for self-rule to the severity of the British response to anti-British nationalism, or to London's equivocation over Burma's constitutional advance. Whatever the case, by late 1941 hard-liner Thakin nationalists and political leaders such as U Saw and Ba Maw were ready to accept Japanese help in freeing Burma from British rule. Collaboration at the height of power in colonial Burma thus had patriotic ends. They sought an independent Burma, even to the extent of switching one colonial yoke for another.

British leaders, however, doubted the extent of Burmese excitement at the new state of affairs. Governor-General Dorman-Smith, for instance, noted in a February 1944 letter that, aside from Ba Maw, no important political leader waited to receive the Japanese with open arms. Dorman-Smith pointed to how Burmese politicians joined Ba Maw's administration at a snail's pace, over the span of months. Collaboration in Ba Maw's government, he argued, "was only achieved after some months—in the initial stages the only people on whom the Japs could rely were the rag-tag and bobtail of the Thakin Party."[142] Dorman-Smith may have been correct in suggesting the lack of any excitement about Burma's new colonial regime. Collaboration may have been limited to a small cadre of individuals, but it was done for patriotic ends nonetheless.

It was these patriotic collaborators who remade Burma and the Philippines into potential showcase regimes in Japan's new empire. Their true importance rested in the fact that they served as national representatives of Japanese imperialism. Their embrace of Japan's Co-Prosperity Sphere, they hoped, could limit the excesses of their new colonial overlord. The patriotic collaborators could help ensure that the Sphere became more than a simple structure of oppression and exploitation. Under their guidance, the Sphere could also be of use in the colonial present. All they had to do was wait for the right opportunity. With Japan's deteriorating war situation in 1943, such an opportunity would come sooner than many had expected.

5

A NEW DEAL FOR GREATER EAST ASIA?

On November 5–6, 1943, at the height of the Pacific War, Japan convened an international conference at the Imperial Diet Building in Tokyo. Forty-six participants from seven Asian nations—Japan, China, Manchukuo, Thailand, Burma, the Philippines, and India—representing close to one billion people, gathered to discuss the war effort and the construction of the Greater East Asia Co-Prosperity Sphere. Ba Maw described this event—the Greater East Asia Conference—as one met with a great deal of anticipation. The conference epitomized a new Asian spirit, the coming together of a single historical family. "Filling the entire hall," he stated, "was a hush and expectancy which could almost be felt."[1] Such anticipation, he thought, was to be expected. The future these Asian leaders discussed represented a new Asian spirit of amity, independence, equality, prosperity, and cooperation—values enshrined in a joint declaration adopted formally the day after the conference. With this conference, East Asia would become a unified community of independent and equal nations.

This was a far cry from earlier visions for the Co-Prosperity Sphere. Although no dominant vision for the Sphere had emerged in 1942, most policy makers and political intellectuals nonetheless understood Japan's mission as building a pan-regional imperium across Greater East Asia. Japan was to become Asia's hegemon, the economic and political leader that would bring true order, security, prosperity, and economic development. As chapter 3 argued, some of the earliest visions for the Sphere in the wake of Japan's dramatic successes at Pearl Harbor and Singapore suggested that Japan could become successor to the greatest empires in history: Rome and Great Britain. At the height of Japan's imperial expansion, intellectuals and policy makers alike dreamed of the Co-Prosperity Sphere as part of an attempt to reorder the world.

Actions taken in the lead up to the conference, however, suggested a significant policy shift. From early 1943, the Japanese government began what might be thought of as its new deal for Greater East Asia. Policy makers abandoned their earlier navel gazing and began to reimagine the Sphere in a way that could win hearts and minds across the region. Japan granted independence to Burma and the Philippines, helped create the Provisional Government of Free India, signed a treaty with the Chinese Nanjing regime that restored autonomy and got rid of the last vestiges of the unequal treaties, and stressed respect for Thai sovereignty and independence. Further, the foreign ministry helped draft a joint declaration that brought Japan's war aims remarkably closer to those found in the Atlantic Charter. From 1943, Japanese rhetoric became more cooperative, inclusive, and liberal, stressing that Japan was to be fighting for Asian independence, autonomy, prosperity, and regional cooperation. On the surface, earlier goals of subordination and control were replaced by those of interdependence and equality. Akira Iriye thus argues that wartime Japan returned to the shared Wilsonian values of the 1920s, and this served as the important first step toward the postwar Japanese-American embrace.[2] Jessamyn R. Abel, too, shows the conference as highlighting an internationalism that never disappeared during the wartime era.[3]

This new vision, however, did not decidedly change the political makeup of the Co-Prosperity Sphere, and it did not represent an unreserved commitment to liberal internationalist ideals. Granted, Japan broadened the scope of its empire of "self-determined" states, with the Philippines and Burma joining Manchukuo and the Chinese Nanjing regime as nominally independent showcases of the benefits of Japan's new order.[4] But the old imperialism of colonial and territorial rule never died out. Japanese leaders did not grant independence to Korea, Taiwan, or Karafuto. Leadership circles instead called for their broader incorporation as inner territories (naichi) of the Japanese Empire. Lacking independence and autonomy, these territories were not represented at the conference. Malaya, Indonesia, and Indochina were excluded as well. These areas would continue to be dependent parts of the empire's outer territories (gaichi), valuable for natural resources and for constructing a system of defense across Asia. The decision to create new showcase "independent" regimes while retaining more traditional modes of imperialism highlights the continued hybridity of Japan's wartime empire, which featured political arrangements mirroring those of the British Empire and Commonwealth.

Moreover, this new liberal internationalist rhetoric gained acceptance across the Japanese political establishment owing to pragmatic concerns. The Greater

East Asia Conference represented an agreement between two approaches to war-time diplomacy.[5] The imperial high command—led by Prime Minister Tōjō Hideki—sought to rally Asian practical and ideological support for the war effort before the true strength of the U.S.-led counterattack was manifest. This show of solidarity, they hoped, might force the Allied powers to the negotiating table. Foreign ministry leaders, however, used the conference to articulate a language of international relations that would resonate positively with enemy and Allied nations alike and generate willingness for peace negotiations. Tokyo, in short, uti-lized liberal internationalist language both to rally Asian nations to make war and to convince the Allied powers to make peace. The rhetoric of liberal internation-alism thus supported imperial ends. In shifting toward such rhetoric, Japanese leaders attempted to ensure that the Japanese Empire survived the Pacific War.

This chapter also highlights the mixed reception of Japan's new rhetoric. Some participants were enthusiastic supporters. Others were more reserved. Burmese representative Ba Maw, for instance, ardently supported the conference and joint declaration, stating, "Asia is one!" Other leaders remained skeptical of Japan's regional designs. They utilized Japan's internationalist rhetoric to curb what they saw as Japanese domination. This use of rhetoric depicts the double-edged nature of internationalist language. Although articulated for the pragmatic purpose of building support, it became part of a common language that weaker states could use to advance their own interests. This is a story, then, of contestation. This new language—used to bolster Tokyo's position in the region—became available for nations to criticize the realities of Japanese rule.

Re-imagined War Aims

Despite a wild rush across Asia, by 1943 the war was not going well for Japan. The battle of Midway in June 1942 resulted in the Imperial Navy's loss of the four air-craft carriers that formed the core of its power projection capabilities. Moreover, the six-month Guadalcanal campaign, which ended in a full-scale Japanese evac-uation in February 1943, placed Japan on the defensive in the Pacific. Guadalca-nal also weakened Japanese forces across all fronts owing to Tokyo's consistent attempts to reinforce failing defenders with fresh supplies and troops. A perhaps more powerful, psychological shock came in April 1943 when Admiral Yama-moto Isoroku, the architect of the surprise attack on Pearl Harbor, was shot down over Bougainville in the South Pacific. One could guess the shock and dismay of navy leader Yoshida Zengo, who called Yamamoto's death "an irrecoverable loss."[6]

The Pacific theater, however, was not the only source of concern. Japanese lead-ers also keenly perceived the deteriorating war situation in Europe. Ambassador to Nanjing Shigemitsu Mamoru, for instance, looked uneasily at German war prospects. He recognized the link between the two theaters of war and realized that a German defeat would allow the Allies to focus their military and technological might into the Asia-Pacific. Nazi Germany's faltering Atlantic submarine warfare and declining air superiority gave additional cause for alarm. Shigemitsu thus began publishing position papers highlighting the shared destiny of the Axis powers. "These military difficulties Germany faces," he insisted, "are not someone else's affair. It directly affects Japan's military affairs, so it is only natural that serious consideration is warranted."[7] He called for increased Axis cooperation to deal with the unfavorable war situation.

Shigemitsu became instrumental in Japan's rethinking of wartime strategy. His widely circulated position papers from 1942 criticized the one-sided, hamfisted, military-first nature of Japan's war. Shigemitsu continually insisted that victory did not depend solely on fortunes met at the field of battle. "Military force," he asserted, "must be met with military force, and diplomacy must be countered with diplomacy." He thus called for a revitalized diplomacy to counter the Allied propaganda of the Atlantic Charter and to secure Asian support for the war effort. Smart foreign policy, he argued in mid-1942, "has the same effect as military affairs in deciding victory or defeat."[8]

Victory in Asia depended on whether Japan could win the hearts and minds of occupied territories. But Japanese policy makers consistently failed to consider how to win sympathy and support from Asia. Shigemitsu believed that Japan paid mere lip service to issues of Asian liberation but geared war aims to secure autarky and regional hegemony. Political discussions failed to focus on how Tokyo could uplift the region. Rather, they revolved around how Asia would serve as a material supply post and subservient political partner. This was anathema to Shigemitsu. He argued that securing material goods alone would be ineffective in building trust with the region. "Asian liberation," he argued, "must be an expression of true friendship toward the Asian peoples. Victory or defeat in this war will likely be decided by this point."[9]

Shigemitsu was calling for a sea change in Japanese policy. Far from rehashing the tired old arguments about Asian "liberation" from the exploitative colonial powers, Shigemitsu was now calling for liberation from the exploitative Japanese Empire as well. He trumpeted a nationalities policy of high ideals, one that could be lauded by friend and foe alike. After all, without true friendship and true liberation, Japan's new order would not amount to much. Thus, Shigemitsu used his position papers to emphasize the necessity of "establishing political equality among all nations." Maintaining dependencies or colonies in Greater East Asia would prove a distraction and dampen any emergent spirit of cooperation in the region. Japan instead had to support *actual* independence: Shigemitsu emphasized that countries in Greater East Asia "must be given the authority of independence and autonomy that will allow them to manage their national affairs."[10]

These views do not imply that Shigemitsu was an anti-imperialist, committed to the end of empire in Asia. Far from it: Shigemitsu was a consummate political realist who recognized the importance of power in international relations. "The world has always been a world of power," he would write shortly after war's end. "International relations have always been policies of power. But it is only the content of that power that changes with both the time and place."[11] Shigemitsu had in fact supported the Manchurian Incident in 1931 and the formation of Manchukuo. Moreover, while vice minister for foreign affairs between May 1933 and April 1936, he called for something akin to an Asian Monroe doctrine, noting that Japan "is in the position to maintain peace in the Far East" and "has the determination to do so."[12] But by 1942, with Japan's empire teetering on the precipice of disaster, Shigemitsu now counseled a diplomacy of reconciliation. Building a voluntary East Asian union would serve as the "biggest weapon" in Japan's fight for Asia. In this sense, Shigemitsu is best understood as a child of Machiavelli, one who sought victory in diplomacy over defeat in war.

Here at last was a call to arms for the foreign policy establishment, an appeal to wage a war of diplomacy. Superficial propaganda, after all, had done little to promote Japanese leadership and could not bolster Japan's faltering international position. Shigemitsu wrote, "If we display a policy of aggression and exploitation abroad where we cry wine and sell vinegar, then our [vision] will be meaningless both during wartime and peacetime." Instead, Shigemitsu advocated pragmatic measures to promote Japan as the moral leader of Asia and to crush the Anglo-American propaganda of the Atlantic Charter. He called for a "voluntary East Asian union" to preserve and strengthen the Japanese Empire. This, he argued, "will become during wartime the biggest weapon, and in the postwar era will become the greatest foundation of the empire's expansion."[13]

To enact this strategy and reassert Japan's moral leadership, Shigemitsu championed a New China Policy and a New Greater East Asia Policy. The New China Policy represented Shigemitsu's understanding that peace with the Chiang Kai-shek regime was the precondition for peace in Asia. Thus, the policy called for the revision of the unequal treaties, respect for Chinese sovereignty, and the eventual withdrawal of troops from Chinese territory. This policy formed the basis for his New Greater East Asia Policy. Shigemitsu argued that extending independence and autonomy to former European colonies would set Japan apart from the Allied powers, which preached high ideals but controlled far-flung empires. More importantly, these two policies represented the core of Shigemitsu's broader wish to bring about "the liberation and rebirth of Asia."[14]

Shigemitsu's ideas struck a chord with Prime Minister Tōjō and other leading policy makers. Facing a string of military failures, even members of the high command began to pine for diplomatic successes. Thus, from December 1942 Japan embarked on a new strategy that mirrored the very policies Shigemitsu had been advocating.[15] The New China Policy, which gave greater independence to the collaborationist Wang Jingwei regime in Nanjing, represented the first link of this new strategy. Japan announced the end of extraterritorial rights and allowed the Nanjing regime to declare war on Britain and the United States, thus eliminating most vestiges of overt political control. This was part of a naïve attempt toward peace with Chiang Kai-shek. Japanese leaders believed that showing a new sincerity of intentions toward China would set the stage for peace talks with the Nationalist government in Chongqing, to be initiated through the Nanjing government.[16] To implement this new policy, Tōjō invited Shigemitsu to join his administration as foreign minister on April 20, 1943. Shigemitsu joined the cabinet the same day, after gaining Tōjō's consent to enact his strategy for Asia.[17]

The extension of independence to other parts of the Co-Prosperity Sphere constituted the second aspect of Japan's reformulated regional strategy. The willingness to do so predated Shigemitsu's return to Tokyo but was no doubt influenced by his position papers and his aggressive promotion of the New Greater East Asia Policy. On January 21 and again on January 28, 1943, Prime Minister Tōjō made statements in the Imperial Diet calling for the extension of independence to Burma and the Philippines.[18] A March 10 liaison conference followed up on this call, agreeing to grant independence to Burma and calling for the country's leadership under Ba Maw.[19] Shortly after, Japan decided to grant independence to the Philippines—with José P. Laurel as president. A May 31 imperial conference solidified and endorsed these decisions to bestow independence. In the end, Burma and the Philippines received independence on August 1 and October 14, respectively, and on October 21 Japan helped establish in Singapore the Provisional Government of Free India (Azad Hind) under nationalist leader Subhas Chandra Bose.

One should be careful to avoid overstating the extent of this independence. This was the independence of the "new imperialism," in which "sovereign" satellite regimes were controlled indirectly by Japan. Neither Burma nor the Philippines gained true self-determination. Independence instead preserved Japanese leadership and control. As chapter 6 will show, on the same day they announced their independence, both regimes signed agreements that gave the Japanese military wide leeway to intervene in their domestic affairs.[20] Japan could mark nearly all demands for aid, facilities, infrastructure, or territory as military necessities, demands that neither government was able to refuse. Thus, Japan merely bestowed nominal independence to Burma and the Philippines and in the process extended the Manchukuo model of semicolonial governance to Southeast Asia.

This was a decidedly Machiavellian strategy. By 1943, after all, the true importance of Burma and the Philippines lay in the realm of propaganda. Political
leaders no doubt believed that bestowing independence would underscore the
benevolence of Japan's new order. Of course, Japan had little choice but to grant
independence to the Philippines, which had been slated to receive independence
from the United States in 1946. But the promise of independence to Burma had
subtler designs: Burmese independence, many hoped, would fan the flames of
anticolonial nationalism in the British Raj. This hope was present even before the
outbreak of the Pacific War. Most notably, a November 15, 1941, liaison conference adopted a draft plan that sought "to hasten Burmese independence and use
that to spur on Indian independence."[21] Burma's main importance, then, rested
on its effect on India. Independence was always tied to pragmatic concerns.

The third link in Japan's new strategy was a public relations campaign across
Asia. Officials traveled across the empire, making state visits to Manchukuo, the
Philippines, Thailand, and Indonesia. These visits were measures to build support and legitimacy and to demonstrate the power of Asia's new overlord. Prime
Minister Tōjō's trip to the Philippines in May 1943, however, provides a fascinating glimpse into the dynamics of empire. On the one hand, the visit produced
a level of control and scripting over the populace comparable to any totalitar-
ian state. Japanese consul Kihara gave a list of orders to Jorge Vargas in advance
of Tōjō's visit. All residents were expected to wave Japanese flags and greet Tōjō
with screams of "*Banzai!*" as the premier went past. Filipinos were also ordered
to attend the ceremonies held at Luneta Park, and they were instructed to wave
Japanese flags to greet the visitors and break out into applause after each speech.
More than four hundred thousand Filipinos, young and old, braved the fierce
summer sun to watch Tōjō speak. This left the Japanese premier trembling with
excitement. After wearing himself out with bowing and saluting, Tōjō took on
Hitler's affectations, walking through Luneta with his hand held high.[22]

Despite this degree of political theater and control, Tōjō's visit gave Philippine
leaders a chance to influence Japan. According to Satō Kenryō, Tōjō's protégé and
the director of the army ministry's powerful Bureau of Military Affairs, the idea
to hold a regional conference emerged during Tōjō's visit to the Philippines. During his stay, Tōjō received a report from Lt. Gen. Wachi Takaji, chief of staff of the
Japanese Military Administration in the Philippines, which outlined future Philippine president José P. Laurel's concerns about the legitimacy of Japanese rule.
Filipinos, Laurel contended, remained suspicious of Japanese motives. To alleviate such suspicions, Laurel recommended that Japan hold a conference outlining
the nature of postwar economic relations within the Co-Prosperity Sphere. Satō
claims that he and Tōjō took this as a hint. After discussion in Tokyo, Japanese
leaders decided to hold a conference that would bring together the leaders of

Greater East Asian nations.[23] This conference would serve as the fourth and final link of Japan's reformulated strategy.

A May 26 liaison conference and May 31 imperial conference solidified the commitment to holding a conference. But instead of a simple conference on economic relations, Japanese leaders believed this Greater East Asia Conference was part of a new charm offensive to build moral and political support. In this context, Japan would invite leaders of Asia's independent countries to declare their support for the war effort and for the Co-Prosperity Sphere.[24] An October 2 liaison conference formalized the conference details. Participation would be limited to Japan, Manchukuo, China, Thailand, Burma, and the Philippines. The Provisional Government of Free India would attend as an observer. To lend the conference legitimacy, heads of government were to attend as delegates. Policy makers also solidified the date and time, the venue, and the seating arrangement and order of speeches. Most importantly, they formalized the topic for discussion as "clarifying to the world both the firm resolution to prosecute the war to a successful conclusion and the policy of establishing the Greater East Asia Co-Prosperity Sphere."[25] In a sense, then, the Philippines—a subject nation—helped motivate the imperial center to reenvision its own empire.

But this would not have been possible without Japanese support. The decision to hold the conference represented an agreement on a new vision for Japanese foreign policy. Prime Minister Tōjō and the imperial high command saw the conference as a practical means of galvanizing Asian support for the war and undermining Allied morale. Foreign minister Shigemitsu no doubt agreed with these goals, but he also saw the conference as the first step toward the creation of a Greater East Asia Confederation, a group of independent states that would provide for cooperation in the postwar international regime.[26] Shigemitsu and other foreign ministry bureaucrats also hoped the drafting of an idealistic joint declaration—modeled after the Atlantic Charter—would create a more positive image of Japan's war aims in both Britain and the United States.[27] Although Japanese historians often highlight the differences between Tōjō and Shigemitsu, both leaders shared a common understanding of the conference's main purpose. It was intended to rally Asian nations to make war and to convince Britain and the United States to make peace.

The Greater East Asia Conference

The Greater East Asia Conference formally convened at 10 a.m. on November 5, 1943. Each delegation filed into the Imperial Diet Building and the leaders took their seats: Prime Minister Tōjō, Japan; president of the Executive Yuan, Wang Jingwei, the China Nanjing regime; Prime Minister Zhang Jinghui, Manchukuo;

FIGURE 4. The leaders of the Greater East Asia Conference. From left to right: Ba Maw (Burma), Zhang Jinghui (Manchukuo), Wang Jingwei (Chinese Nanjing regime), Tōjō Hideki (Japan), Wan Waithayakon (Thailand), José P. Laurel (Republic of the Philippines), and Subhas Chandra Bose (the Provisional Government of Free India). Photo courtesy of *Mainichi shinbun* and Aflo.

FIGURE 5. The attendees of the Greater East Asia Conference. Photo courtesy of *Mainichi shinbun* and Aflo.

Prime Minister Ba Maw, Burma; President José P. Laurel, the Republic of the Philippines; Deputy Prime Minister Prince Wan Waithayakon, Thailand; and Head of State Subhas Chandra Bose, the Provisional Government of Free India. The full attendance at the event was nothing short of miraculous. Both Ba Maw and Prince Wan's planes crashed on the way to Tokyo. Ba Maw's plane crash-landed on some thatched huts, which cushioned the fall and saved him from certain death. And Prince Wan survived a plane crash on takeoff, only to be hit by a fever of 104 degrees Fahrenheit (40 degrees Celsius) after arriving in Tokyo. Prince Wan felt well enough, however, to attend the afternoon session of the first day.

Policy makers carefully scripted the conference to promote the legitimacy of Japan's regional leadership. Conference designers thus took great pains to create an atmosphere of apparent equality. Statements of opinion by each representative were to occur in Japanese alphabetical order (*iroha jun*) so no representative could claim special treatment. More importantly, Prime Minister Tōjō declined to issue a keynote address. He instead took the stage and merely suggested the conference begin with the selection of a chairman. This too had been scripted in advance. Conference planners arranged for the Thai representative to introduce a motion— seconded by the Philippines—nominating the Japanese representative as chairman.

FIGURE 6.   Tōjō greets the delegates of the Greater East Asia Conference. Photo courtesy of *Mainichi shinbun* and Aflo.

The scripting of this motion shows just how far Japanese leaders went to present an air of equality and to demonstrate widespread acceptance of Japan's legitimate political leadership. This act of political theater created an important image. Just as each representative supported Tōjō as the unquestioned leader of the conference, each nation supported Japan as the head of the Co-Prosperity Sphere.

Tōjō's opening speech reflected this attempt to build legitimacy. The premier justified the Greater East Asia War as a Pan-Asian war, a collective struggle in pursuit of self-defense, stability, and progress. In this context, he dismissed U.S. and British war aims and ideologies as smoke screens for "sinister designs of aggression" and colonial intent.[28] Tōjō accused Britain and the United States of hindering world progress "by advocating freedom and equality while oppressing and discriminating against other nations and peoples, by imposing the Open Door on others while monopolizing vast territories and natural resources, and by threatening the existence of others without compunction."[29] Japan's new order, he argued, was thus a dramatic departure, a benign force for peace and prosperity. To this end, Tōjō stressed six building blocks for the new order: close-knit cooperative relations, respect for independence and sovereignty, a spirit of justice endemic to the region, the enhancement of the culture, economic cooperation, and efforts to contribute to the progress of humankind. These points were enshrined in the Greater East Asia Joint Declaration, adopted the following day. It is appropriate to note here that Tōjō's new internationalist language maintained striking similarities to that of the United States and Great Britain. But Tōjō implied that whereas the Anglo-American powers were duplicitous in promoting these ideals, Japan was sincere. Japan's mission was to replace the oppressive and deceitful Anglo-American order with one embodying fairness, justice, prosperity, and understanding.

This speech is a poor indication of Tōjō's personal views. Tōjō indeed believed that Anglo-American rhetoric sugarcoated policies of exploitation and domination across the world. But he had little faith in fostering true independence and autonomy. For instance, despite calling for Burmese independence, Tōjō continually spoke of Burma in colonial terms. In a Privy Council discussion on July 29, 1943, Tōjō declared, "Burma is more a newborn than a child." As a newborn, Burma needed the strong, fatherly guiding hand of Japan. Tōjō recognized the demeaning effect this would have on the Burmese pride. He thus cautioned council members to "outwardly maintain the [façade of] complete equality."[30] But when push came to shove, Tōjō recognized that Japan could keep the Burmese in line. "As long as we have our military power," he boasted, "we know we have Burma by the throat."[31] This statement, made three days before Burma received independence, is a striking admission of the little regard Japanese elites held for independence. But the turning tides of war necessitated the trumpeting of new values. Tōjō acted as the mouthpiece of this new internationalism, regardless of his private beliefs.

Following Tōjō's speech, each representative declared his nation's support for the war and the Greater East Asia Co-Prosperity Sphere. A closer examination, however, reveals a spectrum of reactions to Japan's war aims, from enthusiastic support to passive resistance. Ba Maw, Subhas Chandra Bose, and Zhang Jinghui were the most enthusiastic. Wang Jingwei, José P. Laurel, and Prince Wan Waithayakon were more reserved, even showing signs of passive resistance.

The two leaders who showed the most enthusiasm for Japan's new order were Ba Maw and Bose. Ba Maw's support pervades not only his speech at the conference but also his recollection of the party held at Tōjō's residence the evening prior. He describes the meeting of Asian leaders at Tōjō's residence in melodramatic terms. Although the two were meeting for the first time, it was "as if we had known each other all our lives, and had lost and now found one another again." Ba Maw pushed his melodrama even further, arguing that he was among "Asians rediscovering Asia."[32]

These rosy feelings extended to his speech. Ba Maw spoke of the conference as one of epochal importance. Asians had not been able gather together in years past, as they had been kept divided and estranged by "enemy Powers." Thus, he roared, finally "an East Asiatic-Assembly is sitting in the capital of East Asia. . . . For the first time in history, the East-Asiatic peoples are meeting together as members of a free and equal brotherhood which is founded upon and consecrated to the truth that East Asia is one and indivisible."[33] This new world, Ba Maw stressed, was thanks to Japanese power and purpose. Japan not only vanquished the European colonial powers; it also rallied East Asian peoples and even bestowed independence on Burma and the Philippines. There was still much critical work left for Co-Prosperity Sphere members, most pressingly the creation of a free India. But since the new order would be built on the shared internationalist principles of justice, reciprocity, and mutual respect for independence and autonomy, Ba Maw declared that it "will stand like a rock forever."

Bose, who only spoke once at the end of the second day, made the most forceful and eloquent speech in support of the new order. He began by noting the differences between the Greater East Asia Conference and past international conferences since 1815. The Tokyo conference was unique because it intended neither to victimize nor to defraud weaker powers. Instead, Bose declared the conference "an Assembly of liberated nations" that is trying to create a new order centered on "the sacred principles of justice, national sovereignty, reciprocity in international relations and mutual aid and assistance." Thus the Co-Prosperity Sphere had already garnered great interest from oppressed peoples in West Asia and Africa who had succumbed to Anglo-American imperialism. The colonial world, he believed, could aid Japan in the creation of a better future. Bose thus saw the Greater East Asia Co-Prosperity Sphere as a first step toward an "All-Asia Co-Prosperity Sphere," an entity that would herald "a world federation, a real society of nations, and not the League of robbers that we saw at Geneva." This idea contains an implicit note of caution. By stressing the creation of a "real society" as opposed to a "League of robbers," Bose pressed Japan to avoid becoming another League of Nations, which failed to act in support of its own high ideals of national self-determination.

This enthusiastic support does not mean that Ba Maw and Bose were mere puppets manipulated by Tokyo. Far from it, both leaders were dyed-in-the-wool nationalists. These patriotic collaborators shared an admiration for Japan as the first nation to put the imperialist West on the defensive, and this regard persisted even after witnessing Japanese aggression firsthand.[34] But mere admiration paled by comparison to the political benefits to be gained from working with Japan. Both leaders held the firm conviction that collaboration could bring about the end of British colonial rule and beget the very indigenous rule that the League of Nations failed to support after World War I. Ba Maw, for instance, was keen to defend Burma's war-born independence (and his own political leadership) at all costs. Bose supported Japan for similar reasons. Granted, he had been highly critical of Japan's war in China, and in 1937 he wrote a famous essay that rejected for India's future the very imperialism Japan embraced.[35] But Bose viewed Japan's wartime expansion as creating a unique opportunity to destroy the foundations of British rule over South Asia. Moreover, his government in exile owed its existence to support from Japan. The fate of both Indian and Burmese independent governments thus hinged on Japan's war. Victory could lead to self-government; defeat could bring back the firm grip of British rule to the subcontinent. With such stakes at play, it is small wonder that Bose and Ba Maw threw in their lot with Japan.

Bose profited from such cooperation. With Japan's backing, he served as the leader of the Indian nationalist movement in East Asia and as the head of state of the nationalist government in exile. During the Greater East Asia Conference, he received yet another boon from Japan. Immediately after Bose's speech, Prime Minister Tōjō announced, to thunderous applause, the return of the Andaman and Nicobar Islands in the Bay of Bengal to the Provisional Government of Free India. This was done in response to Bose's request for the Andaman Islands at a November 1 meeting with Tōjō.[36] By returning the Nicobar Islands as well, Tōjō hoped to display to both Bose and the world the magnanimity of Japanese leadership.

Zhang Jinghui, too, demonstrated his support and highlighted the founding of Manchukuo as "the first powerful step toward the construction of the Greater

East Asia Co-Prosperity Sphere." Zhang hinted that his country could be held as a model for the new order. To this end, Zhang went as far as to quote Tōjō's January 1943 statement, which spoke of the Manchukuo of today as showing the potential of "what may be the entire Greater East Asia region of tomorrow."[37] But despite the triumphalism of his language, it is difficult to read anything into this speech other than resigned acquiescence. Zhang was known to be a "yes man," and was derided as the "Give-them-what-they-want" prime minister. Perhaps this owed to the fact that he saw the future of any ethnic Manchurian state as bound to Japan. Both Japan and Manchukuo, he once said, were "two dragonflies tied to the same string." Whatever criticisms he may have harbored about Japanese imperialism, he continually stood at the forefront of pro-Japanese cooperation.[38]

The other three representatives—Wang Jingwei, José P. Laurel, and Prince Wan Waithayakon—demonstrated more reserved support. Both Wang and Laurel subtly used their speeches to voice discontent with Japanese hegemony and to push for an egalitarian international order. Wang's grievances were embedded in the language he used to describe the Co-Prosperity Sphere. He stressed that the Sphere should be built on close-knit relations and a respect for "independence and autonomy" of member states. His speech was replete with such phrases as: "When China has gained independence and autonomy, then she can shoulder her share in the responsibilities for the defence of East Asia; when the defence of East Asia has been secured, then will China's independence and autonomy be guaranteed."[39]

In fact, the most striking aspect of Wang's speech is the extent to which he emphasized the phrase "independence and autonomy."[40] In all, he repeated the phrase as many as twenty times during his three conference speeches. It is reasonable to assume that this resulted from frustrations the nominally independent regime felt under Japanese rule. Wang had defected from Chiang Kai-shek's Nationalist government in 1938 to head the collaborationist Nanjing regime, which was inaugurated in March 1940. But he stepped into a government that lacked sovereignty. Until 1943, Japan did not allow Nanjing to make any important policy moves (such as declaring war against the Allied powers) and refused to end extraterritoriality on Chinese soil. Moreover, even the extension of these new privileges did not dramatically alter the military or political situation on the ground. Military occupation begot political authority, which the Japanese military had not been reluctant to use in the past.[41] Wang's emphasis on independence and autonomy, then, suggests frustrations his weak regime felt toward its stronger partner.

Laurel, too, did not hesitate to utilize Japanese rhetoric in a subtle criticism of Japan's new order. Although the main thrust supported Japan's war and postwar aims, his speech contained underlying currents of dissent. The foremost of these included a discreet reminder that the new order was not meant to benefit Japan alone. Laurel deftly quoted Tōjō's address, highlighting the premier's use of the phrases "independence and autonomy" and "brotherly amity." The significance of these guiding principles, he noted, was that they demonstrated a single important fact. The "Greater East Asia Co-Prosperity Sphere," Laurel argued, "is not being established for the benefit of any integral unit of that Sphere." That is, the new order was not meant to benefit any single country. Instead, the Co-Prosperity Sphere should promote the prosperity of all. "The prosperity of all," he insisted, "is the prosperity of the integral parts, but the prosperity of the integral parts is not necessarily the prosperity of the whole."[42]

Laurel also used the conference to express solidarity with Indonesia, to which Japan had granted neither independence nor an invitation to the conference. The Japanese government refused to grant Indonesia independence owing to the territory's inherent value as a "treasure trove" of aluminum, oil, nickel, rubber, and other resources. In fact, the May 31, 1943, imperial conference noted above decided to incorporate Malaya, Sumatra, Java, Borneo, and the Celebes into the Japanese Empire, to be formally controlled by Japan.[43] It is uncertain whether Laurel knew of this decision, but he clearly recognized Japan's unwillingness to grant Indonesian independence. Moreover, Laurel was not even allowed to use the term "Indonesia" in his speech. Tokyo had banned the use of the term.[44] Laurel instead stressed unity with all parts of East Asia, including "the peoples of Java, Borneo, and Sumatra, whose interests cannot be different from those of other peoples of Greater East Asia."[45] This comment represented a subtle but strong criticism of the contradictions within Japan's new internationalism. The refusal to grant independence to Indonesia belied Japanese rhetoric of promoting independence and autonomy, and of establishing a fair and just order. What did Japan's new order of independence and cooperation really mean if not applied to all nations and peoples?

These criticisms resulted not only from the gap between rhetoric and reality but also from conditions in the Philippines. By 1943, most Filipinos had become disillusioned with the reality of Japanese occupation. Despite attaining independence, Japan maintained a strong military presence on Philippine soil. Moreover, the occupation forces had become notorious for discriminatory, arrogant, and cruel behavior. The imperial army condoned slapping or beating Filipinos on the slightest provocation, jailing people without providing information about the charges against them, forcibly recruiting laborers, exacting collective responsibility for guerrilla acts, and evacuating Philippine homes so that they could be occupied by Japanese forces. And the dungeons of Fort Santiago became well known for the torture and murder of countless Filipinos. The brutality and total domination of the Japanese occupation led to continued protests by Philippine leaders. Most famously, on June 20, 1944, Philippine foreign minister Claro M. Recto wrote an impassioned plea to Lt. Gen. Wachi Takaji (who was then a liaison officer to the Japanese embassy in Manila) protesting the behavior of occupation forces.[46]

Laurel abhorred the realities of occupation. He laid bare this resentment in a February 1944 meeting with Dr. Victor Buencamino. "I am faced with many tremendous difficulties," Laurel complained. "This independence we have is an independence which is not independence. You have the [Japanese] Navy on one side, the [Japanese] Army on the other, the guerrilla, the Embassy and my own government. Five in all!"[47] And Laurel received updates that described the mal-treatment of Filipinos by Japanese soldiers and civilians.[48] Such conditions in the Philippines lend credibility to Laurel's postwar comment comparing the Philip-pines to a concentration camp, with Fort Santiago "as the gruesome center of gloom and horror."[49] The reality of the occupation lay behind Laurel's criticisms of the new order and led him to (ever so subtly) press the Japanese to practice what they preached.

The Wang and Laurel speeches at the conference thus highlight the double-edged nature of Japan's internationalist rhetoric. Once articulated, such rhetoric became part of the language of international relations that could be used by both stronger and weaker states. Whereas Japan developed such rhetoric to promote legitimacy and leadership, leaders of weaker states, such as Wang and Laurel, could co-opt it in pursuit of domestic interests and more equal foreign relations. By repeatedly stressing Japan's newfound rhetoric, Wang and Laurel no doubt hoped to curb Japanese domination and to create a future of true partnership and harmonious relations.

It was the Thai delegation, however, that showed the strongest form of resistance. As noted above, Japanese governmental officials wanted only heads of state to represent their respective countries. The wily Prime Minister Phibun, however, refused to attend the conference, citing health reasons. Tokyo leaders had feared this would be the case and had sent a telegram to the Japanese embassy in Thai-land warning that his absence would "kill the significance of the conference" and "send a message to the world that Japan-Thai relations are unfavorable."[50] Adding insult to injury, Counselor Ishii Kō of the Japanese embassy in Thailand stated that health reasons were a poor excuse, as Phibun talked of playing tennis often.[51] Phibun remained adamant, however, and even threatened to resign rather than take the trip to Tokyo. Japanese authorities were backed into a corner. They did not wish to threaten the legitimacy of the conference by having the Thai premier resign shortly before the opening ceremony, so had no recourse but to choose an alternate representative. Prince Wan "represented the consensus choice."[52] The reality of Phibun's absence, however, weighed on the minds of Japanese leaders even during the conference. Phibun had made a powerful statement in refusing to attend. Hence Satō Kenryō wrote of Phibun's absence as representing the "one stain" on the event, and the Japanese foreign ministry reported that it "diminished the [conference's] significance."[53]

Perhaps as a conciliatory gesture, Prince Wan went to great lengths to stress the strong and close relationship between Thailand and Japan. Prince Wan spoke at length of the two nations as natural military, political, and economic partners, both committed to the "high purpose" of Japan's war and maintaining "a good understanding of one another." He further conveyed appreciation for the return of territories in the Malai and Shan regions, and for Japan's respect of Thai independence and sovereignty.[54] Prince Wan ended his speech by expressing gratitude and pledging cooperation in the Co-Prosperity Sphere. Nonetheless, this conciliatory attitude failed to appease Japanese officials, who maintained a noticeably cold attitude toward the Thai delegation.

The Pacific Charter

The climax of the conference came on November 6, with the unanimous decision to approve the Greater East Asia Joint Declaration. Adopted formally the following day, this declaration articulated the principles that would undergird the new order. This was Japan's Pacific Charter, meant in opposition to the Atlantic Charter:

> It is the basic principle for the establishment of world peace that the nations of the world have each its proper place, and enjoy prosperity in common through mutual aid and assistance.
>
> The United States of America and the British Empire have in seeking their own prosperity oppressed other nations and peoples. Especially in East Asia, they indulged in insatiable aggression and exploitation, and sought to satisfy their inordinate ambition of enslaving the entire region, and finally they came to menace seriously the stability of East Asia. Herein lies the cause of the present war.
>
> The countries of Greater East Asia, with a view to contributing to the cause of world peace, undertake to cooperate toward prosecuting the War of Greater East Asia to a successful conclusion, liberating their region from the yoke of British-American domination, and assuring their self-existence and self-defense, and in constructing a Greater East Asia in accordance with the following principles:
>
> 1. The countries of Greater East Asia through mutual cooperation will ensure the stability of their region and construct an order of common prosperity and well-being based upon justice.

2. The countries of Greater East Asia will ensure the fraternity of nations in their region, by respecting one another's sovereignty and independence and practicing mutual assistance and amity.

3. The countries of Greater East Asia by respecting one another's traditions and developing the creative faculties of each race, will enhance the culture and civilization of Greater East Asia.

4. The countries of Greater East Asia will endeavor to accelerate their economic development through close cooperation upon a basis of reciprocity and to promote thereby the general prosperity of their region.

5. The countries of Greater East Asia will cultivate friendly relations with all the countries of the world, and work for the abolition of racial discriminations, the promotion of cultural intercourse and the opening of resources throughout the world, and contribute thereby to the progress of mankind.[55]

These points can be condensed into five basic ideas: (1) mutual cooperation; (2) independence and friendly relations; (3) the enhancement of cultures and civilizations; (4) mutual economic development and prosperity; and (5) the abolition of racial discrimination and contribution to the progress of mankind. Strikingly, the new language of cooperation, independence, and friendship sat uncomfortably next to older, Japanist notions of "each its proper place."

Japan's Pacific Charter was, in fact, an amalgamation of two documents—one drafted by the Greater East Asia Ministry and the other by the foreign ministry.[56] This accounts for the document's uncomfortable marrying of Japanist and liberal internationalist rhetoric. The Greater East Asia Ministry draft was created by the National Policy Research Association, with detailed input from Ōkawa Shūmei and Yabe Teiji.[57] But general staff leaders did not feel the Greater East Asia Ministry draft to be an acceptable document for highlighting the new era of international relations. On October 14, 1943, the War Guidance section of the general staff complained that draft "is not satisfactory. At times it is crammed full of ideology [rinen ni hashirite] and distant from reality, and at other times it uses expressions like 'spirit of the Imperial Way,' so it will not generate common understanding among the peoples of Greater East Asia."[58]

Much more is known about the foreign ministry drafts, most of which were drawn up and discussed by the War Aims Research Association from August to October 1943. The foreign ministry drafts sponsored, in a variety of forms, the main principles included in the final declaration: political equality and autonomy, respect for culture, economic prosperity, and contributions to humankind.[59] The final drafts from both ministries were combined on October 20 and adopted, with subtle changes, at a liaison conference three days later. This resulted in an ideologically inconsistent document. The introductory statement outlined the official position of the Greater East Asia Ministry, while the five points—the essence of the declaration—constituted that of the foreign ministry.

The Joint Declaration represented Japan's answer to the Atlantic Charter. It is thus of little surprise that the drafters of the foreign ministry's five principles referred to the Atlantic Charter when drawing up the document, and that there are strong similarities between the two documents. The Joint Declaration's emphasis on "sovereignty and independence" is equivalent to the Atlantic Charter's stress on national self-determination and "sovereign rights and self-government." Both documents call for similar measures in the economic realm. Both sought to advance international cooperation for economic development, to promote economic prosperity, and to guarantee equal access to markets and resources. And both the Joint Declaration and the Atlantic Charter stressed stability, peace, and prosperity for all.

The similarity between the two documents was not lost on contemporaries. Japanese intellectuals and newspapermen immediately declared the declaration a "Pacific Charter" or a "Greater East Asia Charter" written in opposition to the Atlantic Charter.[60] Liberal critic Kiyosawa Kiyoshi dryly noted, "It is Japan's tragedy that it had to draft a declaration that resembles the Atlantic Charter, granting independence and freedom to all peoples." Kiyosawa was no doubt criticizing the shift away from Pan-Asian rhetoric, which negated the notion that Japan was waging a war in the name of Asian solidarity.[61] Even foreign minister Shigemitsu could only weakly brush off similarities by stating that the Joint Declaration "is not a simple statement of principles like the Atlantic Charter, but a declaration of policy to be promoted by each country at the conference."[62]

Greater East Asian leaders and conference attendees noted the similarities as well. Philippine president Laurel wrote in his memoirs, "The idea of co-prosperity is found in the Atlantic Charter no less than in the Pacific Charter. Fundamentally, they [charters] coincide in the enunciation of many vital principles!"[63] Burmese prime minister Ba Maw, who was shown a copy of the declaration a week before the conference, immediately recognized that the declaration was meant in opposition to the Atlantic Charter. He then argued to the Japanese ambassador in Burma that the declaration should not be limited to the region. It should be a worldwide call for the support from all peoples who hold negative views of Britain and the United States, including Arabs, Egyptians, and Palestinians.[64] Although the ambassador recognized the merit in this critique, Japanese policy makers had no intention of changing the declaration.[65]

There is good reason why the two documents shared such similarities, and why foreign ministry officials referred to the Atlantic Charter when drafting the

Joint Declaration. Japanese authorities had struggled to forge an ideology that would win the hearts and minds of political elites in the region. This resulted from longer-term trends in Japanese political culture. Foreign policy since the late Meiji period operated as a realist pursuit of national power. Ideology played a mostly negligible role in the attainment of empire. From the 1930s, however, Pan-Asianism took a stronger foothold among Japanese political elites owing to Japan's intellectual and political revolt against the West.[66] Japanese leaders used Pan-Asianism as part of a propaganda campaign in support of war in China and the new order. But Pan-Asianism never had a defined ideological program or systematic doctrine, and it lacked a positive program that Japanese leaders could use to gain allegiance in the region. The urgency of forging a compelling ideology once the war turned against Japan led the foreign ministry drafters of the declaration back to Anglo-American internationalist language. They no doubt found in Wilsonian liberal internationalist language a way to resolve Japan's crisis of legitimacy. Borrowing Wilsonian language does not suggest, as Akira Iriye argues, a return to values held in the 1920s.[67] Instead, it reveals a pragmatic response to the realities of war. Japanese elites were willing to utilize values known to have broad appeal to rally Asian support for Japan's imperial project. Wilsonian values would reinforce Japan's Pan-Asian mission to create an Asia for the Asians.

This pragmatic attitude led Tokyo to accept the greatest difference between the two documents: the clause abolishing racial discrimination. At its core, this clause appears extremely idealistic—more so than the Atlantic Charter, which lacked provisions for racial equality. But conflict within leadership circles over whether to include the clause reveals the pragmatic aims behind the use of such language. According to Lt. Gen. Satō Kenryō, assistant secretaries in the foreign, army, and navy ministries argued that the clause would prove an obstacle to reaching a separate peace with the Allied powers. The Allied powers, after all, had opposed the inclusion of a racial equality clause at the Paris peace conference of 1919. The navy ministry came up with a revision plan that changed the phrase "abolish racial discrimination" to "devotion to mutual love among humankind."[68] But Satō insisted that since Japan was fighting with the very "conquerors" that opposed the clause, Japan ought to call for the abolition of racial discrimination. Moreover, Satō added that this would both "win public sentiment" and breed fear among the Allied powers that the war would devolve into a race war.[69] Satō's arguments held the day, and the clause remained unchanged. The lack of idealism behind this revolutionary clause is telling. Japanese leaders enshrined it in the declaration to provide Tokyo with sufficient leverage to end the war on favorable terms.

The Joint Declaration was thus a formidable weapon for ideological warfare. Many Japanese intellectuals jumped on the bandwagon, dismissing the Atlantic

Charter as propaganda that was worth no more than the paper on which it was written. Granted, many appreciated the Atlantic Charter as an abstract statement for peace and order. "But we too are fighting for the same principles!" declared Tokyo Imperial University professor Yabe Teiji in a paper he wrote between 1943 and 1944.[70] The problem was not whether the Allied powers professed internationalist principles. The issue was instead which order *upheld* such principles. Japanese intellectuals agreed that despite high-sounding ideals, British and American foreign policies stressed realist notions of hard power.

There was much truth to such criticisms. Arch-imperialist British prime minister Winston Churchill, for instance, remained unwilling to return self-rule to India and other countries across Africa and Asia. The Allied powers also allowed the Soviet Union to secure postwar hegemony in Finland, the Baltic States, Poland, and Romania. Furthermore, Japanese intellectuals argued that although free trade and the Open Door might be splendid principles, they only served to undergird British and American domination of global economic life. Thus Tokyo Imperial University professor Kamikawa Hikomatsu contended that the Atlantic Charter established an international society in which the wolves ruled the sheep. The ideas of freedom and equality expressed in the Atlantic Charter, Kamikawa insisted, were freedom and equality for the wolves alone. The sheep remained cowering in an unfree and unequal world of servitude and slavery.[71]

Kamikawa marshaled the most forceful arguments for the authentic morality of the Joint Declaration versus the hypocrisy of the Atlantic Charter. He saw the Joint Declaration as "the firing of the first deadly hemispheric shot at the old world capitalist-imperialist structure favored by Britain and the United States."[72] It represented the birth of a new era of Asian values and ideals, and a new utopian culture of international relations. Kamikawa believed the Joint Declaration phrase emphasizing "common prosperity and well-being based upon justice" served as the cultural-political guiding light behind the new order. Politically, the phrase implied a break from Anglo-American world control that had inhibited true equality, freedom, and cooperation. Economically, it signified the end to profit-oriented economics and Anglo-American capitalist oppression. Henceforth economics would serve not material but ethical ends, and the market would be utilized to promote stability and prosperity among all countries and peoples. Internationally, the phrase highlighted the Co-Prosperity Sphere's role as a progressive force for humankind, one that would ensure global peaceful relations as well as the elimination of Western racial prejudice.[73] Kamikawa thus envisioned a utopian Joint Declaration, which thrust aside the Atlantic Charter's instruments of exploitation for those of understanding, peace, and stability. To Kamikawa, Japan's Pacific Charter was an unmitigated success for Pan-Asian ideals and the harbinger of an Asian renaissance. These understandings of Japan's war aims, as Jessamyn Abel shows, were shared across a wide segment of the Japanese intellectual community.[74]

Not all Japanese pundits, however, supported the Joint Declaration. Yabe Teiji, who led the navy brain trust's September 1942 vision for the Co-Prosperity Sphere, recoiled from Japan's new rhetoric. He remained wed to the idea that Japan must reject Anglo-American notions of "liberty" or "freedom."[75] Japan's task, Yabe believed, was to establish "true liberty" (*shin no jiyū*) through a hierarchical model of international relations, one that imposed family-state norms onto the international system and, in return, provided cultural understanding, respect, and the "right to exist." Yabe thus rejected the Joint Declaration as running counter to Japan's quest for a new order. He even criticized Shigemitsu's turn to Wilsonian internationalist language. "Foreign minister Shigemitsu," Yabe wrote in his diary on October 27, 1943, "like always, is preaching equality and reciprocity."[76] Yabe believed that this was no different from the international order Japan was trying to overthrow.

Yabe, in fact, helped craft a separate draft joint declaration advanced by the National Policy Research Association. This declaration, which would be championed by the Greater East Asia Ministry in the lead-up to the conference, rejected equality and reciprocity in favor of Japanist and Pan-Asian values. Yabe's joint declaration saw "everlasting peace in Greater East Asia" as emerging from ideas of "each to its proper place," Japan's National Founding Spirit, and a region-wide system of "familial communal relations."[77] Instead of pairing Japan's Pan-Asian mission with Wilsonian internationalism, Yabe called on Japanese leaders to double down on Japanism and Asianism alone. But he found few leaders willing to champion his cause. Yabe remained powerless to stop Japan's liberal internationalist turn, and from 1943 he remained on the sidelines of Japan's political life.

For their part, Greater East Asia Conference representatives were ecstatic that Japan committed these new principles to paper. Whether they believed in Japan's ability to practice what it preached was immaterial. Ba Maw publicly expressed his appreciation for the racial equality clause. He further stressed that the declaration was applicable to the whole world.[78] Bose noted that the Joint Declaration was a "charter for liberty," one intended for the "suppressed nations of the whole world."[79] And Wang Jingwei was particularly pleased with the racial equality clause. To Wang, the elimination of racial discrimination set the Joint Declaration apart from the United States, which practiced racial prejudice within its own borders. [80]

José P. Laurel, however, maintained the most conflicted view. On the one hand, he acknowledged the progressive nature of the document, and even after returning to the Philippines he declared the Joint Declaration a "great human charter." Laurel further stressed his respect for the provisions guaranteeing freedom and equality to all, and that these provisions convinced him to cast his vote in favor of the document.[81] But owing to his experience with Japanese occupation forces, Laurel privately doubted the willingness of Japan to enforce such principles. He stated in his memoirs: "Personally, however, I did not believe that the avowed lofty purposes therein embodied could be realized with Japan's militaristic and economic plan of expansion, her background and experience in colonial adventures, and with Japan as 'the centripetal power.' But a small country is a small country and a weak people is a weak people. We had no choice and everything depended on the result of the war. My duty was to tide our people over to better times and lead them to national survival."[82]

Memoirs, of course, should be read with caution. But this postwar statement is consistent with his private views on Japanese policies. It is thus not a far stretch to suggest that Laurel saw the Joint Declaration as little more than propaganda. But since this propaganda formed the new language of Co-Prosperity Sphere international relations, he recognized that it could be used to the advantage of weaker states. And Laurel did just that in a November 20, 1943, speech meant for the people of Japan. He stressed that he voted to approve the declaration owing to its guarantee for "free and equal treatment to all members of the Co-Prosperity Sphere, irrespective of size or strength."[83]

In fact, Laurel even used the Joint Declaration to protest Japanese infringements on Philippine industry. On July 26, 1944, he objected to the Japanese military's use of the Alabang Biological Laboratory, located on the outskirts of Manila. The appropriation of the laboratory inhibited the Philippines' ability to produce biological products, serums, or vaccines necessary to nurture scientific industries. Strikingly, Laurel appealed to both the Greater East Asia Joint Declaration and the Pact of Alliance in making his case. "The fundamental as well as the practical need is collaboration, not absorption," he argued. "If the important activities of the Republic are absorbed or taken over fully by the Imperial Japanese Government, then the Republic will be placed in a position of being obligated to collaborate without the means of effecting that collaboration, and collaboration then becomes purely academic."[84] Laurel insisted that Japan should provide the republic with the opportunity to produce goods, even military necessities, for the Japanese army. Only through actual production would the quality of serums and vaccines improve at Alabang. Nonetheless, there is no evidence that Japan budged on the matter.

The Ba Maw regime also found Japan's Pacific Charter useful to raise objections about Japanese activities in Burma. On his return to Burma, Ba Maw extensively publicized the aims of the Joint Declaration.[85] But when the opportunity arose, he also used the declaration to protest violations of Burmese sovereignty. His government, for instance, tried to gain control over shipping by demanding the registration of all vessels with the Burmese government. This order was aimed at Japanese firms, which had seized Burmese ships or procured them under the new order demand request system. Burmese leaders hoped to utilize these vessels in the interest of local industry. They pointed out to Japanese staff officers the iniquities of this system, which prevented Burma's ability to safeguard civilian interests. Such a "special exemption of Japanese civilian firms," they argued, "was not in keeping with the Greater East Asia Declaration." But Japan refused to budge. Once the issue reached the highest levels of the Burmese and Japanese governments, it was swept under the rug. A scapegoat was found in the director of civil transport, on whom sole blame was laid.[86]

No doubt in response to such demands, in November 1944 Lt. Gen. Kimura Heitarō, commander in chief of Japan's Burma Area Army, spoke in Rangoon to caution restraint. He urged the Burmese to "trust implicitly in Nippon's sincerity" and argued that full independence would be promoted as part of a gradual process, to be completed after war's end. For now, however, Burma needed "to harmonize the civilian and military needs of the country." This required sacrifices, as Burma needed to go through "war time quasi-civil administration" before finally reaching "the normal peacetime form of government" after war's end.[87] Kimura's comments underlined the fact that the Imperial Japanese Army viewed the Pacific Charter as a worthless piece of paper, or as an inconvenience to be summarily dismissed. The Burmese would have to "trust implicitly" in Japan to practice what it preached after war's end.

Given time, Japan's Pacific Charter might have proved as explosive as the Atlantic Charter. Like the Atlantic Charter, it gave subordinate countries a rhetorical means to protest the realities of Japan's informal empire of dependent, nominal independence. And it gave other directly controlled territories a means to demand their independence from Japan. Moreover, the Pacific Charter gave further cause to resist Japan's war effort. By 1944, Japan had lost any remaining support in Burma and the Philippines. This highlights an important irony behind Japan's adoption of Wilsonian internationalist language. Although promoted in the service of empire, Wilsonian internationalist language became a thorn in the side of Japan's imperial project.

A Reimagined Empire

This chapter has highlighted the Greater East Asia Conference and Joint Declaration as epitomizing a major shift in Japan's Co-Prosperity Sphere: the turn to liberal internationalism. Japanese leaders reoriented the nation's policy to supporting limited independence among select countries, and they formulated a new internationalist language for intraregional cooperation. The motives behind such policies, however, were largely pragmatic. With the war looking increasingly bleak, the imperial high command sought to rally support from the very Asian nations Japan dominated. Elites in the foreign ministry had the added goal of crafting language that would convince British and American leaders of the righteousness of Japan's war aims. Thus there were two main goals behind the liberal internationalist turn: to rally Asian nations to fight and to bring the Allied powers to the negotiating table. The ultimate purpose, however, was the survival of the Co-Prosperity Sphere and the Japanese Empire. Internationalism served both imperial and Pan-Asian ends.

This engagement with liberal internationalism would only strengthen as Japan's war situation worsened. On April 23, 1945, less than four months before the emperor made the historic decision to surrender, Japan convened a second Greater East Asia conference. Owing to the dangers of traveling during an increasingly unpromising war, participation was limited mainly to the Japanese foreign minister and Greater East Asia minister Tōgō Shigenori and ambassadors from China, Manchukuo, Burma, the Philippines, and Thailand (India had no ambassador and thus was absent). Since the conference centered around the ambassadors, this second conference has become known as the Greater East Asia Ambassadors Conference.

FIGURE 7.   The much smaller scale of the Greater East Asia Ambassadors Conference, April 1945. Photo courtesy of *Mainichi shinbun* and Aflo.

Much smaller in size and held when defeat loomed just over the horizon, the Ambassadors Conference was but a shell of the former glory of the 1943 conference.

Despite its small scale, the conference's vision was much bigger. Since Japan saw a real need to mobilize Asian sentiment behind Japan's cause, the Ambassadors Conference adopted even more egalitarian measures than those promoted at the 1943 conference. The most important of these include the decisions to support Indochinese and East Indonesian independence.[88] In doing so, Japanese leaders agreed to relinquish their hold over areas (particularly Indonesia) the army had seen as critical for its natural resource needs. Participants also adopted a joint statement—drafted by the foreign ministry—that echoed the 1943 Pacific Charter. But the joint statement went much further. It also called for "the liberation of all peoples from their colonial status" and renounced any moves to intervene in the other countries' domestic affairs. The statement called for free trade and "the elimination of military armaments," which would rid the world of economic and military threats. Finally, it pushed for a collective security mechanism to keep the peace and help prevent any reoccurrence of the scourge of global war. This mutual security organization, however, would be different from the League of Nations. It would not be subject to the arbitrary control of stronger states or the application of uniform methods across the world. Instead, it would be based on a system of "regional security guarantees" that would work in combination with a global organization to keep the global peace.[89]

Owing to these differences, diplomatic historian Hatano Sumio argues that the "regionalism" of the 1943 Joint Declaration became the "universalism" of the 1945 joint statement.[90] This newfound stress on "universal" principles also hinted at a radical reinterpretation of the Pacific War in early 1945. No longer was Japan simply fighting for the liberation of Asia. Japan was now also fighting to do away altogether with war, aggression, and exploitation. The principles of nonaggression, the elimination of military armaments, and the creation of regional and global security organizations to ensure peace across the world had become by April 1945 the very point of Japan's Pacific War. By war's end, then, people could choose to reinterpret both the Pacific War and the Co-Prosperity Sphere as humanitarian projects that would ensure the end of empire and herald the emergence of a peaceful, progressive international order. The closer Japan came to defeat on the battlefield, the more leaders paired Japan's Pan-Asian mission with liberal internationalist norms.

Japan, of course, was not alone in opportunistically using liberal internationalist values in the service of empire. As Japanese intellectuals and pundits were quick to note, Allied propaganda did much the same.[91] While Britain and the United States coproduced the Atlantic Charter, Churchill maintained that it only pertained to the European countries under the yoke of Nazi rule. Moreover, by

June 1943 the British Foreign Office had distanced Britain from the universal application of the Atlantic Charter. In a confidential document (which was not sent to the dominions), the Foreign Office noted that the charter merely "enunciates certain principles" but does not commit its adherents to realize them "in every single case" or to "[treat] all cases alike."[92] Moreover, Churchill remained steadfast in his opposition to self-determination throughout the empire. By 1945, Churchill merely argued, "The Atlantic Charter is a guide, and not a rule."[93] Moreover, although U.S. president Franklin D. Roosevelt was a staunch anticolonialist who lobbied for Indian independence, from 1943 he decided not to confront Churchill over the issue of India's future. Roosevelt also distanced himself from the ideals of the Atlantic Charter, believing instead that any postwar organization to replace the League of Nations must be compatible with a high degree of great power control.[94] The rhetoric and propaganda of both sides of the Pacific War sailed free of real-world constraints.

The rhetoric and reality of the Greater East Asia Conference, however, underscores the dynamism of the Co-Prosperity Sphere ideal. By mid-1943 Japanese leaders had taken the first steps on a different path forward for the new order. They broadened the network of nominally independent satellite regimes and, by holding the Greater East Asia Conference, suggested that these regimes would have critical roles to play in the postwar international order. The lead-up to the conference thus witnessed the height of Japan's new imperialism, appearing at first glance as further support to the notion of the Sphere as an emancipatory creation, or an effort to pursue imperialism without colonies.

A closer look, however, reveals a more interesting dynamic. In important ways, visions for the Co-Prosperity Sphere remained unchanged. The Sphere still constituted an ambitious project for international order, a political hierarchy that joined nominally independent states with colonial territories. Japan only granted independence to the regimes represented at the Greater East Asia Conference (aside from Thailand, which was already independent). Korea and Taiwan received no such guarantees. Instead, both colonies had been given a greater stake in the politics of Japan proper as part of what Takashi Fujitani calls an inclusionary and culturalist regime of "polite racism."[95] Moreover, Malaya and Indonesia were to remain as colonies within the broader Japanese Empire. Throughout the war, then, the Co-Prosperity Sphere embraced both nominally independent, sovereign nations and territories under Japan's direct control. It was only in April 1945 when, in an act of desperation, Japanese leaders called for true independence across Asia. At that point, the Co-Prosperity Sphere was little more than a distant dream.

The rhetoric of the Greater East Asia Conference generated a mixed reaction across Southeast Asia. Some, such as José P. Laurel, viewed independence and

Japan's new internationalism as a fiction designed to perpetuate Japanese control. Others, such as Ba Maw, maintained a sanguine impression of the Greater East Asia Conference for the rest of his life. Despite Japanese occupation-era mistakes, he believed that Japan had fought for a just cause and could have been more successful had the military practiced the Pan-Asianism, the brotherhood, and the trust it preached. Whatever the case, both leaders saw value in Japan's new internationalism and used it to protest infringements on their constrained independence. The rhetoric and reality of independence thus gave subordinate nations a means of criticizing the realities of Japanese rule. Independence, autonomy, and self-determination implied that colonial control would increasingly be met with resistance, if not open rebellion.

This focus on the mixed reaction among participant nations underscores a more significant point: the importance of the periphery in influencing visions of empire. Even with Japan's oppressive wartime empire, the periphery exercised influence, albeit muted, on the metropole. The Greater East Asia Conference, as we have seen, was not solely a Japanese idea. Shigemitsu's push to "counter diplomacy with diplomacy" was no doubt the most important contributing factor. Shigemitsu provided the domestic ideological push to go ahead with the conference. Philippine pressure proved to be yet another driving force behind the conference. Laurel used Tōjō's visit to Manila in May 1943 to warn of Philippine hostility to Japanese rule, and he recommended a conference outlining postwar economic relations within the Co-Prosperity Sphere. Japanese leaders took Laurel's hint and reimagined the nature of the Co-Prosperity Sphere as the embodiment of regional partnership. Granted, this reimagining of the Sphere only happened because it aligned with preexisting ideas held by the Japanese military and political elite. But the very fact of its acceptance highlights the negotiated nature of empire building. In times of discord, visions of empire are prone to be triggered by the weak as well as imposed by the strong.

6

INDEPENDENCE IN TRANSITION

If Burma and the Philippines could be called fortunate in any way during World War II, it would be in their relative unimportance to Tokyo. Japanese leaders coveted their natural resources far less than those of Malaya and the Netherlands Indies, and they had little interest in assuming direct colonial rule. Instead, they saw the true importance of Burma and the Philippines as symbolic. Both polities mattered far more as showcases of Japanese goodwill and as weapons of propaganda against the Allied powers. This desire to wage a propaganda offensive led to early calls to grant independence. As noted in chapter 5, as early as November 1941 Japanese leaders advocated Burmese independence in order to spur on anticolonial nationalism in India, the crown jewel of the British Empire. Japanese involvement in the Philippines, conversely, owed to the strategic necessity of ousting U.S. power from Asia. By demonstrating a commitment to immediate independence, Japanese leaders hoped to paint American promises for independence as disguising imperialist intent. From the outset, bestowing independence to less important regimes constituted a winning hand.

On January 21, January 28, and again on February 26, 1942, Prime Minister Tōjō made statements in the Imperial Diet promising "the honor of independence" to both Burma and the Philippines should they cooperate closely with Japan.[1] As the war situation deteriorated by 1943, Japanese leaders also believed bequeathing independence to select regimes might rally Asia behind Japan's cause and persuade the Allied powers to sue for peace. A January 14, 1943 liaison conference set the basic policy of granting independence. From March for Burma and May for the Philippines, Tokyo moved to fulfill Tōjō's promise.[2] Burma and the Philippines received independence on August 1 and October 14, 1943, respectively.

This independence was in many ways a sham, however. The military regimes maintained control over areas deemed critical to the war effort. Moreover, Japanese forces acted with impunity. They requisitioned agricultural, industrial, and other goods for the war effort, despite noticeable shortages and looming food crises. Physical and emotional abuse abounded. Japanese soldiers became well known in both regimes for unruly, violent behavior, and locals found fearful stories of arrest and torture all too common. In Manila, Fort Santiago became synonymous with the ills of the Japanese occupation, as Japanese forces used its dungeons to mete out inhuman punishments to people suspected of guerrilla or anti-Japanese activities. "The very mention of Fort Santiago," it was said, "would make a crying child quiet down in fear."[3] Even Philippine president José P. Laurel complained that what Japan granted "is not independence." Burmese villagers felt much the same way. Sometimes they protested to the bulls pulling their carts. "Come on, my sons," they screamed, "don't you know this is Independence?" Others, when forced to dig trenches for the Japanese, cynically cried out, "We are digging for independence."[4]

But even sham independence brought opportunity. Nationalist elites in Rangoon and Manila kept their eyes to the future and strove to turn their constrained independence into something more meaningful. They engaged in a process of state building, creating governmental organs their countries lacked in the colonial era. Burmese and Philippine elites populated these new institutions and, in some cases, gained valuable experience in areas of government with which they had little experience. It is this local process of co-opting Japan's new order with which this chapter is concerned. Leaders across the region engaged in what Philippine historian Ricardo T. Jose has called a "test of wills," a diplomacy of duress in which each side pressed for their respective interests.[5] This test of wills in both Manila and Rangoon in small but meaningful ways subverted Japanese informal imperialism to serve local interests. This chapter thus shows the ways in which, for both Burma and the Philippines, Japan's Greater East Asia Co-Prosperity Sphere was useful in the colonial present. Japanese efforts to construct an informal regional imperium ended up playing a role in the eventual transition to postwar independence.

Institutionalizing Independence

Burma was the first to receive independence. On March 10, 1943, a liaison conference adopted a policy plan calling for the creation of an independent Burmese

regime under Ba Maw. To this end, the plan called on Ba Maw to lead a preparatory committee to plan for the structure, organization, and spirit of the new
Burma. But the plan highlighted significant costs for Burma. Although Japanese
advisers did not intervene in preparatory committee deliberations, they were still
expected to play a leadership role over the committee. Further, the plan circumscribed the new regime's independence of action. Burma was expected to sign
an alliance with Japan and to declare war on the United States and Great Britain. The Japanese military would retain control over the Shan and Karen states.
A "small group of elite Japanese" would be posted in Burma to advise the new
government. Finally, Burma was expected to cooperate with Japan across a wide
range of military and economic matters.[6] The range of limitations suggested that
Tokyo would only permit an independent Burma under the umbrella of Japan's
informal imperial control.

On March 22, 1943, Ba Maw flew to Japan with Aung San, Dr. Thein Maung,
Thakin Mya, and three other private secretaries and aides-de-camp to receive
formal notice of Tokyo's decision. The Burmese delegation met that very same
day with Prime Minister Tōjō and other leaders, who gave Ba Maw the official
promise of independence. Official business ended, the stiff atmosphere gave way
to warm-hearted laughter and merrymaking. For the next five days, Ba Maw's
group attended concerts and social evenings, and they even received decorations
at the Imperial Palace.[7] On several occasions they met Tōjō, with whom they
were duly impressed. The night before leaving Japan, Tōjō surprised them by
arranging for the Burmese group to go to a musical concert and sitting with
them until the concert ended. Always proper but personable, Tōjō took care to
laugh at Aung San's jokes (when few others did). "Aung San," Ba Maw later noted,
"was completely won over." The same could be said for Ba Maw, who remembered Tōjō in glowing terms as a man of "uncompromising will" and "astonishing
farsightedness."[8]

Ba Maw was equally won over by the patriotic sentiment in Japan. Wherever
the Burmese group went, they were met with an emotional response "too spon-
taneous and universal to be a put-on show." This surprised him. Few staff officers
in the Japanese military administration sympathized with Burmese nationalist
aspirations, and the rank-and-file troops frequently slapped, beat, detained, and
publicly humiliated the locals. The overbearing attitude of Japanese forces led
one Thakin leader to protest that whereas the British sucked Burmese blood,
"the Japanese are here to suck the marrow out of your bones."[9] Ba Maw was thus
surprised to find in Japan a people who appeared to believe in the mission to
liberate Asia. He grasped a sharp division between Japan proper and the Japanese
forces occupying Burma. Ba Maw later wrote that whereas Japanese forces saw
the Burmese as a conquered people, the masses he met in Japan "saw us mostly

FIGURE 8.   Japanese prime minister Tōjō Hideki discusses the future of Burmese independence with Ba Maw, Thein Maung, Aung San, and other members of his government on March 22, 1943, in Tokyo. Photo courtesy of Getty Images.

as Asian comrades who had come from far away to join them in a common war for Asia."[10]

On returning to Burma in early April, Central Executive Administration leaders established the Burma Independence Preparatory Committee. This group, which was composed of members of the Central Executive Administration and fifteen other officials of intellectual repute, met for the first time on May 8, 1943. Sessions were held in absolute secrecy, and few documents have survived to tell a partial tale of its activities.[11] Taken in tandem with postwar recollections, however, it is possible to recreate a plausible story of its activities. Overall, the committee rubber-stamped a domestic order that elevated Ba Maw to near dictatorial control. Yet the committee was beset by conflict over the nature of the government and its constitution. A group led by Thein Maung fought a losing battle to preserve a semblance of liberal-democratic government.[12] Thakins Ba Sein and Tun Ok, on the other hand, advocated a return of the monarchy to forestall Ba Maw's control over Burmese politics. Ba Sein and Tun Ok were so persistent in their opposition that Ba Maw eventually had them arrested and deported to Malaysia and Indonesia. The rift was camouflaged with an announcement that they would serve as ambassadors to the Chinese Nanjing regime and Manchukuo.[13]

Perhaps owing to this internal conflict, the Japanese military administration intervened in late May to forestall further debate. They made clear Japan's wish "that the Committee will stop for the time being further discussion concerning the constitution." Instead, Japan provided detailed instructions for wartime Burmese governance. The absolute conditions for independence, the Japanese side noted, were Burma's incorporation into the Co-Prosperity Sphere and its cooperation in the Pacific War. To this end, they called on Burma to establish the form of governance best suited to wartime conditions: dictatorship. The basic principles for this dictatorship were that one person would serve as both national representative and prime minister; that the national representative could exercise legislative power; and that a parliament and privy council could exist, but they would "be merely advisory bodies." The ideal candidate to lead this system was a dictator of high ideals, one who could show self-restraint and self-control, and who had in his mind only "the welfare of the nation." Most members of the preparatory committee found these orders unsettling, but they could do little but follow Japan's wishes. They could only emphasize Burma's wholehearted cooperation with Japan and hint that Japan would recognize cooperation as "a mutual obligation."[14]

In the end, the preparatory committee bent to Japanese wishes, preparing an illiberal constitution that resembled those of other fascist regimes. As head of state (*Adipadi*), Ba Maw was accorded dictatorial powers. He could appoint and dismiss the cabinet of ministers, justices of the Supreme Court, and members of the Privy Council, a secret body of elder statesmen who advised in matters of taxation, the budget, national loans, legislation, and treaties. The head of state could only make appointments in consultation with the prime minister. This provision, however, had little meaning, as Ba Maw occupied both positions. No national assembly existed under the new constitution, though the constitution did tentatively call for one "should war conditions permit." Moreover, the head of state retained sole responsibility for passing legislation, on consultation with the cabinet and the privy council. The position of the *Adipadi*, British intelligence noted, resembled that of the British governors-general, who could issue ordinances instead of assenting legislative acts.[15] But he was much more. Government officials were required to take an oath of loyalty to the people of Burma and to the "Supreme Head of the Burmese people."[16] As John Cady notes, the new system "gravitated in the direction of royalty," a direction that may have appealed to Ba Maw's personal inclinations. By the end of 1943, the *Adipadi* made use of the additional title of *Anashin Mingyi Kodaw*, or king.[17]

TABLE 5. The Principal Personnel of Ba Maw's Government, 1943

Head of state and prime minister	Dr. Ba Maw
Deputy prime minister	Thakin Mya
Home minister	U Ba Win
Foreign minister	Thakin Nu
Finance minister	Dr. Thein Maung
Defense minister	Maj. Gen. Aung San
Taxation minister	U Aye
Justice minister	U Thein Maung
Education and health minister	U Hla Min
Agriculture minister	Thakin Than Tun
Forestry and mines minister	U Hla Pe
Commerce and industry minister	U Mya (Pyawbwe)
Communications and irrigation minister	Thakin Lay Maung
Welfare and publicity minister	Bandula U Sein
Cooperation (with Japan) minister	U Tun Aung
Public works recovery minister	Thakin Lun Baw

Burma formally became independent on August 1, 1943. In his memoirs, Ba Maw noted that it was an auspicious day, bright but with slight rain and enough clouds in the sky to keep enemy planes away.[18] It was, in short, a perfect day for such a momentous event. At 10 a.m. Lieutenant General Kawabe Masakazu, Iida Shōjirō's replacement as the supreme commander of Japan's Burma Area Army, officially dissolved the Japanese military administration (outside of the Shan and Karen areas, which remained under Japanese control).[19] More than an hour later, at 11:20 a.m., the Burma Independence Preparatory Committee and dignitaries met in the ballroom of the Government House. There the commission declared Burma an independent state, promulgated the constitution, and appointed Ba Maw as head of state. The main personnel of Ba Maw's government are shown in table 5.

Then followed the inauguration ceremony, held with all the pomp and splendor the new state could muster. Ba Maw, ever interested in building legitimacy, mirrored Burma's old royal tradition of a king's coronation. All attendees attired themselves in their best silks and jewels, celebrating under the new national flag, a tricolor of yellow, green, and red with a proud peacock adorning a circular insert at the center. A dwarf announced the *Adipadi* Ba Maw, who entered the ballroom to music reserved for a king's arrival. Thakin Kodaw Hmaing administered an oath as ministers of old addressed their king.[20] But the inauguration also kept in tune with the trends of the times. Foreign dignitaries from Germany and Thailand, as well as Subhas Chandra Bose, attended the event. And Ba Maw, declaring the Burmese state as "one blood, one voice, one leader," highlighted his polity as in keeping with the authoritarian, fascist trends of the day.

Independence at hand, Ba Maw followed Tōjō's instructions and entered Japan's Greater East Asia War. In a speech that highlighted Burma's long period of suffering under British imperialism, Ba Maw declared war on Great Britain and the United States. The present war, he argued, "is Burma's war also. It is a war for Burma's existence." He vowed to join hands with Japan and to "fight till the insolent British and Americans are vanquished."[21] Following the declaration, Ba Maw and Japanese ambassador Sawada Renzō signed a treaty of alliance between the two nations. The alliance called for the successful prosecution of the war through close cooperation in military, political, and economic matters.[22] With these moves, Burma became a participant in East Asia's clash of empires.

Allied nations dismissed Burmese independence and the declaration of war as meaningless. British leaders spoke of the independence ceremony as a "little comedy" that proved greater subservience to Japan. Echoing this, the *New York Times* on June 23, 1943, spoke of independence as "a means of inducing cooperation for Japanese exploitation of 'Greater East Asia.'"[23] Others derided the declaration of war against the Allied powers as highlighting Burma's lack of control over its own affairs. "Now in one grand comprehensive gesture," asserted the *Times of India*, "the puppet Government of Burma has declared war on the United Nations. Ba Maw may want to vent his spleen on Britain. But why drag America in? The voice is Ba Maw's, but the hands are the hands of Tojo."[24]

These critiques hit close to the mark. On the same day Burma received independence, Ba Maw also signed a secret military agreement that severely constrained Burma's freedom of action. According to the agreement signed with Lieutenant General Kawabe and Vice Admiral Ōkawachi Denshichi, the commander of the First Southern Expeditionary Fleet, Burma guaranteed Japan complete freedom in military operations in Burma and agreed "to provide Japanese forces with every necessary assistance." The implications were drawn out in a separate agreement, signed on the same day. Burma was to provide Japanese forces with anything they found necessary to prosecute the war, from land and buildings to labor, infrastructure, and facilities. Further, Burma agreed not to interfere with anything "essential for military operations" and promised to submit district authorities to Japanese control, if necessary. Finally, Ba Maw entrusted Japan with the administration of the Frontier Areas.[25]

This secret agreement made a mockery of any pretentions to a liberated Burma. Japanese forces could present nearly any demand as a "military necessity," which the Ba Maw government would be unable to refuse. Ba Maw's government thus endorsed the informal imperialism of the Japanese military: Japan could exercise control over Burmese infrastructure, economic institutions, and its means of production. Moreover, the Japanese military retained control over the countryside and Upper Burma and could continue to operate with impunity.

As historian Jan Bečka correctly notes, Burmese independence was nominal, with the Japanese retaining control and turning Burma into little more than a satellite state.[26] Burma, in short, received the very same type of nominal independence that Japan had bequeathed to Manchukuo and the Chinese Nanjing regime. By January 1944, one well-informed observer stated that the Burmese administration "was only a paper one," justifying Allied claims that Ba Maw was heading up a "puppet government."[27] Ba Maw agreed with this assessment in his postwar depositions, noting that he had little power to protect his own people.[28]

Nonetheless, the new Burmese regime sought to make the most of its nominal independence. Rangoon moved to establish institutions it lacked when Burma was a British colony, creating or reforming institutions central to a modern state: a foreign affairs establishment; a central bank; and a ministry of defense and a renamed national army. Moreover, it began a process of economic planning that Burma continued well into the postwar era. Notably, leaders were not averse to seeking Japanese aid in building these new institutions and practices.

First, the Ba Maw government set up a new ministry of foreign affairs, headed by Thakin Nu. As foreign minister, Nu quickly aligned diplomatic policy with the goals of the Greater East Asia Co-Prosperity Sphere. In an August 4, 1943, statement, he declared that Burma would pursue friendly relations with its allies and would become an active member of Japan's new order. More importantly, Nu spoke to his willingness to use Japanese help. Since Burma remained inexperienced in foreign affairs, he revealed that he was consulting Japanese ambassador Sawada to gain advice about how to organize and select personnel for Burma's new foreign ministry.[29] Thakin Nu was not alone in this desire; the independence preparatory committee also indicated its desire to solicit "Japanese assistance in training a diplomatic corps." By the end of August 1943, Thakin Nu and his foreign secretary, Kyaw Nein, headed a small but bustling foreign ministry of more than twenty officers, clerks, and typists.[30]

The government also created a network of ambassadors and diplomats who were to serve as the face of Burma's foreign policy establishment. Dr. Thein Maung, Ba Maw's confidant, took the all-important position of ambassador to Japan. He established the Burmese embassy in the former residence of famous entrepreneur Masuda Takashi, situated on a sunny slope of the fir-crested small hill, Gotenyama, in the Kojimachi district of Tokyo. Altogether, Thein Maung's embassy consisted of a staff of twelve who moved to Japan without their families. The Ba Maw government also designated ambassadors to Co-Prosperity Sphere regimes that recognized Burma as an independent state. U Ba Lwin, for instance, was appointed as ambassador to Thailand. The appointment order reached Ba Lwin in Singapore on his return trip from Japan, so he headed to his position in Bangkok direct from Singapore.[31]

Burma also established a central bank, originally at Japan's behest. This was a new development, as central bank functions had traditionally been performed by the Reserve Bank of India's Rangoon branch. With independence, the Ba Maw government prepared to institutionalize a new, government-run central bank. In July 1943, U Chit Tun, who later served as manager, went to Tokyo to study banking. Shortly after he left, Ba Maw established a Central Bank Preparatory Committee consisting of Finance Minister Thein Maung, U Ba Maung (the bank's first governor), Finance Ministry secretary U Hla Shein, U Set (who had served in the Indian Audit and Accounts Service), and nine others. The committee, with the help of Japanese financial advisers, gave its final report in October 1943. Burma passed the State Bank Act later that year.[32]

The State Bank—Burma's new central bank—was opened with great publicity and fanfare on January 15, 1944. The new leadership included president of the board of directors Ba Maung, manager Chit Tun, and six other directors. They were to be assisted by three Japanese advisers, officials of Japanese banks who had extensive experience with banking and monetary policy. Nonetheless, U Set's opening speech made clear that the State Bank would be a wholly Burmese institution, "a Central Bank for Burma and the Shan States." Set further spoke of the State Bank as undertaking all monetary affairs, from implementing monetary policy to issuing currency notes and coins and helping and supervising the nation's banks.[33] Since Burma had no other indigenous banks, the State Bank acted as a commercial bank as well.[34] The State Bank opened with 10 million rupees in deposits, supposedly provided by the government but in reality lent by the Japanese. The bank did in fact attract some money. Ba Maw made an initial deposit of 100,000 rupees "on behalf of the people." According to the Japanese press agency Dōmei, by the end of January 1944 the State Bank had received around 5.5 million in deposits on current account and granted loans of almost 40 million rupees.[35]

While successful to a degree in attracting initial deposits, there is no evidence that the State Bank made any impact on the Burmese economy. Granted, the bank received 5 million rupees' worth of deposits in its first ten days. But it only reported a mere 11,825 rupees in savings deposits, indicating a lack of public faith in the bank's future. Furthermore, the State Bank did not issue a new set of banknotes or coins as currency for Burma.[36] Nor did it have any impact on economic growth. The hapless central bank instead became saddled with the responsibility for an unknown currency supply as well as the underwriting of a colossal government deficit. In such conditions, Burma's State Bank could never gain relevance within Burmese wartime economic life.

The Ba Maw government also sought to institutionalize independence through a focus on national planning, which became a governmental obsession. Through national planning, the Burmese government hoped to mobilize the masses in service of the state, to instill a sense of patriotism, and to give voice to Burma's official slogan, "one blood, one voice, one leader." The first attempt came with Ba Maw's wordy and vague New Order Plan of 1943–44. The plan's overall objectives were "war-waging and state-making." It argued that the whole life and work of the nation must be geared toward the creation and defense of the new Burmese state.[37] To this end, Ba Maw called for measures to build loyalty toward the state and to give a material stake in the new order. Such measures included land redistribution, guarantees for basic livelihoods, and efforts to inculcate patriotism in the populace. That said, the planning itself was vague at best and nonexistent at worst. The New Order Plan was more a laundry list of guiding principles and hopes than a detailed blueprint for Burma's future. As Robert H. Taylor notes, any appealing rhetoric and style "were belied by the state's inability to implement its plans for lack of both economic resources and coercive power. Planning became talisman."[38]

This focus on planning, however, continued uninterrupted. In May 1944 Ba Maw appointed his brother, Dr. Ba Han, as head of a Burma Special Research Commission, which he sent through the Co-Prosperity Sphere to study models and processes of economic development. Ba Han was joined in this endeavor by U Soe Nyun and U Ba Nyein, both members of the Burmese Planning Board. From May to August, the commission traveled to Japan, Manchukuo, Taiwan, the Philippines, Java, Singapore (renamed Shōnan by Japan), and Thailand. This experience not only forged greater familiarity with Burma's allies; it also generated ideas on how to promote economic growth. The commission's interim report, produced on August 12, 1944, called for strengthening Burma's economy by copying practices Japan had encouraged through the Co-Prosperity Sphere. In all, it championed strengthened state control over economic life and called on Burma to build the foundations of a planned economy. It recommended central planning, state monopolies on foreign trade, the creation of new factories and industries, and the imposition of state controls over production and commodity distribution.[39] These efforts at national planning, pursued piecemeal and half-heartedly, became mainstays of Burmese politics in the ensuing decades. Successions of national plans, many unannounced and some unimplemented, and many beyond the state's capability to implement, defined national politics well into the 1980s.[40]

Most importantly, independence led to the institutionalization of a defense establishment, symbolized by the Burmese army and headed by a ministry of defense. Aung San took great pride in the chance to create an effective, strong military. Thus he no doubt welcomed the Japanese decision in July 1942 to reorganize the bloated and unruly Burma Independence Army into the Burma

Defense Army (BDA), a smaller and more disciplined military force. Over the course of the next year, the BDA developed under Japanese tutelage. Burmese soldiers endured harsh training methods, wore nearly identical uniforms, and occupied positions in a Japanese-style army organization. By mid-1943, the BDA had created six infantry battalions, two anti-aircraft batteries, and two engineer battalions—all subject to extensive Japanese control.[41] Nonetheless, journalist and official reporter Tun Pe saw in the BDA the seeds of a truly *Burmese* army. "As I mingled with the young men of the BDA," Tun Pe later noted, "I got the feeling that despite Japanese direction and control, they had in fact made a very good attempt to create a force with its own distinctive traditions and characteristics."[42]

On September 16, 1943, Burmese leaders renamed its military force the Burma National Army (BNA). The new name carried significant implications, both psychological and tangible. It inspired confidence. Burma, after all, now had its own national army, one of the primary institutions of a functioning nation-state. But more importantly, as General Ne Win hinted in early August, the name change implied that Burma could use its national force to attack national enemies "with courage and determination."[43] Finally, it signified a growing independence from Japan. Brigadier Maung Maung noted that Japan relaxed control over the Burmese forces after the creation of the BNA. "Only selected troops were placed under the operational control of the Japanese," he wrote. Otherwise, commanding officers could recruit more freely, and the BNA gained access to better arms, ammunition, and training facilities. Furthermore, the recruitment, training, and direction of the army became the responsibility of Aung San's new ministry of defense.[44]

The new army paid equal attention to training the next generation of officers and soldiers. From 1942, training centers were established in Mingaladon, Pyinmana, Mandalay, and Maymyo.[45] The Burmese army sent the best graduates of the various training centers to a new officer training school in Mingaladon, fourteen miles north of Rangoon. From September 1942 through the end of the war, four groups of two to three hundred cadets enrolled in the school's seven-month training course. The top thirty to forty graduates of each group were sent to the Japanese Military Academy in Tokyo for further training.[46] Whether in Burma or Japan, however, the new cadets underwent the same strict training methods. Cadets had their heads shaved immediately on arrival. Japanese teachers imposed rigorous study, training, and work schedules. Orders and instructions were carried out wholly in the Japanese language. British intelligence noted that treatment was "harsh and humiliating," leading some cadets to desert before the end of the course.[47] "Every day," one trainee remembered, "Japanese *hsayas* [teachers] cruelly slapped faces during military training. No student escaped this treatment."[48] Those who remained, however, forged deep and abiding relationships with each other, ultimately forming the core of the Burmese resistance movement against the Japanese.

The Ba Maw regime also inaugurated a ministry of defense to direct and oversee its new army. Like the army, the ministry did not emerge from the ether. It grew out of the Japan-sponsored Military Preparations Bureau, an organization established on July 31, 1942, to help create, teach, equip, and maintain the military. Leadership initially rested in Japanese hands, but the bureau included noncommissioned officers from both Japan and Burma.[49] After independence, the Military Preparations Bureau was reorganized into the ministry of defense, headed by minister Aung San and vice minister Aung Than. As Mary P. Callahan has shown, over the following years the ministry gained operational independence from Japan. With each set of military reforms, the nascent ministry of defense became increasingly independent from its Japanese advisers.[50] By 1945, when disenchantment with the Japanese occupation had reached fever pitch, the ministry had become sufficiently independent to plot an anti-Japanese revolt.

The wartime Burmese regime thus made use of its limited independence to engage in a process of state building. Granted, Japanese authorities placed a wide range of restrictions on the autonomy of the new Burmese state. And owing to the exigencies of the war, bodies such as the State Bank never got off the ground. But institution building, particularly the creation of a new defense establishment, had important legacies. It was perhaps a bitter pill for Japanese forces to swallow when the very defense establishment it had trained courted British aid and revolted against Japan. Coming full circle, the very men who helped oust the British from Burma later welcomed them back as liberators.

Philippine independence followed a similar pattern, beginning in late May. A May 31, 1943, imperial conference called on Japan to grant independence by October. Two weeks later, on June 16, Prime Minister Tōjō proudly announced to the Imperial Diet Japan's intentions "to grant the Philippines, too, with the honor of independence later this year."[51]

A June 26, 1943, liaison conference enshrined this objective into policy. It adopted a policy plan, "Outline for the Guiding of Philippine Independence," which confirmed the decision to grant independence in October. In preparation, the "Outline" called for an independence preparatory committee to help build the new Philippines. Japan would provide the Philippine government with the freedom to select its leadership as well as its form of government, country name, flag, and capital. Nonetheless, there would be similar limits to Philippine autonomy to that of Burma. Japan reserved the right to take special measures in Mindanao, owing to the island's strategic, military, and economic importance. Japanese nationals were to receive equal treatment in the Philippines. Japan also expected the Philippines to join Japan's Greater East Asia War "at the appropriate moment." In the meantime, it would provide facilities, transportation, and communications to meet Japan's military needs.[52]

On June 20, one week in advance of the liaison conference decision, Japanese forces ordered the creation of the Preparatory Committee for Philippine Independence. This committee, Japanese leaders hoped, would not merely revise the existing commonwealth constitution. Instead, they wanted the Philippines to remake country and constitution to showcase a new, Asian Philippines. From July 2, the twenty prominent Philippine members began discussions.[53] Japan had originally hoped to offer the leadership of the preparatory committee and the presidency of the new republic to Manuel Roxas. But Roxas declined, throwing his support behind his friend and colleague José P. Laurel.

In many ways, Laurel was the perfect choice. He was well known for his brilliance, administrative ability, and political passion. Born in 1891 in the town of Tanauan, Batangas, Laurel first emerged in the public eye owing to a disastrous misadventure. In 1909, at the age of eighteen, while vacationing in his hometown from his high school studies in Manila, Laurel stabbed a man in a fight over a town beauty. At first convicted of "frustrated murder," he fought in court for three years to reverse the decision. Ultimately, in 1912 the supreme court sided with Laurel, labeling his actions as legitimate self-defense.[54] In the following years Laurel emerged a changed man. He became a devoted Christian and drove himself to excel, receiving a law degree from the University of the Philippines in 1915 and a doctorate of law from Yale University in 1920. By 1922, at the young age of thirty-one, Laurel joined the political elite as secretary of the interior.

His prominence did not last long, however. In 1923 Laurel found himself at the epicenter of a bitter conflict with U.S. governor-general Leonard Wood. The conflict centered on the Conley case, in which a U.S. chief of the vice squad in the Manila Police Department was charged for accepting bribes from gamblers, dealing opium, and keeping a mistress. A devout nationalist, Laurel refused to defend what he considered acts of malfeasance by U.S. officials. Wood, however, sided with the policeman. In response, Laurel led a failed cabinet revolt. The cabinet resigned en masse, but once the dust had settled, the revolting cabinet members returned to their former positions of power, locking Laurel out of office until 1936. Some scholars have argued that this episode left Laurel embittered, influencing his willingness to accept the presidency under Japan.[55] But it is unclear whether Laurel's decision to become president resulted from frustrated ambition (which he never denied) or a sense of responsibility to the nation and desire to change the national character. Whatever the case, the conflict with Wood solidified Laurel's nationalist and anticolonial credentials.

In Laurel, Tokyo hoped they had found a pliable, pro-Japanese leader. Following the Conley case, Laurel had become a well-known critic of both the U.S. Empire and the "craze for Western standards" in the Philippines.[56] He had a closer relationship with Japan than did most Filipinos of the time. Laurel received an honorary law doctorate from Tokyo Imperial University and even sent his own son to study at the Imperial Military Academy in Tokyo. A failed assassination of Laurel on June 5, 1943, further reinforced the sense of his pro-Japanese credentials. Early in the morning, a guerrilla resistance fighter named Little Joe fired seven shots on Laurel as he was playing golf at Wack Wack Country Club, near Manila. Laurel was hit four times, and he only survived thanks to excellent Japanese medical care. According to witness testimony, Little Joe had claimed, "We guerrillas are angry with [Laurel] because he is pro-Japanese."[57] Truth be told, Laurel was no more pro-Japanese than he was pro-American. But this episode convinced Japanese leaders that Laurel was someone with whom they could work.

Laurel and the preparatory committee produced a new constitution, which they approved on September 4, 1943, and the National Assembly ratified three days later.[58] To the dismay of Japanese advisers, however, the new constitution was the direct offspring of its 1935 counterpart. The biggest difference rested in the new strength of the executive branch. The president had near-dictatorial authority with extensive powers of appointment. He could appoint cabinet ministers and vice ministers, ambassadors, bureau heads, higher officers of the armed forces, the advisory council of state, and even judges, provincial governors, and mayors. The constitution also created a unicameral National Assembly, which was to be filled by representatives from the Kalibapi, the sole party of state modeled after Japan's Imperial Rule Assistance Association. The president could appoint one-half of the National Assembly, thus entrenching his executive control.[59] The constitution also weakened the judiciary. The Supreme Court could only declare laws, ordinances, executive orders, or regulations unconstitutional through a unanimous vote (up from a two-thirds vote in the 1935 constitution). This heralded the emergence of a strong executive branch, stronger than Quezon's "de facto dictatorship" of the 1930s. Laurel, nonetheless, spoke of the constitution as "transitory." He believed a strong executive was necessary to weather the global storm of World War II, but he was by no means committed to keeping it after war's end.[60]

After completing the constitution, a Philippine delegation consisting of President-Elect Laurel, retiring Executive Commission chairman Jorge B. Vargas, Speaker Benigno S. Aquino, and two others flew to Tokyo to hash out a pact of alliance with Japan. The delegation arrived on September 30, 1943, and remained in Tokyo for several days, during which they attended banquets, meetings, and

FIGURE 9.   Rally for President-Elect José P. Laurel (center) at the Legislative Building in Manila, September 25, 1943. Photo courtesy of the Jorge B. Vargas Museum and Filipiniana Research Center, University of the Philippines.

other pleasantries and paid their respects to the emperor. The most important event of the trip, however, occurred the day after the delegation arrived. They attended a meeting at the prime minister's residence for nearly an hour, during which time they engaged in discussions with Prime Minister Tōjō, foreign minister Shigemitsu Mamoru, Greater East Asia minister Aoki Kazuo, vice chief of staff of the Southern Expeditionary Army (and Lt. Gen.) Wachi Takaji, ambassador to the Philippines Murata Shōzō, and chief cabinet secretary Hoshino Naoki.[61] The climax of the meeting came when Tōjō asked the Philippine delegation to declare war on the United States and Great Britain.

This was not an order. Tōjō recognized that the situation in the Philippines was different from that of Burma. Owing to the fierce anti-Japanese guerrilla resistance movement and fond memories of U.S. colonial rule, Japan remained willing to grant leeway in the timing of the declaration. This reflected a consensus about Philippine volatility and the potential for foot dragging, evasion, and other types of resistance. On June 19, 1943, Japanese Fourteenth Army commander Kuroda Shigenori told vice chief of the army general staff Hata Hikosaburō, in a message meant to reach Tōjō's ears, that forcing the Philippines into the war would generate "a constant state of great fear."[62] Even Satō Kenryō, director of the army ministry's Bureau of Military Affairs, had argued against forcing the

Philippines into the war. Satō felt that any demands to declare war would be used by enemy propaganda to highlight Japan's weakened military power. Satō's arguments won the day, influencing the June 26, 1943, policy decision to call on the Philippines to declare war "at the appropriate moment," sometime in the future.[63] This explains Tōjō's conciliatory tone. Tōjō nonetheless tried to coax a declaration of war out of the Laurel cabinet, insisting that it "is for the defense of the New Philippines."[64]

Tōjō's statement, however tame, shocked the Philippine delegation and their Japanese liaison and translator, Hamamoto Masakatsu.[65] Although Tōjō carefully worded his statement to allow wiggle room, the Philippine delegation understood it as instructions for an immediate declaration of war. This appeared a heavy price for independence. Laurel took a moment to silently pray. After collecting his thoughts, he gave a delicate reply. Laurel admitted the Philippines should fight on Japan's side, but he insisted that four hundred years of Western rule had changed his nation. A long experience of Western education and propaganda, combined with a lack of knowledge of Japan, had caused the Philippine people to lose their "Oriental spirit." Laurel thus insisted that the Philippine people "will not consent to an immediate declaration of war."[66] He further argued that he was neither a strong nor popular leader like Quezon, Osmeña, or Roxas, and he hinted that he could only govern through responsible leadership and keeping the public trust. "The moment I declare war," Laurel hammered home, "I will be ousted from my position as president of the Philippines."[67] Laurel made an impassioned plea for Japan to allow the postponement of any declaration of war.[68]

Tōjō sympathized with Laurel's position and agreed to wait. But he held firm to Japanese demands. "When the time comes I would like you to join the war as soon as possible," Tōjō insisted. He hinted that continued protests of failing popularity or weakness of leadership were weak excuses that reflected a failure of determination—which Tōjō no doubt saw as a failure of leadership. True leadership, Tōjō advised, emerged not from popularity but from confidence and determination, values that Tōjō sought to instill in his Philippine partner. Tōjō stated: "I have held office as prime minister for two years. In my experience, I think it can be said that the people are a shade of grey. If the leader says white, the people become white. If the leader says black, the people become black. This depends on the leader's determination and leadership; it is not possible for [them] to turn white naturally—that would be like waiting a hundred years for the water in the Yellow River to become clear. I would like Your Excellency to understand this point and lead the people as a good leader."[69] It is unclear how Laurel responded. Tōjō never gave him the chance. Instead, the premier finished by reciting what he considered a particularly poignant and apt *tanka* poem, created by Shingon cleric Sakura Azumao (1811–60).

Kimi ga tame	The road of morning frost
Asashimo fumite	I tread
Iku michi wa	In Thy name
Tōtoku ureshiku	Has been noble and pleasing
Kanashiku ari keri	But also filled with sadness

He explained how his mixed feelings of pleasure and sadness related to the daunt-ing task facing Laurel in constructing the new Philippines.[70] But Tōjō's point, and its relation to the declaration of war, was lost in translation.

From the perspective of the Philippines, Laurel's trip had been an unmitigated success: he managed to stall, avoiding both an offensive alliance and a declara-tion of war.[71] Instead, the Philippine delegation escaped with the promises of a defensive pact of alliance. In return, Tokyo required the Philippines to provide the Japanese military with resources (both mineral and agricultural), facilities, and transportation necessary to prosecute the war. But this was a small price to pay for avoiding war. As Laurel told Burmese journalists U Tun Than and Tun Pe in late November 1943, Philippine public opinion would never consent to a declaration of war on the United States. "What America has done for us in forty years," Laurel told Tun Than, "cannot be undone in six months."[72] Whatever the case, with its important business completed, the Philippine delegation relaxed for the rest of their time in Tokyo. They were wined and dined by the Japanese government, and both sides engaged in mutual flattery and joking. On October 4, 1943, the Philippine delegation returned to the Philippines and prepared for the nation's upcoming independence ceremonies.[73]

The Republic of the Philippines officially became independent on October 14, 1943. At 8 a.m., Japanese Fourteenth Army commander Kuroda dissolved the Japanese military administration. Inauguration festivities continued in front of the legislative building in Manila. Laurel, Vargas, and Aquino, all adorned with decorations received from Japan, stood proudly before a crowd of half a mil-lion Filipinos. Accompanying them were members of the National Assembly, the Council of State, the Supreme Court, the defunct preparatory commission, and the executive commission, as well as Japanese military officials and civilian advisers. At just after 9:30 a.m., Vargas read the proclamation terminating the military administration, to the wild cheers of the crowd. Following this, Gen-erals Emilio Aguinaldo and Artemio Ricarte hoisted the Filipino flag while the national anthem played in the background. President Laurel took his oath of office before delivering his inaugural address, in which he stressed the country's "single purpose and common determination to make our independence stable, lasting, and real."[74] Laurel established a government led by the following officials, outlined in table 6."

TABLE 6.   The José P. Laurel Cabinet, January 1944

President	José P. Laurel
Minister of foreign affairs	Claro M. Recto
Minister of finance	Antonio de las Alas
Minister of justice	Teofilo Sison
Minister of agriculture and natural resources	Rafael R. Alunan
Minister of public works and communications	Quintin Paredes
Minister of health, labor, and public welfare	Emiliano Tría Tirona
Minister of home affairs	José P. Laurel
Minister of economic affairs	José P. Laurel
Minister of education	José P. Laurel
Chief justice of the Supreme Court	José Yulo
Acting executive secretary	José Gil

Following the inauguration ceremony, Japanese ambassador Murata Shōzō and Philippine minister of state for foreign affairs Claro M. Recto signed a pact of alliance in the state reception hall of Malacañan Palace. The National Assembly ratified the pact four days later, on October 18, 1943. This alliance emphasized "mutual respect of sovereignty and territories" between the two nations and called for close cooperation in all affairs. More importantly, it permitted the Philippines to take a passive role in the global conflict. The Laurel government merely promised facilities for Japanese military actions and cooperation to safeguard the territorial integrity of the Philippines.[75]

At the same time, Japan imposed on the new republic a secret agreement that severely limited the scope of Philippine independence. According to the agreement, the Philippines would provide Japanese forces with exclusive control over mines, factories, and workshops connected to war production (especially for copper, manganese, and chromium mines, butanol factories, and shipyards and munitions factories). The Japanese military would also control air transportation, overseas routes, harbors of military importance, and overseas electric communication and radio broadcasts. Most of these, the agreement noted, would be transferred to the Philippine government "if circumstances permit." The Philippines would be expected to provide funds from the national budget to help Japan's war. Moreover, they would also be required to consult with Japan before enacting important foreign exchange, financial, and currency measures. And Japan required that the Philippine government accord Japanese subjects with the same treatment as Philippine nationals.[76] Similar to the Burmese case, the agreement further entrenched Japanese control over Philippine economic and political life.

Many Filipinos viewed independence as a sham—a smoke screen that would allow Japan to rule with impunity. Former governor of Iloilo and outspoken guerrilla leader Tomas Confesor, for instance, protested the establishment of what he believed to be a puppet regime. On October 4, 1943, Confesor wrote to Dr. Fermin Caram challenging the new Philippine constitution, which was scheduled to go into effect ten days hence. He derided the constitution as "a wolf in lamb's skin" and a tool to manipulate Philippine politics. This was an astute analysis. Confesor realized the constitution contained the potential to create a presidential dictatorship, wherein the president, whom he dismissed as a "super puppet," could manipulate Philippine politics to Japanese ends.[77] Confesor wrote a similar letter to Philippine president José P. Laurel on October 26, 1943. "Do you honestly believe," Confesor admonished, "that you have independence, a sovereign legislature, a sovereign government, while the Japanese Imperial Army remains quartered within our shores, free to shoot and murder at will civilians irrespective of sex and age?" He further lambasted Filipino leaders as mere "figureheads" and independence as "a grand farce, with the Samurai as your director and stage-master, for the world to laugh at."[78]

The world was not as clear-cut or black and white as Confesor argued, however. Independence was indeed constrained, but it also provided opportunity. Laurel argued that the whole point of his government and constitution was "the perpetuation of a Republic of the Filipinos, by the Filipinos and for the Filipinos, solely and exclusively."[79] Laurel pointed to this as early as September 7, when he went to the legislative building to plea for the ratification of the new Philippine constitution. "Our problem," he sneered, wandering from his prepared text, "is to remove this flag (pointing at the Japanese flag) and replace it with our own."[80] Even the official text of his speech was surprisingly frank. Laurel noted that the war would result in an Allied victory in six years at most. "The problem of the Filipinos, in the meanwhile," he continued, "is to decide and determine what attitude they should adopt for the duration of that war."[81] Those listening on the radio were shocked, taking Laurel's statement as a challenge. So strong was Laurel's tone that minister of public works and communication Quintin Paredes stated, shortly after war's end, "we thought that Laurel was going to finish his speech with a declaration of war against Japan."[82]

Such feelings notwithstanding, Philippine leaders, like their Burmese counterparts, strove to make the most of their situation. They moved to institutionalize their independence, building new organs of government necessary for a fully functioning state. As Laurel described in October 1943, his regime sought to bring about "the reorganization of our government in order to effect simplicity, efficiency, and economy."[83] To this end, his administration cooperated with Japan to create institutions the Philippines had lacked during the commonwealth era: a central bank, a ministry of foreign affairs, and a limited diplomatic establishment.

One of the Laurel regime's first orders of business was creating a foreign policy establishment. On October 16, 1943—two days after receiving independence— Laurel sent a message to the National Assembly pressing for a ministry of foreign affairs. Two days later he followed up in an address before the National Assembly, insisting on a law creating a new foreign ministry that would allow the Philippines to engage not only with Japan and Greater East Asia but also with the entire world. Laurel noted that the Japanese had already sent an ambassador extraordinary and plenipotentiary to the Philippines, and he suggested that they respond in turn. He thus argued, "It is our duty at once to send to that country an ambassador who would represent the Philippines in her international relations in that country." Laurel also contended that doing so required his government to "add to our departmental organization" through the creation of a new foreign ministry.[84]

The National Assembly responded straightaway, drafting a bill creating the ministry of foreign affairs and freeing up funds for the Philippine diplomatic office. Laurel approved the law on October 20, 1943. That same day, he appointed Claro M. Recto as the first minister of state for foreign affairs, and five days later Emilio Abello took office as vice minister of foreign affairs. The ministry soon began organizing its staff, installing offices on the fourth floor of the former finance building. Other officials were appointed in early 1944. At its height, the ministry of foreign affairs comprised some 140 employees, making it the smallest institution in the wartime Philippine regime.[85]

The Laurel regime also provided the skeleton for a new structure of diplomatic relations with Japan. On October 23, 1943, Laurel appointed former executive commission chairman Jorge B. Vargas as ambassador extraordinary and plenipotentiary to Japan. Vargas took his oath of office two days later at Malacañan Palace.[86] This initial speed notwithstanding, it took more than four more months for the embassy to get up and running in Tokyo, owing to delays in the freeing up of Philippine money and the signing of the contract for the embassy land.[87] On February 10, 1944, Vargas flew to Tokyo and was greeted at Haneda Airport by Japanese diplomat and chief protocol officer Yoshioka Noritake. One week later, the Philippine government approved an act allowing for one million pesos to be used to purchase a site and building, including furniture and equipment, for the new Philippine embassy. The embassy occupied the former Western-style residence of Yasuda Iwajirō (the grandson of Yasuda *zaibatsu* founder Yasuda Zenjirō), located on a hill near Kudanshita in Tokyo. On February 29, Vargas presented his credentials as Philippine ambassador extraordinary and plenipotentiary to the emperor of Japan.[88] By mid-March, once the bitter February cold had passed, Vargas moved with the diplomatic staff to the new embassy.

In February 1944, with the approval of Act No. 60, the Philippines established another cornerstone of an independent regime it had lacked during the commonwealth era: a central bank.[89] In doing so, the Laurel regime hoped to take control, at least to a limited extent, over the country's economic life. A March 1, 1944, press statement issued by the Board of Information revealed the nationalist intent behind the newly created central bank. "One of the most important and urgent problems of the Republic," the statement read, "is financial. The financial system of the Philippines has largely been dominated by foreign banking institutions." This state of affairs, the statement maintained, was wholly unacceptable. It limited the flow of credit to Philippine industry, preventing the nation's much-needed modernization efforts. "Political independence," the Laurel government maintained, "will be meaningless unless we can shake off the financial control which tends to subordinate national welfare to the convenience of financiers and investors."[90]

With the central bank, the Republic of the Philippines hoped to fashion an institution that would help the financial system meet the needs of business. Philippine leaders imagined the central bank would have a broad mandate, from implementing monetary policy and managing the currency system to determining interest rates, managing the country's foreign exchange, regulating and supervising the banking industry to meet the needs of business, serving as a lender of last resort, and creating a new currency.[91] Nonetheless, the central bank was established too late in the war to achieve true economic independence. One of its only major policies, as historian Ricardo T. Jose has discovered, was the creation of a prototype for new peso bills that were never put into circulation. As the Japanese Empire teetered toward collapse by late 1944, so did the central bank's commitment to monetary policy. The central bank, Jose maintains, never had the time to help bring about an independent economy.[92]

Philippine state-building measures thus were implemented in a piecemeal, selective, and incomplete nature. A notable omission from state-building efforts was the creation of a broader defense establishment. Unlike Burma, the wartime Philippine republic refused to create a ministry of defense and a national army. But this does not suggest a lack of commitment to state building. Instead, the decision to forego building a defense establishment resulted from wartime realities and no small amount of foot dragging. The Laurel cabinet, seeking to protect the Philippines and resist Japanese demands to the extent possible, avoided any measures that would end up sending Philippine citizens to fight a war they neither wanted nor supported. In fact, the only fighting force for the Republic was the Japan-sponsored *Makapili*, organized in November 1944 by Benigno Ramos and Artemio Ricarte after it became clear Laurel would not conscript Filipinos into the war effort. In the end, Philippine state building was selective, focusing on those institutions that would not carry a heavy toll for the Philippine people. Wartime state building was thus as focused on the present as the future. While limiting the adverse effects of Japan's wartime occupation, the Laurel regime engaged in a process of preparing for future independence.

Diplomacy in Practice

Philippine and Burmese leaders did not stop at building new governmental institutions. They also used the crucible of war to build a functioning foreign policy establishment and to gain experience in diplomatic affairs. Both countries engaged in a variety of diplomatic activities, from negotiations to protesting Japanese abuses and engaging in cultural diplomacy initiatives. In the process, they co-opted the Greater East Asia Co-Prosperity Sphere as best they could, subverting informal Japanese imperialism to serve national ends and to prepare for future self-governance.

Much of the diplomatic activity of the Republic of the Philippines consisted of foot dragging and resisting Japanese entreaties to enter the war. As noted above, the first mission taken in late September 1943 resulted in the successful negotiation of an alliance that did not commit the Philippines to join the war. Japan at first remained flustered but tolerant of these stall tactics. In a May 29, 1944, discussion with Ambassador Murata, General Terauchi Hisaichi railed against the "spineless Filipinos," but he vowed that Japanese forces "will do whatever it takes to fight."[93] Nonetheless, by the autumn of 1944 the Japanese position in the Pacific had become precarious. In August 1944, U.S. forces had advanced steadily, defeating Japanese forces in Guadalcanal, seizing Guam and the Marianas, and making initial preparations for an invasion of Leyte in the Philippines. By September, U.S. planes had launched aerial bombardments of the cities of Davao and Manila.[94] The imperial general staff, displeased with the state of Philippine defense, sent the so-called Tiger of Malaya, General Yamashita Tomoyuki, to head up the Philippine command. At the same time, Japan became desperate for a Philippine commitment to enter the war.

Murata approached Laurel on August 25 to revisit the issue, reminding him that Japan desired the Philippines' "entry into the war." Murata pushed even harder after the bombing of Manila in September.[95] According to Laurel's memoirs, Murata politely but sternly reminded him of the Pact of Alliance with Japan, noting that Japan's other independent partners had already declared war—including the Chinese Nanjing regime, Thailand, Burma, and even Subhas

Chandra Bose's provisional government of India. Laurel was at a loss for what to do. He called a meeting of the cabinet and Council of State, which hashed out four possible strategies: (1) resist Japanese pressure; (2) escape to the mountains; (3) commit suicide; or (4) make a declaration that U.S. leaders would understand to have been coerced by the Japanese.[96]

Nobody seriously considered the first three alternatives. The Laurel cabinet instead saw equivocation as their only option. They decided to make a declaration that was vague enough to be acceptable to Japan but also avoided conscripting Filipinos for active military service and could be read by policy makers in Washington as imbued with a spirit of resistance. In the end, Foreign Minister Recto came up with a creative solution. Instead of declaring war, he suggested they proclaim "the existence of a state of war." This implied a passive attitude to the war, a mere recognition that war existed with an attack on the republic. Laurel, Roxas, and other cabinet members agreed that declaring a state of war was the only possible move given the serious constraints placed on their freedom of action.[97] The Philippine government officially declared the state of war on September 22 and announced it nationwide in a September 26 radio broadcast. Recto later argued that this declaration constituted an unmitigated diplomatic success. Japan, he argued, got "exactly nothing." Without the commitment to conscript Filipinos into the Japanese military, he believed, the declaration was worthless.[98] Recognizing this, one observer wrote, "Good Work! This compromise complies with Nippon 'recommendations' but . . . does not change materially the previous status quo if at all."[99]

The point was lost on Japan. Ambassador Murata, for instance, praised Laurel's "decisive decision, courage, and ardent love for country" as expressed by his "resolute declaration of war on America and Britain" in a September 23, 1944, diary entry.[100] The imperial general headquarters in Tokyo took note that the Philippines declared a "state of war" (*sensō jōtai*) but failed to distinguish this from making a declaration of war (*sensen fukoku*).[101] Even the semi-official Japanese histories of World War II miss the intended point of Laurel's declaration, noting that "the Republic of the Philippines made known their position to fight with Japan against the United States and Great Britain."[102] In the end, this was primarily a victory in semantics, but it also was a small triumph in that the Laurel government satisfied Japan while ensuring that Filipinos would not be conscripted into fighting a war nobody wanted.

These negotiations, however, constituted the visible tip of an iceberg of diplomatic activity. Broadly speaking, the Laurel government engaged in two types of diplomacy: protests to the Japanese forces and official and cultural diplomacy with Japan proper. Protests of Japanese maltreatment generally took the form of letters to the commander of the Imperial Japanese Army, who had administrative control over the Japanese Fourteenth Army in the Philippines. Otherwise, the fledgling government engaged in such activities as heading diplomatic and cultural missions abroad, sending Filipinos in study-abroad programs to Japan, and receiving statesmen and missions from its fellow Asian nations. Likewise, the new Philippine embassy engaged in supporting operations, preparing visas, telegrams, and *notes verbales*.[103]

Officials in the Laurel regime spent a prodigious amount of time writing letters of protest to the Japanese military. As described in chapter 5, Laurel protested the military's use of the Alabang Biological Laboratory, which he thought inhibited Philippine scientific and pharmaceutical potential and prevented the Philippines from developing its own serums and vaccines. Laurel also protested Japanese atrocities in a May 29, 1944, letter to Lieutenant General Wachi. The letter took issue with meaningless acts of cruelty in the barrio of Nag-iba, located in Mindoro Province's municipality of Calapan. According to Laurel, at midday on April 20 a company of Japanese soldiers apprehended eleven Filipinos, questioning whether they had seen guerrilla fighters in the area. The Filipinos replied that they had not. Not believing them, the Japanese soldiers then tied up five of them (before running out of rope), suspending them horizontally from a tree. They then flogged all eleven with wooden and bamboo sticks as wide as a man's forearm, leaving most of them unconscious by the roadside. One reportedly died of injuries sustained in the beating. Another vomited blood. All sustained severe contusions and bruises, especially around the wrists and ankles. "I wish to protest," Laurel wrote, "against the outlandish procedure adopted by the Japanese soldiers on this particular occasion. Incidents of this nature spoil the morale of the civilian populace and cannot but sow rancor against the Army in the hearts of the people."[104]

Other times, it was the ministry of foreign affairs that protested Japanese actions. Foreign Minister Recto recalled his ministry authoring multiple energetic complaints to the Japanese military. The most famous one came in a letter Recto wrote to Lieutenant General Wachi, dated June 20, 1944, which outlined the abuses, atrocities, and brutality committed by the very Japanese forces that were supposed to have recognized Philippine independence.[105] The letter reads like a feature column, highlighting a litany of grievances the Philippines had with its Japanese partners. Slapping Filipinos in the face, beatings, tying them to posts or making them kneel in public, *Kenpeitai* arrests of Filipinos (who disappeared completely), the seizure of private residences and large tracts of land, and countless cases of torture and murder, Recto argued, constitute a source of mounting dissatisfaction within the Philippines. "The only sign of independence," Recto declared, "is the display of the Filipino flag." But this hardly convinced Filipinos of the benevolence of Japanese motives. Recto thus called on Wachi to resolve such grievances, emphasizing that it was in Japan's interest to do so. "For how, otherwise," Recto contended, "would it be possible to induce the Filipino people, or any people for that matter, to defend a country that they may not call their own, or to safeguard an independence that does not exist?"[106]

The republic also engaged in more cordial official and cultural diplomacy to strengthen relations with its Asian partners. The delegation sent to the Greater East Asia Conference constitutes the best example of official diplomatic activities. The conference provided an opportunity to meet and hobnob with other Asian delegations. It also offered a chance to articulate shared understandings of the Greater East Asia Co-Prosperity Sphere. Laurel, for instance, made use of the conference not only to meet his peers from East and Southeast Asia. He also used it to remind Japan that the new order was not only for Japan's interests. Instead, as noted in chapter 5, Laurel argued that it was for the prosperity of *all* member nations, not for Japan alone. In April 1945, members of the Philippine embassy took part in the follow-up Greater East Asia Ambassadors Conference, during which Ambassador Vargas noted his approval and celebrated the decisions to bequeath independence to the Netherlands Indies and other territories.[107]

The wartime Philippine republic also used cultural diplomacy to foster mutual understanding with Japan. In 1944 the fledgling republic sent a group of 25 *pensionados* to study abroad in Japan. Ambassador Vargas drove home the aim of this program in a March 30, 1944, speech in Tokyo before the Philippine Society of Japan. "What we are after," Vargas stated, "is to get the Japanese and the Filipino peoples to know and understand one another better." Better understanding, he argued, would help both sides see "each other's best points" rather than the ones that breed both prejudice and mutual suspicion.[108] This *pensionado* diplomacy, however, was a mixed bag. Whereas some in fact shared each other's best points, other *pensionados* became the source of never-ending headaches. On one occasion, Ambassador Vargas learned that Japanese forces had detained a *pensionado* named Jose de Ungria for trying to escape to Russia. Ungria had been assigned to a fishing school in Hokkaidō. But he fled to Sakhalin, hoping to find the way to Russia. Unfortunately, however, his escape route brought him to the hands of the Japanese army, which imprisoned him and roughed him up, knocking out a few of his teeth. Ambassador Vargas negotiated his return to the Philippines, succeeding only after arguing that Ungria was "out of his mind with homesickness."[109]

Finally, the Philippine foreign ministry sent and received diplomatic missions. In April 1944, for instance, the Laurel government sent an official gratitude mission to Japan and Manchukuo. This mission was headed by Speaker Benigno S. Aquino and joined by such political heavyweights as Chief Justice José Yulo, finance minister Antonio de las Alas, agriculture minister Rafael R.

Alunan, Kalibapi director-general Camilo Osias, and secretary Andres V. Castillo. In sending the mission the Laurel government hoped to express their appreciation for independence and to promote "mutual understanding." Japan met the mission with pomp and splendor. Aquino, accompanied by Ambassador Vargas, was received by the emperor in the Phoenix Hall, where he was presented with the First Class Order of the Rising Sun. In Manchukuo as well, the delegation met with Emperor Pu-Yi and dined at a fancy court banquet.[110] Other times, the Philippines hosted diplomatic missions. Ba Maw made a stopover to visit the Philippines on November 18, 1943, on his way back to Burma from the Greater East Asia Conference. President Laurel gave a banquet in Ba Maw's honor the following day, mustering all the pageantry and splendor he could for his Burmese peer.[111] And the ministry of foreign affairs also hosted the Burmese Special Research Commission, which visited the Philippines in July 1944. Foreign minister Recto considered the commission's visit as one of the most significant events of the budding Philippine republic.[112]

The Burmese story is more complicated. Most histories dismiss the wartime diplomatic establishment as meaningless. In large part, this owes to Foreign Minister Nu's disdain for his own position and for Burmese foreign affairs. Nu did not feel this way from the outset of his assumption of the foreign ministry. He admitted enjoying discussions of foreign and domestic policies with staff members, and he reveled in his deferential treatment as a governmental elite. Nonetheless, Nu revealed that he was unable to hold his head high as foreign minister. "I felt rather ashamed of my position," Nu later recalled.

> In other independent countries if there was any subject for discussion with a foreign ambassador, not merely the Minister or Deputy Minister but even the Secretary could call him to the Foreign Office to discuss it. But in Burma we received the Japanese Ambassador on his first arrival and he came to call on us once afterwards. That was all we saw of him at the Foreign Office. If I wanted to discuss anything I had to go to his office, but if he wanted to discuss anything the Foreign Minister was not good enough and he went over his head direct to the Adipati [Ba Maw]. If he had any business with the Foreign Office he would not come himself, but only sent his Chargé d'Affaires. I much disliked having to put up with these slights, and as I could not escape being affronted I wanted to clear out.[113]

Nu had not initially wanted any role in government. Nor did he originally want to take part in the Burma Independence Preparatory Committee. In fact, from early 1942 he had actively avoided politics, seeking instead to continue his career as a writer. But after receiving the Japanese go-ahead to prepare for independence, Ba Maw refused to take no for an answer. Ba Maw hinted that he would not be around for much longer, and he told Nu that he had a unique opportunity to help build the new Burma. "Now that you have a chance," he said, "do try to learn the work, and let me give you a good practical training."[114] Nu only agreed on the condition that he would not be included when the committee became a full-fledged government council.

But with independence near, Ba Maw reneged on his promise. On July 30, 1943—two days before Burma received independence—Ba Maw summoned Nu, Thakin Mya, Than Tun, Aung San, and several others to the Government House in Rangoon. Once there, Nu found himself pressured into assuming the position of either minister of home affairs or minister of foreign affairs. The verbal assault continued for a couple of hours. As Nu's only defense was that he wanted to become a writer, he found himself overwhelmed and ultimately relented. Owing to Aung San's advice that the foreign affairs were the more important task, Nu capitulated. The following day, he told Ba Maw that he would take the foreign minister's portfolio.

Nu initially found that he loved the pleasantries of power and the respect accorded to him by his staff. But he ultimately despaired of his yearlong term as foreign minister. He did not take part in the most important diplomatic events of the new Burmese state. Unlike his Philippine counterpart, Nu did not sign the treaty of alliance with Japan. Ba Maw did so in his place, laying bare the discrepancies of power within the Burmese government. Nor did Nu participate in the Greater East Asia Conference as a member of Ba Maw's retinue. Instead, he remained confined to Rangoon, an afterthought within the Burmese foreign policy establishment.

Nu's disdain for the activities of the foreign ministry is palpable in his memoirs. He wrote that his ministry only dealt with three matters of any importance: apologizing for a Burman sentry who wounded a Japanese soldier; negotiating the arrest of a Burman involved in a failed plot to assassinate Ba Maw; and convincing the Japanese ambassador to allow Subhas Chandra Bose the seat of honor at the wedding of Bo Yan Naing to Ba Maw's daughter, Tinsa Maw. "Otherwise," Nu recalled, "there was nothing worth mentioning." He thought of the ministry's daily operations, whether dealing with telegrams or greetings and sending off foreign visitors, as "trifling business," and he noted that sending cables became such an integral part of what the foreign ministry did that it was unofficially dubbed the Telegraph Office.[115] Thakin Mya, who served as foreign minister after Nu resigned in 1944, felt much the same way. Shortly after war's end, Mya told his British interrogator that his main responsibilities were limited to making "broadcast speeches on behalf of the Government" and dealing with the Japanese ambassador.[116] These statements have led postwar scholars to dismiss the foreign ministry as "an emblem of 'independence' and an insignia of prestige."[117]

The wartime foreign ministry was indeed inconsequential, but scholars should not throw the baby out with the bathwater and reject outright all its activities. After all, some leaders, like Foreign Secretary and later Vice Foreign Minister Kyaw Nein, saw a useful purpose for the wartime foreign policy establishment: to train the next generation of Burmese diplomats. They even solicited Japanese assistance in training a Burmese diplomatic corps.[118] In her unpublished memoirs, Khin Myo Chit revealed that her own husband, Latt, was one of those so trained. "It was Ko Kyaw Nein's idea," she wrote, "to train men like Ko Latt to be future diplomats in this bogus foreign office so that they would be ready to serve when Burma became a really independent state."[119] Language classes were opened to prepare future diplomats.[120] Moreover, work such as press reports, cables, and wires—the trifling business that Nu derided—are central to the operations of foreign ministries. The same can be said for multiple types of diplomatic exchanges, from attending functions to making speeches, greeting and sending off visitors, serving as the nation's voice abroad, and always ensuring proper decorum. Those Burmese who joined the ministry gained firsthand experience in these aspects of foreign policy.

Like that of the Philippines, the Burmese government engaged in official diplomacy with Japan, symbolized by its participation in both the 1943 Greater East Asia Conference and the follow-up 1945 Ambassadors Conference. That said, Burmese diplomacy was much less contested than its Philippine counterpart. Although Ba Maw at times protested the realities of Japanese rule, he was much more likely to use personalized diplomacy to celebrate the Japan-Burma relationship and to reaffirm the goals of the Pacific Charter, Japan's Greater East Asia Joint Declaration. For instance, in mid-November 1944, he went to Tokyo with Minister of Cooperation U Tun Aung, Vice Minister of Foreign Affairs U Kyaw Nein, and his personal secretary to celebrate the one-year anniversary of the Greater East Asia Conference. During his stay, he met with the emperor, Prime Minister Koiso Kuniaki, Foreign Minister Shigemitsu, and other leaders, and he continually stressed that an all-out fight was "the only way for us to survive, and also for the Joint Declaration of the East Asiatic Nations to survive."[121] Was this stress on the Pacific Charter a type of mild resistance—an effort to get Japan to practice more fully what it preached? Perhaps. But what is more likely is that Ba Maw saw in his personalized diplomacy the chance to carve out an advantageous position for Burma if the Co-Prosperity Sphere survived the war.

Wartime independence also provided Burmese with opportunities to travel to and interact with foreign countries. During 1943 and 1944, a string of other missions that included politicians, newspapermen, researchers, educators, students, and entrepreneurs visited Japan and other nations in the Co-Prosperity Sphere. With the Burmese Cultural Mission, headed by former school headmaster U Ba Lwin, twenty-eight Burmese toured Japan's principal towns, factories, and other sites.[122] Burma also set up a program of awarding state scholarships tenable in Japan to the ablest of Burmese young students between seventeen and twenty years of age. The program began in 1943 with plans for a modest twelve scholarships. By 1944, Burma had sent fifteen state scholars to study in Japan and proposed to send a total of fifty per year.[123] Moreover, as mentioned above, Dr. Ba Han led the Special Research Commission across the various polities of the Co-Prosperity Sphere. As Ba Maw later noted, this was the only team of its kind touring Southeast Asia during the war.[124]

The importance of such foreign policy efforts in both the Philippines and Burma, however meager, should not be overlooked. As a British policy paper admitted, Burma before the war had little experience in foreign affairs, and few Burmese had either official or unofficial experience of, or connections with, neighboring Thailand, Malaya, China, Ceylon, or India.[125] The same could be said for the Philippines, in which only the Nacionalista oligarchy maintained ties with foreign countries. Granted, both wartime states never witnessed a steady stream of diplomats or businessmen traveling abroad. Nor did they forge a wide-ranging network of diplomatic contacts outside the Greater East Asia Co-Prosperity Sphere. By the time World War II ended, few Burmese or Filipinos had official or unofficial experience abroad. Nonetheless, through participation in conferences, developing relations with regional elites, and engaging in various types of official and cultural diplomacy, the Ba Maw and Laurel regimes had begun the process of institutionalizing their independence.

Imperial Collapse

By 1944, however, Japan's hold over its Co-Prosperity Sphere had become tenuous. Japanese forces could do little to stop the inexorable advance of the Allied powers. U.S. general Douglas MacArthur's return to the Philippines was only a matter of time. On October 20, 1944, MacArthur, whose skill in strategy was perhaps exceeded only by his talent for self-promotion, triumphantly broadcast his return as he landed on the Philippine island of Leyte. With aid from the large anti-Japanese guerrilla resistance movement, U.S. forces managed to take possession of the entire island by the end of the year. From there, MacArthur made haste to recapture Manila. Japanese forces, realizing the fragility of their hold over the archipelago, evacuated the Philippine government first to Baguio in

December 1944, and later to Tokyo via Taiwan in March 1945. By late June 1945, U.S. forces recaptured the entire island of Luzon and moved to clear the entire Philippine archipelago.

Japan fared little better in Burma. From late 1943, the Burma campaign had shifted decisively in the Allied powers' favor. Disastrous Japanese defeats in the Indian territories of Imphal and Kohima between March and June 1944 to a large extent broke Japanese power in Burma. Just as military disasters made defeat from without inescapable, poor treatment of the Burmese set the stage for revolt from within. Japan's earlier expansion across Southeast Asia had relied on a combination of hard power and the active support of transnational elite groups. From mid-1944, it became increasingly clear that Japan had neither. The weakening of Japan's hard power, the chafing of the Burmese under the cruelties of occupation, and repeated infringements on Burmese independence had undermined Japanese support. Revolt was but a matter of time.

Resistance came in fits and starts. The Army Young Resistance Group, a group of junior officers in the Military Preparations Bureau and ministry of defense, began circulating anti-Japanese propaganda from as early as October 1942. The group gradually increased its clout within the ministry of defense, giving officers such as Maung Maung, Aug Gyi, Tin Pe, and Khin Maung Gale the chance to build a cadre of loyal officers and soldiers. The group aimed at an uprising against the Japanese as soon as possible. In the summer of 1944, their labors bore fruit. They linked up with Thakin Soe, the communist insurgent leader hiding in the Arakan countryside, and even convinced the far more cautious Aung San to ready the BNA for a full-scale revolt.[126] By August 1944, Aung San had begun to publicly criticize the state of affairs in Burma, giving speeches in Rangoon that denounced Burmese independence as little more than a sham. "What is freedom," he cried out in an August 1 speech at the Jubilee Hall, "and where is it? The truth is that the freedom we have in Burma today is only on paper."[127]

By early August 1944, the Army Young Resistance Group helped create what ultimately became known as the Anti-Fascist People's Freedom League (AFPFL)— a political alliance between Aung San's BNA, Thakin Soe's Communist Party of Burma, and the People's Revolutionary Party. Aung San was appointed president and military leader, and Thakin Soe as political leader. At the meeting, Aung San read out the AFPFL's new manifesto, "Drive out the Japanese Fascist barbarian Imperialists." The manifesto denounced Japanese exploitation and persecution, railed against the shameful treatment of Burmese monks and monasteries, and called on Burma "to drive out the Japanese militarists and their capitalists, big and small."[128] The AFPFL called for the sabotage of Japanese war efforts, the denial of labor and materiel to Japan, the revolt of the BNA, the assassination of known traitors or collaborators, and the uniting of the people, irrespective of rank, religion, or ethnic group. The young revolutionaries also divided the country into eight resistance areas, in which they planned to open hostilities as early as October 1944. But from the outset Thakin Soe gave only half-hearted support, despite the enthusiasm of his younger followers. Even Aung San and the BNA dithered, postponing the uprising to 1945.[129]

Ba Maw was not unaware that members of his inner circle were engaged in political activities against the Japanese. It is doubtful, however, whether he realized the full extent of AFPFL plans. An Anglophobe, Ba Maw was reluctant to welcome back the British. Even though he himself had strained relations with Japan, Ba Maw continued to warn the Burmese that they would lose all should the British return. Despite these feelings, when he finally learned of the plot from Thakins Nu and Than Tun in early 1945, Ba Maw refused to betray it to Japan. In his discussions with Nu, he warned that the plotters "are playing with fire," but he admitted that all he cares about is independence and advised that they take great care.[130] Any further efforts to court Ba Maw were met with rebuff. Whatever Burmese leaders thought of Ba Maw's opportunism, narcissism, and lust for political power, most held a grudging respect for his nationalism and his unwillingness to betray his compatriots.

On March 27, 1945, the BNA revolted against Japan. Resistance groups across Burma, many working independently, began attacking Japanese forces.[131] Carrying a new flag—a red base with a white star in the upper left side—the resistance armies fought alone until Aung San met up with British lieutenant general William Slim, who had recaptured Rangoon in early May.[132] Slim was immediately impressed with Aung San, whom he regarded as a genuine nationalist and an honest, intelligent man. "Go on, Aung San," Slim remembered taunting Aung San. "You only come to us because you see we are winning!" To this, Aung San retorted, "It wouldn't be much good coming to you if you weren't, would it?" Once working together, Slim also viewed the BNA troops favorably. He believed the Burmese troops obeyed orders well and were useful in intelligence operations and in tying down Japanese troops. They were a valuable, if junior, partner in Britain's fight to reclaim Burma.[133]

The irony of the turn back to Britain is palpable. The mercurial patriotic collaborators, who had turned to Japan to oust the British just three years earlier, now looked to Britain to help recapture "independent" Burma from Japan. This did not, however, imply that Burmese nationalists were giving up on independence. Far from it. By this time, they saw little value in serving as a pawn in Japan's Co-Prosperity Sphere, and they considered Britain the better partner in securing freedom from Japanese oppression and interference. Aung San thus promised Slim that he would continue to work with British military forces and delay talks of independence until after Japan's defeat.

After the British recapture of Rangoon on May 3, 1945, British forces and the BNA worked together to pacify the rest of Burma, often encountering hard-fought pockets of resistance. Japanese forces continued fighting until late October 1945, well after the emperor's August 15 broadcast of Japan's intention to surrender. Finally, on October 24, Burma Area Army commander Kimura Heitarō surrendered his forces in a ceremony at Rangoon University. Kimura and the Japanese officers under his command unfastened their swords and presented them to Mountbatten's representative, Lt. Gen. Sir Montagu Stopford.[134] With this act, the war for Burma had finally ended. Yet as one struggle ended, the political struggle for self-government began anew.

Japan's role in Burma's push for independence was perhaps best symbolized in a June 15, 1945, BNA parade in Rangoon. This parade, held months before war's end, witnessed the BNA in its pride and glory. Burmese soldiers, attired in their full (albeit tattered) Japanese-style military garb, goose-stepped through the streets of Rangoon to the considerable displeasure of British onlookers.[135] With not a hint of irony, Burmese soldiers wore the garb of Japanese imperialism while reveling in their liberation from Japanese rule. This is highly symbolic. Burmese nationalists used the very institution Japan built to help destroy the Japanese position in Burma. Local leaders took what they could from Japan, using the Co-Prosperity Sphere for anticolonial ends.

Independence in Transition

In the middle of 1944, Aung San reportedly sought out Ba Maw to complain about the state of Burmese independence. "The Japanese are insincere and over-bearing," he protested. "They are only using us." Ba Maw agreed, but he retorted, "What you say is only a part of the truth. There are other parts too. If the Japanese use us, let us use them in turn."[136] It is unclear whether this conversation occurred, as Ba Maw recorded it nearly two decades after the war's end. Nonetheless, Ba Maw's statement can still be taken as emblematic of the actions taken by Burma's political establishment during the wartime years. Rangoon built new governmental institutions they had lacked in the colonial era. Kyaw Nein and others sought to use the "bogus foreign office" to train the future diplomats of Burma. In this situation, Hla Pe later noted, "civil servants began to share with politicians a pride in what Burmese could accomplish on their own."[137] Finally, Aung San led the very army Japan built in revolt, helping expel Japanese power from Burma.

A similar story occurred in the Philippines. Like in Burma, Philippine politicians were more than the mere puppets the Allied powers portrayed them to be. "Laurel and his cabinet-men privately admitted that they were puppets," wrote Sergio Osmeña, Jr., the son of the Nacionalista politician in exile. But, he argued, "they were puppets with a subtle purpose . . . of making the republic a shield and a rampart of the people against the atrocities and machinations of Japan and her scheming rapacious warlords."[138] Osmeña was correct in noting the Laurel regime's desire to protect the Philippines. But he might have also mentioned another subtle purpose: state building. Laurel sought to reorganize the government to be simple and efficient, and he created new governmental institutions the country had lacked under U.S. rule. And Philippine leaders gained firsthand experience in these new institutions. This was particularly true of the Philippine diplomatic establishment, which, as historian Ricardo Jose notes, provided "hands-on training to a number of Philippine diplomats."[139]

Although a similar process may have occurred in both countries, Philippine collaboration differed from its Burmese counterpart in the extent to which the Laurel regime made use of subtle everyday resistance, or what James C. Scott calls the "weapons of the weak."[140] Instead of overt opposition to Japan, they employed such strategies as stalling, foot dragging, noncompliance, and resistant mutuality. This resistance was by no means total. Refusing to declare war and protesting self-serving policies constituted part of a protracted struggle the Laurel government used both to make its presence felt and to shield the Philippines from Japanese abuses of power. In the process, elites in Manila attempted to preserve the Philippine order while awaiting MacArthur's return and Japan's ultimate defeat. In the Philippines, then, subtle resistance and collaborative institution building happened side by side, and elites in Manila were far more likely to employ the weapons of the weak than their counterparts in Rangoon.

In the end, Japan benefited from Philippine and Burmese state building far more than did either of its partners. The establishment of functioning independent governments in both Burma and the Philippines was a propagandist's dream. Bequeathing independence was part and parcel of attempts to showcase Japanese benevolence and to rally Asia behind Japan's cause. More importantly, however, in some sense state building had the potential to bind each regime even more firmly in a semicolonial embrace. A perfect example of this are central banks, which Japan helped establish in Taiwan (1899), Korea (1910), Manchukuo (1932), Inner Mongolia (1937), Beijing (1938), and the Chinese Nanjing regime (1941). The new central banks in the Philippines and Burma joined them as important instruments of Japanese monetary imperialism. By fixing their local currencies to the yen, and by using the yen as their reserve currency and as the currency to settle their balance-of-payments accounts, Japan's "money doctors" believed central banks would help pull the region into a self-sufficient yen bloc, led by Japan.[141]

Nonetheless, this process of institutionalizing independence had unintended consequences that lasted into the postwar era. For the Philippines, the main impact of the war was in the training of its diplomatic establishment. Many officials who served in the wartime ministry of foreign affairs (1943–44) continued on to have careers in the postwar department of foreign affairs. Press and publications officer Salvador P. Lopez became a secretary of foreign affairs as well as an ambassador to the United States, France, and the United Nations. Vice Minister of State for Foreign Affairs Emilio Abello in 1949 served as minister plenipotentiary to the United States. First Secretary at the Philippine embassy in Tokyo Leon Ma. Guerrero by 1954 had risen to the position of undersecretary of foreign affairs. A number of other diplomatic officers also transitioned directly into the postindependence Philippine diplomatic establishment, as shown in table 7.

TABLE 7. Phillipine Diplomatic Personnel

NAME	MINISTRY OF FOREIGN AFFAIRS (1943–1944)	DEPARTMENT OF FOREIGN AFFAIRS (1946–)
Emilio Abello	Vice minister of state for foreign affairs	Minister plenipotentiary to the United States (1949)
Teodoro Evangelista	Counselor	Counselor, political and cultural affairs (1946)
Salvador P. Lopez	Press and publications officer	Undersecretary of foreign affairs (1961–1963); secretary of foreign affairs (1963–1964); ambassador to the United Nations, the United States, and France
Mauro Calingo	Secretary	Chief, division of controls (1946)
Octavio L. Maloles	Law officer	Special assistant, office of legal affairs (1946)
Jacinto C. Borja	Chief protocol officer	Chief, division of European and African affairs (1946)
Leon Ma. Guerrero	Second secretary and first secretary, Philippine embassy in Tokyo	Assistant chief, division of European and African affairs (1946); undersecretary of foreign affairs (1954)

Compiled from Republic of the Philippines, *Official Gazette* 1, no. 6 (March 1944): 630; Ministry of Foreign Affairs, *Bulletin* 1, no. 2 (February 16–March 31, 1944), 59; Japanese Occupation Papers reel 4, UP; Public Relations Office, *Official Directory of the Republic of the Philippines*, 1946 (Manila: Bureau of Printing, 1946), 9–10; J. L. Vellut, "Foreign Relations of the Second Republic of the Philippines, 1943–1945," *Journal of Southeast Asian History* 5, no. 1 (March 1964): 133–34.

The Burmese case paralleled that of the Philippines, with some wartime personnel filling positions in the postindependence government. Wartime vice foreign minister U Kyaw Nein served as minister of foreign affairs in late 1948, and again when Burma reestablished diplomatic relations with Japan in 1952. U (Thakin) Nu became minister of foreign affairs for a few days in April 1949, and he also held the post of prime minister of Burma through most of the period between 1948 and 1962. Ba Lwin, too, later served as minister and later as ambassador to the dominion of Ceylon (Sri Lanka).[142]

For Burma, however, the primary legacy of the war years for Burma was military in nature. The war militarized Burmese society. Independence brought about the creation and consolidation of the first ethnic Burman army since the British annexation of Burma into the Indian Empire. Under Japanese tutelage, Burma trained the next generation of leaders in military and political affairs. The rebirth of the Burmese army, governor Dorman-Smith wrote in his unpublished memoirs, stood as the visible sign of Burmese sovereignty. "Aung San," he further noted, "stood for the revival of Burma's old glory as an independent nation."[143] Of course, the revival of Burma's army was a turning point in another sense as well. After 1942 military men, not politicians or colonial officials, dominated the political stage. This was most dramatically realized with General Ne Win's coup d'état on March 2, 1962, and subsequent rule by military junta.

By the time Burma received independence from Britain in 1948, Burmese leaders had largely eschewed the Japanese military system for its British counterpart. But the wartime era was still significant for personnel and structural innovations. The wartime regime trained a core of officers that led the postwar Burmese military, including well-known generals Aung San and Ne Win. Moreover, certain Japanese military innovations such as the Military Preparations Bureau had an afterlife in the postcolonial era. A decade after the war, Maung Maung and Aung Gyi used the Military Preparations Bureau as a model for Burma's new Military Planning Staff, the agency responsible for reorganizing the Tatmadaw (the Burma Armed Forces).[144] Although Maung Maung did not fully succeed in streamlining the army administration, his Military Planning Staff built new institutions throughout the 1950s with little civilian oversight.

The Greater East Asia Co-Prosperity Sphere was thus not wholly one-sided. Certainly, Japan's wartime empire was oppressive and domineering, callous and brutal. But it also provided limited space that enterprising leaders in the periphery could use to their advantage. The patriotic collaborators in Manila and Rangoon used this space, creating new governmental institutions and gaining experience in governmental affairs. The fall of the Japanese Empire in

August 1945 and the brief return of the colonial empires to the Philippines and Burma stalled or undermined many of these efforts. But whether through military or diplomatic issues, the wartime period had lingering legacies well into the postwar era of decolonization. The Co-Prosperity Sphere was thus a contested process that served both imperial and anti-imperial ends, and left its traces on Asia well after its collapse.

THE CO-PROSPERITY
SPHERE IN HISTORY

There were only two times that the leaders of Greater East Asia assembled in Tokyo. The first was at the Greater East Asia Conference in November 1943. There the region's leaders spoke triumphantly of creating a new and just order, one that ensured friendly, fair relations and future political-economic cooperation. The second time, however, was in much less fortuitous circumstances. By 1946, after the Co-Prosperity Sphere's collapse, many Greater East Asia Conference participants now shared a life as inmates of Sugamo Prison, where some awaited war crimes trials. The incarceration of Japan's wartime leadership and Class A war criminals at Sugamo Prison is well known. Much less known, however, is that Burmese and Philippine leaders were also imprisoned there. Ba Maw, Thein Maung, José P. Laurel, Jorge B. Vargas, Benigno S. Aquino, and others shared a stifling loneliness in Sugamo. And they were housed in the very same prison as Tōjō Hideki, Matsuoka Yōsuke, Shigemitsu Mamoru, Kido Kōichi, Nagano Osami, Tōgō Shigenori, Hoshino Naoki, and other Japanese elites who had imagined building a new order for the region. Life at Sugamo served as a constant reminder of Japan's failed wartime dreams.

The Burmese and Philippine inmates forged intimate relations under the watchful eyes of their American prison wards. In fact, the Filipinos usually took their meals with their Burmese counterparts. This closeness was not simply one of convenience. Both parties spoke a common language: English. But more importantly, both groups were cut from the same colonial cloth. They shared ideals, had comparable educations, and had similar experiences under liberal colonial rule. The Philippine and Burmese legations in Tokyo, in particular, had maintained warm relations even before their time in Sugamo Prison. Leon Ma. Guerrero, the second secretary and later first secretary at the Philippine embassy in Tokyo, often visited the Burmese embassy (at Ambassador Thein Maung's invitation) for intimate meals. The discussions at embassy dinners often turned to the failures of Japan's idealistic new order. "Surely," Guerrero remembered, "there was no irony more significant or poignant in the capital of Asianism than the heated homesick discussions I used to have with the Burmese military attaché on who was more understanding and generous and democratic, the Americans or the British."[1]

The fact that such arguments took place in the capital of Pan-Asianism highlights the tensions within Japan's new order. As most Southeast Asians attested, any idealism Japan professed flew in the face of the realities on the ground. Many Japanese did believe in the idealistic mission to liberate Asia from Western domination. But at the same time, they thought that this idealism could only be accomplished by asserting Japanese self-interest. Asia could only be saved through Japanese political-economic dominance. These tensions between idealism and self-interest, between utopian dreams of and the realist pursuit of national power, were shared among modern empires. All modern colonial empires believed in a moral component to imperialism—that colonialism benefited colonizer and colonized alike. Japan, in this sense, might be best described as engaging in the Asian counterpart of the white man's burden.

Despite the promise of a new and inclusive Pan-Asian order, Japan delivered little more than war, oppression, control, cruelty, and hardship. But the Co-Prosperity Sphere's imperial dreams had unintended consequences: it initiated a broader process of decolonization that played out in the following decades. Ba Maw noted this in his postwar memoirs without a hint of irony. "The case of Japan is indeed tragic," he noted. "Looking at it historically, no nation has done so much to liberate Asia from white domination, yet no nation has been so misunderstood by the very peoples whom it has helped either to liberate or to set an example in many things." Ba Maw believed that Japan missed its chance to garner the respect and admiration of Asia. Japan's imperial mission started a process that brought about the end of imperialism and colonialism. But Japanese actions, especially those of the fanatical military, undid much of the love it would have otherwise garnered. He continued:

> Had her Asian instincts been true, had she only been faithful to the concept of Asia for the Asians that she herself had proclaimed at the beginning of the war, Japan's fate would have been very different. No military defeat could then have robbed her of the trust and gratitude of

half of Asia or even more, and that would have mattered a great deal in finding for her a new, great, and abiding place in the postwar world in which Asia was coming into her own. Even now, even as things actually are, nothing can ever obliterate the role Japan has played in bringing liberation to countless colonial peoples.[2]

This incisive critique, however, focuses more on outcomes than process. Had he access to the decisions made in Tokyo, Ba Maw would have recoiled in shock and dismay. The Co-Prosperity Sphere, after all, was not intended to be emancipatory in nature. It was a Janus-faced entity. One face looked forward to Asian liberation from the West. The other looked backward to the age of high imperialism, when great powers carved up much of the globe. This other face highlighted dreams of Japanese imperial control. Unfortunately for the region, both the forward- and backward-looking faces pointed to the same ambition—Asia under Japanese rule.

The crucible of 1940–45 could in many ways be thought of as the era of the two Pacific Wars. This notion, outlined in greatest detail by political historian Shinobu Seizaburō, reflects the fact that the wartime era witnessed not one but two concurrent conflicts that shaped the fate of Asia. The first Pacific War, he argues, was a war of empires. It was a fight primarily between imperial Japan and the combined forces of the U.S. and British empires for ascendancy in the Asia-Pacific. By the time Japan broadcast its desire to surrender on August 15, 1945, the conflict had ravaged Asia. This war of empires ended in tragedy, leading to the deaths of as many as thirty million people. But, as Shinobu contends, this was only one side of the Pacific War. At the same time, the era witnessed a second Pacific War, an anticolonial war fought by occupied territories in Southeast Asia for their independence. Japan both inspired and aided this process, and served as a catalyst for a surging ethnic nationalism that shaped the region in ensuing decades. For Shinobu, the very point of highlighting these two Pacific Wars was to show that Asian independence was a by-product of the war, rather than the intent of the Japanese policy.[3]

The stories of these two Pacific Wars, however, are better told through the lens of the Greater East Asia Co-Prosperity Sphere. The Sphere, after all, epitomized both aspects of the two Pacific Wars. On the one hand, the story of the Co-Prosperity Sphere is the story of Japan's revolt against the old order and its aggressive war of empires. The Co-Prosperity Sphere merged the realities of Japan's total empire with its emerging total war, and it became the focus of a process by which military and civilian elites imagined a new order in international politics, one that asserted Japanese leadership over the expanse of Greater East Asia under the guise of "Asian liberation." It thus represented more than a war of empires. The Co-Prosperity Sphere highlighted the fact that the Pacific War was also a war of visions for the future. And despite the fact that it was created in part to keep Germany out of Asia, the Sphere linked Japan with Germany and Italy in an ideological effort to forge a new world order.

As this study has shown, however, Japanese visions were by no means static. The Co-Prosperity Sphere was a moving target—a shifting, mutable, and contested notion, one that meant different things to different people at different times. It was reshaped and refined in accordance with the changing geopolitical situation in Asia. When Japanese power appeared ascendant, the Co-Prosperity Sphere took on a distinctly *imperial* cast. Foreign minister Matsuoka Yōsuke's vision of the Sphere signaled the return to sphere-of-influence politics reminiscent of late nineteenth-century imperialism. By 1942, while Japanese forces savaged Asia, political intellectuals and politicians alike reimagined it as a political-economic hierarchy of nations and territories under Japanese leadership. Japan was to succeed the Western colonial empires as the dominant power, the ruler of a united Greater East Asia. It was a powerful elder-brother nation, one that would both uplift and guide its regional family of nations and ethnicities. Nonetheless, by 1943 the changing tides of war led to yet another reimagining of the Sphere. At the Greater East Asia Conference of November 1943, Japan opportunistically signaled a new commitment to liberal internationalist ideals of independence, equality, and cooperative regionalism. Whereas earlier ideas envisioned Japanese domination, the conference reestablished a trend toward cooperative internationalism that lasted well beyond the end of the Pacific War.

The Pacific War thus served as the bloody stage for an erratic, unstable drama. This drama played out in the periphery of Japan's wartime empire, where military correspondents such as Kawachi Uichiro lamented the war's ever-shifting nature. "You couldn't tell what was really going on," he bewailed. "A place on a map would be declared Japan's 'life-line.' Then we'd be defeated and that place was no longer a 'life-line.' We'd use the phrase 'point of decisive battle' to describe a place like Leyte. Then it would change. It was constantly changing."[4] The same could be said for understandings of the Greater East Asia Co-Prosperity Sphere. *It was constantly changing.* When the Japanese Empire swelled in size and scope, the nature of the Sphere was vague and unclear, and the subject of continued debate among key agencies and leaders. It took the specter of defeat before policy makers finally resolved in 1943 to insert true meaning into the Sphere. But those ideas were never fully implemented and were opportunistically used by nationalist elites across Southeast Asia for their own ends. In short, the Sphere never emerged into a consistent ideology, a system of ideas and ideals that brought order to both public policy and private lives. The Sphere was little more than an illusion; political scientist Hashikawa Bunzō was correct to deride attempts to imagine it to "trying to work in another man's loincloth."[5]

Japan never had any master plan for regional hegemony. Nor was the Asian conflict the conscious policy of a group of cunning, Machiavellian conspirators. Instead, it is safer to say that the expanding visions for order were piecemeal and opportunistic, brought about by policy makers who desired regional ascendancy but remained at odds over how best to accomplish this aim. Opportunism in the pursuit of national power, in fact, had been a constant theme in Japanese foreign policy since the nation entered the international system in the middle of the nineteenth century. The Greater East Asia Co-Prosperity Sphere constituted the quintessence of such opportunism. German military victories in Europe led Japan to commit to its own regional order. Believing the world was breaking into large blocs, Japanese leaders resolved not to miss their chance to seize their own bloc through expansion into Southeast Asia. It was this resolve that led Foreign Minister Matsuoka to declare the establishment of the Co-Prosperity Sphere. When Japanese power reached its zenith, so did visions for a regional system with Japan at the helm. When Japanese power ebbed, Tokyo imagined a cooperative regionalism that would rally Asia to war and convince the Allies to make peace. If any widely understood grand strategy was at work during the wartime years, it was the grand strategy of opportunism.[6] Such policies, however, served Japan poorly. They led to imperial overreach and the catastrophic fall of the Japanese Empire.

The Co-Prosperity Sphere, on the other hand, was also the story of an anticolonial war fought within occupied territories for their independence. It was partly a military war, one in which nationalist leaders sought national liberation through force of arms. The Burma Independence Army and Sub-has Chandra Bose's Indian National Army, for instance, represented the main examples of this war for independence, and they have been the subject of many histories.[7] They collaborated with Japan for anticolonial ends, hoping to topple the British regimes and seize independence for themselves. This collaboration was primarily patriotic in character. Bose even shocked Japanese Pan-Asian leader Ōkawa Shūmei with the force of his conviction. "I am prepared," Bose told Ōkawa, "to shake hands even with Satan himself to drive out the British from India."[8]

This war, however, was not simply fought on the battlefields. The Co-Prosperity Sphere was also the site of a political war for national liberation waged by patriotic collaborators in the colonial capitals of Manila and Rangoon. Strikingly, the Philippine and Burmese patriotic collaborators sought to make use of the unfolding conflict as best they could and to use the Japanese Empire for anti-colonial ends. In this sense, they were every bit as opportunistic as their Japanese overlords. They engaged in a process of state building, creating new institutions and gaining experience in governmental affairs. Both Philippine and Burmese elites, for instance, built new diplomatic establishments and received on-the-job training in diplomatic affairs. Moreover, the Co-Prosperity Sphere in Burma not only witnessed the revival of the national army. Japanese institutions had legacies well into the 1950s. Burmese leaders used Japanese military innovations such as the Military Preparations Bureau as a model for the new Military Planning Staff, the institution responsible for reorganizing the country's armed forces. Nationalist elites in both countries thus attempted to use their *sham* independence to enact *real* gains. This highlights a major irony of Japan's imperial project: although part of an effort to construct a regional imperium, Japan ended up helping create institutions in Burma and the Philippines that eased the transition to postwar independence.

The Co-Prosperity Sphere witnessed conflicting, contradictory visions and processes. On the one hand, for leaders and intellectuals in Japan, it was the battle cry for centrality in regional affairs and world history. Envisioning and defining the Co-Prosperity Sphere became an important path toward establishing Japanese preeminence in Asia. In this sense, the Co-Prosperity ideal, like the Pacific War itself, betrayed Japan's imperial dreams. It epitomized efforts to institute hegemony and to convey to the rest of the world the benefits of Japanese regional domination. Like Hitler's empire in Europe, however, the Japanese new order never provided a convincing answer to a basic question: why should the region accept Japanese leadership except under duress? Failing to do so, Japan ended up producing ideas of "co-prosperity" that were derided in the Philippines as "prosperity-*ko*," or "me-first prosperity."[9] On the other hand, for the patriotic collaborators in Burma and the Philippines, the Co-Prosperity Sphere was not only the story of engaging with Japanese imperialism. It was also the backdrop against which they worked to gain or preserve future independence. Whereas Japanese leaders dreamt of a new order that would preserve Japanese leadership, often in highly oppressive and domineering ways, Philippine and Burmese nationalist leaders worked toward national goals of an independent future.

Asia was savaged in the process. World War II tore apart Burma. The war destroyed more economic and other infrastructure in Burma than in any other country in Southeast Asia, leaving the country in total disarray. It initiated what Robert H. Taylor describes as a twenty-year "contest between competing groups over which would resurrect the state, in what form, and in whose interest."[10] Even the triumph of independence in 1948 was tarnished by an emerging

Burmese-Karen ethnic and religious conflict that festered in ensuing decades. In fact, the Pacific War militarized Burmese society, serving as catalyst for what has been called "the world's longest-running civil war," a conflict that has lasted longer and has been far more destructive than the struggles against British and Japanese imperialism.[11] The war was no kinder to the Philippines. The Japanese occupation left the Philippines in a state of economic devastation, with agriculture and manufacturing in ruins. Owing to the misdeeds, brutal treatment, and wanton cruelty of Japanese forces, some historians write of the Japanese invasion in wholly negative terms: it was a national trauma that made many Filipinos more eager for the return of U.S. colonial rule.[12] A year after war's end, a newly independent Philippines had only begun the long process of recovery. But any recovery was complicated by a deepening peasant insurgency, the Hukbalahap Rebellion (1946–55), which grew out of the wartime anti-Japanese guerrilla movement. So successful was the Huk revolt that by 1950 it had brought the new Philippine government to the verge of collapse. Even the aggressor nation, Japan, found itself in ruins. By the time the atomic bombs fell on Hiroshima and Nagasaki, a large portion of the home islands had been destroyed. Japan's industrial capacity was crippled, its infrastructure in ruins, and millions suffered from poverty, homelessness, and starvation.

The era of the Co-Prosperity Sphere, however, was not merely a time of destruction. It was also a period of creation—when "order building," nation building, and vast destruction progressed side by side. These processes reshaped the landscape of the modern world. The Pacific War remapped Asia, heralding both the end of empire in Asia and the first wave of Asian decolonization. The conflict ended in catastrophe for the enfeebled European empires in Asia. The wartime humiliation and disarray of colonial administrations across Asia had undercut European prestige. Lacking the wherewithal and desire to contend with growing nationalist movements across the region, the European empires began a process of imperial retreat, often reluctantly and only after great bloodshed. From a long-term perspective, then, the conflict initiated the first wave of global decolonization. Within the first five years of the postwar era, the Philippines (1946), British India (1947), Burma (1948), Ceylon (1948), and Indonesia (1949) had all gained independence from their former colonial masters, and Vietnam was locked in a war of independence against a weakened France. In Burma's case, the war also engendered a sense of self-confidence in their struggle for independence. This newfound self-confidence was perhaps best stated by Thakin Ba Sein in a letter to Sir Hubert Elvin Rance on August 31, 1946. "The war has, however, drastically changed the whole situation," Ba Sein wrote. "It has brought forth most convincing proofs that [Burma's] aspiration is fully justified and that it is the national duty of her people to continue to struggle until full realization is achieved."[13]

By the end of the 1940s, it had become clear that Asia was fast approaching the end of the age of high imperialism.

The war remapped Japan as well, clarifying the boundaries of the Japanese nation in both territorial and psychological terms. The postdefeat settlements reduced Japan to its current territorial borders (minus Okinawa, which the United States returned to Japan in 1972). But the more important shift in Japan was psychological. According to Nakano Satoshi, it was Japan, not Southeast Asia, that was liberated by the global conflict. The tragedy of war, he argues, spiritually liberated Japan from the chains of the Japanese Empire.[14] The war, in this context, was the harbinger of the death of Japanese imperialism. But out of the ashes of imperialism rose a growing trend toward peaceful expansionism. Since the crucible of World War II, an economically vibrant Japan has maintained a fierce pacifist orientation in global affairs. Indeed, pacifism has been, through the second half of the twentieth century, perhaps the defining component of Japanese nationalism.

Even before war's end, some Japanese began recasting the Co-Prosperity Sphere in a way that would fit with the postwar order. By the time of the Greater East Asia Ambassadors Conference in April 1945, foreign minister Tōgō maintained that the purpose of the war was not only to liberate Greater East Asia but also to create "an international order that will bring prosperity to all nations of the world."[15] An even better example, however, can be found in a top-secret memorandum drafted by retired general Ugaki Kazushige on August 11, 1945, four days before the emperor broadcast the decision to surrender. Ugaki, who had left politics in 1944 to become president of Takushoku University, now confidently argued the blessings of Japan's Greater East Asia War. He wrote:

> The Greater East Asia War is [being fought] for the revival and defense of Greater East Asia, and for the liberation of all colonies across the world. It is for the realization of coexistence and co-prosperity for all humanity, and for the fulfillment of the grand ideals of *hakkō ichiu* and the construction of moral states. This has been expressed clearly in the Greater East Asia Declaration. Moreover, on the other hand, the ultimate aims [of the enemy]—as expressed in the Atlantic Charter as well as the Yalta Conference, the United Nations Conference on International Organization, and the Potsdam Conference—in the end have clearly converged with the fundamental principles of the Greater East Asia Declaration.[16]

Ugaki thus highlighted the meaninglessness of further hostilities. After all, both sides remained at war for the same ends: to create a world of "coexistence and co-prosperity for all humanity." The language of the Co-Prosperity Sphere, which had once justified Japan's war, now justified peace with the Allied powers. Even in surrendering, Japan had still won through its advancement of universal principles.

In the following months, Ugaki took this argument even further. By late September, he predicted a fallout between the victors of World War II, and he contended that Japan could take advantage of the postwar confrontations to realize its unfulfilled wartime dreams. Ugaki noted in a September 30 diary entry that conflicts would likely emerge between the United States and the Soviet Union for global leadership, and between the United States and Great Britain for leadership among the capitalist democracies. This constituted a unique opportunity to reassert Japan's dreams of global leadership, but in a different form. Ugaki believed that Japan should become "the most advanced pacifist nation," one that could mediate the disputes between the United States, Britain, and the Soviet Union. By becoming a model pacifist power, Japan in defeat could "establish itself in a leadership position so as to save them all from destruction and ensure true peace in the world." Ugaki even argued that this postwar pacifist identity could become the key to "realizing the vast strategy of *hakkō ichiu*." In this sense, Japan's wartime dream of *hakkō ichiu* was still achievable through pacifist leadership in international affairs. Strikingly, Ugaki was employing the defining principle of the Co-Prosperity Sphere—Japan's imagined East Asian bloc—both to reject any postwar imperialist division of the world into Soviet and American blocs and to legitimize Japan's reemergence into international politics.[17]

Former foreign minister Shigemitsu Mamoru justified the Sphere in similar terms. On December 20, 1945, four months after the surrender, he wrote of his vision for the Co-Prosperity Sphere as something that brought Japan in line with the democratic powers. "Though the Empire was a latecomer [to democratic global policy]," Shigemitsu argued, "the establishment of the wartime new policy that made use of nationalism and called for East Asian liberation and the revival of Asia was a unique policy, secured through war, that followed along with global trends. Perhaps this is because the policy is in line with the most important global trend: the principle of international democracy."[18] For Shigemitsu, the birth of Japan's postwar foreign policy of international engagement began not in 1945. Instead, it began in 1943, during the lead-up to the Greater East Asia Conference.

It is of no little significance that Shigemitsu Mamoru, the man who helped redefine Japanese wartime diplomacy, became a major player in Japan's reintegration into the postwar diplomatic world. Shigemitsu served as deputy prime minister and foreign minister when Japan attended the Bandung Conference in 1955 (although he did not attend the conference). Shigemitsu also oversaw Japan's admission to the United Nations. On December 18, 1956, he addressed the UN General Assembly to offer his sincere appreciation of Japan's admittance into international society. He spoke of Japan's relations with Asia in terms of "mutual cooperation and common destiny," terms reminiscent of the Greater East Asia Joint Declaration of 1943. The main difference, however, rested in his promise that Japan would be a progressive force, a "bridge between the East and the West."[19] Shigemitsu also oversaw the normalization of relations with the Philippines and the Soviet Union. In a June 1956 radio address celebrating the war reparations agreement with the Philippines, he highlighted Japan's desire to build relations of "common prosperity" and thereby "to contribute to the prosperity of Southeast Asia and to world peace."[20] Eleven years after the war's end, Shigemitsu continued to use his language of co-prosperity to reenter international society as a peaceful nation.

Some Asians, too, saw in international society the ghosts of Japan's Co-Prosperity Sphere. Ba Maw, who had a conflicted but sympathetic view, spoke of the Greater East Asia Conference as the first step toward the Bandung Conference, the first large-scale meeting of Asian and African states in 1955. He wrote in his memoirs, "There may be a controversy over the conflict between words and deeds in Japanese policy towards the rest of East Asia, but Tojo's statement of principles still remains true for Asia, as the Bandung Conference of 1955 has borne witness." Moreover, Ba Maw remained spellbound by the 1943 conference, which he saw as "the first time Asia became real and luminous for Asians," and the "first time Asians met together by themselves to plan and pursue their future."[21] Ba Maw was by no means alone in these beliefs. At the Asian Congress for World Federation, which was held in Hiroshima in 1952, Kagawa Toyohiko was surprised at the reaction from the Indian delegation. "What got our attention," he wrote, "was a remark from everyone in the Indian delegation. They said we, the Asian Congress for World Federation, can achieve what Japan has forever advocated: the East Asia Co-Prosperity Sphere ideal."[22]

Wartime apologists and historical revisionists no doubt welcomed such a reassessment, which validated the war many wartime figures believed they were fighting. Satō Kenryō, a retired lieutenant general and former head of the army's Bureau of Military Affairs, offered a compelling apologia for the Co-Prosperity Sphere. He wrote, "The Greater East Asia Co-Prosperity ideal, which we hoisted as our broad war aims, got rid of the colonial order of conquest and exploitation, and in its place attempted to build a new order of co-prosperity" that "represents the only path to eternal world peace." Although Japan lost its opportunity to build the new order in war, Satō argued that the ideal still lives on through such institutions as the European Economic Community.[23] Other authors are more simplistic, arguing that Japan martyred itself for Asian freedom from white imperialism. The resilience of these ideas is a worrying legacy of the war and has led Japanese historians such as Gotō Ken'ichi to fight for what should be an obvious point: that Japan used its "lofty ideals" as a smokescreen for its "aggressive war" for mastery over Asia.[24]

It has only been a vocal minority, however, who have attempted to recast Japanese imperialism in a positive light. The savagery and cruelty of Japan's occupation regimes were hard forgotten. The distrust and wariness they engendered were highlighted in 1957, as the Philippines prepared for a state visit from Prime Minister Kishi Nobusuke, a former minister in the Tōjō cabinet and planner of Japanese wartime policies. Teodoro F. Valencia, a renowned journalist and political commentator who had an influential column in the *Manila Times* called "Over a Cup of Coffee," wrote of the passions of memory that Kishi's visit inspired. "It is no secret," Valencia wrote, "that Filipinos have always felt themselves Asians. What happened during the Second World War under the feet of Japan has killed whatever germ of Asian brotherhood we felt. The Philippines is turning to nationalism today but the idea of Asian brotherhood is not gaining ground. We have Japan to blame for this."[25] By the late 1980s, suspicions of Japan remained. As Margaret Shapiro wrote in the *Washington Post* in October 1988, "Where Japan's military once led the charge to create a Greater East Asia Co-Prosperity Sphere, today yen-wielding businessmen and government bureaucrats representing new, rich Japan have fanned out across the Pacific. And they are welcomed, albeit warily, almost anywhere they go."[26] For better or for worse, the Co-Prosperity Sphere provided a lexicon from which Asia and the world could draw.

The ghosts of the Co-Prosperity Sphere have been difficult to exorcise. Japan's history disputes with China and South Korea have kept the past alive and relevant in the present. Likewise, the ghosts of Japan's wartime empire are equally palpable in the geography of Manila and Rangoon (now called Yangon). The tree-lined Jose Laurel Street, which runs through north-central Manila to the Malacañan Palace, pays homage to the wartime president of the Philippines. North-central Manila's principle commercial thoroughfare, Claro M. Recto Avenue, is named after the wartime minister of foreign affairs, and it intersects with roads named for two other national heroes, Manuel Quezon and José Rizal.[27] Aung San has likewise been memorialized across Yangon, with Bogyoke Aung San Park and the major thoroughfare Bogyoke Aung San Road, on which sits one of Yangon's major markets: Bogyoke Aung San Market. Other roads and parks are also named after Thakin Tun Shein (Bo Yan Naing) and Thakin Mya. In both cities, the wartime past remains alive in the geography of the present.

But the ghosts of Japan's Co-Prosperity Sphere throughout the rest of Southeast Asia were gradually overshadowed by the realities of the age of empire's end. The burgeoning Cold War turned areas of decolonization into theaters of conflict between liberal democratic and communist power blocs. It was these postwar wars of decolonization, internal conflicts, and the gradual stabilization of independence that shaped the region in the ensuing decades. Japan's dreams of creating a new international order were thus relegated to history and memory. The postwar order would be affected by different processes and guided by different dreams.

Abbreviations

APAC-BL	Asia, Pacific and Africa Collections, British Library
AFPFL	Anti-Fascist People's Freedom League
BDA	Burma Defense Army
BIA	Burma Independence Army
BIB	Burma Intelligence Bureau
BKS	*Biruma kōryaku sakusen*
BNA	Burma National Army
DGFP	Documents on German Foreign Policy
DR	*Daihon'ei rikugunbu*
FRUS	Foreign Relations of the United States
GCBA	General Council of Burmese Associations
GRIPS	National Graduate Institute for Policy Studies, Tokyo
HL-HU	Houghton Library, Harvard University
JACAR	Japan Center for Asian Historical Records
JFMA	Japan Foreign Ministry Archives, Diplomatic Records Office
JPLML	José P. Laurel Memorial Library
KSS-NDL	*Kensei Shiryōshitsu*, National Diet Library
LC	Library of Congress
MGC	Mauro Garcia Collection
NAD-Y	The National Archives Department, Yangon
NDL	National Diet Library
NIDS	National Institute of Defense Studies, Tokyo
NLP	National Library of the Philippines
PEC	Philippine Executive Commission
ROP	Republic of the Philippines
SSKSS	*Shōwa shakai keizai shiryō shūsei*
TG-NDL	*Teikoku gikai kaigiroku*, National Diet Library
TNA	The National Archives (UK)
UP	University of the Philippines

Notes

INTRODUCTION

1. Japan maintained forces in the Beiping area owing to the Boxer Protocol of 1901. Japan had taken part in the international expedition to quell the Boxer Uprising (1900–1901). The ensuing Boxer Protocol of 1901 permitted each of the powers to station soldiers in the railway towns in the Beiping area in order to protect the foreign legations from any future siege by enraged Chinese. These occupying forces had the right to engage in field exercises. But many Chinese believed that Japan's occupation was in contravention of the Boxer Protocol. Whereas other powers had at most two thousand soldiers, the Japanese occupation force by 1937 was composed of at least seven thousand soldiers. It was this force that first became embroiled in the China Incident.

2. Although they were supposed to serve as advisory bodies, liaison conferences in the wartime era constituted the highest level of Japanese decision making. They were liaisons between the cabinet and the high command. While membership varied, the liaison conferences always included the army chief of staff, the navy chief of staff, and the four principal ministers of the cabinet (the prime minister, army minister, navy minister, and foreign minister). Therefore, it was always heavily dominated by the military. Even an ad hoc inclusion of other members could not shift the balance in favor of civilian leaders.

3. Heraclitus wrote, "War is the father of all and the king of all; and some he shows as gods, others as men, some he makes slaves, others free." Taken from Diané Collinson and Kathryn Plant, *Fifty Major Philosophers*, 2nd ed. (London: Routledge, 2007), 12.

4. Bōeichō Bōei Kenshūjo, Senshishitsu, *Daihon'ei rikugunbu*, vol. 1 (Tokyo: Asagumo Shinbunsha, 1968), 526–30. Henceforth, all books in the ten-volume series will be abbreviated as DR. All translations from Japanese are mine unless otherwise noted.

5. This story is best told in Kenneth B. Pyle, *Japan Rising: The Resurgence of Japanese Power and Purpose* (New York: PublicAffairs, 2007), 66–136.

6. Matsuoka Yōsuke, *Kōa no taigyō* (Tokyo: Dai'ichi Kōronsha, 1941), 266–99.

7. "Dairisō, chokusai ni hyōgen," *Tokyo Asahi shinbun*, December 13, 1941, 1.

8. "Naikaku sōridaijin no enzetsu," January 22, 1941, *Kanpō gōgai*, Kizokuin giji sokkiruoku dai 2 gō, *Teikoku gikai kaigiroku* database (http://teikokugikai-i.ndl.go.jp/). Henceforth cited as TG-NDL.

9. Kawanishi Kōsuke, *Teikoku Nihon no kakuchō to hōkai: "Dai Tōa Kyōeiken" e no re-kishiteki tenkai* (Tokyo: Hōsei Daigaku Shuppankai, 2012), 7. See also Sugiyama Hajime, *Sugiyama memo: Daihon'ei seifu renraku kaigi tō hikki*, vol. 2 (Tokyo: Hara Shobō, 1967), 41–44 (hereafter cited as *Sugiyama memo*).

10. *Sugiyama memo*, 2:42–43.

11. The entire quote is as follows: "If anyone asks how you conceive the new Europe, we have to reply that we don't know. Of course we have some ideas about it. But if we were to put them into words it would immediately create more enemies for us. . . . When the time comes we will know very well what we want." Quoted in Mark Mazower, *Hitler's Empire: How the Nazis Ruled Europe* (New York: Penguin, 2008), 121.

12. The dominions included Canada, Australia, South Africa, New Zealand, and the Irish Free State. They shared a common sovereign with Britain but were formally independent of any British control.

13. See Sir Reginald Dorman-Smith Papers, Mss Eur E215/32A, Asia, Pacific and Africa Collections, British Library (hereafter abbreviated as APAC-BL).

14. Hatano Sumio, *Taiheiyō Sensō to Ajia gaikō* (Tokyo: Tokyo Daigaku Shuppankai, 1996), 104.

15. Takeshima Yoshinari, *Nihon senryō to Biruma no minzoku undō: Thakin seiryoku no seijiteki jōshō* (Tokyo: Ryūkei Shosha, 2003), 190–91.

16. See, for instance, Kobayashi Hideo, *"Dai Tōa Kyōeiken" no keisei to hōkai*, 2nd ed. (Tokyo: Ochanomizu Shobō, 2006); Kobayashi Hideo, *Dai tōa kyōeiken* (Tokyo: Iwanami Shoten, 1988); Hikita Yasuyuki, ed., *Nanpō Kyōeiken: Senji Nihon no Tōnan Ajia keizai shihai* (Tokyo: Taga Shuppan, 1995); Itō Takashi, *Nihon no rekishi, 30: Jūgōnen sensō* (Tokyo: Shōgakukan, 1976); Ienaga Saburō, *Taiheiyō Sensō* (Tokyo: Iwanami Shoten, 1968); Shinobu Seizaburō, *"Taiheiyō Sensō" to "mō hitotsu no Taiheiyō Sensō": Dainiji taisen ni okeru Nihon to Tōnan Ajia* (Tokyo: Keisō Shobō, 1988); Eguchi Keiichi, *Jūgōnen sensō shōshi* (Tokyo: Aoki Shoten, 1991); W. G. Beasley, *Japanese Imperialism, 1894–1945* (Oxford: Clarendon, 1987), 233. See also Arima Manabu, *Teikoku no Shōwa* (Tokyo: Kōdansha, 2010), 280–83.

17. See, for instance, Nicholas Tarling, *A Sudden Rampage: The Japanese Occupation of Southeast Asia, 1941–1945* (Honolulu: University of Hawaii Press, 2001); Jan Pluvier, *South-East Asia from Colonialism to Independence* (Kuala Lumpur: Oxford University Press, 1974); Christopher Bayly and Tim Harper, *Forgotten Armies: The Fall of British Asia, 1941–1945* (Cambridge, MA: Harvard University Press, 2004).

18. Kobayashi, *"Dai Tōa Kyōeiken" no keisei to hōkai*, 534.

19. Hayashi Fusao, "Dai Tōa Sensō kōteiron," *Chūō kōron* 80, no. 4 (April 1965): 222–44; and Hayashi Fusao, *Zoku - Dai Tōa Sensō kōteiron* (Tokyo: Tsubasa Shoin, 1967), 21, 485. For other revisionist works, see Hasegawa Michiko, "Sengo sedai ni totte no Dai Tōa Sensō," *Chūō kōron* (April 1983): 96–111; Fukada Yūsuke, *Reimei no seiki: Dai Tōa Kaigi to sono shuyakutachi* (Tokyo: Bungei Shunjū, 1991); Fukuda Yūsuke and Miura Shumon, "'Shinryaku no gyakusetsu': Dai Tōa Kaigi 1943," *Shokun!* 24, no. 2 (February 1992): 178–93.

20. Ienaga, *Taiheiyō Sensō*, 208. Another good example is found in the writings of Shinobu Seizaburō, who actively focused on wartime interactions between Japan and Southeast Asia. Shinobu maintains that independence was a by-product of the war, not the intent of Japanese policy. See Shinobu, *"Taiheiyō Sensō" to "mō hitotsu no Taiheiyō Sensō."* More recently, Kawanishi Kōsuke has shown that Japanese professions of "independence" and "liberation" meant little more than ousting the European colonial empires from Asia and replacing them with Japanese control. For a collection of his writings, see Kawanishi, *Teikoku Nihon no kakuchō to hōkai.*

21. Tamogami made similar comments in 2008 as well. See *Yomiuri shinbun*, November 1, 2008, 1. Strikingly, Tamogami ran for the governorship of Tokyo, garnering more than half a million votes.

22. *Asahi shinbun*, December 26, 2013, 11.

23. See Matsu'ura Masataka, *"Dai Tōa Sensō" wa naze okitanoka? Han Ajiashugi no seiji keizaishi* (Nagoya: Nagoya Daigaku Shuppankai, 2010); Eri Hotta, *Pan-Asianism and Japan's War, 1931–1945* (New York: Palgrave Macmillan, 2007). See also Sven Saaler and J. Victor Koschmann, eds., *Pan-Asianism in Modern Japanese History: Colonialism, Regionalism and Borders* (London: Routledge, 2007); and Abe Hirozumi, "'Dai Tōa Kyōeiken' kōsō no keisei," *Kitakyūshū daigaku hōsei ronshū* 16, no. 2 (January 1989): 121–46.

24. Eizawa Kōji, *"Dai Tōa Kyōeiken" no shisō* (Tokyo: Kōdansha Gendai Shinsho, 1995), 10.

25. Akazawa Shirō, "Senchū, sengo bunkaron," *Iwanami kōza Nihon tsūshi*, vol. 19 (Tokyo: Iwanami Shoten, 1993), 285–89.

26. Examples of scholarship in this school include Kawanishi, *Teikoku Nihon no kakuchō to hōkai*; Peter Duus, "Imperialism without Colonies: The Vision of a Greater East Asia Co-Prosperity Sphere," *Diplomacy and Statecraft* 7, no. 1 (1996): 70; Peter Duus, "The Greater East Asian Co-Prosperity Sphere: Dream and Reality," *Journal of Northeast Asian History* 5, no. 1 (June 2008): 143–54; Ikeda Hiroshi, ed., *Dai Tōa Kyōeiken no bunka kensetsu* (Tokyo: Jinbun Shoin, 2007); Janis Mimura, *Planning for Empire: Reform Bureaucrats and the Japanese Wartime State* (Ithaca, NY: Cornell University Press, 2011); John W. Dower, *War without Mercy: Race and Power in the Pacific War* (New York: Pantheon, 1986), 262–90; Aaron Stephen Moore, *Constructing East Asia: Technology, Ideology, and Empire in Japan's Wartime Era, 1931–1945* (Stanford, CA: Stanford University Press, 2013); and Gordon M. Berger, "The Three-Dimensional Empire: Japanese Attitudes and the New Order in Asia, 1937–1945," *Japan Interpreter* 12, nos. 3–4 (1979): 355–82. See also Francis Clifford Jones, *Japan's New Order in East Asia: Its Rise and Fall, 1937–45* (London: Oxford University Press, 1954), 330–400.

27. Adachi Hiroaki, *"Dai Tōa Kyōeiken" no keizai kōsō: Ken'nai sangyō to dai tōa kensetsu shingikai* (Tokyo: Yoshikawa Kōbunkan, 2013).

28. See Akira Iriye, *Power and Culture: The Japanese-American War, 1941–1945* (Cambridge, MA: Harvard University Press, 1981); Hatano, *Taiheiyō Sensō to Ajia gaikō*, and Hatano Sumio, "Senji gaikō to shūsen kōsō" (Ph.D. diss., Keio University, 1996). More recent work also notes this trend as well. See Takato Mori, *'Co-Prosperity' or 'Commonwealth'? Japan, Britain and Burma, 1940–1945* (Berlin: VDM, 2009).

29. The only major attempt, by Joyce Lebra-Chapman, is more an introduction of documents in translation than a full-scale study of the Co-Prosperity Sphere. See Joyce Lebra-Chapman, *Japan's Greater East Asia Co-Prosperity Sphere in World War II: Selected Readings and Documents* (Kuala Lumpur: Oxford University Press, 1975).

30. Ugaki Kazushige, *Ugaki Kazushige nikki*, vol. 1: *Meiji 35-nen 9-gatsu—Shōwa 6-nen 6-gatsu* (Tokyo: Misuzu Shobō, 1968), 150.

31. For an excellent analysis of the rise of total war thought in Japan, see Michael A. Barnhart, *Japan Prepares for Total War: The Search for Economic Security, 1919–1941* (Ithaca, NY: Cornell University Press, 1987), 22–49; Kurosawa Fumitaka, "Tanaka gaikō to rikugun," *Gunji shigaku* 21, no. 3 (December 1985): 17–34.

32. Robert Gerwarth and Erez Manela, eds., *Empires at War: 1911–1923* (Oxford: Oxford University Press, 2014).

33. See Sadao Asada, *From Mahan to Pearl Harbor: The Imperial Japanese Navy and the United States* (Annapolis: Naval Institute Press, 2006).

34. Yoshihisa Tak Matsusaka, *The Making of Japanese Manchuria, 1904–1932* (Cambridge, MA: Harvard University Asia Center, 2001), 391.

35. See Konoe Fumimaro, "Ei-Bei hon'i no heiwashugi o haisu," *Nihon oyobi Nihonjin*, December 15, 1918, 23–26.

36. Frederick R. Dickinson, *World War I and the Triumph of a New Japan* (Cambridge: Cambridge University Press, 2013), 65.

37. See Danny Orbach, *Curse on This Country: The Rebellious Army of Imperial Japan* (Ithaca, NY: Cornell University Press, 2017), 193–224; and Matsusaka, *Making of Japanese Manchuria*, 377–87.

38. Akira Iriye calls the Manchurian Incident "Japan's negative response to the Chinese idea of a new order." See Akira Iriye, *After Imperialism: The Search for a New Order in the Far East, 1921–1931* (Cambridge, MA: Harvard University Press, 1965), 300.

39. Prasenjit Duara, "The Imperialism of 'Free Nations': Japan, Manchukuo, and the History of the Present," in Ann Stoler, Carole McGranahan, and Peter Perdue, eds. *Imperial Formations* (Santa Fe, NM: SAR Press, 2007), 211–39.

40. Quoted in Yamamuro Shin'ichi, *Manchuria under Japanese Dominion*, trans. Joshua A. Fogel (Philadelphia: University of Pennsylvania Press, 2006), 36–37.

41. Hatano, *Taiheiyō Sensō to Ajia gaikō*, 103–4.

42. Louise Young, *Japan's Total Empire: Manchuria and the Culture of Wartime Imperialism* (Berkeley: University of California Press, 1998).

43. Mimura, *Planning for Empire*, 41–69.

44. Gaimushō, *Nihon gaikō nenpyō narabini shuyō monjo: 1840–1945*, vol. 2 (Tokyo: Hara Shobō, 1955), 401. Konoe further elaborated on this statement on December 22, asserting that the goals of the new order rested in the three points of "neighborly friendship, joint defense against communism, and economic linkages." Ibid., 407.

45. There was one other, shorter-term goal of Konoe's call for a new order in East Asia. The declaration also represented an attempt to establish a friendly satellite regime in China. Konoe had earlier refused to deal with the Nationalist regime and even gave a venomous call for the regime's "annihilation." Within a few months Konoe regretted this rash action. By calling for the cooperation with the Nationalist regime, the declaration also epitomized a new search for collaborators in China. The following month, Wang Jingwei left the Nationalist government in Chongqing and began his tortuous route to establishing a collaborationist regime in Nanjing. Wang became the president of the Japan-sponsored Republic of China in March 1940. After Manchukuo, this so-called Chinese Nanjing regime was the second major "independent" polity in Japan's Sphere, to be later joined by Thailand, the Philippines, and Burma.

46. Gaimushō, *Gaimushō no hyakunen*, vol. 2 (Tokyo: Hara Shobō, 1969), 299. See also U.S. Department of State, *Foreign Relations of the United States: Japan: 1931–1941*, vol. 1 (Washington, D.C.: Government Printing Office, 1943), 800, 803. Henceforth this volume will be abbreviated as *FRUS, Japan: 1931–1941*.

47. See Hori Kazuo, *Higashi Ajia shihonshugi shiron*, vol. 1 (Minerva Shobō, 2009).

48. In fact, in the 1930s more than 97 percent of Korean exports were sent to destinations within the Japanese Empire. See Hori Kazuo, "Higashi Ajia ni okeru shihonshugi no keisei," *Shakai keizai shigaku* 76, no. 3 (November 2010): 33.

49. Hori, *Higashi Ajia shihonshugi shiron*, 1:243.

50. Duus, "Imperialism without Colonies," 54–72.

51. Inclusivity was offered in myriad ways. Koreans and Taiwanese were allowed to volunteer for, and were later conscripted into, the Japanese military. Moreover, when Japan's colonial ministry was abolished in November 1942, its jurisdiction over the government-generals of Korea and Taiwan was transferred to the home ministry. In a law promulgated on April 1, 1945, Koreans and Taiwanese also received the right to vote for and send representatives to the Imperial Diet. Another law in 1945 even made it possible for Koreans and Taiwanese to join the House of Peers. Japan also expanded social welfare and other social services to both colonies. This was all part of what Takashi Fujitani calls a more inclusionary and culturalist regime of "polite racism," which replaced the "vulgar racism" of earlier years. See Takashi Fujitani, *Race for Empire: Koreans as Japanese and Japanese as Americans during World War II* (Berkeley: University of California Press, 2013).

52. Quoted in Arima, *Teikoku no Shōwa*, 285.

53. The British had three classes of mandates that corresponded to their supposed civilizational levels. Class A mandates envisaged a "provisional recognition" of their independence, whereas Class B and C mandates were colonies in all but name. See Mark Mazower, *Governing the World: The History of an Idea* (New York: Penguin, 2012), 169.

54. See Rebecca West, *The Meaning of Treason*, 3rd ed. (London: Virago, 1982), 276. See also Hernando J. Abaya, *Betrayal in the Philippines* (New York: A. A. Wyn, 1946). Even David Joel Steinberg, who writes about Philippine collaborators in positive terms, is trapped by this pejorative view of collaboration. He sees the country's failure to deal with the issue of collaboration as perhaps "an infection below the skin of the body politic, an infection that might have carried silently the germs of the collaboration crisis elsewhere into Philippine life. As with a cancer that is secretly feared but consciously ignored in the hope that it might vanish by itself, Filipinos have gone to some lengths to avoid examining the consequences of collaboration." David Joel Steinberg, *Philippine Collaboration in World War II* (Manila: University of Michigan Press, 1967), 164–65.

55. The classic study of Vichy France is Robert O. Paxton, *Vichy France: Old Guard and New Order, 1940–1944* (New York: Columbia University Press, 1972).

56. Mazower, *Hitler's Empire*, 102–4.

57. Yamamuro, *Manchuria under Japanese Dominion*, 54–61.

1. INTO THE TIGER'S DEN

1. Grew to Franklin Mott Gunther, February 1941, Joseph C. Grew Papers, MS AM 1687 v. 111 (24), Houghton Library, Harvard University, Cambridge, Massachusetts (hereafter HL-HU).

2. Shigemitsu Mamoru, *Shōwa no dōran*, vol. 2 (Tokyo: Chūō Kōronsha, 1952), 21.

3. Johanna Menzel Meskill, *Nazi Germany and Imperial Japan: The Hollow Diplomatic Alliance* (London: Aldine Transaction, 2012), 25.

4. For more on the scholarship surrounding the pact, see Jeremy A. Yellen, "Into the Tiger's Den: Japan and the Tripartite Pact, 1940," *Journal of Contemporary History* 51, no. 3 (July 2016): 556–57.

5. Mimura, *Planning for Empire*, 16, 114–16.

6. Akira Iriye, *Pearl Harbor and the Coming of the Pacific War: A Brief History with Documents and Essays* (Boston: Bedford/St. Martin's, 1999), 6.

7. See Gaimushō, *Gaimushō no hyakunen*, 2:435–36; and Harada Kumao, *Saionji-kō to seikyoku*, vol. 7 (Tokyo: Iwanami Shoten, 1952), 258–59.

8. Galeazzo Ciano, *Ciano's Diary, 1939–1943* (London: William Heinemann, 1947), March 8 entry: 41. Negotiations with Germany and Italy to form a united front against England, France, and the Soviet Union began in earnest in January 1939. See DR, 1:582–83.

9. Hattori Takushirō, *Dai Tōa Sensō zenshi* (Tokyo: Hara Shobō, 1965), 13; *Ushinawareshi seiji: Konoe Fumimaro kō no shuki* (Tokyo: Asahi Shinbunsha, 1946), 29, 41; see also Gaimushō, *Gaimushō no hyakunen*, 2:433; and DR, 1:607, 2:1.

10. "Teikoku taigai hōshin," April 27, 1940, *Shina jihen kankei ikken* vol. 15, file A.1.0.0 30, Ministry of Foreign Affairs Office of Diplomatic Records, Tokyo, Japan. Henceforth this will be abbreviated as JFMA.

11. "Dainiji taigai shisaku hōshin yōkō," May 1940, *Teikoku no taigai seisaku kankei ikken*, file A.1.0.0. 6, JFMA.

12. Satō Kenryō, *Dai Tōa Sensō kaikoroku* (Tokyo: Tokuma Shoten, 1966), 94.

13. Arita gave his first request to Ambassador Ott on May 11, 1940. See Telegram, Ott to the Foreign Ministry, May 11, 1940, *Documents on German Foreign Policy, 1918–1945*, series D, vol. 9, document no. 234, 327 [Series henceforth labeled DGFP]. Ambassador Kurusu followed up in Berlin. For an account of the meeting, see State Secretary Weizsäcker Memorandum, May 17, 1940, DGFP, series D, vol. 9, document no. 262, 360–62. Japanese initiatives concerning French colonial possessions began in late June, when Kurusu met Weizsäcker on June 21, 1940. DGFP, series D, vol. 9, document no. 511, 642–43.

14. Hatano Sumio, "Nanshin e no senkai," *Ajia keizai* 26, no. 5 (May 1985): 39.

15. Matsumoto Shun'ichi and Andō Yoshirō, *Nihon gaikōshi*, vol. 22, *Nanshin mondai* (Tokyo: Kajima Heiwa Kenkyūjo, 1972), 182. Henceforth labeled *Nihon gaikōshi* 22.

16. Taken from Hosoya Chihiro, "Sangoku dōmei to Nisso chūritsu jōyaku (1939–1941)," *Taiheiyō Sensō e no michi: kaisen gaikōshi*, vol. 5: *Sangoku dōmei, Nisso chūritsu jōyaku* (Tokyo: Asahi Shinbunsha, 1963), 173.

17. Ribbentrop stated, "This German-Dutch conflict was an exclusively European affair and had nothing to do with overseas questions. Germany, therefore, had no interest in occupying herself with such overseas problems." May 20, DGFP, series D, vol. 9, document no. 280, Telegram, Foreign Minister to the Embassy in Japan, 386.

18. Horinouchi Kensuke, *Nihon gaikōshi*, vol. 21, *Nichi-Doku-I dōmei, Nisso chūritsu jōyaku* (Tokyo: Kajima Heiwa Kenkyūjo, 1971), 232. Henceforth labeled *Nihon gaikōshi* 21.

19. Telegram, Ambassador Kurusu to Foreign Minister Arita, July 10, 1940, in Ōkubo Tatsumasa et al., eds., *Kaigunshō shiryō* document 1168: *Shōwa shakai keizai shiryō shūsei* [henceforth SSKSS], vol. 10 (Tokyo: Daitō Bunka Daigaku Tōyō Kenkyūjo, 1985), 170. I was led to this by Kawanishi Kōsuke's excellent study on the foreign ministry. Kawanishi Kōsuke, "Gaimushō 'Dai Tōa Kyōeiken' kōsō no keisei katei," *Rekishigaku kenkyū*, no. 798 (February 2005): 8.

20. See Cemil Aydin, *The Politics of Anti-Westernism in Asia: Visions of World Order in Pan-Asian and Pan-Islamic Thought* (New York: Columbia University Press, 2007).

21. "Ōshū no shinjōsei ni sokuō suru Nanpō seisaku," *Teikoku Nanpō seisaku kankei ikken*, file A.1.0.0. 7, JFMA. Also see Japan Center for Asian Historical Records (JACAR), Reference Code B02030016300.

22. Tanemura Sakō, *Daihon'ei kimitsu nisshi* (Tokyo: Fuyō Shobō, 1985), entry for May 10, 1940, 33–35.

23. Quoted in Gaimushō, *Gaimushō no hyakunen*, 2:436.

24. *Tokyo Asahi shinbun*, June 22, 1940, 1; and *Tokyo Asahi shinbun*, June 21, 1940, 1.

25. Gaimushō, *Nihon gaikō nenpyō*, 2:434.

26. See Hatano Sumio, "Arita hōsō (1940 nen 6-gatsu) no kokunaiteki bunmyaku to kokusaiteki bunmyaku," Kindai gaikōshi kenkyūkai, ed., *Hendōki no gaikō to gunji* (Tokyo: Hara Shobō, 1987), 137–64.

27. "Sekai jōsei no hendō ni taisho subeki: teikoku gaikō shisaku yōkō (an)" in *Shina jihen kankei ikken*, vol. 7, file A.1.0.0–30, JFMA. Also see JACAR, reference code B02030010900.

28. Hatano, "Nanshin e no senkai," 38.

29. Gaimushō, *Gaimushō no hyakunen*, 2:438–39.

30. The participants included: (1) foreign ministry Bureau of Eurasian Affairs section 1 chief Andō Yoshirō; (2) foreign ministry Bureau of Eurasian Affairs section 3 chief Ishizawa Yutaka; (3) army ministry Lt. Col. Takayama Hikoichi; (4) foreign ministry Bureau of Eurasian Affairs section chief Tajiri Akiyoshi; (5) foreign ministry secretary Tokunaga; (6) army general staff office representative Major Tanemura Sakō; and (7) navy ministry representative Commander Shiba Katsuo.

31. "Nichi-Doku-I teikei kyōka ni kan suru riku-kai-gai sanshō keikan kyōgikai," JACAR, Reference Code B04013489500. Also see *Nichi-Doku-I dōmei jōyaku kankei ikken*, file B.1.0.0. J/X3, JFMA. I was led to this quote through Hatano, "Nanshin e no senkai," 40–41, and Kawanishi, "Gaimushō," 13.

32. Hatano, "Nanshin e no senkai," 39; Kawanishi, *Teikoku Nihon no kakuchō to hōkai*, 113–60.

33. Shigemitsu, *Shōwa no dōran*, 1:277–78.

34. Barbara J. Brooks, *Japan's Imperial Diplomacy: Consuls, Treaty Ports, and War in China, 1895–1938* (Honolulu: University of Hawaii Press, 2000).

35. Ott to the Foreign Ministry, June 24, 1940, DGFP, series D, vol. 10, document no. 273, 5.

36. In fact, Lord Keeper of the Privy Seal Yuasa Kurahei and Admiral Okada Keisuke maneuvered to have him chosen as premier in January 1940 precisely because of Yonai's moderate aims and headstrong opposition to the army in matters of foreign policy.

37. Hattori, *Dai Tōa Sensō zenshi*, 15.

38. For an excellent analysis of this, see Hosoya, "Sangoku dōme," 182–84.

39. Gaimushō, *Nihon gaikō nenpyō*, 2:436–37; Bōeichō Bōei Kenshūjo Senshishitsu, *Daihon'ei rikugunbu Dai Tōa Sensō kaisen keii*, vol. 2 (Tokyo: Asagumo Shinbunsha, 1973), 178 (henceforth all volumes in this five-volume series will be labeled *Kaisen keii*); *Nihon gaikōshi*, 21:238–39.

40. *Kaigunshō shiryō*, SSKSS, 10: document 1193, 257.

41. Kawanishi, "Gaimushō," 14; *Kaigunshō shiryō*, SSKSS, 10: document 1196, 263.

42. See "Sekai jōsei no suii ni tomonau jikyoku shori yōkō," in *Sugiyama memo*, 1:11–12; Gaimushō, *Nihon gaikō nenpyō*, 2:436–37.

43. *Sugiyama memo*, 1:12; Gaimushō, *Nihon gaikō nenpyō*, 2:437.

44. Kido Kōichi, *Kido Kōichi nikki*, vol. 2 (Tokyo: Tokyo Daigaku Shuppankai, 1966), 812.

45. For "The Main Principles," see "Kihon kokusaku yōkō," in *Sugiyama memo*, 1:7–10; and in Nihon keizai renmeikai, *Kihon kokusaku yōkō* (Tokyo, 1941).

46. *Tokyo Asahi shinbun*, August 2, 1940, Evening edition, 1. Matsuoka Yōsuke's address is also reprinted in *Shūhō*, no. 199, August 7, 1943, 2–3.

47. Matsuoka Yōsuke, *Nichi-Doku bōkyō kyōtei no igi* (Tokyo: Dai'ichi Shuppansha, 1937), 78–79.

48. Saitō Yoshie, *Azamukareta rekishi: Matsuoka to sangoku dōmei no rimen* (Tokyo: Yomiuri Shinbunsha, 1955), 27. See chapters 2 and 3 for his mistrust of Germany.

49. Matsuoka, *Kōa no taigyō*, 294–95.

50. Shigemitsu Mamoru, *Shigemitsu Mamoru shuki* (Tokyo: Chūō Kōronsha, 1986), 132. The military also spoke of Matsuoka's "leave diplomacy to me attitude." See *Kaisen keii*, 3:219. See also Gunjishi Gakkai, *Daihon'ei rikugunbu sensō shidōhan kimitsu sensō nisshi*, 2 vols. (Tokyo: Kinseisha, 1999). Henceforth *Kimitsu sensō nisshi*.

51. Tanemura, *Daihon'ei kimitsu nisshi*, September 29, 1940, 52.

52. *Kaisen keii*, 2:181.

53. Ott to the Foreign Ministry, August 7, 1940, DGFP, series D, vol. 10, document no. 273, 394.

54. *Nihon gaikōshi*, 21:242; Gaimushō, *Gaimushō no hyakunen*, 2:441. Ott cabled Ribbentrop, "I left the Foreign Minister in no doubt that Japan had much to make up for in order even to bring about a state of really benevolent neutrality toward Germany." Ott to the Foreign Ministry, August 7, 1940, DGFP, series D, vol. 10, document no. 273, 395.

55. *Tokyo Asahi shinbun*, August 2, 1940, evening edition, 1.

56. *Kaisen keii*, 2:195.

57. Ibid.

58. *Nihon gaikōshi*, 21:240; Gaimushō, *Gaimushō no hyakunen*, 2:440. As Hosoya Chihiro explains, this was Matsuoka's favorite phrase. See Hosoya, "Sangoku dōmei," 181. A more colloquial translation is "Nothing ventured, nothing gained."

59. *Kaisen keii*, 2:185–91.

60. DR, 2:109–11. By this time, Navy Minister Yoshida Zengo, who had been against the Tripartite Pact, took sick and was admitted to a hospital.

61. *Sugiyama memo*, 1:39; DR, 2:111–12; Gaimushō, *Nihon gaikō nenpyō*, 2:443–44, 452–53.

62. *Sugiyama memo*, 1:35; Gaimushō, *Nihon gaikō nenpyō*, 2:445–46.

63. *Kaisen keii*, 2:223–64.

64. Ibid., 258–59.

65. Ott to Matsuoka, September 27, 1940, DGFP, series D, vol. 11, document no. 119, 205–6. For the Japanese records of the exchange, see *Nichi-Doku-I dōmei jōyaku kankei ikken*, vol. 1, file B.1.0.0 – 057, JFMA; JACAR Reference Code B04013489700.

66. Hosoya, "Sangoku dōmei," 202–4; Meskill, *Nazi Germany and Imperial Japan*, 20.

67. Hoshina Zenshirō, *Dai Tōa Sensō hishi: ushinawareta wahei kōsaku: Hoshina Zenshirō kaisōroku* (Tokyo: Hara Shobō, 1975), 15. See also Yoshida Zengo, *Moto kaigun taishō Yoshida Zengo dan shūroku*, in file 25, *Yoshida Zengo kankei monjo*, Kensei Shiryōshitsu, National Diet Library, Tokyo (henceforth KSS-NDL).

68. Hosoya, "Sangoku dōmei," 202–4.

69. Barnhart, *Japan Prepares for Total War*, 162–75; Mori Shigeki, "Sūjiku gaikō oyobi nanshin seisaku to kaigun," *Rekishigaku kenkyū*, September 1999, 1–18, 64.

70. Sakai Saburō, *Shōwa Kenkyūkai* (Tokyo: TBS Britannica, 1979), 185–87.

71. Konoe, *Ushinawareshi seiji*, 33. The original aim of including the Soviet Union in the Tripartite Pact was to maintain a balance of power with the United States and Great Britain. See Konoe Fumimaro, *Konoe nikki* (Tokyo: Kyōdō Tsūshinsha, 1968), 148. See also Konoe Fumimaro, *Konoe Fumimaro shuki: heiwa e no doryoku* (Taihoku: Taiwan Geijutsusha, 1947), 12–13. Konoe even assumed that strengthened tripartite relations would bring the United States to the negotiating table. *Kaisen keii*, 1:404.

72. *Sugiyama memo*, 1:49–50. Also see Tanemura, *Daihon'ei kimitsu nisshi*, September 29, 1940, 53.

73. See Joseph C. Grew, Diary (July-December 1940), 4555-56, 4493, Joseph C. Grew Papers, MS AM 1687 v. 101, HL-HU.

74. See, for instance, Mori Shigeki, "Matsuoka gaikō ni okeru tai Bei oyobi tai Ei saku: Nichi-Doku-I dōmei teiketsu zengo no kōsō to tenkai," *Nihonshi kenkyū*, no. 421 (September 1997): 35–62.

75. *Tokyo Asahi shinbun*, August 2, 1940, Evening edition, 1.

76. Kawanishi Kōsuke, *Dai Tōa Kyōeiken: Teikoku Nihon no Nanpō taiken* (Tokyo: Kōdansha, 2016), 31–35.

77. State Secretary (Weizsäcker) Memorandum, August 7, 1940, DGFP, series D, vol. 10, document no. 304, 432–33.

78. Kudō Akira, "The Reality of Wartime Economic Cooperation: From Germany's Blitzkrieg Victory to Its War with the Soviet Union," in Akira Kudō, Tajima Nobuo, and Erich Pauer, eds., *Japan and Germany: Two Latecomers to the World Stage, 1890–1945*, vol. 2 (Folkestone, UK: Global Oriental, 2009), 357.

79. Ciano, *Ciano's Diary*, March 10, 1942, 444.

80. Ōda Ichirō and Ikeda Chikata, eds., *Nihon gaikōshi*, vol. 24: *Dai Tōa Sensō, senji gaikō* (Tokyo: Kajima Heiwa Kenkyūjo, 1971), 118–23. Henceforth *Nihon gaikōshi 24*.

81. Leon Ma. Guerrero, "Twilight in Tokyo," in *Ang Buong Ulat Ng Buhay Ni Laurel: Ang Mga Huling Araw Ng Imperyong Hapones: Takip-silim Sa Tokyo* (Manila, 1949), 104.

82. Reto Hofmann, *The Fascist Effect: Japan and Italy, 1915–1952* (Ithaca, NY: Cornell University Press, 2015), 109–35.

83. Konoe, *Ushinawareshi seiji*, 41–42.

84. Ciano, *Ciano's Diary*, August 11, 1939, 124.

85. Matsuoka, *Kōa no taigyō*, 293.

86. Saitō, *Azamukareta rekishi*, 5.

2. ORDER BEGETS WAR

1. Japanese studies in the past two decades, however, have paid greater attention to this and have influenced my own views. Mori Shigeki argues that the Sphere was part of Matsuoka's bilateral diplomacy "to get the United States to recognize Japan's position as 'the stabilizing power of East Asia.'" See Mori, "Matsuoka gaikō," 61. Kawanishi Kōsuke's

fantastic study shows Matsuoka's end goals as building a world of co-prosperity spheres. See Kawanishi, *Dai Tōa Kyōeiken*.

2. Matsuoka Yōsuke, "Sekai daihenkyoku ni chokumen shite," *Taiheiyō* 3, no. 5 (May 1940): 2–11.

3. "Teikoku gaikō hōshin yōkō," September 28, 1940. See JACAR, reference code B02030515200; *Shina jihen kankei ikken*, vol. 2, file A.1.0.0 30_002, JFMA. All subsequent references to the "Main Points" come from this document.

4. Kawanishi, *Dai Tōa Kyōeiken*, 35–40. Kawanishi also speaks of something akin to sphere-of-influence diplomacy, placing emphasis on Matsuoka's idea that each great power will "respect each other's co-prosperity spheres" (*sorezore no kyōeiken sonchō*).

5. The Soviet Union still chafed over Japan annexing southern Sakhalin (Karafuto) in the wake of the Russo-Japanese War of 1904–5, as well as the oil and coal concessions Japan held in northern Sakhalin.

6. Jonathan Haslam, *The Soviet Union and the Threat from the East, 1933–41: Moscow, Tokyo and the Prelude to the Pacific War* (Pittsburgh: University of Pittsburgh Press, 1992), 44.

7. Negotiations for a neutrality pact had been started by the previous cabinet, but Matsuoka largely opposed the traditional policies of nonconciliation held by the previous foreign minister, Arita Hachirō. For Arita's diplomacy of avoidance, see Hosoya, "Sangoku dōmei," 244–46. Arita finally made an offer for a neutrality pact on August 14, 1940.

8. M. F. Lindley, *The Acquisition and Government of Backward Territory in International Law* (New York: Longmans, Green, 1926), 209–10. See 207–36 for details on spheres of influence and interest.

9. *Kaisen keii*, 3:258.

10. Kawanishi, *Dai Tōa Kyōeiken*, 39.

11. David J. Lu, *Agony of Choice: Matsuoka Yōsuke and the Rise and Fall of the Japanese Empire, 1880–1946* (Lanham, MD: Lexington, 2002), 183.

12. U.S. Department of State, *Foreign Relations of the United States Diplomatic Papers, 1940*, vol. 4: *The Far East* (Washington, D.C.: Government Printing Office, 1955), 129. See also *Nihon gaikōshi*, 22:132–34; *Kaisen keii*, 3:162.

13. See, for instance, Kobkua Suwannathat-Pian, *Thailand's Durable Premier: Phibun through Three Decades, 1932–1957* (Kuala Lumpur: Oxford University Press, 1995), 254. The author does include a brief discussion of an unsuccessful 1926 convention seeking the return of some "lost territories."

14. Numerous academic works discuss the border dispute. See Edward Thaddeus Flood, "Japan's Relations with Thailand: 1928–1941" (Ph.D. diss., University of Washington, 1967), 316–594; E. Bruce Reynolds, *Thailand and Japan's Southern Advance, 1940–1945* (New York: St. Martin's, 1994), 25–51; Kobkua, *Thailand's Durable Premier*, 254–62; Nagaoka Shinjirō, "Nanpō shisaku no gaikōteki tenkai (1937–1941)," in *Taiheiyō Sensō e no michi*, vol. 6: *Nanpō shinshutsu* (Tokyo: Asahi Shinbunsha, 1963), 112–30; Hattori, *Dai Tōa Sensō zenshi*, 44–50. For the West's involvement and response, see Richard J. Aldrich, *The Key to the South: Britain, the United States, and Thailand during the Approach of the Pacific War, 1929–1942* (Kuala Lumpur: Oxford University Press, 1993), 256–310.

15. Lu, *Agony of Choice*, 189.

16. See DR, 2:172; *Kaisen keii*, 3:184; *Nihon gaikōshi*, 22:272. The policy called on Thailand to support Japan's new order and engage in stronger economic, political, and material ties. The policy called on Thai political and economic support for Japan's new order. In return, Japan would not only return Luang Prabang and Pakse but also promise "other lost territories (particularly British) in the future." On the French side, Japan would limit Thai demands and in return expect greater military cooperation in southern

Indochina. Whether through favors or coercion, Japan would play both parties against each other to achieve these ends.

17. *Kimitsu sensō nisshi*, 1:51; Nagaoka, "Nanpō shisaku," 121.

18. See the December 21, 1940, entry in army general staff department chief Tanaka Shin'ichi's memoirs. Tanaka Shin'ichi, *Dai Tōa Sensō e no zentei*, vol. 1: *Futsuin Tai funsō chōtei*, 17–18, National Institute for Defense Studies, Japan (henceforth labeled NIDS). See also Flood, "Japan's Relations with Thailand," 376–77.

19. *Kimitsu sensō nisshi*, 1:51.

20. Tanaka, *Dai Tōa Sensō e no zentei*, 1:17, NIDS; see also Tanaka Shin'ichi's diary entry of December 21, 1940, *Tanaka Shin'ichi chūjō gyōmu nisshi*, part 2, 173, NIDS.

21. His notes of the liaison conferences, the *Sugiyama memo*, provide one of the major sources of our knowledge of decision making during the wartime period.

22. See Kojima Noboru, *Sanbō* (Tokyo: Bungei Shunjū, 1972), 149; Hata Ikuhiko, "Nit-Chū sensō no gunjiteki tenkai (1937-nen – 1941-nen)," in *Taiheiyō Sensō e no michi*, vol. 4: *Nit-Chū sensō* (Tokyo: Asahi Shinbunsha, 1963), 48; Edward J. Drea, *In the Service of the Emperor: Essays on the Imperial Japanese Army* (Lincoln: University of Nebraska Press, 1998), 177.

23. Kojima, *Sanbō*, 148–56.

24. For the best understanding of Matsuoka, see Tsunoda Jun, "Nihon no tai-Bei kaisen (1940-nen – 1941-nen)," in *Taiheiyō Sensō e no michi*, vol. 7: *Nichi-Bei kaisen* (Tokyo: Asahi Shinbunsha, 1963), 98–101. He includes a list of these contradictory statements. Also see Nagaoka, "Nanpō shisaku," 121; Tanaka, *Dai Tōa Sensō e no zentei*, 1: 43–44 (and esp. January 1941 entries in vol. 1), NIDS; and *Kaisen keii*, 3:190, 191, 211. See Tanaka, *Dai Tōa Sensō e no zentei*, 1:43–44, NIDS.

25. Flood, "Japan's Relations with Thailand," 380.

26. Hattori, *Dai Tōa Sensō zenshi*, 46.

27. *Kimitsu sensō nisshi*, 1:67. Kido Kōichi recorded a similar statement in his diary. See the January 24, 1941 entry, Kido, *Kido Kōichi nikki*, 2:851. Tanemura Sakō also records a similar statement in his entry dated January 24, 1941. See Tanemura, *Daihon'ei kimitsu nisshi*, 66–67. Tanemura also shows how embarrassed Sugiyama was.

28. As David J. Lu explains, Matsuoka's humiliation of Sugiyama was in part payback for the callous treatment he received from Sugiyama in 1937. Matsuoka—who was then president of the South Manchurian Railway—was twice summoned to Sugiyama's office, only to be met by his subordinates. Lu, *Agony of Choice*, 194.

29. *Sugiyama memo*, 1:178–79.

30. Ambassador Grew to the Secretary of State, March 11, 1941, *Foreign Relations of the United States, Diplomatic Papers, 1941*, vol. 5: *The Far East* (Washington, D.C.: Government Printing Office, 1956), 108–9 (hereafter *FRUS, 1941*). Also see E. Bruce Reynolds, *Thailand and Japan's Southern Advance*, 49.

31. *Tokyo Asahi shinbun*, March 11–12, 1941.

32. See the March 11, 1941 entry, Tanaka, *Dai Tōa Sensō e no zentei*, 1:77, NIDS. The other two extraordinarily influential staff officers were army ministry Bureau of Military Affairs director Mutō Akira and navy ministry Bureau of Naval Affairs director Oka Takazumi.

33. "Shōwa 16-nen 3-gatsu 11-nichi Nichi-Tai, Nichi-Futsu kōkan seimei," JACAR, reference code C12120377100; Chūō sensō shidōhan jūyō kokusaku bunsho 1312, NIDS. Drafts of the documents can also be found in *Sugiyama memo*, 1:193–95.

34. *Nihon gaikōshi*, 22:192–93.

35. For the full plans, see "Tai Ran'in keizai hatten no tame no shisaku" and "Tai Futsuinshi keizai hatten no tame no shisaku," *Nihon gaikōshi*, 22:214–16, 247–49.

36. Cited in Mori Shigeki, "Dainiji Nichi-Ran kaishō o meguru Matsuoka gaishō to Gaimushō: 'kōki binjōteki nanshin' setsu no saikentō," *Rekishigaku kenkyū* 766 (September 2002): 17.

37. "Gaimudaijin no enzetsu," January 22, 1940. *Kanpō gōgai*, Kizokuin giji sokkiruoku dainigō, TG-NDL.

38. *Kaisen keii*, 4:8. The spirit of universal brotherhood implicit in *hakkō ichiu*, of course, posited Japan as the elder brother or family head in East Asia, poised to take its rightful place as leader of the region.

39. *Nichi Ran tsū jōyaku kankei ikken, Shōwa 15, 16 nen Nichi-Ran kaishō kankei*, vol. 2, file B.2.0.0. J/N2–3, JFMA.

40. *FRUS, 1941*, 5:174.

41. *Sugiyama memo*, 1:219.

42. *FRUS, Japan: 1931–1941*, 2:171–73; see also Joseph C. Grew, *Ten Years in Japan* (New York: Simon & Schuster, 1944), 341–43, 345.

43. Mori, "Matsuoka gaikō," 61.

44. Peter Mauch, "Revisiting Nomura's Diplomacy: Ambassador Nomura's Role in the Japanese-American Negotiations, 1941," *Diplomatic History* 28, no. 3 (June 2004): 359. An additional reason for the selection of Nomura (initially in August 1940) was that Matsuoka sought to alleviate naval concerns over the impact of the German alliance on relations with the United States. See Peter Mauch, *Sailor Diplomat: Nomura Kichisaburō and the Japanese-American War* (Cambridge, MA: Harvard University Asia Center, 2011), 118.

45. *Japan Times and Advertiser*, December 19, 1940, 1.

46. Matsuoka Yōsuke, *Address of Yosuke Matsuoka Delivered at the America-Japan Society Luncheon*, December 19, 1940, 6–8, NDL.

47. Ibid., 9.

48. Quoted in Lu, *Agony of Choice*, 12.

49. Gaimushō, *Gaimushō no hyakunen*, 2:540; *Kaisen keii*, 3:457–58.

50. *Kaisen keii*, 3:458–60.

51. The United States, however, had no interest in sphere-of-influence politics. With the December 1938 Declaration of Lima, the United States joined other American countries in reaffirming the "sovereignty, and independence of each American state" and reasserted that there would be no intervention in each other's affairs. See U.S. Department of State, *Peace and War: United States Foreign Policy, 1931–1941* (Washington, D.C.: Government Printing Office, 1943), 438–49.

52. *FRUS, 1941*, 4: 33.

53. Kido, *Kido Kōichi nikki*, 2:863.

54. Much has been made of Nomura's English-language failings. But a similar point could be made against the American side. The State Department provided a specialist, Joseph W. Ballantine, to explain conference proceedings to Nomura in Japanese. The Japanese, however, dismissed Ballantine's command of Japanese in much the same way that Hull, Grew, and others spoke of Nomura's English. Nomura's aide, special envoy Iwakuro Hideo, wrote, "I couldn't call that halting Japanese fluent, even in flattery." Clearly, linguistic problems were evident on both sides of the Pacific conversations. See Iwakuro Hideo, *Shōwa rikugun bōryaku hishi* (Tokyo: Nihon Keizai Shinbun Shuppansha, 2015), 286.

55. The argument that Matsuoka aimed to build a "four-power entente" has been most forcefully argued in Hosoya, "Sangoku dōmei," 261–82; Lu, *Agony of Choice*, 197–212; and Hattori Satoshi, *Matsuoka gaikō: Nichi-Bei kankei o meguru kokunai yōin to kokusai kankei* (Tokyo: Chikura Shobō, 2012). Miwa Munehiro, however, finds no evidence or documentation to support the idea of a "four-power entente" as Matsuoka's end goal. See Miwa Munehiro, "Nichi-Doku-I Sangoku dōmei teiketsu toki ni okeru, Nichi-Doku-I-So kōsō e no gimon: Matsuoka kōsōsetsu e no gimon," *Nihon Daigaku seisan kōgakubu kenkyū hōkoku* 25, no. 1 (June 1992): 21–39. Finally, Hattori Satoshi and Hatano Sumio both argue that by the time of his European trip, Matsuoka understood no such alliance was possible. See Hattori, *Matsuoka gaikō*; Hatano, "Nanshin e no senkai," 30–31.

56. Quoted in Eri Hotta, *Japan 1941: Countdown to Infamy* (New York: Knopf, 2013), 59.

57. Kawanishi, *Dai Tōa Kyōeiken*, 61.

58. *Kaisen keii*, 3:357–58; *Nihon gaikōshi*, 21:276–77; *Sugiyama memo*, 1:176–77. Readers may notice here a subtle difference with Matsuoka's September 1940 policy paper, in which Japan was to seek Soviet recognition of Japan's paramount interests in Outer Mongolia.

59. *Kimitsu sensō nisshi*, 1:63.

60. February 10, 1941 entry, *Shōwa Tennō jitsuroku*, vol. 28 (Tokyo: Kunaichō), 24–25.

61. The minutes of these meetings can be found in R. Sontag and S. Beddie, eds., *Nazi-Soviet Relations: Documents from the Archives of the German Foreign Office* (Washington, 1948), 281–98. The meetings are described in detail in *Kaisen keii*, 3:385–95, and separate reports can be found in Gaimushō, *Nihon gaikō bunsho: dainiji Ōshū taisen to Nihon*, vol. 1: *Nichi-Doku-I sangoku dōmei, Nisso chūritsu jōyaku* (Tokyo: Gaimushō, 2012), 334–37. Henceforth *NGB*.

62. Sontag and Beddie, *Nazi-Soviet Relations*, 298–303.

63. Akira Iriye, *The Origins of the Second World War in Asia and the Pacific* (London: Longman, 1987), 133.

64. Lu, *Agony of Choice*, 148.

65. *Nihon gaikōshi*, 21:282.

66. *NGB*, 1:347–49; *Nihon gaikōshi*, 21:284–85; *Kaisen keii*, 3:416–17.

67. Ambassador Tatekawa to Konoe, "Kita Karafuto riken ni kan suru fuzoku giteisho o nozoku chūritsu jōyaku an e no chōin o waga hō teigi ni tsuite," April 10, 1941, *NGB*, 1:339–40.

68. *Sugiyama memo*, 1:201.

69. Saionji Kinkazu, *Saionji Kinkazu kaikoroku* (Tokyo: Ipec, 1991), 197.

70. Quoted in Haslam, *Soviet Union*, 162.

71. Incidentally, Matsuoka's messages were suppressed by Secretary of State Cordell Hull, so Roosevelt never saw them. Lu, *Agony of Choice*, 209.

72. This group was spearheaded by Bishop James E. Walsh and Father James M. Drought, with input from Igawa (Wikawa) Tadao, a former finance ministry bureaucrat and director of the Industrial Federation Central Bank, and staff officer Col. Iwakuro Hideo. For an engrossing history of this group as well as the exploratory conversations between Japan and the United States, see Robert J. C. Butow, *The John Doe Associates: Backdoor Diplomacy for Peace, 1941* (Stanford, CA: Stanford University Press, 1974). See also Jun Tsunoda, "Confusion Arising from a Draft Understanding between Japan and the United States," in James William Morley, ed., *Japan's Road to the Pacific War: The Final Confrontation* (New York: Columbia University Press, 1994), 1–105.

73. April 21, 1941 entry, *Shōwa Tennō jitsuroku*, 28:66. This is the first time I have seen the Co-Prosperity Sphere spoken of as "national policy." Within the next few months, policy documents also began describing the Sphere as "national policy."

74. See, for instance, *FRUS, Japan: 1931–1941*, 2: 333, 420–26.

75. Ibid., 485.

76. *DR*, 2:312.

77. *Sugiyama memo*, 1:254–64.

78. Hatano Sumio, *Bakuryōtachi no Shinjuwan* (Tokyo: Yoshikawa Kōbunkan, 2013), 91.

79. *Sugiyama memo*, 1:260.

80. *Kimitsu sensō nisshi*, 1:73; *Nihon gaikōshi*, 22:337–40.

81. Quoted in Kawanishi, *Dai Tōa Kyōeiken*, 85.

82. Asada, *From Mahan to Pearl Harbor*, 253.

83. Barnhart, *Japan Prepares for Total War*, 227–28.

84. For a detailed understanding of the charter, see Iriye, *Origins of the Second World War*, 152–57. For a broader discussion of Wilsonianism during World War II, see Jeremy A. Yellen, "Wartime Wilsonianism and the Crisis of Empire, 1941–1943," *Modern Asian Studies* (2018), 1–34, doi:10.1017/S0026749x17000397.

85. Iwakuro, *Sensō rikugun*, 327. The notion of an "ABCD encirclement" was widely publicized throughout the Japanese media from August 1941.

86. *Sugiyama memo*, 1:312. A text of the imperial conference is provided in *Sugiyama memo*, 1:306–12. The minimum demands required to prevent war included noninterference in the China war, an avoidance of any action that might threaten the defense of Japan's empire, and more active cooperation to help Japan secure vital natural resources.

87. Iwakuro, *Sensō rikugun*, 327.

88. Ballantine stressed this in his discussions with Iwakuro on April 7, 1941, when he spoke of "the inconsistency between assertions that Japan intended to respect the principle of the open door and the economic bloc idea underlying the so-called 'co-prosperity sphere in East Asia.'" See Memorandum of a Conversation, by Joseph W. Ballantine, April 7, 1941. *FRUS, 1941*, 4:128.

89. Nomura to Tōgō, October 29, 1941 (received on October 30). In *Nichi-Bei gaikō kankei zassan: Taiheyō no heiwa narabini Tōa mondai ni kan suru Nichi-Bei kōshō kankei*, vol. 4, file A.1.3.1.1–3, JFMA.

90. Grew, *Ten Years in Japan*, 479. Grew had been worrying since late 1940 that "unless we are prepared . . . to withdraw bag and baggage from the entire sphere of 'Greater East Asia including the South Seas' (which God forbid), we are bound eventually to come to a head-on clash with Japan." See Joseph C. Grew, *Turbulent Era: A Diplomatic Record of Forty Years, 1904–1945*, vol. 2 (Boston: Houghton Mifflin, 1952), 1257.

91. *FRUS, Japan: 1931–1941*, 2:363, 754.

92. Cordell Hull, *The Memoirs of Cordell Hull*, vol. 2 (New York: Macmillan, 1948), 1091.

93. Memorandum by Mr. Joseph W. Ballantine to the Secretary of State, December 7, 1941. *FRUS, 1941*, 4:729.

94. "Amō jikan iken," October 13, 1941. *Nichi-Bei gaikō kankei zassan: Taiheyō no heiwa narabini Tōa mondai ni kan suru Nichi-Bei kōshō kankei*, vol. 5, file A.1.3.1.1–3, JFMA.

95. "Nichi-Bei kōshō ni kan suru gaimudaijin setsumei an," December 1, 1941. *Nichi-Bei gaikō kankei zassan: Taiheyō no heiwa narabini Tōa mondai ni kan suru Nichi-Bei kōshō kankei*, vol. 6, file A.1.3.1.1–3, JFMA; *Sugiyama memo*, 1:549–50. See also Nobutaka Ike, ed., *Japan's Decision for War: Records of the 1941 Policy Conferences* (Stanford, CA: Stanford University Press, 1967), 270.

96. See *Nichi-Bei gaikō kankei zassan: Taiheyō no heiwa narabini Tōa mondai ni kan suru Nichi-Bei kōshō kankei*, vol. 14, file A.1.3.1.1–3, JFMA. The entire statement can also be found in *FRUS, Japan: 1931–1941*, 2:787–92.

97. *Kimitsu sensō nisshi*, 1:201; *Sugiyama memo*, 1:568.

98. "Dai Tōa Sensō to yobu," *Yomiuri shinbun*, December 13, 1941; see also *Kimitsu sensō nisshi*, 1:203.

99. *Japan Times and Advertiser*, December 14, 1941, 1.

3. IMAGINING CO-PROSPERITY

1. Mustapha Hussain, *The Memoirs of Mustapha Hussain: Malay Nationalism before UMNO* (Singapore: Singapore University Press, 2005).

2. See, for instance, Walter LaFeber, *The Clash: U.S.-Japanese Relations throughout History* (New York: W. W. Norton, 1997), 214–56; Pyle, *Japan Rising*, 170–209; Mark R. Peattie, *A Historian Looks at the Pacific War* (Stanford, CA: Hoover Institution, 1995), Hoover Essays, No. 13, 3–4.

3. Document 1625, "Gaikō kondankai (sensō mokuteki wa nan to nasu beki ka, Nichi-Bei kōshō no gidai)," October 7, 1941, *Kaigunshō shiryō*, SSKSS, 14: 285–86, 292.

4. Tamura Tokuji, "Dai Tōa Kyōeiken no sosei," *Gaikō jihō*, no. 881 (August 15, 1941): 1–27.

5. Rōyama Masamichi, "Dai Tōa Kyōeiken no chiseigakuteki kōsatsu," *Kaizō* 23, no. 7 (April 1941): 97, 101–2.

6. Japanese scholars have noticed this as well. See Minagawa Masaki, "'Dai Tōa Kyōeiken' shisō no ronri to sono kiketsu—seijigakusha Yabe Teiji o chūshin ni," *Jinbun gakuhō* 306 (March 2000): 107–44; Arima Manabu, "Dare ni mukatte kataru no ka: 'Dai Tōa Sensō' to shinchitsujo no gensetsu," in Sakai Tetsuya, ed., *"Teikoku" Nihon no gakuchi*, vol. 1: *"Teikoku" hensei no keifu* (Tokyo: Iwanami Shoten, 2006), 252–85.

7. Tōjō's response was that it included all territories occupied by Japan: Burma, Malaya, the Netherlands Indies, and the islands across the Pacific. They also agreed that, depending on the state of Japan's war, India and Australia might also be included. For the whole exchange, see *Sugiyama memo*, 2:40–41.

8. Dai Tōa Kensetsu Shingikai, "Dai san bukai giji sokkiroku," March 1942, in Dai Kikakuin and Dai Tōa Kensetsu Shingikai, *Dai tōa kensetsu shingikai kankei shiryō: sōkai, bukai, sokkiroku*, vol. 2, ed. Akashi Yōji and Ishii Hitoshi (Tokyo: Ryūkei Shosha, 1995), 16. Henceforth this will be referred to as *Dai tōa kensetsu shingikai kankei shiryō*. Part of Ōtani's statements were also quoted in Kawanishi, *Teikoku Nihon no kakuchō to hōkai*, 7.

9. Gotō Ken'ichi, *Nihon senryōki Indonesia kenkyū* (Tokyo: Ryūkei Shosha, 1989), 21.

10. Sanbō Honbu Dai'ichi kenkyūhan, *Nanpō sakusen ni okeru senryōchi tōchi yōkōan*, esp. 2–20, NIDS.

11. See "Tai Bei-Ei-Ran-Shō sensō shūmatsu sokushin ni kan suru fukuan," *Sugiyama memo*, 1:523–25.

12. *Sugiyama memo*, 1:527; JACAR, reference code B02032867900.

13. Watanabe Wataru, *Watanabe Wataru shōshō gunsei kankeishi shiryō*, vol. 2 (Tokyo: Ryūkei Shosha, 1998), 421–23.

14. "Nanpō keizai taisaku yōkō," in Ishikawa Junkichi, *Kokka sōdōinshi*, vol. 8 (Tokyo: Kokka Sōdōinshi Kankōkai, 1979), 524.

15. Ishikawa, *Kokka sōdōinshi*, 8:524–29. For an English translation of this document, see Harry J. Benda, James K. Irikura, and Koichi Kishi, eds., *Japanese Military Administration in Indonesia: Selected Documents* (New Haven, CT: Yale University Press, 1965), 17–25.

16. Benda et al., *Japanese Military Administration*, 26–46.

17. Iriye, *Power and Culture*, 67.

18. *Yomiuri shinbun*, October 1, 1940.

19. The first class of "research students" included technocratic heavyweights such as Mōri Hideoto, Minobe Yōji, Sakomizu Hisatsune, Okumura Kiwao, and others.

20. Sōryokusen Kenkyūjo, *Dai Tōa Kyōeiken kensetsu gen'an* (January 27, 1942), Chūō sensō hidō sono hoka 83, NIDS.

21. Notable intellectuals associated with the navy brain trust include Nishida Kitarō, Kōyama Iwao, Yabe Teiji, Kamikawa Hikomatsu, Tanabe Hajime, and Nishitani Keiji.

22. See *Kaigunshō shiryō*, SSKSS 15:41–49, 98–102. See documents 1680, 1681, and 1689 for the first meetings that led to the report.

23. Document 1796, "Dai Tōa Kyōeikenron," *Kaigunshō shiryō*, SSKSS, 17:8–50. Henceforth this study will be listed as "Dai Tōa Kyōeikenron."

24. The Shōwa Kenkyūkai had dissolved by November 1940 and thus was not involved in crafting visions for the Co-Prosperity Sphere.

25. Yatsugi Kazuo, *Shōwa dōran shishi*, vol. 1 (Tokyo: Keizai Ōraisha, 1971), 257.

26. See "Kyōeiken wa kaku aru beshi," *Kokusai Kenkyūkai shūhō*, vol. 4, no. 14, in Kokusai Kenkyūkai, *Senji seiji keizai shiryō*, vols. 4–5 (Tokyo: Hara Shobō, 1982), 279. This citation comes from vol. 4 of the series.

27. See *Kokusai Kenkyūkai shūhō*, vol. 4, no. 45, in Kokusai Kenkyūkai, *Senji seiji keizai shiryō*, 5:339.

28. Peter Duus notices this debate as well, but he focuses his analysis only on economic issues. See Duus, "Imperialism without Colonies."

29. Kokusaku Kenkyūkai, *Dai Tōa Kyōeiken seiji keizai taiseiron* (Tokyo: Dai tōa mondai chōsakai kenkyū hōkoku 1, 1943), 38.

30. "Dai Tōa Kyōeikenron," 21. The National Policy Research Association referred to this in a similar way, calling the new order an "organic body" (*yūkiteki tōitsutai* or *tōitsuteki yūkitai*). See Kokusaku Kenkyūkai, *Dai Tōa Kyōeiken seiji keizai taiseiron*, 44–46.

31. Kokusai Kenkyūkai, *Senji seiji keizai shiryō*, 4:352.

32. *Dai Tōa Kyōeiken kensetsu gen'an*, NIDS.

33. The navy brain trust, for instance, discussed independent states within the Sphere with the following caveat: "Even though independent, they will submit to guidance over internal affairs." See "Dai Tōa Kyōeikenron," 25. The National Policy Research Association, too, called for "true independent countries" but argued that Japan must "lead the independent countries [of the Sphere]." "Partner countries have autonomy," concludes the study, "but this must not be thought of as absolute autonomy." Kokusai Kenkyūkai, *Senji seiji keizai shiryō*, 4:347–48.

34. Kawanishi Kōsuke, "'Teikoku' to 'dokuritsu': Dai Tōa Kyōeiken' ni okeru 'jishu dokuritsu' mondai no kyōshin." *Nenpō Nihon gendaishi* 10 (2005): 47–84.

35. *Dai Tōa Kyōeiken kensetsu gen'an*, NIDS. The navy study had a similar understanding of protectorates but labeled them "independent protectorates" owing to propaganda and political concerns. The navy draft hoped to appeal to desires for self-determination across the world by providing the impression of a willingness to bestow independence. The report thus noted, "For propaganda purposes, we cannot avoid the use of the term 'independent country,' but strictly speaking they are different from the independent countries. Rather, they are incomplete independent countries." See "Dai Tōa Kyōeikenron," 21.

36. Strikingly, these intellectuals were perhaps unintentionally reproducing for the Greater East Asia Co-Prosperity Sphere the mandate system used by the British after World War I. For more on Class A, B, and C mandates proposed by the British, see Mazower, *Governing the World*, 169.

37. Kokusaku Kenkyūkai, *Dai Tōa Kyōeiken seiji taisei ni kan suru kenkyū*, Dai Tōa Mondai Chōsakai toku sei 012 (Tokyo: Kokusai Kenkyūkai Jimukyoku), 78. The National Policy Research Association even stated that, generally speaking, member countries would be able to interact or pursue trade with subordinate territories in other regional spheres. But as leader of the Sphere, Japan should be formally involved in the process of establishing and overseeing such relations. See Kokusaku Kenkyūkai, *Senji seiji keizai shiryō*, 5:355.

38. "Dai Tōa Kyōeikenron," 25.

39. Ibid., 43. For Matsushita's views on international law, see ibid., 41–50; Masatoshi Matsushita, "Greater East Asia International Law," *Contemporary Japan*, December 1942, 1712–19; Masatoshi Matsushita, "Greater East Asia International Law II," *Contemporary Japan*, January 1943, 30–37.

40. The National Policy Research Association perhaps best stated the complex nature of international law, as future relations would be held between multiple actors, including (1) the Co-Prosperity Sphere or other regional spheres of influence; (2) states affiliated with a regional sphere; and (3) nonaligned countries. Kokusaku Kenkyūkai, *Senji seiji keizai shiryō*, 5:354–55. Other legal scholars, such as Maehara Mitsuo, argued that international law in the future will have to recognize ethnicities in the same way that it currently

recognizes states as legitimate types of political organization. See Maehara Mitsuo, "Dai Tōa Kyōeiken no riron," in Maehara Mitsuo, Noguchi Hoichirō, and Kobayashi Hajime, eds., *Dai Tōa Kyōeiken no minzoku* (Tokyo: Rokumeikan, 1943), 99. See also Kevin M. Doak, "The Concept of Ethnic Nationality and Its Role in Pan-Asianism in Imperial Japan," in Sven Saaler and J. Victor Koschmann, eds., *Pan-Asianism in Modern Japanese History: Colonialism, Regionalism, and Borders* (London: Routledge, 2007), 174.

41. Hatano Sumio calls this the "Manchukuo model" of "dependent independence." Hatano, *Taiheiyō Sensō to Ajia gaikō*, 103–4.

42. Strikingly, military men often did not think these plans went far enough. For instance, Yabe's ideas in the Naval Intelligence Division's plan drew opposition from the navy brain trust's director, Ōgi Kazuto, as well as from the organization's founder, Rear Admiral Takagi Sōkichi. Both navy men were opposed to a restrained occupation policy. See Arima, "Dare ni mukatte," 268–69.

43. Mimura, *Planning for Empire*, 189.

44. Peter Duus has noticed a similar trend. See Duus, "Imperialism without Colonies," 67.

45. According to the National Policy Research Association's plan for the new economic system, trade would be highly regulated. It had two main principles on trade:

1. "In principle, component countries and regions within the Co-Prosperity Sphere will be forbidden from [engaging in] trade outside of the Sphere."
2. Thus, all trade outside of the Sphere will be managed by the leading country, which will systematically and single-handedly negotiate [deals for foreign trade]."

Component states, however, would have a greater level of freedom to trade nonstrategic goods to other states within the Co-Prosperity Sphere. See Kokusai Kenkyūkai, *Senji seiji keizai shiryō*, 5:373.

46. See *Dai Tōa Kyōeiken kensetsu gen'an*, chapter 7, NIDS.

47. Quoted in Mimura, *Planning for Empire*, 188.

48. "Dai Tōa Kyōeikenron," 30.

49. Kokusaku Kenkyūkai, *Senji seiji keizai shiryō*, 5:375.

50. "Dai Tōa Kyōeikenron," 31.

51. As some argued, however, Japan's Co-Prosperity Sphere was influenced as much by the British bloc economy (imperial preference) as it was by the German idea of *Grossraumwirtschaft*. Geographer Noguchi Hoichirō, for instance, argued: "The Greater East Asia Co-Prosperity ideal comes from a shared parentage of the German idea of regional economics (*Grossraumwirtschaft*) and the English bloc economy." See Noguchi Hoichirō, "Dai Tōa Kyōeiken no minzoku," *Dai Tōa Kyōeiken no minzoku*, 1.

52. See *Dai tōa kensetsu shingikai kankei shiryō*, 1:2.

53. Adachi, *"Dai Tōa Kyōeiken" no keizai kōsō*, 25–51. For a condensed version, see Adachi Hiroaki, "'Dai Tōa Kyōeiken' ron," *Iwanami Kōza Nihon rekishi*, vol. 18, Kin-Gendai 4 (Tokyo: Iwanami Shoten, 2015), 144–48.

54. The navy got involved as well, seeking to include the southern areas in this "core region."

55. Adachi, *"Dai Tōa Kyōeiken" no keizai kōsō*, 58–62.

56. Established by the cabinet planning board in September 1941, the control associations were headed by businessmen who had detailed knowledge about production in their respective fields. For more on the control associations, see Richard Rice, "Economic Mobilization in Japan: Business, Bureaucracy, and Military in Conflict," *Journal of Asian Studies* 38, no. 4 (August 1979): 689–706.

57. The original draft of the cabinet planning board document, "Dai tōa keizai kensetsu kihon hōsaku," can be found in *Dai tōa kensetsu shingikai kankei shiryō*, 2:20. See also JACAR, reference codes C01000321400 and C12121909300, for the April 17 plan; Adachi, *"Dai Tōa Kyōeiken" no keizai kōsō*, 70.

58. Adachi, *"Dai Tōa Kyōeiken" no keizai kōsō*, 70.

59. May 19 entry, *Kimitsu sensō nisshi*, 1:247. Gen. Sugiyama Hajime records this liaison conference as occurring on May 20. See *Sugiyama memo*, 2:124–25.

60. See Adachi, *"Dai Tōa Kyōeiken" no keizai kōsō*, 77–105.

61. This view is best laid out in Baba Akira, "Dai Tōa Shō setchi mondai," *Nit-Chū kankei to gaisei kikō no kenkyū: Taishō-Shōwa Ki*. Meiji hyakunenshi sōsho 333 (Tokyo: Hara Shobō, 1983), 383–471.

62. Document 1795, "Dai Tōashō setchi ni kan suru ken," September 1, 1942. *Kaigunshō shiryō*, SSKSS, 17:1–7. See also Gaimushō, *Gaimushō no hyakunen*, 2:706–8.

63. Gaimushō, *Gaimushō no hyakunen*, 2:706–12.

64. Kido Kōichi noted his surprise at Tōgō's gambit. See Kido, *Kido Kōichi nikki*, 2:980–81.

65. *Shōwa Tennō jitsuroku*, 30:150.

66. "Tōjō kokumu daijin no enzetsu," February 17, 1941. *Kanpō gōgai*, TG-NDL. See also "Dai tōa kensetsu hōshin," document 1546, reel 36, *Hatta Yoshiaki kankei monjo* Waseda Daigaku Gendai Seiji Kenkyūsho.

67. *Sugiyama memo*, 1:7; Bōeichō Bōei Kenkyūjo Senshibu, *Nanpō no gunsei* (Tokyo: Asagumo Shinbunsha, 1985), 35. Henceforth labeled *Nanpō no gunsei*.

68. Kawanishi, *Dai Tōa Kyōeiken*, 119–21.

69. Document 1623: "Shisō kondankai (hyōgo no kentō)," September 30, 1941, *Kaigunshō shiryō*, SSKSS, 14:263–66.

70. Document 1812: "Gaikō kondankai (Taiheiyō kenshō seitei ni tsuite)," September 26, 1942, *Kaigunshō shiryō*, SSKSS, 17:132–33.

71. He mentioned Tamura in the same brain trust meeting, stating, "I reread Tamura Tokuji's book and it is very sincere and excellent." He continued, referring to Tamura's notions of a new internationalism based on the Japanese concept of *musubi*, stating, "I eagerly anticipate an 'ideology' that is both rational and universal." See ibid., 133.

72. See, for instance, Tamura Tokuji, *Nihon to shin kokusai shugi: jinsei, shakai, kokka, kokkō, sekinin ni kan suru konpon riron* (Kyoto: Ritsumeikan Shuppanbu, 1939); Tamura Tokuji, "Shin kokusaishugi joron," *Gaikō jihō* 820 (February 1, 1939): 1–18; Tamura Tokuji, "Rekishiteki hitsuzensei no kengen to shin kokusaishugi," *Gaikō jihō* 826 (May 1, 1939): 1–32.

73. Tamura, "Rekishiteki hitsuzensei," 1.

74. Tamura Tokuji, "Kokusai shakai to hakkō ichiu no risō," *Gaikō jihō*, no. 908 (October 1, 1942): 2, 8, 16.

75. Tamura Tokuji, "Dai Tōa Kyōeiken kensetsu shuisho (1)," *Dōshisha ronsō* 77 (November 2, 1942): 2. See also Tamura Tokuji, "Kokusaihō no shōrai to Nihon seishin," *Hōritsu jihō* (October 1942), 958–62.

76. Tamura Tokuji, "Dai Tōa Kyōeiken kensetsu shuisho (2)," *Dōshisha ronsō*, no. 78 (January 31, 1943): 125.

77. The -isms include total cooperativism (*zenbu kyōdōshugi*); totalism (*sōtaishugi*); state-ism (*hōhonshugi*), meaning that the state is the purpose of life and that developments in global society begin with developments at home; ultranationalism, which highlighted respect for an institution (the state) that has a duty of bringing out the development of all humankind; new internationalism; and harmonism.

78. Even the Greater East Asia Construction Council's "Fundamental Policy" viewed *hakkō ichiu* as the "basic principle [*kihon rinen*] behind the construction of Greater East

Asia." See, for instance, "Dai tōa kensetsu ni kan suru kiso yōken," May 4, 1942, in Kikakuin, *Dai tōa kensetsu kihon hōsaku* (July 1942), JACAR, reference code C12120393700.
79. Noguchi, "Dai Tōa Kyōeiken no minzoku," 209–11.
80. Quoted in Shinobu, *"Taiheiyō Sensō" to "mō hitotsu no Taiheiyō Sensō,"* 194.
81. Mazower, *Hitler's Empire*, 326, 555.
82. See "Dai Tōa Kyōeikenron," 15–17. Yabe made similar points in a 1943 article, "Rōma teikoku, Ei teikoku, Dai Tōa Kyōeiken," *Hōritsu jihō* 15, no. 3 (March 1943): 19–23. Another similar comparison was done by the National Policy Research Association. See "Sekai shinchitsujoron," *Kokusaku Kenkyūkai shūhō* 4, no. 48, in *Senji seiji keizai shiryō*, 5:408–9.
83. "Dai Tōa Kyōeikenron," 17–18; Yabe, "Rōma teikoku, Ei teikoku, Dai Tōa Kyōeiken," 23.
84. Nogi Harumichi, interview in Haruko Taya Cook and Theodore F. Cook, *Japan at War: An Oral History* (New York: New Press, 1992), 106–7.

4. THE PATRIOTIC COLLABORATORS

1. Royal Arch Gunnison, "The Filipinos Fight On," *Collier's*, July 1, 1944, 46.
2. Bo Let Ya (Hla Pe), "The March to National Leadership," in Maung Maung, ed., *Aung San of Burma* (The Hague: Published for Yale University, Southeast Asia Studies by M. Nijhoff, 1962), 47. Hereafter this book will be cited as *Aung San of Burma*. See also Ba Maw, *Breakthrough in Burma: Memoirs of a Revolution, 1939–1946* (New Haven, CT: Yale University Press, 1968), 139; Izumiya Tatsurō, *The Minami Organ* (Rangoon: Translation and Publications Dept., Higher Education Dept., 1981), 99.
3. *Sugiyama memo*, 1:527.
4. Perhaps the most important for the Philippines are Steinberg, *Philippine Collaboration*; Theodore Friend, *Between Two Empires: The Ordeal of the Philippines, 1929–1946* (New Haven, CT: Yale University Press, 1965); Teodoro A. Agoncillo, *The Fateful Years: Japan's Adventure in the Philippines*, 2 vols. (Quezon City: R. P. Garcia, 1965); and Alfred W. McCoy, "'Politics by Other Means': World War II in the Western Visayas, Philippines," in Alfred W. McCoy, ed., *Southeast Asia under Japanese Occupation* (New Haven, CT: Monograph Series No. 22, Southeast Asia Studies, Yale University, 1980), 191–245. For research on Burma, however, see especially Dorothy Hess Guyot, "The Political Impact of the Japanese Occupation of Burma" (Ph.D. diss., Yale University, 1966); Maung Maung, *Burma and General Ne Win* (Bombay: Asia Publishing House, 1969), 62–125; Jan Bečka, *The National Liberation Movement in Burma during the Japanese Occupation Period, 1941–1945* (Prague: Oriental Institute in Academia, 1983), 51–104; Robert H. Taylor, *The State in Burma* (Honolulu: University of Hawaii Press, 1987); Nemoto Kei, *Teikō to kyōryoku no hazama: kindai Birumashi no naka no Igirisu to Nihon* (Tokyo: Iwanami Shoten, 2010).
5. Important exceptions include Pluvier, *South-East Asia*, 206–10; Tarling, *Sudden Rampage*.
6. H. W. Brands, *Bound to Empire: The United States and the Philippines* (New York: Oxford University Press, 1992), 24–26.
7. Usha Mahajani, *Philippine Nationalism: External Challenge and Filipino Response, 1565–1946* (St. Lucia: University of Queensland Press, 1971), 399–400.
8. Friend, *Between Two Empires*, 4.
9. The law originally included the Clarke Amendment, which called for independence between two to four years of the passage of the Jones Law. But the Clarke Amendment failed to pass the House of Representatives.
10. Roy Watson Curry, "Woodrow Wilson and Philippine Policy," *Mississippi Valley Historical Review* 41, no. 3 (December 1954): 448; see also Friend, *Between Two Empires*, 4.

11. Frederic S. Marquardt, *Before Bataan and After: A Personalized History of Our Philippine Experiment* (New York: Bobbs-Merrill, 1943), 133.

12. Friend, *Between Two Empires*, 4.

13. Ibid., 123.

14. See Christopher Capozzola, "The Philippines and the Politics of Anticipation," in David Farber and Beth Bailey, eds., *Pearl Harbor and the Attacks of December 8, 1941: A Pacific History*. Manuscript under contract at University Press of Kansas.

15. Pio Duran, *Philippine Independence and the Far Eastern Question* (Manila: University of the Philippines Press, 1935), 123–24, 194–95.

16. Grant K. Goodman, *Four Aspects of Philippine-Japanese Relations, 1930–1940* (New Haven, CT: Southeast Asia Studies, Monograph No. 9, Yale University, 1967), 133–94.

17. Eufronio M. Alip, *Japan-Philippine Relations: Historical, Political, Social, Economic* (Manila: Santo Tomas University Press, 1938), 22–23.

18. "Dewey Foresaw a Japanese Controlled Philippines," *The Philippines* (Spring 1938), 10.

19. Uchiyama to Foreign Minister Ugaki, July 19, 1938, JACAR, reference code B02031588000.

20. *Life*, August 8, 1938, 24.

21. Quezon Papers, series III, box 16, National Library of the Philippines (henceforth NLP).

22. Ibid.

23. Ricardo Trota Jose, *The Philippine Army, 1935–1942* (Manila: Ateneo de Manila University Press, 1992), 114, 165.

24. Sayre to Roosevelt, April 23, 1941, Frances Bowe Sayre Papers, box 7, Library of Congress (henceforth LC).

25. Jose, *Philippine Army*, 164–65. For Quezon's concerns about Philippine defense plans, see 162–76. See also Brands, *Bound to Empire*, 178–81; Joseph Ralston Hayden, *The Philippines: A Study in National Development* (New York: Macmillan, 1942), 730–59.

26. Sergio Osmeña, "Quezon of the Philippines," *Foreign Affairs* 21, no. 2 (January 1943): 289; Sayre to Roosevelt, June 18, 1941, Frances Bowe Sayre Papers, box 7, LC.

27. They accounted for 425 of 429 members. "Problems of the Post-War Settlement in the Far East," Burma Office Records, IOR: M/5/26, Asia, Pacific and Africa Collections, British Library (hereafter APAC-BL).

28. "Ba Maw to U Pu," *Time*, March 6, 1939.

29. Burma Office Records, IOR: M/5/48, APAC-BL.

30. See Paul H. Kratoska, "The Karen of Burma under Japanese Rule," in Paul H. Kratoska, ed., *Southeast Asian Minorities in the Wartime Japanese Empire* (London: RoutledgeCurzon, 2002), 21–23.

31. Albert D. Moscotti, *British Policy and the Nationalist Movement in Burma, 1917–1937* (Honolulu: University Press of Hawaii, 1974), 34–35.

32. The best treatment of this is in Maung Maung, *From Sangha to Laity: Nationalist Movements of Burma, 1920–1940* (New Delhi: Manohar, 1980), 83–107.

33. For a good understanding of U Saw, see Robert H. Taylor, "Politics in Late Colonial Burma: The Case of U Saw," *Modern Asian Studies* 10, no. 2 (1976): 161–93.

34. Khin Myo Chit, *Many a House of Life Hath Held Me*, Burmese Politics Collection, Mss Eur D1066/1, 78, APAC-BL.

35. For concerns about U Saw's ambitions, see, for instance, IOR: M/3/1113, APAC-BL.

36. Burma Office Records, IOR M/5/9, APAC-BL; Maung Maung, *Burma and General Ne Win*, 53; Martin Smith, *Burma: Insurgency and the Politics of Ethnicity*, 2nd ed. (London: Zed, 1999), 54.

37. "The 1936 Rangoon University Strike," Miscellaneous Papers on Life and Politics in Burma, Mss Eur D 1066/2, APAC-BL.

38. Douglas MacArthur, *Reminiscences* (New York: McGraw-Hill, 1964), 124.

39. Sanbō Honbu Dai'ichi Kenkyūhan, *Nanpō sakusen ni okeru senryōchi tōchi yōkōan*, 82–87, NIDS.

40. Bōeichō Bōei Kenshūjo, Senshishitsu, *Hitō kōryaku sakusen* (Tokyo: Asagumo Shinbunsha, 1966), 208.

41. The following are taken from "Actas de las Reuniones de Prominentes Filipinos Celebradas en la residencia del ex-Speaker José Yulo en la Calle Peñafrancia No. 353 Distrito de Paco, Ciudad de Manila, Filipinas, Enero 5 á 10, 12 y 23, 1942," in Mauro Garcia Collection (MGC), Sophia University. Henceforth labeled "Reuniones en la Calle Peñafrancia No. 353." These citations were taken from the January 6 and 7, 1942, meetings. All the Peñafrancia meetings can also be found in Mauro Garcia, ed., *Documents on the Japanese Occupation of the Philippines* (Manila: Philippine Historical Association, 1965).

42. "Reuniones en la Calle Peñafrancia No. 353," January 5, 1942, MGC; José P. Laurel, *War Memoirs of Dr. José P. Laurel* (Manila: José P. Laurel Memorial Foundation, 1962), 7.

43. "The Filipinos Fight on," *Collier's*, July 1, 1944, 15. See also Laurel, *War Memoirs*, 5–6; Ricardo Trota Jose, ed., *World War II and the Japanese Occupation* (Diliman, Quezon City: University of the Philippines Press, 2006), 111. Quezon's memoirs also hint at instructions to collaborate. He wrote, "My last instructions to my colleagues who were left behind were that they should do everything in their power to minimize the sufferings of the civilian population." See Manuel L. Quezon, *The Good Fight* (New York: D. Appleton-Century, 1946), 208. A similar statement can also be found on 260.

44. "Reuniones en la Calle Peñafrancia No. 353," January 7, 1942, MGC.

45. Ibid., January 9, 1942, MGC.

46. Recto was likely referring to either former Sakdalista leader Benigno Ramos or General Artemio Ricarte. Ibid., January 12, 1942, MGC; Garcia, *Documents*, 28.

47. "Politics, Pure Politics," July 16, 1949, in Claro M. Recto, *The Complete Works of Claro M. Recto*, vol. 7 (Pasay City: Claro M. Recto Memorial Foundation, 1990), 91. See also Jose, *World War II and the Japanese Occupation*, 112.

48. For the various edits to the official reply, see "Reuniones en la Calle Peñafrancia No. 353," January 10–12, 1942, MGC. The reply is also quoted in Philippines Executive Commission (PEC), *Official Gazette* 1, no. 1 (January 1942): 20.

49. PEC, *Official Gazette* 1, no. 1 (January 1942): 6–7; see also Philippines (Japanese Military Administration, 1942–1943), *Official Journal of the Japanese Military Administration*, vol. 1 (January 1942): 7–8.

50. "Acta de la Lectura y Entrega del Mensaje de Contestacion del Alcalde Jorge B. Vargas de la Ciudad de Manila Mas Grande al Comandante en Jefe de las Fuerzas Imperiales Japoneses, Teniente General Toshinari Maeda, en la Antigua Mansion del Alto Comisionado Americano en el Dewey Boulevard, Distrito de la Ermita, Ciudad de Manila, Filipinas, el Dia Viernes, Veinte y Tres de Enero de 1942," MGC, Sophia University. See also Garcia, *Documents*, 34–36.

51. See "Actas de las Sesiones del Consejo de Estado Filipino Celebrados en el Salon del Consejo de Estado Malacañan, Ciudad de Manila, Filipinas," January 24, 1942, MGC. See also PEC, *Official Gazette* 1, no. 1 (January 1942): 15.

52. PEC, *Official Gazette* 1, no. 2 (February 1942): 52–54; PEC, *Official Gazette* 1, no. 3 (March 1942): 160; Steinberg, *Philippine Collaboration*, 34–43.

53. *Official Journal of the Japanese Military Administration*, 1:34–35, 2:1–2.

54. The Hukbalahap was a radical peasant movement in central Luzon that held a deep antipathy toward not only the Japanese incursion but also Philippine landlordism

and the exploitation of an impoverished peasantry. The Hukbalahap launched a civil war against the Philippine government after the end of World War II.

55. David Bernstein, *The Philippine Story* (New York: Farrar, Straus, 1947), 172.

56. José P. Laurel Papers, series 3 (Japanese Occupation Papers), part II, Laurel War Papers, box 1 (hereafter Laurel War Papers), José P. Laurel Memorial Library, Manila (hereafter JPLML). See also MacArthur to Adams, January 28, 1942, U.S. Department of State, *Foreign Relations of the United States, Diplomatic Papers, 1942: General; the British Commonwealth; the Far East*, vol. 1 (Washington, D.C.: Government Printing Office, 1960), 888–89. Hereafter cited as *FRUS 1942*.

57. Laurel War Papers, box 1, JPLML.

58. MacArthur, *Reminiscences*, 130.

59. Charles A. Willoughby, *MacArthur: 1941–1951* (New York: McGraw-Hill, 1954), 55–56. See also Agoncillo, *Fateful Years*, 1:275; Friend, *Between Two Empires*, 218.

60. "Naikaku sōridaijin no enzetsu," January 22, 1941, *Kanpō gōgai*, TG-NDL. See also "Dai tōa kensetsu konpon hōshin," document 1546, reel 36, *Hatta Yoshiaki kankei monjo*. See also *Nihon gaikōshi*, 24:432. The text of Tōjō's Diet speech was confirmed six days earlier, at a January 15, 1942, liaison conference. See *Nanpō no gunsei*, 39; Gaimushō, *Nihon gaikō nenpyō*, 2:577.

61. MacArthur to Chief of Staff Marshall, February 10, 1942, *FRUS 1942*, 1:898–99. See also Quezon, *Good Fight*, 266.

62. Quezon Papers, series III, box 8, NLP.

63. The timing of the article's publication is suggestive. It was published in the immediate aftermath of the January 28, 1948 proclamation of amnesty, which set free members of the Philippine political elite on trial for collaborating with Japan. Thus, aside from being a testament to Cruz's activities, this article no doubt constituted part of a public relations campaign aimed at cleaning up the images of "collaborators" and "traitors" to the Philippines and the United States.

64. Lt. Col. Emigdio Cruz, "Quezon's Secret Agent," *Philippines Free Press*, February 7, 1948, 37; Cruz, "Quezon's Secret Agent," *Philippines Free Press*, February 14, 1948, 21.

65. Quezon to Mrs. Pilar H. Lim, November 29, 1943, Quezon Papers, Series II, Box 28, NLP.

66. José P. Laurel Papers, Series 3, Box 15, JPLML.

67. Claro M. Recto, "Un Discurso Historico," in *Complete Works of Claro M. Recto*, 5:364. Jorge B. Vargas justified his collaboration in a similar manner. See Abaya, *Betrayal in the Philippines*, 36.

68. Sergio Osmeña Jr., *Dear Dad*, microfilm roll 415a, no. 4154a, iii. Unpublished manuscript, Rare Books and Manuscripts, NLP.

69. Takeuchi Tatsuji, "Manila Diary, December 1942–October 1943," in Rōyama Masamichi and Takeuchi Tatsuji, *The Philippine Polity: A Japanese View*, trans. Takeuchi Tatsuji, ed. Theodore Friend (New Haven, CT: Southeast Asia Studies, Yale University, 1967), 213.

70. Agoncillo, *Fateful Years*, 1:ix.

71. Ba Maw, *Breakthrough in Burma*, 49.

72. Guyot, "Political Impact," 22; Bečka, *National Liberation Movement*, 54. See also Robert H. Taylor, "Burma in the Anti-Fascist War," in McCoy, *Southeast Asia under Japanese Occupation*, 163.

73. Ba Maw, *Breakthrough in Burma*, 62–63, 71–74.

74. Taken from *Extract from the Proceedings of the First House of Representatives, Volume VII, No. 7, at a meeting held on Friday, the 23rd February 1940*, 16, in Burma Office Records, IOR: M/3/1112, APAC-BL; Ba Maw, *Breakthrough in Burma*, 84–85.

75. Burma Office Records, IOR: M/3/897, APAC-BL.

76. "Policy in Burma" (May 1945 War Cabinet Report), Burma Office Records, IOR: M/3/1573, APAC-BL.

77. The full text for the Atlantic Charter can be found at Yale University's online archive, The Avalon Project, http://avalon.law.yale.edu/wwii/atlantic.asp (accessed August 21, 2018).

78. August 14, 1941, diary entry, in Leo Amery, *The Empire at Bay: The Leo Amery Diaries, 1929–1945* (London: Hutchinson, 1988), 710.

79. See Dorman-Smith Papers, Mss Eur E.215.32A, APAC-BL.

80. U Saw, "Self Government in Burma," *Times*, October 16, 1941.

81. The first statement was made on November 1, 1929, by the governor-general of India on behalf of the British government. Burma Office Records, IOR: M/3/733 and IOR: M/3/734, APAC-BL.

82. Of course, the resolution was weakened by phrases such as "as soon as practicable" and "in so far as it is possible in the immediate present." See Burma Office Records, IOR: M/3/730, APAC-BL.

83. CO 54/973/15, The National Archives (UK), henceforth cited as TNA.

84. FRUS, *1941*, 3:182.

85. See Burma Office Records, IOR: M/3/732 and IOR: M/3/734, APAC-BL.

86. U Saw in a press interview on November 3, 1941. See Papers of Sir John Clague, Mss E.252.45, APAC-BL. See also Burma Office Records, IOR: M/3/733, APAC-BL; *Times*, November 4, 1941; FRUS, *1941*, 3:183.

87. Burma Office Records, IOR: M/3/732, APAC-BL. For Churchill's statement, see IOR: M/3/18, APAC-BL.

88. Burma Office Records, IOR: M/3/1113, APAC-BL.

89. Bayly and Harper, *Forgotten Armies*, 103.

90. "U Saw's Bet," *Time*, January 26, 1942. See also "The Devil We Know," *New York Times*, January 20, 1942.

91. *FRUS, 1941*, 3:183.

92. After his detention, U Saw continued to deny any wrongdoing. He protested that he sought out the Japanese consul to ask him "to look after Burmese students in Tokyo." See FO 371/31776 and PREM 4/50/2, TNA. British records state that "Saw's statements of his visit to the Japanese Consul at Lisbon and his movements at San Francisco are unconvincing." See Private Office Papers of Sir Anthony Eden, Earl of Avon, Secretary of State for Foreign Affairs, FO 954/1B/474, TNA.

93. British authorities kept him imprisoned (without trial) to maintain secrecy over the fact that they had cracked Japanese diplomatic codes. See PREM 4/50/2, TNA. Tin Tut, however, was cleared of any wrongdoing and eventually made his way back to the Burmese government in exile in Simla.

94. R. Dorman Smith to L. S. Amery, October 17, 1944, IOR: L/PO/9/7 (ii), APAC-BL; Dorman-Smith Papers, "Unfinished Memoirs," 186, Mss Eur E.215.32b, APAC-BL.

95. Joyce C. Lebra, *Japanese-Trained Armies in Southeast Asia* (New York: Columbia University Press, 1977), 46–47.

96. Quoted in Shinobu, *"Taiheiyō Sensō" to "mō hitotsu no Taiheiyō Sensō,"* 163.

97. Bōeichō Bōei Kenshūjo, Senshishitsu, *Biruma kōryaku sakusen* (Tokyo, 1967), 9. Henceforth listed solely as *BKS*.

98. U Nu, *Burma under the Japanese* (London: MacMillan, 1954), 24–25.

99. Keiji Suzuki, "Aung San and the Burma Independence Army," *Aung San of Burma*, 58–59.

100. Quoted in Guyot, "Political Impact," 44.

101. Bo Yan Aung, "Our Lonely Mission," *Aung San of Burma*, 41–42; Izumiya, *Minami Organ*, 23; U Ba Than, *The Roots of the Revolution: Brief History of the Defence Services of the Union of Burma and the Ideals for Which They Stand* (Rangoon: Director of Information, 1962), 15.

102. *BKS*, 10; Sugii Mitsuru, *Minami Kikan gaishi*, 6, Mss Eur L614, APAC-BL; Izumiya, *Minami Organ*, 23; Aung San, "Burma's Challenge, 1946," in Josef Silverstein, ed., *The Political Legacy of Aung San* (Ithaca, NY: Cornell University Southeast Asia Program, 1972, 82–83; Keiji Suzuki, "Aung San and the Burma Independence Army," *Aung San of Burma*, 54–55; Aung San, "A First-Hand Report," *Aung San of Burma*, 33; Aung San, *The Writings of General Aung San* (Rangoon: Govt. Employees' Co-operative [Education] Pub. Committee, Universities Historical Research Centre, 2000), 71.

103. Aung San's speech is reprinted in *Aung San of Burma*, 33–34; Silverstein, *Political Legacy of Aung San*, 84. See also Nemoto Kei, *Aun San: Fūin sareta dokuritsu Biruma no yume* (Tokyo: Iwanami Shoten, 1996), 100.

104. *BKS*, 10, 117.

105. Bo Let Ya, "The March to National Leadership," *Aung San of Burma*, 44.

106. Nemoto, *Aun San: Fūin sareta dokuritsu Biruma no yume*, 104.

107. Bo Yan Aung, "Our Lonely Mission," *Aung San of Burma*, 42; Ba Maw, *Breakthrough in Burma*, 132–33.

108. *BKS*, 11–14, 72–73.

109. Izumiya, *Minami Organ*, 67.

110. Keiji Suzuki, "Aung San and the Burma Independence Army," *Aung San of Burma*, 58; Izamiya, *Minami Organ*, 70–71.

111. *BKS*, 117, 127.

112. Ibid., 124–25. The army still recognized the Minami Kikan and did not dissolve it until June 10, 1942.

113. Burma Intelligence Bureau, *Burma during the Japanese Occupation*, vol. 1 (Simla, 1943), 58–60 (henceforth referred to as BIB). See also Won Z. Yoon, *Japan's Scheme for the Liberation of Burma: The Role of the Minami Kikan and the "Thirty Comrades"* (Athens: Ohio University Press, 1973), 47.

114. Guyot, "Political Impact," 85.

115. *BKS*, 134.

116. BIB, 1:59. There are wide discrepancies on the size and strength of the BIA, perhaps owing to the loose nature of its organization. Ōta Tsunezō suggests that there were anywhere between 10,000 regulars and 100,000 soldiers in civilian clothes. See Ōta Tsunezō, *Biruma ni okeru Nihon gunseishi no kenkyū* (Tokyo: Yoshikawa Kōbunkan, 1967), 45. Japanese official sources list estimates at 15,000. See *BKS*, 448. U Ba Than gave an estimate of 23,000. See U Ba Than, *Roots of the Revolution*, 33.

117. BIB, 1:59.

118. U Hla Pe, "U Hla Pe's Narrative of the Japanese Occupation of Burma," Data Paper no. 41, Southeast Asia Program, Cornell University, March 1961, 9.

119. U Ba U, *My Burma: The Autobiography of a President* (New York: Taplinger, 1959), 150.

120. William Joseph Slim, *Defeat into Victory* (London: Cassell, 1956), 115. Slim provides fascinating insights into the nature of Japan's victories in Burma (115–21).

121. Maung Maung, *To a Soldier Son* (Rangoon: Sarpay Beikman, 1974), 16.

122. Nu, *Burma under the Japanese*, 3.

123. Hla Pe, "U Hla Pe's Narrative," 6.

124. Gaimushō, *Nihon gaikō nenpyō*, 2:577; *Kimitsu sensō nisshi*, 1:215; *Tokyo Asahi shinbun*, January 22, 1941, 1; *Nihon gaikōshi*, 24:432; *BKS*, 125–26.

125. *Tokyo Asahi shinbun*, January 23, 1941, 1.

126. "Biruma ni kan suru bōryaku jisshi nado ni kan suru ken," *BKS*, 122–23.

127. *BKS*, 123, 446. See also Won Z. Yoon, "Military Expediency: A Determining Factor in the Japanese Policy regarding Burmese Independence," *Journal of Southeast Asian Studies* 9, no. 2 (September 1978): 254–55.

128. BIB, 1:1–3, 4.

129. Guyot, "Political Impact," 139–46.

130. BIB, 1:32–33.

131. *BKS*, 450–52.

132. Frank N. Trager, ed., *Burma: Japanese Military Administration, Selected Documents, 1941–1945* (Philadelphia: University of Pennsylvania Press, 1971), 105. See also *BKS*, 455.

133. Ōta, *Biruma ni okeru Nihon gunseishi no kenkyū*, 526–28; Trager, *Burma*, 117–21.

134. Khin Myo Chit, *Many a House of Life Hath Held Me*, 42.

135. For a useful synthetic work on modes of collaboration, see Jorge I. Dominguez, "Responses to Occupations by the United States: Caliban's Dilemma," *Pacific Historical Review* 48, no. 4 (November 1979): 591–605.

136. March 11, 1943, letter to Dean Leoncio Monzon, in José P. Laurel, *Selected Correspondence of Dr. José P. Laurel* (Manila: Lyceum of the Philippines, 1997), 97.

137. Abaya, *Betrayal in the Philippines*, 38. Quezon loyalist and pro-American Leon Ma. Guerrero, however, noted that the war showed him his mistake in remaining loyal to the Americans. "I became anti-American in Bataan and Corregidor. We ate raw onions and bad rice, while they had steak at the table. We wore coconut helmets, the Americans wore regulation steel." Quoted in Erwin S. Fernandez, *The Diplomat-Scholar: A Biography of Leon Ma. Guerrero* (Singapore: ISEAS—Yusof Ishak Institute, 2017), 81.

138. Fernandez, *Diplomat-Scholar*, 91.

139. Tanigawa Yoshihiko, "Taiheiyō Sensō to Tōnan Ajia minzoku dokuritsu undō," *Hōsei kenkyū* 53, no. 3 (1987): 384–85.

140. McCoy, "'Politics by Other Means,'" 191–245.

141. Marcial P. Lichauco, *"Dear Mother Putnam": A Diary of the War in the Philippines* (Manila, 1949), 90. This is taken from Lichauco's diary entry from April 12, 1943.

142. Dorman-Smith to Wallace, February 25, 1944, Dorman-Smith Papers, Mss Eur E 215/6, APAC-BL.

5. A NEW DEAL FOR GREATER EAST ASIA?

1. Ba Maw, *Breakthrough in Burma*, 338–39.

2. Iriye, *Power and Culture*, 112–21.

3. Jessamyn Abel, *The International Minimum: Creativity and Contradiction in Japan's Global Engagement, 1933–1964* (Honolulu: University of Hawaii Press, 2015), 194–217.

4. Thailand, however, operated in a unique situation. The Thai regime had been independent before the war and resisted in all ways possible Japanese efforts to extend further informal control.

5. Hatano Sumio has provided the best account of this to date. See Hatano, *Taiheiyō Sensō to Ajia gaikō*, 161–244. See also Yasuda Toshie, "Dai Tōa Kaigi to Dai Tōa Kyōdō Sengen o megutte," *Hōgaku kenkyū* 63, no. 2 (February 1990): 369–422.

6. File 4–1, *Yoshida Zengo kankei monjo*, KSS-NDL.

7. Shigemitsu Mamoru, *Shigemitsu Mamoru: Gaikō ikenshoshū*, vol. 2: *Chū Ka taishi, gaimudaijin jidai* (Tokyo: Gendai Shiryō Shuppan, 2007), 259.

8. Ibid., 302, 119.

9. Ibid., 124.

10. Ibid., 268.

11. Shigemitsu Mamoru, *Shigemitsu Mamoru shuki*, vol. 2 (Tokyo: Chūō Kōronsha, 1988), 335.

12. Usui Katsumi, "Gaimushō: hito to kikō," in Hosoya Chihiro, Saitō Makoto, Imai Sei'ichi, and Rōyama Michio, eds., *Nichi-Bei kankeishi: kaisen ni itaru 10-nen (1931–41-nen)*, vol. 1: *Seifu shunō to gaikō kikan* (Tokyo: Tokyo Daigaku Shuppankai, 1971), 119–23.

13. Shigemitsu, *Gaikō ikenshoshū*, 2:245–46.

14. Shigemitsu, *Shōwa no dōran*, 2:171.

15. This began with an imperial conference in December 1942, which decided to abolish the unequal treaties and forge a more equal partnership with China.

16. Iriye, *Power and Culture*, 96–112.

17. Shigemitsu, *Shigemitsu Mamoru shuki*, 1:321–23, 328–29. See also Itō Takashi, Hirohashi Tadamitsu, and Katashima Norio, eds., *Tōjō naikaku sōridaijin kimitsu kiroku: Tōjō Hideki Taishō genkōroku* (Tokyo: Tokyo Daigaku Shuppankai, 1990), 175. Henceforth referred to as *Tōjō naikaku sōridaijin kimitsu kiroku*.

18. *DR*, 7:361.

19. *Sugiyama memo*, 2:386–88; "Kanpō," *Gōgai*, January 22, 1942, TG-NDL.

20. *BKS*, 544–45; for the Philippine case, see "Memorandum on Questions between Japan and the Philippines Arising from the Philippine Independence," October 1943. Taken from Agoncillo, *Fateful Years*, 977–82.

21. The November 15, 1941, liaison conference is in the *Sugiyama memo*, 1:523–24. See also "Tai Ei-Bei-Ran-Shō sensō shūmatsu sokushin ni kan suru fukuan," JACAR reference code B02032969200.

22. Armando J. Malay, *Occupied Philippines: The Role of Jorge B. Vargas during the Japanese Occupation* (Manila: Filipiniana Book Guild, 1967), 114–16; Teodoro A. Agoncillo, *The Burden of Proof: The Vargas-Laurel Collaboration Case* (Manila: University of the Philippines Press, 1984), 48.

23. Satō, *Dai Tōa Sensō kaikoroku*, 313–14.

24. *DR*, 6:536, 538; *Sugiyama memo*, 2:411, 414. Shigemitsu argued for limiting the conference to independent countries. He argued that inviting representatives from all areas of the Sphere might negatively impact Japan's relations with its "independent" partners. *DR*, 7:382.

25. *Sugiyama memo*, 2:497–98.

26. This is apparent in his policy papers. Others have also argued this point as well. See Yasuda, "Dai Tōa Kaigi," 373, 382; also see Hatano, "Shigemitsu Mamoru," 40.

27. Yasuda, "Dai Tōa Kaigi," 373–74; Hatano, "Shigemitsu Mamoru," 42.

28. Text of the conference taken from *Tōjō naikaku sōridaijin kimitsu kiroku*, 306, and Ministry of Greater East-Asiatic Affairs, *Addresses Before the Assembly of Greater East-Asiatic Nations* (Tokyo: Dai Tōashō, 1943), 2–3, hereafter cited as *Addresses Before the Assembly*.

29. *Tōjō naikaku sōridaijin kimitsu kiroku*, 308–9; *Addresses Before the Assembly*, 6–7.

30. "Nichi-Bi dōmei jōyaku oyobi zai Bi teikoku taishikan sechhi no ken narabini Nichi-Ka kazeiken ni kan suru jōyaku, sūmitsuin shinsa iinkai gijiroku," July 29, 1943, in *Dai tōa shojōyaku teiketsu keii kankei ikken 2: Nihonkoku "Biruma" kokkan dōmei jōyaku*, file B.1.0.0.J/X5, JFMA; JACAR reference code B04013494600. Also cited in Kawanishi Kōsuke, "'Dokuritsu' koku to iu 'shikkoku,'" in Wada Haruki et al., eds., *Higashi Ajia kindai tsūshi*, vol. 6: *Ajia Taiheiyō Sensō to "Dai Tōa Kyōeiken," 1935–1945 nen* (Tokyo: Iwanami Kōza, 2011), 347.

31. "Nichi-Bi dōmei jōyaku," file B.1.0.0.J/X5, JFMA; JACAR reference code B04013494600.

32. Ba Maw, *Breakthrough in Burma*, 337.

33. *Addresses Before the Assembly*, 37. Subsequent quotations from Ba Maw's and Sub-has Chandra Bose's speeches come from pages 41, 53, and 57, respectively.

34. Ba Maw's recollection of such admiration extends to his childhood. He wrote in his memoirs, "I can even now recall the Russo-Japanese war and the emotion with which we heard about the Japanese victories. I was then just a little boy at school, but the feeling was so widespread that even the little ones caught it. For instance, in the war games that became popular then we fought each other to be on the Japanese side. . . . Historically, that victory could be called the beginning, or perhaps the beginning of the beginning, of an awakening in Asia." See Ba Maw, *Breakthrough in Burma*, 47.

35. Subhas Chandra Bose, "Japan's Role in the Far East," *Modern Review*, October 1937, in Subhas Chandra Bose, *Netaji: Collected Works*, vol. 8: *Letters, Articles, Speeches and Statements, 1933–1937* (Calcutta: Netaji Research Bureau, 1994), 411–29.

36. *Tōjō naikaku sōridaijin kimitsu kiroku*, 287–88.

37. Ibid., 319, 321.

38. Yamamuro, *Manchuria under Japanese Dominion*, 173–74.

39. "Proceedings of the Assembly of Greater East Asiatic Nations Held on November 5 and 6, 1943, at the Diet Building, Tokyo," *Contemporary Japan*, November 1943, 1351–52.

40. Yasuda Toshie has noticed the use of this as well. See Yasuda, "Dai Tōa Kaigi," 413.

41. Historian Usui Katsumi writes of two instances of such use of authority. In 1939 Japanese Imperial Army troops mobilized Beijing middle school students to spell out, in human formation, the Chinese characters for "New Order in East Asia." The previous fall, middle school students were forced to take part in a marathon celebrating the Japanese takeover of the Wuhan triangle. Owing to this, Katsumi argues that students like them "witnessed the reality of the 'Provisional Government' and the Japanese colonial administration, and became profoundly skeptical of the 'New Order in East Asia.'" See Usui Katsumi, "Gen'ei o ou mono: Tōa shinchitsujo," Asahi jānaru, ed. *Shōwashi no shunkan*, vol. 1 (Tokyo: Asahi Shinbunsha, 1966), 285.

42. *Addresses Before the Assembly*, 27.

43. The May 31, 1943, imperial conference adopted the "Outline to Guide Greater East Asia Policy." One part of the outlines states: "It is decided that Malaya, Sumatra, Java, Borneo, and the Celebes are imperial territories (*teikoku ryōdo*), and [Japan] should make great efforts to develop the territory to supply important raw materials and to gain the understanding of the people." See *Sugiyama memo*, 2:411; *DR*, 6:536.

44. Gotō Ken'ichi, "Cooperation, Submission, and Resistance of Indigenous Elites of Southeast Asia in the Wartime Empire," in Peter Duus, Ramon H. Myers, and Mark R. Peattie, eds., *The Japanese Wartime Empire, 1931–1945* (Princeton, NJ: Princeton University Press, 1996), 288.

45. *Addresses Before the Assembly*, 32–33.

46. The Claro M. Recto letter was dated June 20, 1944. The entire letter appears in Recto, *Complete Works*, 5:378–93; Garcia, *Documents*, 109–24; Jose, *World War II and the Japanese Occupation*, 182–90.

47. Garcia, *Documents*, 190–91.

48. One example is a memorandum titled "Maltreatment of Filipinos by the Japanese," which Laurel received in mid-1944. This memorandum discussed instances of mistreatment that had occurred since September 1943. See ibid., 130–38.

49. Laurel, *War Memoirs*, 19, 63. His memoirs were written while he was in Sugamo Prison in 1945. And while he was no doubt attempting to distance himself from being labeled a pro-Japanese collaborator, I find that conditions in the Philippines lend credibility to his account.

50. Telegram quoted in *Nihon gaikōshi*, 24:368. The reasons Japanese authorities feared that Phibun would not attend were described in a telegram from Japanese ambassador to Thailand Tsubokami Teiji. According to Tsubokami, other reasons preventing Phibun from attending included a desire to distance Thailand from other client regimes, and domestic conditions, which would not tolerate a sign of Thailand submitting to Japan. See *Kimitsu sensō nisshi*, 2:438.

51. *Nihon gaikōshi*, 24:370.

52. E. Bruce Reynolds, *Thailand and Japan's Southern Advance*, 165.

53. Satō Kenryō, *Satō Kenryō no shōgen* (Tokyo: Fuyō Shobō, 1976), 429. Also see *Dai Tōa Sensō kankei ikken: Dai Tōa Kaigi kankei*, file A.7.0.0.9–48, 497, JFMA.

54. *Addresses Before the Assembly*, 17–19.

55. The original draft, which was written in English, can be found in ibid., 63–65. The Japanese versions that accompanied the English original can be found in *Shūhō* no. 369 (November 10, 1943); *Sugiyama memo*, 2:504; Gaimushō, *Shūsen Shiroku*, vol. 1 (Tokyo: Hokuyōsha, 1977), 99.

56. For a detailed discussion of the creation of the declaration, including earlier foreign ministry drafts, see Hatano, *Taiheiyō Sensō to Ajia gaikō*, 161–86, and Yasuda, "Dai Tōa Kaigi," 402–11. For the full foreign ministry drafts and discussions about them, see Gaimushō Jōyakukyoku, *Gaimushō shitsumu hōkoku*, vol. 2: *Shōwa 14-nen – 18-nen* (Tokyo: Kuresu Shuppan, 1995), 137–72.

57. Hatano, *Taiheiyō Sensō to Ajia gaikō*, 170. Hatano neglects to mention Yabe Teiji, who played an important role in drafting the Greater East Asia Ministry's draft. A copy of the draft can be found in Yabe's personal papers. See "Dai tōa kensetsu sengen an," document 4050, folder no. 24–83, *Yabe Teiji kankei monjo*, National Graduate Institute for Policy Studies, Tokyo (hereafter GRIPS).

58. *Kimitsu sensō nisshi*, 2:440–41.

59. Some drafts went so far as to include principles against threats or military invasions. See, for instance, the Andō draft and the Committee on Special Problems in International Law (*kokusai hōgaku tokubetsu mondai iinkai*) draft. Gaimushō, *Gaimushō shitsumu hōkoku*, 2:159, 170.

60. Kiyosawa Kiyoshi, *Ankoku nikki* (Tokyo: Hyōronsha, 1995), 179. The *Asahi shinbun* labeled it a "Greater East Asia Charter." See "Sekai ni rui naki kaigi," *Tokyo Asahi shinbun*, November 7, 1943, 2.

61. Kiyosawa, *Ankoku nikki*, 180. See also Iriye, *Power and Culture*, 119.

62. Shigemitsu, *Shōwa no dōran*, 2:179.

63. Laurel, *War Memoirs*, 60.

64. *Nihon gaikōshi*, 24:478.

65. The Greater East Asia minister demonstrated this unwillingness to modify the Joint Declaration in a telegram sent out to the region's ambassadors. This telegram stated, "We do not mean to act as an empire, forcing the document on the region. But as you can see from the above explanation, we created the document taking into serious consideration the perspectives of all countries. So we simply seek each nation's consent. Should the countries wish to state their opinions, they will have the opportunity to do so at the conference." *Nihon gaikōshi*, 24:475.

66. Tetsuo Najita and Harry D. Harootunian, "Japan's Revolt against the West," in B. T. Wakabayashi, ed., *Modern Japanese Thought* (Cambridge: Cambridge University Press, 1998), 207–72.

67. See Iriye, *Power and Culture*.

68. The Navy Ministry's plan also wanted to change "voluntarily open up their natural resources" to "provide for natural resources to be widely shared." See *Nihon gaikōshi*, 24:473–74.

69. Satō, *Satō Kenryō no shōgen*, 437; Satō, *Dai Tōa Senso kaikoroku*, 319.

70. Yabe Teiji, "Ei-Bei sensō mokuteki oyobi sengo keieiron no hihan," 9, *Yabe Teiji kankei monjo*, document 4103, folder 24–46, GRIPS. Henceforth "Ei-Bei sensō mokuteki."

71. Kamikawa Hikomatsu, "Dai Tōa Kaigi to Dai Tōa Kyōdō Sengen," *Kokusaihō gaikō zasshi* 43, no. 1 (January 1944): 77.

72. Kamikawa, "Asia Declaration and Atlantic Charter," *Contemporary Japan* 12, no. 12 (December 1943): 1555–56.

73. Kamikawa, "Dai Tōa Kaigi to Dai Tōa Kyōdō Sengen," 74–80.

74. Abel, *International Minimum*, 204–12.

75. This owed to Yabe's understanding of "liberty" or "freedom" (*jiyū*) as inherently contradictory. Traditional conceptions of liberty, he argued, are impossible in current foreign affairs. "Thinking of liberty from the standpoint of one state or people," he insisted, "inevitably contradicts with the liberty of another state or people." The right of one group for living space or economic advantage, for instance, necessarily contradicted that of another. Moreover, taken to its logical extreme, promoting such ideals as "self-rule" and "self-determination" could bring about anarchy in international relations. This being the case, Yabe argued that the "liberty" that Britain and the United States preached was not true liberty. Instead, he maintained that the Anglo-American powers sought their own "liberty" through the subordination of other countries or people. Anglo-American liberty, in short, was illiberal. Yabe, "Ei-Bei sensō mokuteki," 16–17.

76. Yabe Teiji, *Yabe Teiji nikki*, vol. 1, *Ichō no maki* (Tokyo: Yomiuri Shinbunsha, 1974), 661 (entry for October 27, 1943).

77. See "Dai tōa kensetsu sengen an," document 4050, folder no. 24–83, *Yabe Teiji kankei monjo*, GRIPS.

78. *Tōjō naikaku sōridaijin kimitsu kiroku*, 335–36.

79. *Addresses Before the Assembly*, 60.

80. *Tōjō naikaku sōridaijin kimitsu kiroku*, 333.

81. The November 13, 1943, statement can be found in Republic of the Philippines (ROP), *Official Gazette*, vol. 1, no. 2 (November 1943): 162; see also J. P. Laurel, "Fair and Equal Treatment to All," "A New Code of International Relations," and "Most Historic and Most Significant Conference," in *His Excellency José P. Laurel, President of the Second Philippine Republic: Speeches, Messages and Statements, October 14, 1943 to December 19, 1944* (Manila: Lyceum of the Philippines, 1997), 26–31.

82. Laurel, *War Memoirs*, 60.

83. Laurel, *His Excellency José P. Laurel*, 31.

84. José P. Laurel Papers, series 3, box 7, JPLML.

85. See Burma Office Records, IOR: M/3/864, APAC-BL.

86. U Hla Pe, "U Hla Pe's Narrative of the Japanese Occupation of Burma," Data Paper No. 41, Southeast Asia Program, Cornell University, March 1961, 59.

87. Burma Office Records, IOR: M/5/88, APAC-BL.

88. *Nihon gaikōshi*, 24:493. Japan was in a position to grant Indochina independence owing to the coup of March 9, 1945.

89. Ibid., 24:492–93.

90. Hatano, *Taiheiyō Senso to Ajia gaikō*, 208.

91. For a more detailed comparison of the British and Japanese engagement with Wilsonianism during World War II, see Yellen, "Wartime Wilsonianism."

92. "Legal Effect of the 'Atlantic Charter,'" file U 232, FO 371/34349, TNA.

93. FO 371/50778, TNA.

94. Mazower, *Governing the World*, 196. Roosevelt instead sought to highlight achievements international cooperation could make in eliminating hunger and poverty.

95. Fujitani, *Race for Empire*.

6. INDEPENDENCE IN TRANSITION

1. "Naikaku sōridaijin no enzetsu," January 22, 1941, *Kanpō gōgai*, TG-NDL; "Dai tōa kensetsu konpon hōshin," document 1546, reel 36, *Hatta Yoshiaki kankei monjo*.

2. *DR*, 7:356–65.

3. Yomiuri Shinbunsha, *Shōwashi no Tennō*, vol. 10 (Tokyo: Yomiuri Shinbunsha, 1970), 360.

4. Civil Affairs Staff (Burma) Weekly Report No. 61, December 9, 1944, in IOR: R/8/43, APAC-BL. For Laurel's statement, see Garcia, *Documents*, 190–91.

5. Ricardo T. Jose, "Test of Wills: Diplomacy between Japan and the Laurel Government," in Ikehata Setsuho and Lydia N. Yu-Jose, ed., *Philippines-Japan Relations* (Honolulu: University of Hawaii Press, 2003), 185–222.

6. *Sugiyama memo*, 2:388–91; *BKS*, 531–34.

7. *Tōjō naikaku sōridaijin kimitsu kiroku*, 168–70. See also Ba Maw, *Breakthrough in Burma*, 307.

8. Ba Maw, *Breakthrough in Burma*, 310–11.

9. Tun Pe, *Sun over Burma* (Rangoon: Rasika Ranjani Press, 1949), 40.

10. Ba Maw, *Breakthrough in Burma*, 309–10.

11. Judicial Department, General Branch, "Discussions of the First Meeting between the Japanese Side and the Special Committee," Series 10/1, Acc. No. 219 (hereafter "Discussions of the First Meeting"), National Archives Department, Yangon (hereafter NAD-Y). See also Tun Pe, *Sun over Burma*, 70; BIB, 1:9–10.

12. Nu, *Burma under the Japanese*, 63.

13. John F. Cady, *A History of Modern Burma* (Ithaca, NY: Cornell University Press, 1958), 455.

14. To this end, the Burmese side requested the creation of a Joint Co-operation Board. There is no evidence that such an organization was ever created. See "Discussions of the First Meeting."

15. BIB, 2:247–52 for the full text of the constitution. BIB, 2:10–18 provides an excellent discussion of its provisions.

16. See "Form of Oath Taken by Government Servants," BIB, 2:258.

17. Cady, *History of Modern Burma*, 456.

18. Ba Maw, *Breakthrough in Burma*, 325.

19. *BKS*, 541.

20. Tun Pe, *Sun over Burma*, 73.

21. BIB, 2:256–58.

22. BIB, 1:12; *Nihon gaikōshi*, 24:424–25; Ōta, *Biruma ni okeru Nihon gunseishi no kenkyū*, 373–74; Trager, *Burma: Japanese Military Administration*, 152.

23. "Tokyo Defines 'Freedom,'" *New York Times*, June 23, 1943, 6.

24. *Times of India*, August 18, 1943.

25. *BKS*, 544–45; see also Trager, *Burma: Japanese Military Administration*, 153–55.

26. Bečka, *National Liberation Movement*, 123.

27. BIB, 2:17.

28. "Transcript of Statement Made by Dr. Ba Maw before Lt. Colonel Figgess on January 17, 1946." Series IOL 2/1, Acc. No. 397 Media 448, 312 b, NAD-Y.

29. "Director, Intelligence Bureau, Government of Burma Fortnightly Report No. 23," IOR: M/4/2597; Clague Papers, IOR: Mss Eur 252/41, APAC-BL (hereafter Clague Papers); *Burma, the Struggle for Independence, 1944–1948: Documents from Official and Private Sources* (London: HMSO, 1983), 38.

30. See IOR: R/8/13, and Clague Papers.

31. See Clague Papers; *Burma, the Struggle for Independence*, 38.

32. "Fortnightly Report No. 23," August 15, 1943, in Clague Papers; BIB, 2:15, 105–6; Tun Pe, *Sun over Burma*, 87; BIB, 1:70.

33. BIB, 2:105; see also IOR: M/3/864, APAC-BL.

34. This came from a condensed report from *The Foreign Affairs Association*, Burma (September 1944). See U Hla Shain, ICS, "Civil Activities in War-time Burma," *Burma Digest* 1, no. 4 (April 1946): 15–16.

35. BIB, 2:106–7.

36. BIB, 2:234; U Hla Pe, "U Hla Pe's Narrative," 69. Hla Pe mistakenly thought it was only a commercial bank.

37. Burma, *Burma's New Order Plan* (Rangoon Bureau of State Print, 1944), 6.

38. Taylor, *State in Burma*, 254.

39. "The Interim Report of the Burma Special Research Commission," in Maung Ba Han, *The Planned State* (Rangoon, 1946), appendix A, i–iv, xxiv–xxv.

40. Tin Maung Maung Than, *State Dominance in Myanmar: The Political Economy of Industrialization* (Singapore: ISEAS, 2007), 35–39.

41. Ba Than, *Roots of the Revolution*, 38.

42. Tun Pe, *Sun over Burma*, 68.

43. BIB, 2:155.

44. See Brigadier Maung Maung, "On the March with Aung San," *Aung San of Burma*, 68.

45. BIB, 2:160; Ba Than, *Roots of the Revolution*, 38; Maung Maung, *Burma and General Ne Win*, 145.

46. Maung Maung, *To a Soldier Son*, 38–39.

47. BIB, 2:159.

48. Quoted in Mary P. Callahan, *Making Enemies: War and State Building in Burma* (Ithaca, NY: Cornell University Press, 2003), 63. Callahan provides an excellent discussion of the Officers Training School. See esp. 60–63.

49. Ōta, *Biruma ni okeru Nihon gunseishi no kenkyū*, 348.

50. Callahan, *Making Enemies*, 63.

51. *Nihon gaikōshi*, 24:434; *DR*, 6:548.

52. See "Hitō dokuritsu shidō yōkō," JACAR, reference code B02032953100; *Nihon gaikōshi*, 24:434–38.

53. *Nihon gaikōshi*, 24:438; José P. Laurel Papers, Series 3: Japanese Occupation Papers, Box 12, JPLML.

54. Remigio E. Agpalo, *José P. Laurel: National Leader, Political Philosopher* (Quezon City: Vera-Reyes, 1992), 37–38.

55. Steinberg, *Philippine Collaboration*, 80; Bernstein, *Philippine Story*, 167–69.

56. José P. Laurel, *Assertive Nationalism: A Collection of Articles and Addresses on Local Problems* (Manila: The National Teachers College, 1931; Theodore Friend, *The Blue-Eyed Enemy: Japan against the West in Java and Luzon, 1942–1945* (Princeton, NJ: Princeton University Press, 1988), 89.

57. Laurel Papers, Series 3: Japanese Occupation Papers, Box 9, JPLML.

58. The full text can be found in the Laurel Papers, Series 3: Japanese Occupation Papers, Box 12, JPLML.

59. U.S. Department of State, *Foreign Relations of the United States, Diplomatic Papers, 1943, The British Commonwealth, Eastern Europe, the Far East*, vol. 3 (Washington, D.C.:

Government Printing Office, 1963), 1111. See also Confesor to Dr. Fermin Caram, October 4, 1943, Tomas Confesor Correspondence, Japanese Occupation Papers, Reel 4, University of the Philippines (hereafter Confesor Correspondence).

60. Philippine Executive Commission (henceforth PEC), *Official Gazette* 2, no. 9 (September 1943): 876.

61. *Tōjō naikaku sōridaijin kimitsu kiroku*, 261. See also "Raureru daitōryō totomo ni," *Intabyū kiroku: Nihon no Firipin senryō*, Nanpō Gunsei Kankei Shiryō 15 (Tōkyō: Ryūkei Shosha, 1994), 102.

62. *DR*, 6:549.

63. See "Hitō dokuritsu shidō yōkō," JACAR reference code B02032953100. See also *DR*, 6:548–49, 7:362.

64. *Tōjō naikaku sōridaijin kimitsu kiroku*, 261.

65. "Raureru daitōryō totomo ni," *Intabyū kiroku*, 102. See also Laurel, *War Memoirs*, 17.

66. *Tōjō naikaku sōridaijin kimitsu kiroku*, 262; Laurel, *War Memoirs*, 17.

67. "Raureru daitōryō totomo ni," *Intabyū kiroku*, 103; a similar, but less pithy, quote can be found in *Tōjō naikaku sōridaijin kimitsu kiroku*, 262. See also Laurel, *War Memoirs*, 17.

68. *Tōjō naikaku sōridaijin kimitsu kiroku*, 262.

69. Ibid., 263–64.

70. *Tōjō naikaku sōridaijin kimitsu kiroku*, 264.

71. Theodore Friend also emphasizes this point. See *Blue-Eyed Enemy*, 126–30.

72. Tun Pe, *Sun over Burma*, 94. Tun Pe was struck at how different Laurel was from Ba Maw, whom he felt sacrificed the Burmese people for his own designs.

73. *Tōjō naikaku sōridaijin kimitsu kiroku*, 264–66.

74. Republic of the Philippines (henceforth ROP), *Official Gazette* 1, no. 1 (October 14–31, 1943): 71. For the plans for the inauguration ceremony, see *Dai Tōa Sensō kankei ikken: Hitō dokuritsu to Nichi-Bi dōmei jōyaku teiketsu kankei*, JFMA. JACAR reference code B02032955200. A great narrative of the inauguration ceremony is also provided in Agoncillo, *Fateful Years*, 1:392–97.

75. ROP, Ministry of Foreign Affairs, *Bulletin* I, 8; ROP, *Official Gazette* 1, no. 1 (October 14–31, 1943): 82; "Nichi-Bi dōmei jōyaku," JACAR reference code B02032955100; *Nihon gaikōshi*, 24:442–43.

76. This document is titled "Memorandum on Questions between Japan and the Philippines arising from the Philippine Independence," October 1943. Taken from Agoncillo, *Fateful Years*, 2:977–82 (appendix C).

77. Confesor to Dr. Fermin Caram, October 4, 1943, Confesor Correspondence.

78. Confesor to Laurel, October 26, 1943, Confesor Correspondence.

79. Published as José P. Laurel, "The Republic's Goals," *Philippine Review*, November 1944, 3.

80. Sergio Osmeña Jr., *Dear Dad*, 230. Unpublished manuscript, Rare Books and Manuscripts, NLP. Osmeña's statement is confirmed by Quintin Paredes in a December 27, 1945, meeting of former cabinet members. See "Reunion del Gabinete del Presidente José P. Laurel Celebrada el Dia Jueves, 27 de Diciembre de 1945, a las 4:30 PM," in Garcia, *Documents*, 228 (hereafter "Reunion del Gabinete del Presidente José P. Laurel").

81. PEC, *Official Gazette* 2, no. 9 (September 1943): 876. See also José P. Laurel, "One Nation, One Heart, One Republic," September 7, 1943, 17, Record Group 65, Classification 105: Foreign Counterintelligence, Box 181, U.S. National Archives.

82. "Reunion del Gabinete del Presidente José P. Laurel."

83. ROP, *Official Gazette* 1, no. 1 (October 14–31, 1943): 82.

84. ROP, *Official Gazette* 1, no. 1 (October 14–31, 1943): 81; see also ROP, Ministry of Foreign Affairs, *Bulletin* 1, no. 1 (October 14, 1943–February 15, 1944): 3.

85. See ROP, *Official Gazette* 1, no. 1 (October 14–31, 1943): 30, 85; ROP, Ministry of Foreign Affairs, *Bulletin* 1, no. 1 (October 14, 1943–February 15, 1944): 3, 5; ROP, Ministry of Foreign Affairs, *Bulletin* 1, no. 2 (February 16, 1944–March 31, 1944): 59. See also J. L. Vellut, "Foreign Relations of the Second ROP, 1943–1945," *Journal of Southeast Asian History* 5, no. 1 (March 1964): 134.

86. ROP, *Official Gazette* 1, no. 1 (October 14–31, 1943): 89; ROP, Ministry of Foreign Affairs, *Bulletin* 1, no. 1 (October 14, 1943–February 15, 1944): 26.

87. Guerrero, "Twilight in Tokyo," 101.

88. ROP, Ministry of Foreign Affairs, *Bulletin* 1, no. 1 (October 14, 1943–February 15, 1944): 31–32; ROP, *Official Gazette* 1, no. 5 (February 1944): 464, 469.

89. ROP, *Official Gazette* 1, no. 5 (February 1944): 526.

90. ROP, *Official Gazette* 1, no. 6 (March 1944): 687–88.

91. Ibid.

92. Jose, "Test of Wills," 204.

93. Murata Shōzō, *Murata Shōzō tsuisōroku* (Osaka: Ōsaka Shōsen, 1959), 359–60, entry for May 29, 1944. The memoirs will be hereafter cited as *Murata Shōzō tsuisōroku.*

94. *Kimitsu senso nisshi*, 2:587; "Raureru daitōryō totomo ni," *Intabyū kiroku*, 103; *DR*, 9:279, 280.

95. *Murata Shōzō tsuisōroku*, 361, entry for August 25, 1944; "Raureru daitōryō totomo ni," *Intabyū kiroku*, 103.

96. Laurel, *War Memoirs*, 24.

97. The best description of Recto's role and of the Philippine declaration of a "state of war" can be found in Agoncillo, *Burden of Proof*, 69–71; Agoncillo, *Fateful Years*, 2:828–29. For more, see Friend, *Blue-Eyed Enemy*, 126–30; Laurel, *War Memoirs*, 24.

98. Recto, *Three Years of Enemy Occupation*, 51.

99. "Souvenirs of Troubled Times in Manila, 1941–1945," 79, American Historical Collection, Ateneo de Manila University.

100. *Murata Shōzō tsuisōroku*, September 23, 1944, diary entry: 364.

101. *Kimitsu senso nisshi*, 2:588.

102. *DR*, 9:280.

103. Guerrero, "Twilight in Tokyo," 102.

104. Laurel Papers, Series 3: Japanese Occupation Papers, Box 6, JPLML.

105. See Recto, *Complete Works*, 5:378–93; Garcia, *Documents*, 109–24; Jose, *World War II and the Japanese Occupation*, 182–90.

106. Recto, *Complete Works*, 5:384, 386, 392. Recto speaks of his multiple protests in his postwar memoirs. He argues that on many occasions they "so embarrassed the Japanese that they had to resort to trickery to deny such practices, as by securing through intimidation or duress, affidavits and other declarations of denial from those Filipinos in whose behalf the protests were made." See Recto, *Three Years of Enemy Occupation*, 43–44.

107. "Firipin Taishi shoken yōshi," *Dai Tōa kankei ikken: Dai Tōa Taishi Kaigi kankei*, file A.7.0.0.9.53, JFMA. See JACAR reference code B02032975600.

108. ROP, *Official Gazette* 1, no. 7 (April 1944): 766.

109. Taken from Fernandez, *Diplomat-Scholar*, 92.

110. ROP, *Official Gazette* 1, no. 7 (April 1944): 768, 880.

111. ROP, Ministry of Foreign Affairs *Bulletin* 1, no. 1 (October 14, 1943–February 15, 1944): 42.

112. Recto, *Complete Works*, 5:400–402.

113. Nu, *Burma under the Japanese*, 87.

114. Ibid., 30.

115. Ibid., 84–85.

116. FO 643/3, TNA.

117. Maung Maung, *Burma in the Family of Nations* (Amsterdam: Djambatan, 1957), 102. Others echo his claim. See, for instance, Bečka, *National Liberation Movement in Burma*, 125; Richard Butwell, *U Nu of Burma* (Stanford, CA: Stanford University Press, 1963), 40–42.

118. See IOR: R/8/13, APAC-BL.

119. Khin Myo Chit, *Many a House of Life Hath Held Me*, Mss Eur D 1066/1, 84, APAC-BL.

120. Hla Pe, "U Hla Pe's Narrative," 37.

121. *Nippon Times*, November 18, 1944, 1.

122. BIB, 2:49; see also Cady, *History of Modern Burma*, 467.

123. "Award of State Scholarships Tenable in Nippon," Series 1/15 (d), Acc. No. 3823, NAD-Y. See also BIB, 2:49.

124. Ba Maw, *Breakthrough in Burma*, 330.

125. See India Office Departmental Records IOR/L/PO Private Office Papers, 1904–1948, IOR: L/PO/9/7(ii), APAC-BL.

126. See Callahan, *Making Enemies*, 74–75; Ba Than, *Roots of the Revolution*, 46, 49–50; Bečka, *National Liberation Movement*, 166–67.

127. Tun Pe, *Sun over Burma*, 103.

128. *Burma, the Struggle for Independence*, 110–12. The AFPFL was also known as the Anti-Fascist Organization (AFO) and the Anti-Fascist League (AFL).

129. Ba Than, *Roots of the Revolution*, 49–52.

130. Nu, *Burma under the Japanese*, 96.

131. For a firsthand account, see Maung Maung, *To a Soldier Son*, 62–70.

132. Bayly and Harper, *Forgotten Armies*, 429–34; Ba Than, *Roots of the Revolution*, 52–58. British Force 136 had channels of communication with Burmese nationalists, so when the revolt occurred they were ready to work with the BNA. Slim, *Defeat into Victory*, 516.

133. Slim, *Defeat into Victory*, 485, 518, 520.

134. "Formal Surrender in Burma," *Times*, October 25, 1945.

135. See Bayly and Harper, *Forgotten Armies*, 445; Lewis Balfour Oatts, *The Jungle in Arms* (London: W. Kimber, 1962), 203.

136. Ba Maw, *Breakthrough in Burma*, 335.

137. See Guyot, "Political Impact," 237.

138. Sergio Osmeña, Jr., *Dear Dad*, 251, NLP.

139. Jose, "Test of Wills," 213.

140. James C. Scott, *Weapons of the Weak: Everyday Forms of Peasant Resistance* (New Haven, CT: Yale University Press, 1985).

141. For more on financial imperialism, see Mark Metzler, *Lever of Empire: The International Gold Standard and the Crisis of Liberalism in Prewar Japan* (Berkeley: University of California Press, 2006); Michael Schiltz, *The Money Doctors from Japan: Finance, Imperialism, and the Building of the Yen Bloc, 1895–1937* (Cambridge, MA: Harvard University Asia Center, 2012).

142. See Burma, Foreign Office, *Burma Foreign Service List 1962* (Rangoon, 1962), 16, 18.

143. Dorman-Smith Papers, Mss Eur E 215/32b, APAC-BL.

144. Callahan, *Making Enemies*, 64.

CONCLUSION

1. Guerrero, "Twilight in Tokyo," 105–7.

2. Ba Maw, *Breakthrough in Burma*, 185.

3. Shinobu, *"Taiheiyō Sensō" to "mō hitotsu no Taiheiyō Sensō."* Shinobu's book was deeply influenced by Tanigawa Yoshihiko's "Taiheiyō Sensō to Tōnan Ajia minzoku

dokuritsu undo," and Maruyama Shizuo, *Indo Kokumingun: mō hitotsu no Taiheiyō Sensō* (Tokyo: Iwanami Shoten, 1985), from whom he borrowed the notion of a "second" Pacific War.

4. Kawachi Uichiro, interview in Cook and Cook, *Japan at War*, 220.

5. "Zadankai: Dai Tōa Kyōeiken no rinen to genjitsu," *Shisō no kagaku* 21 (December 1963): 6.

6. The existence of a "grand strategy" implies not only that an actor has long-term objectives but also that it has consistent tactics or strategies to meet those objectives. Wartime Japan had the objective of leading Greater East Asia but no stable or consistent strategies to bring this about.

7. These were by no means the only "forgotten armies" of the war. In Indonesia, the Pembela Tanah Air (PETA) served as the volunteer army, with a total of sixty-nine battalions. Similar Japanese-trained volunteer armies sprung up in Sumatra, Malaya, and French Indochina. For more on these "forgotten armies," see, for instance, Lebra, *Japanese-Trained Armies in Southeast Asia*; Bayly and Harper, *Forgotten Armies*; Christopher Bayly and Tim Harper, *Forgotten Wars: Freedom and Revolution in Southeast Asia* (Cambridge, MA: Harvard University Press, 2007). See also Shinobu, *"Taiheiyō Sensō" to "mō hitotsu no Taiheiyō Sensō*, 93–176.

8. Taken from "Subhas Chandra Bose and Japan," 4th Section, Asian Bureau, Ministry of Foreign Affairs, Japan, August 1956. This document, translated into English by Joyce Lebra, can be found in Sisir Kumar Bose, ed., *Netaji and India's Freedom* (Calcutta: Netaji Research Bureau, 1975), 368.

9. Friend, *Between Two Empires*, 269.

10. Taylor, *State in Burma*, 217–18.

11. Ivan Watson, Javed Iqbal, and Manny Maung, "Myanmar's Hidden War," *CNN*, November 11, 2015, http://edition.cnn.com/2015/11/11/asia/myanmar-shan-rebels-civil-war/index.html.

12. See Renato Constantino and Letizia R. Constantino, *The Philippines: The Continuing Past* (Quezon City: Foundation for Nationalist Studies, 1978), 27.

13. FO 643/84, TNA.

14. Nakano Satoshi, "Shokuminchi tōchi to Nanpō gunsei: teikoku, Nihon no kaitai to Tōnan Ajia," Kurosawa Aiko et al., eds., *Shihai to bōryoku*, Iwanami Kōza Ajia Taiheiyō Sensō, vol. 7 (Tokyo: Iwanami Shoten, 2006), 24–25.

15. Quoted in Hatano, *Taiheiyō Sensō to Ajia gaikō*, 208.

16. Ugaki Kazushige, "Dai Tōa Sensō no sekaishiteki igi," August 11, 1945. *Ugaki Kazushige kankei monjo*, KSS-NDL.

17. Watanabe Akio, "Sengo Nihon no shuppatsuten," in Watanabe Akio, ed., *Sengo Nihon no taigai seisaku* (Tokyo: Yūhikaku, 1985), 10–17. Part of this is also cited in Yukiko Koshiro, *Imperial Eclipse: Japan's Strategic Thinking about Continental Asia before August 1945* (Ithaca, NY: Cornell University Press, 2013), 264.

18. Shigemitsu, *Shigemitsu Mamoru shuki*, 2:339.

19. "Kokusai Renmei dai 51 sōkai ni okeru Shigemitsu Gaimudaijin no enzetsu," December 18, 1956, taken from Gaimushō, http://www.mofa.go.jp/mofaj/press/enzetsu/18/esm_1218.html. An English translation of the speech is also available on the foreign ministry website.

20. Shigemitsu's radio address can be found in Gaikō Kiroku, No. A'-0193, JFMA.

21. Ba Maw, *Breakthrough in Burma*, 340, 347.

22. Kagawa Toyohiko, "Ajia renpō gikai e no dai'ippo," *Sekai kokka* 7, no. 1 (January 1953): 3.

23. Satō, *Dai Tōa Sensō kaikoroku*, 417.

24. Gotō Ken'ichi, "'Dai Tōa Sensō' no imi," in Yano Tōru, ed., *Tōnan Ajia to Nihon* (Kōza Tōnan Ajiagaku, vol. 10 (Tokyo: Kōbundō, 1991), 169.

25. Teodoro F. Valencia, "Japan Philippine Relations Today," *Manila Times*, 1957. Taken from Gaikō Kiroku, No. A'-0193, JFMA. Even those Filipinos, such as Carlos P. Garcia, who in 1954 had argued for "Asia for the Asians" as a "statement of an eternal reality," admitted that Japan had used it "for imperialistic purposes in the last war." See Gaikō Kiroku, No. A'-0159, JFMA.

26. Margaret Shapiro, "Once Shunned, Japan Is Again a Giant in Asia," *Washington Post*, October 14, 1988.

27. Konrad Lawson has a wonderful section in his dissertation on the geography of power in the Philippines. See Konrad Lawson, "Wartime Atrocities and the Politics of Treason in the Ruins of the Japanese Empire, 1937–1953" (Ph.D. diss., Harvard University, 2012), 171–73.

Bibliography

Archival Collections

India
Netaji Research Bureau, Kolkata

Japan
Ministry of Foreign Affairs Office of Diplomatic Records, Tokyo
The National Archives of Japan, Tokyo
National Diet Library, Tokyo
National Institute for Defense Studies, Tokyo

Myanmar
National Archives Department, Yangon

Philippines
Jose P. Laurel Memorial Library, Manila
Jorge B. Vargas Museum and Filipiniana Research Center
The National Library of the Philippines, Manila

United Kingdom
British Library, Asia, Pacific and Africa Collection, London
The National Archives of the UK, Richmond

United States
Houghton Library, Harvard University, Cambridge, Massachusetts
Library of Congress, Manuscript Division, Washington, DC
National Archives, College Park, Maryland

Digital Collections
The American Presidency Project — http://www.presidency.ucsb.edu/
Foreign Relations of the United States — http://digicoll.library.wisc.edu/FRUS/
Franklin D. Roosevelt Presidential Library and Museum — http://www.fdrlibrary.marist.edu
Japan Center for Asian Historical Records — http://www.jacar.go.jp/
Kokuritsu kōbun shokan — http://www.digital.archives.go.jp/
Teikoku gikai kaigiroku — http://teikokugikai-i.ndl.go.jp/

Newspapers and Other Periodicals

Chicago Daily Tribune
Diamondo
Ekonomisuto
The Guardian (Rangoon)
Japan Times and Advertiser
Mainichi shinbun
Manila Tribune
Manila Times
New York Times
Tokyo Asahi shinbun
Washington Post
Yomiuri shinbun
Time
Times of India

Intellectual Journals

Chūō kōron
Contemporary Japan
Dōshisha ronsō
Gaikō jihō
Hōritsu jihō
Kaizō
Kokusai keizai kenkyū
Kokusaihō gaikō zasshi
Pacific Affairs
Sekai kokka

Unpublished Manuscript Collections

Asia, Pacific and Africa Collection, British Library, London

Burma Office Records, 1932–1948 (IOR/M/1~M/8)
Governor of Burma's Secretariat Files, 1942–1947 (IOR/R/8)
India Office Departmental Records, Private Office Papers, 1904–1948
Papers of Major General Sir Hubert Elvin Rance (Mss Eur F169)
Papers of Sir Frederick Blackmore Arnold (Mss Eur F145)
Papers of Sir John Clague (Mss Eur E252)
Papers of Sir Reginald Dorman-Smith (Mss Eur E215)
Papers of Walter Ian James Wallace (Mss Eur E338)

Gendai Seiji Kenkyūsho, Waseda University, Tokyo

Hatta Yoshiaki kankei monjo
Minobe Yōji monjo

Houghton Library, Harvard University, Cambridge, Massachusetts

Joseph C. Grew Papers

José P. Laurel Memorial Library, Manila
José P. Laurel Papers

Kensei Shiryāshitsu, National Diet Library, Tokyo
Abe Nobuyuki kankei monjo
Amō Eiji kankei monjo
Araki Sadao kankei monjo
Kamei Kan'ichirō kankei monjo
Konoe Fumimaro kankei monjo
Ugaki Kazushige kankei monjo
Yoshida Zengo kankei monjo

Manuscript Division, Library of Congress, Washington, DC
The Papers of Francis Bowes Sayre
The Personal Papers of Harold L. Ickes

The National Archives of the UK, Richmond
Private Office Papers of Sir Anthony Eden, Earl of Avon, Secretary of State for Foreign Affairs

National Graduate Institute for Policy Studies, Tokyo
Yabe Teiji kankei monjo

The National Library of the Philippines, Manila
Cornelio Balmaceda Collection
Sergio Osmeña Papers
Sergio Osmeña, Jr., *Dear Dad* (Microfilm Roll 415a, Item 4154a)
Manuel L. Quezon Papers

Sophia University, Tokyo
Mauro Garcia Collection

University of the Philippines, Diliman, Quezon City
Japanese Occupation Papers (MCF 7527–7531, Microfilm Reels 1–5)

Government Primary Sources

Burma

Burma during the Japanese Occupation. 2 vols. Simla: Burma Intelligence Bureau, 1943–44.
Burma Gazette. Rangoon, 1940–41.

Burma's New Order Plan. Rangoon: Bureau of State Print, 1944.

District Administration (Reconstruction) Committee. *Report.* Simla: Govt. of India Press, 1944.

Interim Report of the Riot Inquiry Committee. Rangoon: Govt. Printing and Stationery, 1939.

Burma, the Struggle for Independence, 1944–1948: Documents from Official and Private Sources. London: HMSO, 1983.

The Revolutionary Government of the Union of Burma. Foreign Office, Administrative and Personnel Division. *Burma Foreign Service List* 1962. Rangoon: Administrative and Personnel Division, Foreign Office, 1962.

Germany

Auswärtiges Amt. *Documents on German Foreign Policy, 1918–1945,* series D, vols. 9–13. London: H. M. Stationery Office, 1949–83.

Sontag, R., and S. Beddie, eds. *Nazi-Soviet Relations: Documents from the Archives of the German Foreign Office.* Washington, DC, 1948.

Japan

Bōeichō Bōei Kenshūjo. Senshishitsu. *Biruma kōryaku sakusen.* Tokyo: Asagumo Shinbunsha, 1966.

———. *Daihon'ei rikugunbu.* 10 vols. Tokyo: Asagumo Shinbunsha, 1973.

———. *Daihon'ei rikugunbu Dai Tōa Sensō kaisen keii.* 5 vols. Tokyo: Asagumo Shinbunsha, 1973–74.

———. *Hitō kōryaku sakusen.* Tokyo: Asagumo Shinbunsha, 1966.

———. *Marē shinkō sakusen.* Tokyo: Asagumo Shinbunsha, 1966.

Bōeichō Bōei Kenkyūjo. Senshibu. *Nanpō no gunsei: shiryōshū.* Tokyo: Asagumo Shinbunsha, 1985.

Dai Nippon Genron Hōkokukai. *Dai Tōa Kyōdō Sengen.* Tokyo: Dai Nippon Genron Hōkokukai, 1944.

Gaimushō. *Gaimushō no hyakunen.* Vol. 2. Tokyo: Hara Shobō, 1969.

———. *Nihon gaikō bunsho: dainiji Ōshū taisen to Nihon,* vol. 1: *Nichi-Doku-I sangoku dōmei, Nisso chūritsu jōyaku* (Tokyo: Gaimushō, 2012).

———. *Nihon gaikō nenpyō narabini shuyō monjo: 1840–1945.* Vol. 2. Tokyo: Hara Shobō, 1955.

———. *Shūsen shiroku.* 6 vols. Tokyo: Hokuyōsha, 1977–78.

Gaimushō Jōyakukyoku. *Gaimushō shitsumu hōkoku,* vol. 2: *Shōwa 14-nen –18-nen.* Tokyo: Kuresu Shuppan, 1995.

———. Jōyakukyoku. *Dai Tōa Kyōeiken dainiji Ōshū taisen kankei jōyakushū.* Tokyo: Nihon Kokusai Kyōkai, 1941.

Gunjishi Gakkai. *Daihon'ei rikugunbu sensō shidōhan kimitsu sensō nisshi.* 2 vols. Tokyo: Kinseisha, 1999.

Kaigunshō. *Tōa Shinchitsujo no kensetu to teikoku kaigun.* Tokyo: Kaigunshō Gunji Fukyūbu, 1939.

Kikakuin and Dai Tōa Kensetsu Shingikai. *Dai Tōa Kensetsu Shingikai kankei shiryō: sōkai, bukai, sokkiroku.* 4 vols. Tokyo: Ryūkei Shosha, 1995.

Kōseishō. *Minzoku jinkō seisaku kenkyū shiryō: senjika ni okeru Kōseishō Kenkyūbu Jinkō Minzokubu shiryō.* 8 vols. Kōseishō Kenkyūbu, undated.

Kunaichō. *Shōwa Tennō jitsuroku,* vols. 27–30 (1940–42). Unpublished manuscripts.

Ministry of Greater East-Asiatic Affairs. *Addresses Before the Assembly of Greater East-Asiatic Nations.* Tokyo: Dai Tōashō, November 1943.
Naikaku Jōhōkyoku. *Shūhō.* Tokyo, 1940–45.
Nihon Keizai Renmeikai. *Kihon kokusaku yōkō.* Tokyo, 1941.
Sanbō Honbu. *Haisen no kiroku.* Tokyo: Hara Shobō, 1967.

Philippines

Foreign Service Institute. *History of the Department of Foreign Affairs, 1898–1991.* Manila: Department of Foreign Affairs, 1991.
Japanese Military Administration, 1942–43. *The Official Journal of the Japanese Military Administration.* 13 vols. Manila, 1942–43.
Philippines Executive Commission. *Official Gazette.* Manila, 1942–43.
Public Relations Office. *Official Directory of the Republic of the Philippines, 1946.* Manila: Bureau of Printing, 1946.
Republic of the Philippines. Ministry of Foreign Affairs. *Ministry of Foreign Affairs Bulletin* 1, nos. 1–3. Manila, 1943–44.
Republic of the Philippines. *Official Gazette.* Manila, 1943–44.

United States

Department of State. *Foreign Relations of the United States: Diplomatic Papers. 1935,* vol. 3: *The Far East.* Washington, DC: Government Printing Office, 1953.
——. *Foreign Relations of the United States Diplomatic Papers. 1940,* vol. 4: *The Far East.* Washington, DC: Government Printing Office, 1955.
——. *Foreign Relations of the United States Diplomatic Papers. 1941.* 5 vols. Washington, DC: Government Printing Office, 1956.
——. *Foreign Relations of the United States Diplomatic Papers. 1942,* vol. 1: *General; the British Commonwealth; the Far East.* Washington, DC: Government Printing Office, 1960.
——. *Foreign Relations of the United States Diplomatic Papers. 1943,* vol. 3: *The British Commonwealth; Eastern Europe; the Far East.* Washington, DC: Government Printing Office, 1963.
——. *Foreign Relations of the United States, Japan: 1931–1941,* 2 vols. Washington, DC: Government Printing Office, 1943.
——. *Peace and War: United States Foreign Policy, 1931–1941.* Washington, DC: Government Printing Office, 1943.
Office of Strategic Services. *The Programs of Japan in the Philippines,* 2 vols. Honolulu, 1944.

Published Primary Sources

Alip, Eufronio M. *Japan-Philippine Relations: Historical, Political, Social, Economic.* Manila: Santo Tomas University Press, 1938.
Amery, Leo. *The Empire at Bay: The Leo Amery Diaries, 1929–1945.* London: Hutchinson, 1988.
Anti-Fascist People's Freedom League. *The New Burma in the New World: From Fascist Bondage to New Democracy.* Rangoon: Nay Win Kyi Press, 1945[?].

Aung San. *The Political Legacy of Aung San*. Edited by Josef Silverstein. Data paper no. 86. Ithaca, NY: Southeast Asia Program, Cornell University, 1972.
——. *The Writings of General Aung San*. Rangoon: Govt. Employees' Co-operative (Education) Pub. Committee, Universities Historical Research Centre, 2000.
Ba Han, Maung. *The Planned State: An Evaluation of the Social and Economic Foundations of the State in the Light of a Comparative Study of the Conditions in the East Asiatic and Western Countries*. Rangoon: Rasika Ranjani, 1947.
Ba Maw. *Breakthrough in Burma: Memoirs of a Revolution, 1939–1946*. New Haven, CT: Yale University Press, 1968.
Ba Swe, U. *The Burmese Revolution*. Rangoon: People's Literature House, 1957.
Ba Than, U. *The Roots of the Revolution: Brief History of the Defence Services of the Union of Burma and the Ideals for Which They Stand*. Rangoon: Director of Information, 1962.
Ba U, U. *My Burma: The Autobiography of a President*. New York: Taplinger, 1959.
Benda, Harry J., James K. Irikura, and Koichi Kishi, eds. *Japanese Military Administration in Indonesia: Selected Documents*. New Haven, CT: Yale University Press, 1965.
Bose, Subhas Chandra. *Netaji: Collected Works*, vols. 8–12. Edited by Sisir Kumar Bose and Sugata Bose. Calcutta: Netaji Research Bureau, 1994–2007.
Buencamino, Felipe. *Memoirs and Diaries of Felipe Buencamino III, 1941–1944*. Makati City, 2003.
Calica, Pio C., ed. *Japan-Philippine Relations*. Manila: Publisher's Bureau, 1936.
Ciano, Galeazzo. *Ciano's Diary, 1939–1943*. London: William Heinemann, 1947.
Cruz, Emigdio (Lt. Col.). "Quezon's Secret Agent," *Philippines Free Press*, February 7 and 14, 1948.
de Asis, Leocadio. *From Bataan to Tokyo: Diary of a Filipino Student in Wartime Japan, 1943–1944*. Lawrence: Center for East Asian Studies, University of Kansas, 1979.
Duran, Pio. *Philippine Independence and the Far Eastern Question*. Manila: University of the Philippines Press, 1935.
——. "Philippine Independence in the Light of Japanese Political Philosophy." *Philippine Review*, October 1943, 31–37.
Fukai Eigo. *Sūmitsuin jūyō giji oboegaki*. Tokyo: Iwanami Shoten, 1953.
Gallego, Manuel V. *The Price of Philippine Independence under the Tydings-McDuffie Act (An Anti-View of the So-Called Independence Law)*. Manila: Barrister's Book Co., 1939.
Garcia, Mauro, ed. *Documents on the Japanese Occupation of the Philippines*. Manila: Philippine Historical Association, 1965.
Glass, Leslie. *The Changing of Kings: Memories of Burma, 1934–1949*. London: P. Owen, 1985.
Grew, Joseph C. *Turbulent Era: A Diplomatic Record of Forty Years, 1904–1945*, vol. 2. Boston: Houghton Mifflin, 1952.
——. *Ten Years in Japan*. New York: Simon & Schuster, 1944.
Guerrero, Leon Ma. *Ang Buong Ulat Ng Buhay Ni Laurel: Ang Mga Huling Araw Ng Imperyong Hapones: Takip-silim Sa Tokyo*. Manila, 1949.
Hla Pe, U. "U Hla Pe's Narrative of the Japanese Occupation of Burma." Data Paper no. 41, Southeast Asia Program, Cornell University, March 1961.
Horinouchi Kensuke. *Nihon gaikōshi*, vol. 21: *Nichi-Doku-I dōmei, Nisso chūritsu jōyaku*. Tokyo: Kajima Heiwa Kenkyūjo, 1971.
Hoshina Zenshirō. *Dai Tōa Sensō hishi: ushinawareta wahei kōsaku: Hoshina Zenshirō kaisōroku*. Tokyo: Hara Shobō, 1975.
Hull, Cordell. *The Memoirs of Cordell Hull*. 2 vols. New York: Macmillan, 1948.

Hussain, Mustapha. *The Memoirs of Mustapha Hussain: Malay Nationalism before UMNO.* Singapore: Singapore University Press, 2005.

Ike, Nobutaka, ed. *Japan's Decision for War: Records of the 1941 Policy Conferences.* Stanford, CA: Stanford University Press, 1967.

International Military Tribunal for the Far East. *The Tokyo War Crimes Trial.* 22 vols. New York: Garland, 1981.

Ishikawa Junkichi. *Kokka sōdōinshi (shiryō hen)*, vol. 8. Tokyo: Kokka Sōdōinshi Kankōkai, 1979.

Itō Takashi, Hirohashi Tadamitsu, and Katashima Norio, eds. *Tōjō naikaku sōridaijin kimitsu kiroku: Tōjō Hideki Taishō genkōroku.* Tokyo: Tokyo Daigaku Shuppankai, 1990.

Iwakuro Hideo. *Shōwa rikugun bōryaku hishi.* Tokyo: Nihon Keizai Shinbun Shuppansha, 2015.

Izumiya Tatsurō. *The Minami Organ.* Rangoon: Translation and Publications Dept., Higher Education Dept., 1981.

Jose, Ricardo T., ed. *World War II and the Japanese Occupation.* Diliman, Quezon City: University of the Philippines Press, 2006.

Kagawa Toyohiko. "Ajia renpō gikai e no daiippo." *Sekai kokka* 7, no. 1 (January 1953): 3–7.

Kajima Morinosuke. *Kajima Morinosuke gaikōron zenshū.* Vols. 3–12. Tokyo: Kajima Kenkyūjo Shuppankai, 1971–73.

Kamikawa Hikomatsu. "Asia Declaration and Atlantic Charter." *Contemporary Japan* 12, no. 12 (December 1943): 1554–62.

———. "Dai Tōa Kaigi to Dai Tōa Kyōdō Sengen." *Kokusaihō gaikō zasshi* 43, no. 1 (January 1944): 72–81.

———. *Kamikawa Hikomatsu zenshū*, vols. 9–10. Tokyo: Keisō Shobō, 1966–72.

Kase Toshikazu. *Journey to the Missouri.* New Haven, CT: Yale University Press, 1950.

———. *Nihon gaikō no shuyakutachi.* Tokyo: Bungei Shunjū, 1974.

———. *Nihon gaikōshi*, vol. 23: *Nichi-Bei kōshō.* Tokyo: Kajima Heiwa Kenkyūjo, 1970.

Kido Kōichi. *Kido Kōichi nikki.* 2 vols. Tokyo: Tokyo Daigaku Shuppankai, 1966.

Kido Nikki Kenkyūkai and Nihon Kindai Shiryō Kenkyūkai. *Iwakuro Hideo shi danwa sokkiroku.* Tokyo: Nihon Kindai Shiryō Shūsho B, 1977.

Kiyosawa Kiyoshi. *Ankoku Nikki.* Tokyo: Hyōronsha, 1995.

———. *Nihon gaikōshi.* 2 vols. Tokyo: Tōyō Keizai Shinpōsha Shuppanbu, 1942.

Kokusai Kenkyūkai. *Dai Tōa Kyōeiken seiji keizai taiseiron.* Tokyo: Dai Tōa Mondai Chōsakai Kenkyū Hōkoku 1, 1943.

———. *Dai Tōa Kyōeiken seiji taisei ni kan suru kenkyū.* Dai Tōa Mondai Chōsakai toku sei 012. Tokyo: Kokusai Kenkyūkai Jimukyoku.

———. *Senji seiji keizai shiryō.* 8 vols. Tokyo: Hara Shobō, 1982–83.

Konoe Fumimaro. "Ei-Bei hon'i no heiwashugi o haisu." *Nihon oyobi Nihonjin*, December 15, 1918, 23–26.

———. *Konoe Fumimaro shuki: heiwa e no doryoku.* Taihoku: Taiwan Geijutsusha, 1947.

———. *Konoe nikki.* Tokyo: Kyōdō Tsūshinsha, 1968.

———. *Ushinawareshi seiji: Konoe Fumimaro kō no shuki.* Tokyo: Asahi Shinbunsha, 1946.

Kyaw Min. *The Burma We Love.* Calcutta: Bharati Bhavan, 1945.

Laurel, José P. *Address of His Excellency José P. Laurel, President of the Philippines on the Occasion of the First Anniversary of the Republic of the Philippines, October 14, 1944.* Manila, 1944.

———. *Assertive Nationalism: A Collection of Articles and Addresses on Local Problems.* Manila: The National Teachers College, 1931.

——. *Forces That Make a Nation Great*. Manila, 1944.

——. *His Excellency José P. Laurel, President of the Second Philippine Republic: Speeches, Messages and Statements, October 14, 1943, to December 19, 1944*. Manila: Lyceum of the Philippines, 1997.

——. *Selected Correspondence of Dr. José P. Laurel*. Manila: Lyceum of the Philippines, 1997.

——. *War Memoirs of Dr. José P. Laurel*. Manila: José P. Laurel Memorial Foundation, 1962.

Lebra-Chapman, Joyce. *Japan's Greater East Asia Co-Prosperity Sphere in World War II: Selected Readings and Documents*. Kuala Lumpur: Oxford University Press, 1975.

Lichaucho, Marcial P. *"Dear Mother Putnam": A Diary of the War in the Philippines*. Manila, 1949.

MacArthur, Douglas. *Reminiscences*. New York: McGraw-Hill, 1964.

Maehara Mitsuo. "Dai Tōa Kyōeiken no riron." In Maehara Mitsuo, Noguchi Hoichirō and Kobayashi Hajime, eds., *Dai Tōa Kyōeiken no minzoku*. Tokyo: Rokumeikan, 1943, 1–99.

Matsumoto Shun'ichi and Andō Yoshirō. *Nihon gaikōshi*, vol. 22: *Nanshin mondai*. Tokyo: Kajima Heiwa Kenkyūjo, 1972.

——. *Nihon gaikōshi*, vol. 25: *Dai Tōa Sensō, shūsen gaikō*. Tokyo: Kajima Heiwa Kenkyūjo, 1972.

Matsushita Masatoshi. "Greater East Asia International Law." *Contemporary Japan* (December 1942): 1712–19.

——. "Greater East Asia International Law II." *Contemporary Japan* (January 1943): 30–37.

Matsuoka Yōsuke. *Doku-I-So no jōsei to waga genjō*. Tokyo: Kokumin Kyōiku Kenkyūkai, 1942.

——. *Kōa no taigyō*. Tokyo: Dai'ichi Kōronsha, 1941.

——. *Matsuoka Gaishō enzetsushū*. Tokyo: Nihon Kokusai Kyōkai, 1941.

——. *Nichi-Doku bōkyō kyōtei no igi*. Tokyo: Dai'ichi Shuppansha, 1937.

——. "Sekai daihenkyoku ni chokumen shite." *Taiheiyō* 3, no. 5 (May 1940): 2–11.

——. *Sūjikukoku ni shi shite*. Tokyo: Katsuragi Shoten, 1941.

Marquardt, Frederic. *Before Bataan and After: A Personalized History of Our Philippine Experiment*. New York: Bobbs-Merrill, 1943.

Maung Maung, U. *Aung San of Burma*. The Hague: Published for Yale University, Southeast Asia Studies by M. Nijhoff, 1962.

——. *To a Soldier Son*. Rangoon: Sarpay Beikman, 1974.

McKelvie, Roy. *The War in Burma*. London: Methuen, 1948.

Mill, Edward W. "The Philippines Prepares for Independence." *Department of State Bulletin*, June 9, 1946. Department of State Publication no. 2558.

Molina, Antonio M. *Dusk and Dawn in the Philippines: Memoirs of a Living Witness of World War II*. Quezon City: New Day, 1996.

Murata Shōzō. *Hitō nikki*. Tokyo: Hara Shobō, 1969.

——. *Murata Shōzō tsuisōroku*. Osaka: Osaka Shōsen, 1959.

Nakao Yūji. *Shōwa Tennō hatsugen kiroku shūsei*. 2 vols. Tokyo, 2003.

Netherlands East Indies. *Ten Years of Japanese Burrowing in the Netherlands East Indies*. New York: Netherlands Information Bureau, 1942.

Nihon Kokusai Kyōkai. *Tōa Shinchitsujo to Nihon gaikō seisaku*. Taiheiyō mondai shiryō 6. Tokyo: Nihon Kokusai Kyōkai Taiheiyō Mondai Chōsabu, 1939.

Nihon no Firipin senryō: intabyū kiroku. Nanpō Gunsei Kankei Shiryō 15. Tokyo: Ryūkei Shosha, 1994.

Nishimura Shinji. *Dai Tōa Kyōeiken*. Tokyo: Hakubunkan, 1942.

Noguchi Hoichirō. "Dai Tōa Kyōeiken no minzoku." In Maehara Mitsuo, Noguchi Hoichirō and Kobayashi Hajime, eds., *Dai Tōa Kyōeiken no minzoku.* Tokyo: Rokumeikan, 1943, 1–211.

Nu, U. *Burma under the Japanese: Pictures and Portraits.* London: Macmillan, 1954.

———. *From Peace to Stability: Translation of Selected Speeches.* Rangoon: Ministry of Information, Government of the Union of Burma, 1951.

———. *U Nu, Saturday's Son.* New Haven, CT: Yale University Press, 1975.

Oatts, Lewis Balfour. *The Jungle in Arms.* London: W. Kimber, 1962.

Ōda Ichirō and Ikeda Chikata. *Nihon gaikōshi,* vol. 24: *Dai Tōa Sensō, senji gaikō.* Tokyo: Kajima Heiwa Kenkyūjo, 1971.

Ōkawa Shūmei. "Dai Tōa Kyōeiken kakuritsu no konpon rinen," in Nanpō Keizai Kondankai, ed., *Nanpō kensetsu no kihon mondai.* Tokyo: Naigai Shobō, 1942, 23–40.

———. *Ōkawa Shūmei nikki.* Tokyo, 1986.

Ōkubo Tatsumasa et al., eds. *Kaigunshō shiryō.* Shōwa shakai keizai shiryō shūsei, vols. 10–23. Tokyo: Daitō Bunka Daigaku Tōyō Kenkyūjo, 1985–96.

———. *Shōwa Kenkyūkai shiryō.* Shōwa shakai keizai shiryō shūsei, vols. 31–37. Tokyo: Daitō Bunka Daigaku Tōyō Kenkyūjo, 2004–10.

Osmeña, Sergio. "Quezon of the Philippines." *Foreign Affairs* 21, no. 2 (January 1943): 289–96.

Porter, Catherine. *Crisis in the Philippines.* New York: A. A. Knopf, 1942.

"Proceedings of the Assembly of Greater East Asiatic Nations Held on November 5 and 6, 1943, at the Diet Building, Tokyo." *Contemporary Japan,* November 1943, 1339–86.

Quezon, Manuel L. *The Good Fight.* New York: Appleton-Century, 1946.

Recto, Claro M. *The Complete Works of Claro M. Recto.* vols. 5–7. Pasay City: Claro M. Recto Memorial Foundation, 1990.

———. *Three Years of Enemy Occupation: The Issue of Political Collaboration in the Philippines.* Manila, 1946.

Romulo, Carlos P. *Crusade in Asia: Philippine Victory.* New York: J. Day, 1955.

———. *I Saw the Fall of the Philippines.* London: George G. Harrap, 1943.

———. *I See the Philippines Rise.* Garden City, NY: Doubleday, 1946.

Rōyama Masamichi. "Sekai keizaishi yori mitaru Dai Tōa Kyōeiken." *Dai Nippon Takushoku Gakkai nenpyō 1: dai tōa seisaku no shomondai.* Tokyo, 1943.

———. *Tōa to sekai: shinchitsujo e no ronsaku.* Tokyo: Kaizōsha, 1941.

Rōyama Masamichi and Takeuchi Tatsuji. *The Philippine Polity: A Japanese View.* Translated by Takeuchi Tatsuji. Edited by Theodore Friend. New Haven, CT: Monograph Series No. 12, Southeast Asia Studies Yale University, 1967.

Saionji Kinkazu. *Saionji Kinkazu kaikoroku.* Tokyo: Ipec, 1991.

Satō Kenryō. *Dai Tōa Sensō kaikoroku.* Tokyo: Tokuma Shoten, 1966.

———. *Satō Kenryō no shōgen.* Tokyo: Fuyō Shobō, 1976.

Sen, Nirmal Chandra. *A Peep into Burma Politics, 1917–1942.* Allahabad: Kitabistan, 1945.

Shigemitsu Mamoru. *Gaikō kaikoroku.* Tokyo: Chūō Kōronsha, 2011.

———. *Shigemitsu Mamoru: Gaikō ikenshoshū,* vols. 2–3. Tokyo: Gendai Shiryō Shuppan, 2007–8.

———. *Shigemitsu Mamoru shuki.* 2 vols. Tokyo: Chūō Kōronsha, 1986–88.

———. *Shōwa no dōran.* 2 vols. Tokyo: Chūō Kōronsha, 1952.

Singh, Balwant. *Independence and Democracy in Burma, 1945–1952: The Turbulent Years.* Ann Arbor: Center for South and Southeast Asian Studies, University of Michigan, 1993.

Slim, William Joseph. *Defeat into Victory.* London: Cassell, 1956.

Sugiyama Hajime. *Sugiyama memo: Daihon'ei seifu renraku kaigi tō hikki.* 2 vols. Tokyo: Hara Shobō, 1967.

Takagi Sōkichi. *Kaigun Taishō Yonai Mitsumasa oboegaki.* Tokyo: Kōjinsha, 1978.

———. *Taiheiyō Sensō to rikukaigun no kōsen.* Tokyo: Keizai Ōraisha, 1967.

Takahashi Kamekichi. *Kyōeiken keizai kensetsuron.* Tokyo: Tōshi Keizaisha, 1942.

Tamura Tokuji. "Dai Tōa Kyōeiken kensetsu shuisho (1)." *Dōshisha ronsō* 77 (November 2, 1942): 1–36.

———. "Dai Tōa Kyōeiken kensetsu shuisho (2)." *Dōshisha ronsō* 78 (January 31, 1943): 100–136.

———. "Dai Tōa Kyōeiken no sosei," *Gaikō jihō* 881 (August 15, 1941): 1–27.

———. "Kokusai shakai to hakkō ichiu no risō." *Gaikō jihō* 908 (October 1, 1942): 1–18.

———. "Kokusaihō no shōrai to Nihon seishin," *Hōritsu jihō* (October 1942): 958–62.

———. *Nihon to shin kokusai shugi: jinsei, shakai, kokka, kokkō, sekinin ni kan suru konpon riron.* Kyoto: Ritsumeikan Shuppanbu, 1939.

———. "Rekishiteki hitsuzensei no kengen to shin kokusaishugi," *Gaikō jihō* 826 (May 1, 1939): 1–32.

———. "Shin kokusaishugi joron," *Gaikō jihō* 820 (February 1, 1939): 1–18.

Tanemura Sakō. *Daihon'ei kimitsu nisshi.* Tokyo: Fuyō Shobō, 1985.

T'ang Leang-li (Tang Liangli). *Fundamentals of National Salvation: A Symposium by Wang Ching-wei and Others.* Shanghai, 1942.

Thein Pe Myint, Thakin. *What Happened in Burma.* Allabahad, 1943.

———. *Wartime Traveler.* In Robert H. Taylor, *Marxism and Resistance in Burma, 1942–1945: Thein Pe Myint's Wartime Traveler.* Southeast Asia Translation Series, vol. 4. Athens: Ohio University Press, 1984.

Tōa Keizai Kondankai. *Dai Tōa keizai kensetsu shingikai sōkai ni okeru tōshin tsuzuri.* Tokyo: Tōa Keizai Kondankai, 1942.

Trager, Frank N., ed. *Burma: Japanese Military Administration, Selected Documents, 1941–1945.* Philadelphia: University of Pennsylvania Press, 1971.

Tun Pe, U. *Sun over Burma.* Rangoon: Rasika Ranjani, 1949.

Ugaki, Kazushige. *Ugaki Kazushige nikki* vol. 1: *Meiji 35-nen 9-gatsu—Shōwa 6-nen 6-gatsu.* Tokyo: Misuzu Shobō, 1968.

van Mook, H. J. *The Netherlands Indies and Japan: Their Relations, 1940–1941.* London: George Allen & Unwin, 1944.

Wa, Theippan Maung. *Wartime in Burma: A Diary, January to June 1942.* Athens: Ohio University Press, 2009.

Wang Jingwei. "Nihon ni yosu: Chūgoku to Tōa." *Chūō kōron* 625 (October 1939): 476–80.

Ward, Robert S. *Asia for the Asiatics? The Techniques of Japanese Occupation.* Chicago, 1945.

Watanabe Wataru. *Watanabe Wataru shōshō gunsei kankeishi shiryō,* 5 vols. Tokyo: Ryūkei Shosha, 1998.

Watari Shūdan Gunseibu. *Gunsei kōhō.* 13 vols. Manila Nichi Nichi Shinbunsha, 1942–43.

Wells, H. G. *Travels of a Republican Radical in Search of Hot Water.* London: Penguin, 1939.

Willoughby, Charles A. (Maj. Gen.). *The Guerrilla Resistance Movement in the Philippines: 1941–1945.* New York: Vantage, 1972.

———. *MacArthur: 1941–1951.* New York: McGraw-Hill, 1954.

Yabe Teiji. "Rōma teikoku, Ei teikoku, Dai Tōa Kyōeiken." *Hōritsu jihō* 15, no. 3 (March 1943): 19–23.

——. *Saikin Nihon gaikōshi*. Tokyo: Nihon Kokusai Kyōkai, 1940.

——. *Shinchitsujo no kenkyū*. Tokyo: Kōbundō Shobō, 1945.

——. *Yabe Teiji nikki: ichō no maki*. Tokyo: Yomiuri Shinbunsha, 1974.

Yatsugi Kazuo. *Shōwa dōran shishi*. 3 vols. Tokyo: Keizai Ōraisha, 1971.

Yomiuri Shinbunsha. *Shōwashi no Tennō*, vols. 8–13. Tokyo: Yomiuri Shinbunsha, 1969–70.

Zhou Fohai. *Zhou Fohai riji*. Vol. 2. Beijing: Zhongguo she hui ke xue chu ban she: Xin hua shu dian Beijing fa xing suo fa xing, 1986.

Secondary Sources in Japanese

Abe Hirozumi. "'Dai Tōa Kyōeiken' kōsō no keisei." *Kitakyūshū Daigaku hōsei ronshū* 16, no. 2 (January 1989): 121–46.

Adachi Hiroaki. "'Dai Tōa Kensetsu Shingikai' to 'keizai kensetu' kōsō: 'Dai Tōa keizai kensetu kihon hōsaku' no keisei o megutte." *Shien* 65, no. 1 (November 2004): 58–79.

——. "'Dai Tōa Kensetsu Shingikai' to 'keizai kensetsu' kōsō no tenkai: 'Dai Tōa sangyō (kōgyō, kōgyō oyobi denryoku) kensetsu kihon hōsaku' o chūshin ni." *Shien* 66, no. 1 (November 2005): 4–27.

——. *"Dai Tōa Kyōeiken" no keizai kōsō*. Tokyo: Yoshikawa Kōbunkan, 2013.

——. "'Dai Tōa Kyōeiken' ron." *Iwanami Kōza Nihon rekishi*, vol. 18, Kin-Gendai 4. Tokyo: Iwanami Shoten, 2015, 141–76.

Akazawa Shirō. "Senchū, sengo bunkaron." *Iwanami Kōza Nihon tsūshi*, vol. 19. Tokyo: Iwanami Shoten, 1993, 281–328.

Aoki Masami. *Senjika no shomin nikki*. Tokyo: Nihon Tosho Sentā, 1987.

Aoki Tokuzō. *Taiheiyō Sensō zenshi*. 3 vols. Tokyo: Gakujutsu Bunken Fukyūkai, 1956.

Arima Manabu. "Dare ni mukatte kataru no ka: 'Dai Tōa Sensō' to shinchitsujo no gensetsu." In Sakai Tetsuya, ed., *"Teikoku" Nihon no gakuchi*, vol. 1: *"Teikoku" hensei no keifu*. Tokyo: Iwanami Shoten, 2006, 252–85.

——. *Teikoku no Shōwa*. Tokyo: Kōdansha, 2010.

ASEAN Sentā. *Ajia ni ikiru Dai Tōa Sensō: genchi dokyumento*. Tokyo: Tantensha, 1988.

Baba Akira. *Nit-Chū kankei to gaisei kikō no kenkyū: Taishō-Shōwaki*. Meiji hyakunenshi sōsho 333. Tokyo: Hara Shobō, 1983.

Duus, Peter. "Shokuminchi naki teikokushugi." *Shisō* 814, April 1992.

Eguchi, Keiichi. *Jūgonen sensō shōshi*. Tokyo: Aoki Shoten, 1991.

Eizawa Kōji. *"Dai Tōa Kyōeiken" no shisō*. Tokyo: Kōdansha Gendai Shinsho, 1995.

Fukada Yūsuke. *Reimei no seiki: Dai Tōa Kaigi to sono shuyakutachi*. Tokyo, 1991.

Fukada Yūsuke and Miura Shumon. "'Shinryaku no gyakusetsu': Dai Tōa Kaigi 1943." *Shokun!* 24, no. 2 (February 1992): 178–93.

Fukutomi Ken'ichi. *Shigemitsu Mamoru: Rengōgun ni mottomo osorerareta otoko*. Tokyo: Kōdansha, 2011.

Furukawa Takahisa. *Tōjō Hideki: Taiheiyō Sensō o hajimeta gunjin saishō*. Tokyo: Yamakawa Shuppansha, 2009.

Gotō Ken'ichi. "Ajia Taiheiyō Sensō to 'Dai Tōa Kyōeiken,' 1935–1945." In Wada Haruki et al., eds., *Higashi Ajia kindai tsūshi*, vol. 6: *Ajia Taiheiyō Sensō to 'Dai Tōa Kyōeiken,' 1935–1945*. Tokyo: Iwanami Kōza, 2011, 1–41.

——. "'Dai Tōa Sensō' no imi." In Yano Tōru, ed., *Tōnan Ajia to Nihon*. Kōza Tōnan Ajiagaku, vol 10. Tokyo: Kōbundō, 1991, 166–83.

——. *Kindai Nihon to Tōnan Ajia: Nanshin no "shōgeki" to "isan."* Tokyo: Iwanami Shoten, 1995.

——. *Nihon senryōki Indonesia kenkyū*. Tokyo: Ryūkei Shosha, 1989.

———. *Shōwaki Nihon to Indonesia*. Tokyo: Keisō Shobō, 1986.

Harada Kumao. *Saionji-kō to seikyoku*, vols. 6–8. Tokyo: Iwanami Shoten, 1952.

Hasegawa Michiko. "Sengo sedai ni totte no Dai Tōa Sensō." *Chūō kōron*, April 1983, 96–111.

Hata Ikuhiko. "Nit-Chū sensō no gunjiteki tenkai (1937-nen – 1941-nen)." In *Taiheiyō Sensō e no michi*, vol. 4: *Nit-Chū sensō 2*. Tokyo: Asahi Shinbunsha, 1963.

Hatano Sumio. "Arita hōsō (1940-nen 6-gatsu) no kokunaiteki bunmyaku to kokusaiteki bunmyaku." In Kindai Gaikōshi Kenkyūkai, ed., *Hendōki no gaikō to gunji*. Tokyo: Hara Shobō, 1987, 137–64.

———. *Bakuryōtachi no Shinjuwan*. Tokyo: Yoshikawa Kōbunkan, 2013.

———. "Nanshin e no senkai: 1940-nen." *Ajia keizai* 26, no. 5 (May 1985): 25–48.

———. "Nihon kaigun to 'nanshin': sono seisaku to riron no shiteki tenkai." In Hajime Shimizu, ed., *Ryō taisenkanki Nihon Tōnan Ajia kankei no shosō*. Tokyo: Institute of Developing Economies, 1986, 207–36.

———. "Senji gaikō to shūsen kōsō." Ph.D. diss., Keio University, 1996.

———. "Shigemitsu Mamoru to Dai Tōa Kyōdō Sengen." *Kokusai seiji* 109, no. 5 (May 1995): 38–53.

———. *Taiheiyō Sensō to Ajia gaikō*. Tokyo: Tokyo Daigaku Shuppankai, 1996.

Hattori Satoshi. *Matsuoka gaikō: Nichi-Bei kankei o meguru kokunai yōin to kokusai kankei*. Tokyo: Chikura Shobō, 2012.

Hattori Takushirō. *Dai Tōa Sensō zenshi*. Tokyo: Hara Shobō, 1965.

Hayashi Fusao. "Dai Tōa Sensō kōteiron." *Chūō kōron* 80, no. 4 (April 1965): 222–44.

———. *Dai Tōa Sensō kōteiron*. Tokyo: Tsubasa Shoin, 1967.

Hikita Yasuyuki, ed. *"Nanpō Kyōeiken": Senji Nihon no Tōnan Ajia keizai shihai*. Tokyo: Taga Shuppan, 1995.

Hori Kazuo. "Higashi Ajia ni okeru shihonshugi no keisei." *Shakai keizai shigaku* 76, no. 3 (November 2010): 27–51.

———. *Higashi Ajia shihonshugi shiron*. 2 vols. Tokyo: Minerva Shobō, 2009.

Hoshino Tsutomu. *Hōdō sarenakatta nyūzu: senji jōhō yoroku*. Tokyo: Keyaki Shuppan, 1994.

Hosoya Chihiro. "Sangoku dōmei to Nisso chūritsu jōyaku (1939–1941)." In *Taiheiyō Sensō e no michi: kaisen gaikōshi*, vol. 5. Tokyo: Asahi Shinbunsha, 1963.

Hosoya Chihiro et al., eds. *Taiheiyō Sensō*. Tokyo: Tokyo Daigaku Shuppankai, 1993.

Hosoya Chihiro, Iriye Akira, Gotō Ken'ichi, and Hatano Sumio, eds. *Taiheiyō Sensō no shūketsu: Ajia Taiheiyō no sengo keisei*. Tokyo: Kashiwa Shobō, 1997.

Ienaga Saburō. *Taiheiyō Sensō*. Tokyo: Iwanami Shoten, 1986.

Ikeda Hiroshi, ed. *Dai Tōa Kyōeiken no bunka kensetsu*. Tokyo: Jinbun Shoin, 2007.

Ikehata, Setsuho. *Nihon senryōka no Firipin*. Tokyo: Iwanami Shoten, 1996.

Itō Takashi. *Nihon no rekishi*, vol. 30: *Jūgonen sensō*. Tokyo: Shōgakukan, 1976.

Karube Tadashi. "'Shigen' to shokuminchi seijigaku: 1940-nendai no Nakamura Akira." In Sakai Tetsuya, ed., *"Teikoku" Nihon no gakuchi*, vol. 1: *"Teikoku" hensei no keifu*. Tokyo: Iwanami Shoten, 2006, 231–49.

Katō Yōko. *Soredemo, Nihonjin wa "sensō" o eranda*. Tokyo: Asahi Shuppansha, 2009.

———. *Sensō made: rekishi o kimeta kōshō to Nihon no shippai*. Tokyo: Asahi Shuppansha, 2016.

———. *Sensō no ronri: Nichi-Ro Sensō kara Taiheiyō Sensō made*. Tokyo: Keisō Shobō, 2007.

Kawanishi Kōsuke. *Dai Tōa Kyōeiken: Teikoku Nihon no Nanpō taiken*. Tokyo: Kōdansha, 2016.

———. "'Dokuritsu' koku to iu 'shikkoku.'" In Wada Haruki et al., eds., *Higashi Ajia kindai tsūshi*, vol. 6: *Ajia Taiheiyō Sensō to "Dai Tōa Kyōeiken," 1935–1945 nen*. Tokyo: Iwanami Kōza, 2011, 347–67.

———. "Gaimushō 'Dai Tōa Kyōeiken' kōsō no keisei katei." *Rekishigaku kenkyū* 798 (February 2005): 1–21.

———. "Gaimushō to Nanyō Kyōkai no renkei ni miru 1930-nendai Nanpō shinshutsu no ichi danmen: 'Nanyō shōgyō jisshūsei seido' no bunseki o chūshin toshite." *Ajia keizai* 44, no. 2 (February 2003): 40–60.

———. "Nichi Bei kōshō to 'Dai Tōa Kyōeiken' mondai: 'Igawa kōshō' o chūshin ni." *Tōhoku Gakuin Daigaku ronshū: rekishi to bunka* 43 (2008): 209–24.

———. *Teikoku Nihon no kakuchō to hōkai: "Dai Tōa Kyōeiken" e no rekishiteki tenkai.* Tokyo: Hōsei Daigaku Shuppankai, 2012.

———. "'Teikoku' to 'dokuritsu': 'Dai Tōa Kyōeiken' ni okeru 'jishu dokuritsu' mondai no kyōshin." *Nenpō Nihon gendaishi* 10 (2005): 47–84.

Keene, Donald. *Nihonjin no sensō: sakka no nikki o yomu.* Tokyo: Bungei Shunjū, 2009.

Kobayashi Hideo. *"Dai Tōa Kyōeiken" no keisei to hōkai.* 2nd ed. Tokyo: Ochanomizu Shobō, 2006.

———. *Dai Tōa Kyōeiken.* Tokyo: Iwanami Shoten, 1988.

Kojima Noboru. *Sanbō.* Tokyo: Bungei Shunjū, 1972.

Kōsaka Masataka. *Saishō Yoshida Shigeru.* Tokyo: Chūō Kōronsha, 1968.

Kurasawa Aiko. *Shigen no sensō: "Dai Tōa Kyōeiken" no jinryū, butsuryū.* Tokyo: Iwanami Shoten, 2012.

———. "Teikokunai no butsuryū: kome to tetsudō." In Kurosawa Aiko et al., *Shihai to bōryoku: Iwanami Kōza Ajia Taiheiyō Sensō,* vol. 7. Tokyo: Iwanami Shoten, 2006, 125–55.

Kurosawa Fumitaka. "Tanaka gaikō to rikugun." *Gunji shigaku* 21, no. 3 (December 1985): 17–34.

Maruyama Shizuo. *Indo Kokumingun: Mō hitotsu no Taiheiyō Sensō.* Tokyo: Iwanami Shoten, 1985.

Matsumoto Toshirō. *Shinryaku to kaihatsu: Nihon shihonshugi to Chūgoku shokuminchika.* Tokyo: Ochanomizu Shobō, 1988.

Matsu'ura Masataka, ed. *Ajiashugi wa nani o kataru no ka? Kioku, kenryoku, kachi.* Kyoto: Minerva Shobō, 2013.

———. *"Dai Tōa Sensō" wa naze okitanoka? Han Ajia shugi no seiji keizashi.* Tokyo: Nagoya Daigaku Shuppankai, 2010.

Minagawa Masaki. "'Dai Tōa Kyōeiken' shisō no ronri to sono kiketsu—seijigakusha Yabe Teiji o chūshin ni." *Jinbun gakuhō* 306 (March 2000): 107–44.

Miwa Kimitada. *Nihon 1945-nen no shiten.* Tokyo: Tokyo Daigaku Shuppankai, 1986.

Miwa Kimitada and Tobe Ryōichi, eds. *Nihon no kiro to Matsuoka gaikō: 1940–41-nen.* Tokyo: Nansōsha, 1994.

Miwa Munehiro. "Nichi-Doku-I sangoku dōmei teiketsu toki ni okeru, Nichi-Doku-I-So kōsō e no gimon: Matsuoka kōsō setsu e no gimon." *Nihon Daigaku Seisan Kōgakubu kenkyū hōkoku* 25, no. 1 (June 1992): 21–39.

Mori Shigeki. "Dainiji Nichi-Ran kaishō o meguru Matsuoka gaishō to Gaimushō: 'kōki binjōteki nanshin' setsu no saikentō." *Rekishigaku kenkyū* 766 (September 2002): 15–32.

———. "Matsuoka gaikō ni okeru tai Bei oyobi tai Ei saku: Nichi-Doku-I dōmei teiketsu zengo no kōsō to tenkai." In *Nihonshi kenkyū* 421 (September 1997): 35–62.

———. "Sūjiku gaikō oyobi nanshin seisaku to kaigun." *Rekishigaku kenkyū,* September 1999, 1–18, 64.

Moriyama Atsushi. "'Nanshin' ron to 'hokushin' ron." In Kurosawa Aiko et al., *Shihai to bōryoku: Iwanami Kōza Ajia Taiheiyō Sensō,* vol. 7. Tokyo: Iwanami Shoten, 2006, 189–218.

———. *Nihon wa naze kaisen ni fumikittaka: "ryōronheiki" to "hikettei".* Tokyo: Shinchōsha, 2012.

Mutō Shūtarō. "Uno Kōzō no kōiki keizairon—sōryokusen taisei to Higashi Ajia." *Nihon kenkyū* 25 (April 2002): 241–62.

Nagaoka Shinjirō. "Nanpō shisaku no gaikōteki tenkai (1937–1941)." In *Taiheiyō Sensō e no michi*, vol. 6: *Nanpō shinshutsu*. Tokyo: Asahi Shinbunsha, 1963.

Nakano Satoshi. *Rekishi keiken toshite no Amerika teikoku: Bei-Hi kankeishi no gunzō*. Tokyo: Iwanami Shoten, 2007.

———. "Shokuminchi tōchi to Nanpō gunsei: teikoku Nihon no kaitai to Tōnan Ajia." In Kurosawa Aiko et al., *Shihai to bōryoku: Iwanami Kōza Ajia Taiheiyō Sensō*, vol. 7. Tokyo: Iwanami Shoten, 2006, 3–28.

Nemoto Kei. *Aun San: Fūin sareta dokuritsu Biruma no yume*. Tokyo: Iwanami Shoten, 1996.

———. *Teikō to kyōryoku no hazama: kindai Birumashi no naka no Igirisu to Nihon*. Tokyo: Iwanami Shoten, 2010.

———. "Tōnan Ajia ni okeru 'tai Nichi kyōryokusha': 'dokuritsu Biruma' Ba Maw seifu no jirei o chūshin ni." In Kurosawa Aiko et al., *Shihai to bōryoku: Iwanami Kōza Ajia Taiheiyō Sensō*, vol. 7. Tokyo: Iwanami Shoten, 2006, 313–44.

Nomura Yoshimasa. *"Dai Tōa Kyōeiken" no keisei katei to sono kōzō: Rikugun no senryōchi gunsei to gunji sakusen no kattō*. Tokyo: Kinseisha, 2016.

Ohno Tōru. "Birumakoku gunshi (sono ichi)." *Tōnan Ajia kenkyū* 8, no. 2 (September 1970): 218–51.

———. "Birumakoku gunshi (sono ni)." *Tōnan Ajia kenkyū* 8, no. 3 (December 1970): 347–77.

———. "Birumakoku gunshi (sono san)." *Tōnan Ajia kenkyū* 8, no. 4 (March 1971): 534–65.

Okabe Makio. "Dai Tōa Kyōeiken to Tōjō seiken." *Rekishi hyōron* 508 (August 1992): 2–11.

Ōta Kōki. "Taisei yokusankai no 'Dai Tōa Kyōeiken' ni kan suru san chōsa hōkoku." *Seiji keizai shigaku* 171 (August 1980): 26–42.

Ōta Tsunezō. *Biruma ni okeru Nihon gunseishi no kenkyū*. Tokyo: Yoshikawa Kōbunkan, 1967.

Saitō Yoshie. *Azamukareta rekishi: Matsuoka to sangoku dōmei no rimen*. Tokyo: Yomiuri Shinbunsha, 1955.

Sakai Naoki and Isomae Jun'ichi, eds. *"Kindai no chōkoku" to Kyōto Gakuha: kindaisei, teikoku, fuhensei*. Tokyo: Kokusai Nihon Bunka Kenkyū Sentā, 2010.

Sakai Saburō. *Shōwa Kenkyūkai: Aru chishikijin shūdan no kiseki*. Tokyo: TBS Britannica, 1979.

Sakai Tetsuya. *Kindai Nihon no kokusai chitsujoron*. Tokyo: Iwanami Shoten, 2007.

———. "'Kokusai kankeiron' no seiritsu: kindai Nihon kenkyū no tachiba kara kangaeru." *Sōbun* (May 2001): 6–10.

———. "Kokusai chitsujoron to kindai Nihon kenkyū." *Rebaiasan* (*Leviathan*) 40 (Spring 2007): 51–56.

———. "Senkanki ni okeru teikoku saihen to kokusaishugi." *Kokusai mondai* 546 (September 2005): 23–34.

———. "Senkanki no kokusai chitsujoron." *Rekishigaku kenkyū* 794 (2004): 84–92.

Shinobu Seizaburō. *"Taiheiyō Sensō" to "mō hitotsu no Taiheiyō Sensō."* Tokyo: Keisō Shobō, 1988.

Shōda Tatsuo. *Jūshintachi no Shōwashi*. 2 vols. Tokyo: Bungei Shunjū, 1981.

Sugimura Masaru. *Nikki ni miru Taiheiyō Sensō*. Tokyo: Bungeisha, 1999.

Suzuki Tamon. *"Shūsen" no seijishi, 1943–1945*. Tokyo: Tokyo Daigaku Shuppankai, 2011.

Tahara Sōichirō and Kobayashi Yoshinori. *Sensōron sōsen*. Tokyo: Bunkasha, 1999.

Taiheiyō Sensō Kenkyūkai, ed. *Taiheiyō Sensō ga yoku wakaru: "Shinjuwan" kara hajimatta Nichi-Bei no shitō no subete*. Tokyo: Nihon Bungeisha, 2009.

Takeshima Yoshinari. *Nihon senryō to Biruma no minzoku undō: Thakin seiryoku no seijiteki jōshō*. Tokyo: Ryūkei Shosha, 2003.

Tanigawa Yoshihiko. "Taiheiyō Sensō to Tōnan Ajia minzoku dokuritsu undō." *Hōsei kenkyū* 53, no. 3 (1987): 361–98.

Taura Masanori. "Shōwa jūnendai Gaimushō kakushinha no jōsei ninshiki to seisaku." *Nihon rekishi* 493 (June 1989): 65–82.

Tobe Ryōichi. *Gaimushō kakushinha: Sekai shinchitsujo no gen'ei*. Tokyo: Chūō Kōron Shinsha, 2010.

———. "Gaimushō kakushinha to shinchitsujo." In Miwa Kimitada and Tobe Ryōichi, eds., *Nihon no kiro to Matsuoka gaikō: 1940–41-nen*. Tokyo: Nansōsha, 1994.

Tsunoda Jun. "Nihon no tai-Bei kaisen (1940-nen – 1941-nen)." In *Taiheiyō Sensō e no michi*, vol. 7: *Nichi-Bei kaisen*. Tokyo: Asahi Shinbunsha, 1963.

Usui Katsumi. "Gaimushō: hito to kikō." In Hosoya Chihiro, Saitō Makoto, Imai Sei'ichi, and Rōyama Michio, eds., *Nichi-Bei kankeishi: kaisen ni itaru 10-nen (1931–41-nen)*, vol. 1: *seifu shunō to gaikō kikan*. Tokyo: Tokyo Daigaku Shuppankai, 1971, 113–40.

———. "Gen'ei o ou mono: Tōa Shinchitsujo." Asahi jānaru, ed. *Shōwashi no shunkan*, vol. 1 (Tokyo, 1966): 285–93.

Wada Haruki et al., eds. *Higashi Ajia kin gendai tsūshi*, vol. 6: *Ajia Taiheiyō Sensō to "Dai Tōa Kyōeiken," 1935–1945 nen*. Tokyo: Iwanami Kōza, 2011.

Watanabe Akio, ed. *Sengo Nihon no taigai seisaku*. Tokyo: Yūhikaku, 1985.

Yamada Munetatsu, Takeuchi Yoshimi, Hashikawa Bunzō, and Tsurumi Shunsuke. "Zadankai: Dai Tōa Kyōeiken no rinen to genjitsu." *Shisō no kagaku* 21 (December 1963): 2–19.

Yamamuro Shin'ichi. *Shisō kadai toshite no Ajia: kijiku, rensa, tōki*. Tokyo: Iwanami Shoten, 2001.

Yasuda Toshie. "Dai Tōa Kaigi to Dai Tōa Kyōdō Sengen o megutte." *Hōgaku kenkyū* 63, no. 2 (February 1990): 369–422.

Yoshida Yutaka. *Shōwa Tennō no shūsenshi*. Iwanami shinsho, No. 257. Tokyo: Iwanami Shoten, 1992.

Yoshii Hiroshi. *Nichi-Doku-I sangoku dōmei to Nichi-Bei kankei: Taiheiyō Sensō mae kokusai kankei no kenkyū*. Tokyo: Nansōsha, 1987.

Yoshimi Yoshiaki. *Kusa no ne fashizumu: Nihon minshū no sensō taiken*. Tokyo: Tokyo Daigaku Shuppankai, 1987.

Yui Masaomi, ed. *Taiheiyō Sensō*. Kindai Nihon no kiseki, vol. 5. Tokyo: Yoshikawa Kōbunkan, 1993.

Secondary Sources in English

Abaya, Hernando J. *Betrayal in the Philippines*. New York: A. A. Wyn, 1946.

Abel, Jessamyn. *The International Minimum: Creativity and Contradiction in Japan's Global Engagement, 1933–1964*. Honolulu: University of Hawaii Press, 2015.

Agoncillo, Teodoro A. *The Burden of Proof: The Vargas-Laurel Collaboration Case*. Manila: University of the Philippines Press, 1984.

———. *The Fateful Years: Japan's Adventure in the Philippines*. 2 vols. Quezon City: R. P. Garcia, 1965.

Agpalo, Remigio E. *José P. Laurel: National Leader, Political Philosopher*. Quezon City: Vera-Reyes, 1992.

Aldrich, Richard J. *The Key to the South: Britain, the United States, and Thailand during the Approach of the Pacific War, 1929–1942*. Kuala Lumpur: Oxford University Press, 1993.

Allen, Louis M. "Fujiwara and Suzuki: Patterns of Asian Liberation." In William H. Newell, ed., *Japan in Asia, 1942–1945*. Singapore: Singapore University Press, 1981, 83–103.

Ampiah, Kweku. "Japan at the Bandung Conference: The Cat Goes to the Mice's Convention." *Japan Forum* 7, no. 1 (1995): 15–24.

Ansprenger, Franz. *The Dissolution of the Colonial Empires*. London: Routledge, 1989.

Asada, Sadao. *From Mahan to Pearl Harbor: The Imperial Japanese Navy and the United States*. Annapolis, MD: Naval Institute Press, 2006.

Aung-Thwin, Maitrii. *The Return of the Galon King: History, Law, and Rebellion in Colonial Burma*. Athens: Ohio University Press, 2011.

Aydin, Cemil. "Japan's Pan-Asianism and the Legitimacy of Imperial World Order, 1931–1945." *Asia-Pacific Journal: Japan Focus*, March 12, 2008, http://www.japanfocus.org/-Cemil-Aydin/2695.

——. *The Politics of Anti-Westernism in Asia: Visions of World Order in Pan-Asian and Pan-Islamic Thought*. New York: Columbia University Press, 2007.

Ba Than, U. *The Roots of the Revolution: Brief History of the Defence Services of the Union of Burma and the Ideals for Which They Stand*. Rangoon: Government Printing Press, 1962.

Barnhart, Michael A. *Japan Prepares for Total War: The Search for Economic Security, 1919–1941*. Ithaca, NY: Cornell University Press, 1988.

Bayly, Christopher, and Tim Harper. *Forgotten Armies: The Fall of British Asia, 1941–1945*. Cambridge, MA: Harvard University Press, 2004.

——. *Forgotten Wars: Freedom and Revolution in Southeast Asia*. Cambridge, MA: Harvard University Press, 2007.

Beasley, W. G. *Japanese Imperialism, 1894–1945*. Oxford: Clarendon, 1987.

Bečka, Jan. *The National Liberation Movement in Burma during the Japanese Occupation Period, 1941–1945*. Dissertationes Orientales, vol. 42. Prague: Oriental Institute in Academia, 1983.

Berger, Gordon M. *Parties Out of Power in Japan, 1931–1941*. Princeton, NJ: Princeton University Press, 1977.

——. "The Three-dimensional Empire: Japanese Attitudes and the New Order in East Asia, 1937–1945." *Japan Interpreter* 12, nos. 3–4 (1979): 355–82.

Bernstein, David. *The Philippine Story*. New York: Farrar, Straus, 1947.

Bingham, June. *U Thant: The Search for Peace*. New York: Knopf, 1966.

Boorman, Howard L. "Wang Ching-Wei: China's Romantic Radical." *Political Science Quarterly* 79, no. 4 (December 1964): 504–25.

Boyd, Carl. "The Berlin-Tokyo Axis and Japanese Military Initiative." *Modern Asian Studies* 15, no. 2 (1981): 311–38.

Boyle, John Hunter. *China and Japan at War, 1937–1945: The Politics of Collaboration*. Stanford, CA: Stanford University Press, 1972.

Brands, H. W. *Bound to Empire: The United States and the Philippines*. New York: Oxford University Press, 1992.

Brooks, Barbara J. "The Japanese Consul in China, 1895–1937." *Sino-Japanese Studies* 10, no. 1 (October 1997): 8–32.

——. *Japan's Imperial Diplomacy: Consuls, Treaty Ports, and War in China, 1895–1938*. Honolulu: University of Hawaii Press, 2000.

Bunker, Gerald E. *The Peace Conspiracy: Wang Ching-wei and the China War, 1937–1941*. Cambridge, MA: Harvard University Press, 1972.

Butow, Robert J. C. *The John Doe Associates: Backdoor Diplomacy for Peace, 1941*. Stanford, CA: Stanford University Press, 1974.

——. *Tojo and the Coming of the War*. Princeton, NJ: Princeton University Press, 1961.

Butwell, Richard. *U Nu of Burma.* Stanford, CA: Stanford University Press, 1963.

Cady, John F. *A History of Modern Burma.* Ithaca, NY: Cornell University Press, 1958.

Callahan, Mary P. *Making Enemies: War and State Building in Burma.* Ithaca, NY: Cornell University Press, 2003.

Chamberlain, M. E. *Decolonization.* 2nd ed. Oxford: Blackwell, 1999.

Charney, Michael W. *A History of Modern Burma.* Cambridge: Cambridge University Press, 2009.

Chaudhry, I. *The Indonesian Struggle.* Lahore: Ferozsons, 1950.

Coble, Parks M. *Facing Japan: Chinese Politics and Japanese Imperialism, 1931–1937.* Harvard East Asian Monographs. Cambridge, MA: Council on East Asian Studies, Harvard University, 1991.

Colbert, Evelyn S. *Southeast Asia in International Politics, 1941–1956.* Ithaca, NY: Cornell University Press, 1977.

Collis, Maurice. *Last and First in Burma (1941–1948).* London: Faber & Faber, 1956.

Connaughton, Richard, John Pimlott, and Duncan Anderson. *The Battle for Manila.* Novato, CA: Presidio, 1995.

Constantino, Renato, and Letizia R. Constantino. *The Philippines: The Continuing Past.* Quezon City: Foundation for Nationalist Studies, 1978.

Cook, Haruko Taya, and Theodore F. Cook. *Japan at War: An Oral History.* New York: New Press, 1993.

Corpuz, O. D. *An Economic History of the Philippines.* Quezon City: University of the Philippines Press, 1997.

Costello, John. *The Pacific War.* New York: Collins, 1981.

Crowley, James B. "Intellectuals as Visionaries of the New Asian Order." In James Morley, ed., *Dilemmas of Growth in Prewar Japan.* Princeton, NJ: Princeton University Press, 1971, 319–73.

——. *Japan's Quest for Autonomy: National Security and Foreign Policy, 1930–1938.* Princeton, NJ: Princeton University Press, 1966.

Curry, Roy Watson. "Woodrow Wilson and Philippine Policy." *Mississippi Valley Historical Review* 41, no. 3 (December 1954): 435–52.

Darwin, John. *Britain and Decolonisation: The Retreat from Empire in the Postwar World.* New York: St. Martin's, 1988.

——. *The End of the British Empire: The Historical Debate.* Oxford: Basil Blackwell, 1991.

Dickinson, Frederick R. *War and National Reinvention: Japan in the Great War, 1914–1919.* Cambridge, MA: Harvard University Asia Center, 1999.

——. *World War I and the Triumph of a New Japan, 1919–1930.* Cambridge: Cambridge University Press, 2013.

Dominguez, Jorge I. "Responses to Occupations by the United States: Caliban's Dilemma." *Pacific Historical Review* 48, no. 4 (November 1979): 591–605.

Dower, John W. *Empire and Aftermath: Yoshida Shigeru and the Japanese Experience, 1878–1954.* Cambridge, MA: Council on East Asian Studies, Harvard University Press, 1979.

——. *Japan in War and Peace: Selected Essays.* New York: New Press, 1993.

——. *War without Mercy: Race and Power in the Pacific War.* New York: Pantheon, 1986.

Drea, Edward J. *In the Service of the Emperor: Essays on the Imperial Japanese Army.* Lincoln: University of Nebraska Press, 1998.

Dreifort, John E. "Japan's Advance into Indochina, 1940: The French Response." *Journal of Southeast Asian Studies* 13, no. 2 (September 1982): 279–95.

Duara, Prasenjit. "The Imperialism of 'Free Nations': Japan, Manchukuo, and the History of the Present." In Ann Stoler, Carole McGranahan, and Peter Perdue, eds., *Imperial Formations* (Santa Fe, NM: SAR Press, 2007), 211–39.

——. *Sovereignty and Authenticity: Manchukuo and the East Asian Modern*. Lanham: Rowman & Littlefield, 2003.

Duus, Peter. "The Greater East Asia Co-Prosperity Sphere: Dream and Reality." *Journal of Northeast Asian History* 5, no. 1 (June 2008): 143–54.

——. "Imperialism without Colonies: The Vision of a Greater East Asia Co-Prosperity Sphere." *Diplomacy and Statecraft* 7, no. 1 (1996): 54–72.

Duus, Peter, Ramon H. Myers, and Mark R. Peattie, eds. *The Japanese Wartime Empire, 1931–1945*. Princeton, NJ: Princeton University Press, 1996.

Elsbree, Willard H. *Japan's Role in Southeast Asian Nationalist Movements, 1940 to 1945*. Cambridge, MA: Harvard University Press, 1953.

Farber, David, and Beth Bailey, eds. *Pearl Harbor and the Attacks of December 8, 1941: A Pacific History*. Manuscript forthcoming at University Press of Kansas.

Feis, Herbert. *The Road to Pearl Harbor*. Princeton, NJ: Princeton University Press, 1950.

Ferguson, Niall. *The War of the World: Twentieth-century Conflict and the Descent of the West*. New York: Penguin, 2006.

Fernandez, Alejandro. *The Philippines and the United States: The Forging of New Relations*. Quezon City, 1977.

Fernandez, Erwin S. *The Diplomat-Scholar: A Biography of Leon Ma. Guerrero*. Singapore: ISEAS—Yusof Ishak Institute, 2017.

Fieldhouse, D. K. *The Colonial Empires: A Comparative Survey from the Eighteenth Century*. New York: Delacorte, 1965.

Flood, Edward Thaddeus. "Japan's Relations with Thailand: 1928–1941." Ph.D. diss., University of Washington, 1967.

Francia, Luis. *A History of the Philippines: From Indios Bravos to Filipinos*. New York: Overlook, 2010.

Frey, Marc, Ronald W. Pruessen, and Tan Tai Yong, eds. *The Transformation of Southeast Asia: International Perspectives on Decolonization*. New York: M. E. Sharpe, 2003.

Friend, Theodore. *Between Two Empires: The Ordeal of the Philippines, 1929–1946*. New Haven, CT: Yale University Press, 1965.

——. *The Blue-Eyed Enemy: Japan against the West in Java and Luzon, 1942–1945*. Princeton, NJ: Princeton University Press, 1988.

Fujitani, Takashi. *Race for Empire: Koreans as Japanese and Japanese as Americans during World War II*. Berkeley: University of California Press, 2013.

Furnivall, J. S. *Colonial Policy and Practice: A Comparative Study of Burma and Netherlands India*. New York: New York University Press, 1956.

Gerwarth, Robert, and Erez Manela, eds. *Empires at War: 1911–1923*. Oxford: Oxford University Press, 2014.

Ginn, John L. *Sugamo Prison, Tokyo: An Account of the Trial and Sentencing of Japanese War Criminals in 1948, by a U.S. Participant*. Jefferson, N.C.: McFarland, 1992.

Goodman, Grant K. *Four Aspects of Philippine-Japanese Relations, 1930–1940*. New Haven, CT: Monograph Series no. 9, Yale University Southeast Asia Studies, 1967.

——. *Imperial Japan and Asia, a Reassessment*. New York: East Asian Institute, Columbia University, 1967.

Gotō Kenichi. *Tensions of Empire: Japan and Southeast Asia in the Colonial and Postcolonial World*. Singapore: Singapore University Press, 2003.

Grimal, Henri. *Decolonization: The British, French, Dutch, and Belgian Empires, 1919–1963*. Boulder, CO: Westview Press, 1978.

Guyot, Dorothy Hess. "The Political Impact of the Japanese Occupation of Burma." Ph.D. diss., Yale University, 1966.

Hack, Karl. *Defence and Decolonisation in Southeast Asia: Britain, Malaya and Singapore, 1941–1968*. Richmond, UK: Curzon, 2001.

Harootunian, H. D. *Overcome by Modernity: History, Culture, and Community in Interwar Japan*. Princeton, NJ: Princeton University Press, 2001.

Haslam, Jonathan. *The Soviet Union and the Threat from the East, 1933–41: Moscow, Tokyo and the Prelude to the Pacific War*. Pittsburgh: University of Pittsburgh Press, 1992.

Hayden, Joseph Ralston. *The Philippines: A Study in National Development*. New York: Macmillan, 1942.

Hofmann, Reto. *The Fascist Effect: Japan and Italy, 1915–1952*. Ithaca, NY: Cornell University Press, 2015.

Holland, R. F. *European Decolonization, 1918–1981: An Introductory Survey*. New York: Macmillan, 1985.

——. "The Imperial Factor in British Strategies from Atlee to Macmillan, 1945–1963." *Journal of Imperial and Commonwealth History* 12, no. 2 (1984): 165–86.

Hopkins, A. G., and P. J. Cain. *British Imperialism: Crisis and Deconstruction, 1914–1990*. London: Longman, 1993.

Hotta, Eri. *Japan 1941: Countdown to Infamy*. New York: Knopf, 2013.

——. *Pan-Asianism and Japan's War, 1931–1945*. New York: Palgrave Macmillan, 2007.

Ienaga, Saburō. *The Pacific War: World War II and the Japanese, 1931–1945*. New York: Pantheon, 1978.

Ikehata, Setsuho. *The Japanese Military Administration in the Philippines and the Tragedy of General Artemio Ricarte*. Singapore: NUS, 1991.

Ikehata, Setsuho, and Lydia N. Yu-Jose, ed. *Philippines-Japan Relations*. Honolulu: University of Hawaii Press, 2003.

Ikehata, Setsuho, and Ricardo Trota Jose, ed. *The Philippines under Japan: Occupation Policy and Reaction*. Quezon City: Ateneo de Manila University Press, 1999.

Iriye, Akira. *After Imperialism: The Search for a New Order in the Far East, 1921–1931*. Cambridge, MA: Harvard University Press, 1965.

——. *The Origins of the Second World War in Asia and the Pacific*. London: Longman, 1987.

——. *Pearl Harbor and the Coming of the Pacific War: A Brief History with Documents and Essays*. Boston: Bedford/St. Martin's, 1999.

——. *Power and Culture: The Japanese-American War, 1941–1945*. Cambridge, MA: Harvard University Press, 1981.

——. "Wartime Japanese Planning for Postwar Asia." In Ian Nish, ed., *Anglo-Japanese Alienation, 1919–1952*. Cambridge: Cambridge University Press, 1982.

Jo, Yung-Hwan. "Japanese Geopolitics and the Greater East Asia Co-Prosperity Sphere." Ph.D. diss., American University, 1964.

Jones, Francis Clifford. *Japan's New Order in East Asia: Its Rise and Fall, 1937–45*. London: Oxford University Press, 1954.

Jose, Ricardo Trota. *Captive Arms: The Constabulary under the Japanese, 1942–1944*. Manila: University of the Philippines, 1997.

——. "Food Production and Food Distribution Programmes in the Philippines during the Japanese Occupation." In Paul H. Kratoska, ed., *Food Supplies and the Japanese Occupation in South-East Asia*. London: Macmillan, 1998, 67–100.

——. *The Philippine Army, 1935–1942*. Manila: Ateneo de Manila University Press, 1992.

Kahin, George McTurnan, ed. *Governments and Politics of Southeast Asia*. Ithaca, NY: Cornell University Press, 1959.

——. *Nationalism and Revolution in Indonesia*. Ithaca, NY: Cornell University Press, 1952.

Kennedy, Paul. *The Rise and Fall of the Great Powers*. New York: Random House, 1987.

Khin Let Ya. *Burma's Fate: Vision and Struggles for Independence, Unity and Development*. Yangon: Zunn Pwint, 2017.

Khin Yi. *The Dobama Movement in Burma (1930–1938)*. Ithaca, NY: Southeast Asia Program Publications, Cornell University Press, 1988.

Kobkua Suwannathat-Pian. *Thailand's Durable Premier: Phibun through Three Decades, 1932–1957*. Kuala Lumpur: Oxford University Press, 1995.

Komatsu, Keiichiro. *Origins of the Pacific War and the Importance of "Magic."* New York: St. Martin's, 1999.

Kratoska, Paul H., ed. *Southeast Asian Minorities in the Wartime Japanese Empire*. London: RoutledgeCurzon, 2002.

Kreager, Philip, Michael Aris, and Aung San Suu Kyi. *Freedom from Fear*. London: Viking, 1991.

Kudō, Akira, Tajima Nobuo, and Erich Pauer, eds., *Japan and Germany: Two Latecomers to the World Stage, 1890–1945*, 3 vols. Folkeston, UK: Global Oriental, 2009.

LaFeber, Walter. *The Clash: U.S.-Japanese Relations throughout History*. New York: W. W. Norton, 1997.

Lawson, Konrad. "Wartime Atrocities and the Politics of Treason in the Ruins of the Japanese Empire, 1937–1953." Ph.D. diss., Harvard University, 2012.

Lebra, Joyce C. *Japanese-Trained Armies in Southeast Asia: Independence and Volunteer Forces in World War II*. New York: Columbia University Press, 1977.

Lee, Loyd E., ed. *World War II in Asia and the Pacific and the War's Aftermath, with General Themes: A Handbook of Literature and Research*. Westport, CT: Greenwood, 1998.

Licuanan, Virginia. *Money in the Bank: The Story of Money and Banking in the Philippines and the PCI Bank Story*. Manila, 1985.

Lindley, M. F. *The Acquisition and Government of Backward Territory in International Law*. New York: Longmans, Green, 1926.

Littlejohn, David. *The Patriotic Traitors: A History of Collaboration in German-Occupied Europe*. London, 1972.

Longmuir, Marilyn. *The Money Trail: Burmese Currencies in Crisis, 1937–1947*. DeKalb: Southeast Center for Southeast Asian Studies, Northern Illinois University, 2002.

Louis, William Roger. *Ends of British Imperialism: The Scramble for Empire, Suez, and Decolonization*. London: Palgrave Macmillan, 2006.

———. *Imperialism at Bay: The United States and the Decolonization of the British Empire, 1941–1945*. New York: Oxford University Press, 1978.

Louis, William Roger, and Ronald Robinson. "The Imperialism of Decolonization." *Journal of Imperial and Commonwealth History* 22, no. 3 (1994): 462–511.

Lu, David J. *Agony of Choice: Matsuoka Yōsuke and the Rise and Fall of the Japanese Empire, 1880–1946*. Lanham, MD: Lexington, 2002.

———. "From the Marco Polo Bridge to Pearl Harbor: Japan's Entry into the Second World War." Ph.D. diss, Columbia University, 1960.

Mahajani, Usha. *Philippine Nationalism: External Challenge and Filipino Response, 1565–1946*. St. Lucia: University of Queensland Press, 1971.

Malay, Armando J. *Occupied Philippines: The Role of Jorge B. Vargas during the Japanese Occupation*. Manila, 1967.

Mañalac, Fernando J. *Manila: Memories of World War II*. Quezon City, 1995.

Manela, Erez. "Imagining Woodrow Wilson in Asia: Dreams of East-West Harmony and the Revolt against Empire in 1919." *American Historical Review* 111, no. 5 (January 2008): 1327–51.

———. *The Wilsonian Moment: Self-Determination and the International Origins of Anticolonial Nationalism*. New York: Oxford University Press, 2007.

Maruyama, Masao. *Thought and Behavior in Modern Japanese Politics*. London: Oxford University Press, 1963.

Matsusaka, Yoshihisa Tak. *The Making of Japanese Manchuria, 1904–1932*. Cambridge, MA: Harvard University Asia Center, 2001.

Mauch, Peter. "A Bolt from the Blue? New Evidence on the Japanese Navy and the Draft Understanding between Japan and the United States, April 1941." *Pacific Historical Review* 78, no. 1 (2009): 55–79.

———. "Dissembling Diplomatist: Admiral Toyoda Teijirō and the Politics of Japanese Security." In Masato Kimura and Toshihiro Minohara, eds., *Tumultuous Decade: Empire, Society, and Diplomacy in 1930s Japan*. Toronto: University of Toronto Press, 2013, 234–57.

———. "Revisiting Nomura's Diplomacy: Ambassador Nomura's Role in the Japanese-American Negotiations, 1941." *Diplomatic History* 28, no. 3 (June 2004): 353–83.

———. *Sailor Diplomat: Nomura Kichisaburō and the Japanese-American War*. Cambridge, MA: Harvard University Asia Center, 2011.

Maung Maung, U. *Burma and General Ne Win*. Bombay: Asia Publishing House, 1969.

———. *Burma in the Family of Nations*. Amsterdam: Djambatan, 1957.

———. *Burmese Nationalist Movements, 1940–1948*. Edinburgh: Kiscadale, 1989.

———. *From Sangha to Laity: Nationalist Movements of Burma, 1920–1940*. New Delhi: Manohar, 1980.

———. *A Trial in Burma: The Assassination of Aung San*. The Hague: M. Nijhoff, 1962.

Mazower, Mark. *Governing the World: The History of an Idea*. New York: Penguin, 2012.

———. *Hitler's Empire: How the Nazis Ruled Europe*. New York: Penguin, 2008.

McCoy, Alfred W. "'Politics by Other Means': World War II in the Western Visayas, Philippines." In Alfred W. McCoy, ed., *Southeast Asia under Japanese Occupation*. New Haven, CT: Monograph Series No. 22, Southeast Asia Studies, Yale University, 1980, 191–245.

———. *Southeast Asia under Japanese Occupation*. New Haven, CT: Monograph Series No. 22, Southeast Asia Studies, Yale University, 1980.

McIntyre, W. David. *British Decolonization, 1946–1997*. New York: St. Martin's, 1998.

Mercado, Stephen C. *The Shadow Warriors of Nakano: A History of the Imperial Japanese Army's Elite Intelligence School*. Washington, DC: Brassey's, 2002.

Meskill, Johanna Menzel. *Nazi Germany and Imperial Japan: The Hollow Diplomatic Alliance*. London: Aldine Transaction, 2012.

Metzler, Mark. *Lever of Empire: The International Gold Standard and the Crisis of Liberalism in Prewar Japan*. Berkeley: University of California Press, 2006.

Meyer, Milton. *A Diplomatic History of the Philippine Republic*. Honolulu: University of Hawaii Press, 1965.

Mimura, Janis. "Japan's New Order and Greater East Asia Co-Prosperity Sphere: Planning for Empire." *Asia-Pacific Journal*, vol. 9, issue 49, no. 3 (December 5, 2011), https://apjjf.org/2011/9/49/Janis-Mimura/3657/article.html.

———. *Planning for Empire: Reform Bureaucrats and the Japanese Wartime State*. Ithaca, NY: Cornell University Press, 2011.

Moore, Aaron Stephen. *Constructing East Asia: Technology, Ideology, and Empire in Japan's Wartime Era, 1931–1945*. Stanford, CA: Stanford University Press, 2013.

Mori, Takato. *"Co-Prosperity" or "Commonwealth"? Japan, Britain, and Burma, 1940–1945*. Berlin: VDM, 2009.

Morley, James William, ed., *Japan's Road to the Pacific War: The Final Confrontation*. New York: Columbia University Press, 1994.

Moscotti, Albert D. *British Policy and the Nationalist Movement in Burma, 1917–1937*. Honolulu: University Press of Hawaii, 1974.

Myers, Ramon H., and Mark R. Peattie, eds. *The Japanese Colonial Empire, 1895–1945*. Princeton, NJ: Princeton University Press, 1984.

Najita, Tetsuo, and Harry D. Harootunian. "Japan's Revolt against the West." In Bob Tadashi Wakabayashi, ed., *Modern Japanese Thought*. Cambridge: Cambridge University Press, 1998, 207–72.

Nakano Satoshi. "Appeasement and Coercion." In Ikehata Setsuho and Ricardo Trota Jose, eds., *The Philippines Under Japan: Occupation Policy and Reaction*. Manila: Ateneo de Manila University Press, 1999, 21–58.

Naw, Angelene. *Aung San and the Struggle for Burmese Independence*. Chiang Mai: Silkworm, 2001.

Nemoto, Kei, ed. *Reconsidering the Japanese Military Occupation in Burma*. Tokyo: Research Institute for Languages and Cultures of Asia and Africa, Tokyo University of Foreign Studies, 2007.

Okamoto, Shumpei, and Dorothy Borg. *Pearl Harbor as History: Japanese-American Relations, 1931–1941*. Studies of the East Asian Institute. New York: Columbia University Press, 1973.

Ooi Keat Gin. *The Japanese Occupation of Borneo, 1941–1945*. New York: Routledge, 2011.

Orbach, Danny. *Curse on This Country: The Rebellious Army of Imperial Japan*. Ithaca, NY: Cornell University Press, 2017.

Paxton, Robert O. *Vichy France: Old Guard and New Order, 1940–1944*. New York: Columbia University Press, 1972.

Peattie, Mark R. *A Historian Looks at the Pacific War*. Stanford, CA: Hoover Institution, 1995.

——. *Ishiwara Kanji and Japan's Confrontation with the West*. Princeton, NJ: Princeton University Press, 1975.

Peschanski, Denis. *Collaboration and Resistance: Images of Life in Vichy France, 1940–44*. New York: Harry N. Abrams, 2000.

Pluvier, Jan M. *South-East Asia from Colonialism to Independence*. Kuala Lumpur: Oxford University Press, 1974.

Pomeroy, William. *The Philippines: Colonialism, Collaboration, and Resistance*. New York: International Publishers, 1992.

Pye, Maung Maung. *Burma in the Crucible*. Rangoon: Khittaya, 1951.

Pyle, Kenneth B. *Japan Rising: The Resurgence of Japanese Power and Purpose*. New York: PublicAffairs, 2007.

Quirino, Carlos. *The Laurel Story: The Life and Times of Dr. José P. Laurel, President of the Second Republic of the Philippines*. Manila: José P. Laurel Memorial Corporation, 1992.

Rajshekhar. *Myanmar's Nationalist Movement (1906–1948) and India*. New Delhi: South Asian Publishers, 2006.

Reynolds, Craig J., ed. *National Identity and Its Defenders: Thailand, 1939–1989*. Clayton, Victoria: Monash Papers on Southeast Asia No. 25, 1991.

Reynolds, E. Bruce. "Aftermath of Alliance: The Wartime Legacy in Thailand-Japanese Relations." *Journal of Southeast Asian Studies* 21, no. 2 (March 1990): 66–87.

——. *Thailand and Japan's Southern Advance, 1940–1945*. New York: St. Martin's, 1994.

Rice, Richard. "Economic Mobilization in Japan: Business, Bureaucracy, and Military in Conflict." *Journal of Asian Studies* 38, no. 4 (August 1979): 689–706.

Saaler, Sven, and J. Victor Koschmann, eds. *Pan-Asianism in Modern Japanese History: Colonialism, Regionalism, and Borders*. London: Routledge, 2007.

Schiltz, Michael. *The Money Doctors from Japan: Finance, Imperialism, and the Building of the Yen Bloc, 1895–1937*. Cambridge, MA: Harvard University Asia Center, 2012.

Scott, James C. *Weapons of the Weak: Everyday Forms of Peasant Resistance*. New Haven, CT: Yale University Press, 1985.

Seekins, Donald M. *Burma and Japan since 1940: From "Co-Prosperity" to "Quiet Dialogue."* Copenhagen: NIAS Press, 2007.
Selth, Andrew. *The Anti-Fascist Resistance in Burma, 1942–1945: The Racial Dimension.* Nathan, Queensland: James Cook University of North Queensland, 1983.
Silverstein, Josef. *Southeast Asia in World War II: Four Essays.* Monograph Series no. 7. New Haven, CT: Southeast Asia Studies, Yale University, 1966.
Singh, Balwant. *Independence and Democracy in Burma, 1945–1952: The Turbulent Years.* Michigan Papers on South and Southeast Asia, No. 40. Ann Arbor: University of Michigan Press, 1993.
Singh, Kumar. *Freedom Struggle in Burma.* New Delhi: Commonwealth, 1989.
Smith, Martin J. *Burma: Insurgency and the Politics of Ethnicity.* 2nd ed. London: Zed, 1999.
Smith, Tony. *The End of the European Empire: Decolonization after World War II.* Lexington, MA: D.C. Heath, 1975.
Spector, Ronald H. *Eagle against the Sun: The American War with Japan.* New York: Free Press, 1985.
———. *In the Ruins of Empire: The Japanese Surrender and the Battle for Postwar Asia.* New York: Random House, 2007.
Springhall, John. *Decolonization since 1945: The Collapse of European Overseas Empires.* New York: Palgrave Macmillan, 2001.
Stanley, Peter. *Reappraising an Empire: New Perspectives on Philippine-American History.* Cambridge, MA: Committee on American-East Asian Relations and Council on East Asian Studies, Harvard University, 1984.
Steinberg, David Joel. "José P. Laurel: A 'Collaborator' Misunderstood." *Journal of Asian Studies* 24, no. 4 (August 1965): 651–65.
———. *Philippine Collaboration in World War II.* Manila: University of Michigan Press, 1967.
Stephan, John J. *Hawaii under the Rising Sun: Japan's Plans for Conquest after Pearl Harbor.* Honolulu: University of Hawaii Press, 1984.
Storry, Richard. *The Double Patriots: A Study of Japanese Nationalism.* London: Chatto & Windus, 1957.
Sturtevant, David R. *Popular Uprisings in the Philippines, 1840–1940.* Ithaca, NY: Cornell University Press, 1976.
Tarling, Nicholas. *The Fall of Imperial Britain in South-East Asia.* Singapore: Oxford University Press, 1993.
———. *Imperialism in Southeast Asia: "A fleeting, passing phase."* London: Routledge, 2001.
———. *Southeast Asia and the Great Powers.* New York: Routledge, 2010.
———. *A Sudden Rampage: The Japanese Occupation of Southeast Asia, 1941–1945.* Honolulu: University of Hawaii Press, 2001.
Tarling, Nicholas, ed. *The Cambridge History of Southeast Asia.* Cambridge: Cambridge University Press, 1992.
Taylor, Robert H. *Marxism and Resistance in Burma, 1942–1945.* Athens: Ohio University Press, 1984.
———. "Politics in Late Colonial Burma: The Case of U Saw." *Modern Asian Studies* 10, no. 2 (1976): 161–93.
———. *The State in Burma.* Honolulu: University of Hawaii Press, 1987.
Thant Myint-U. *The Making of Modern Burma.* Cambridge: Cambridge University Press, 2001.
Tin, Maung Maung Than. *State Dominance in Myanmar: The Political Economy of Industrialization.* Singapore: ISEAS, 2007.
Toland, John. *The Rising Sun: The Decline and Fall of the Japanese Empire.* New York: Random House, 1970.

Tucker, Shelby. *Burma: The Curse of Independence*. London: Pluto, 2001.

Vellut, J. L. "Foreign Relations of the Second Republic of the Philippines, 1943–1945." *Journal of Southeast Asian History* 5, no. 1 (March 1964): 126–42.

von Albertini, Rudolf. *Decolonization: The Administration and Future of the Colonies, 1919–1960*. New York: Africana, 1982.

Walinsky, Louis Joseph. *Economic Development in Burma, 1951–1960*. New York, 1962.

Watanabe Tsuneo, ed. *From Marco Polo Bridge to Pearl Harbor: Who Was Responsible?* Tokyo: Yomiuri Shinbunsha, 2006.

West, Rebecca. *The Meaning of Treason*. 3rd ed. London: Virago, 1982.

Willoughby, Charles. *MacArthur, 1941–1951*. New York: McGraw-Hill, 1954.

Yamamuro Shin'ichi. *Manchuria under Japanese Dominion*. Translated by Joshua A. Fogel. Philadelphia: University of Pennsylvania Press, 2006.

Yellen, Jeremy A. "Into the Tiger's Den: Japan and the Tripartite Pact, 1940." *Journal of Contemporary History* 51, no. 3 (2016): 555–76.

——. "The Specter of Revolution: Reconsidering Japan's Decision to Surrender." *The International History Review* 35, no. 1 (March 2013): 205–26.

——. "Wartime Wilsonianism and the Crisis of Empire, 1941–1943." *Modern Asian Studies* (2018), 1–34. doi:10.1017/S0026749x17000397.

Yellen, Jeremy, and Andrew Campana. "Japan, Pearl Harbor, and the Poetry of December 8th." *Asia-Pacific Journal: Japan Focus*, vol. 14, issue 24, no. 2 (December 2016), https://apjjf.org/2016/24/Yellen.html.

Yoon, Won Z. *Japan's Scheme for the Liberation of Burma: The Role of the Minami Kikan and the "Thirty Comrades."* Papers in International Studies. Southeast Asia Series No. 27. Athens: Ohio University, Center for International Studies, 1973.

——. "Military Expediency: A Determining Factor in the Japanese Policy Regarding Burmese Independence." *Journal of Southeast Asian Studies* 9, no. 2 (1978): 248–67.

Young, Louise. *Japan's Total Empire: Manchuria and the Culture of Wartime Imperialism*. Berkeley: University of California Press, 1998.

Yu-Jose, Lydia N. *Japan Views the Philippines*. Manila: Ateneo de Manila University Press, 1992.

Index

Page numbers in italics indicate figures; those with a *t* indicate tables.

Manchurian Incident (1931), 9, 15–16, 34, 145
Marco Polo Bridge Incident (1937), 1–3, 16–17. *See also* China Incident
Masuda Takashi, 176
Matsumiya Jun, 54, 56
Matsumoto Shigeharu, 59
Matsuoka Yōsuke, 4, 17, 58–71, 205, 208, 209, 228n28; on American character, 61; on Co-Prosperity Sphere, 36–37, 43, 46–52, 58, 62; fall of, 47, 68–70; on *hakkō ichiu*, 95; on New Order in East Asia, 35–38; on Pearl Harbor attack, 45; on Philippine independence, 111; Roosevelt and, 66, 68; on Soviet influence in China, 49, 63; sphere-of-influence diplomacy of, 46–68; Stalin and, 50, 66–70, 67; on Thai border dispute, 51–55, 58; on Tripartite Pact, 26–27, 37–42, 45, 68–69; U.S. diplomacy of, 68
Matsushita Masatoshi, 78, 82, 86
Matsu'ura Masataka, 10
Mauch, Peter, 59
Maung Gyi, J. A., 114
Maung Maung, 179, 198, 203
Maung Pu, 127
Mazower, Mark, 100
McCoy, Alfred W., 139
McKinley, William, 107
Meiji Constitution, 74
Meiji emperor, 17
Midway, battle of (1942), 143
migrant workers, 108
Miki Kiyoshi, 17
Minami Masuyo (Suzuki Keiji), 129–36
Molotov, Vyacheslav, 66, 68
Mongolia, 65–67; central bank of, 201; Soviet attacks in, 28, 49
Monroe Doctrine, 62, 63, 70; "Asian," 71, 109–10, 145
Mori Shigeki, 41, 59, 226n1
Morley-Minto reforms (1909), 6–7, 112
Mountbatten, Louis, 200
Murata Shōzō, 183, 186, 190, 191
Mussolini, Benito, 28, 114
Mutō Akira, 4–5, 34, 79
Mya, Thakin, 136t, 171, 174t, 195–96, 216
Mya, U (Pyawbwe), 174t
Myanmar. *See* Burma

Nagano Osami, 72, 205
Nagata Kiyoshi, 82
Nakano Satoshi, 212
national defense sphere (*kokubōken*), 4–5

National Policy Research Association (*Kokusaku Kenyūkai*), 81–88, 158, 162, 233n33, 233n37, 233n40, 234n45
Naval Intelligence Division (*Kaigunshō Chōsaka*), 78, 81–82, 85–88, 95–96, 100
Nazi Germany, 2–3, 5, 28–29, 74, 100; Anti-Comintern Pact, 27; Asian interests of, 26, 29–34, 37–38, 42–43; Denmark and, 20–21, 28; economic policies of, 88; Japanese views of, 12, 28–35, 144; Matsuoka's trip to, 64–66; "patriotic collaboration" with, 20–21; Soviet nonaggression pact with, 28; USSR invasion by, 45, 65–66, 69; Yugoslavia invasion by, 66. *See also* Tripartite Pact
Ne Win, 179, 203
Netherlands, Nazi conquest of, 28–29, 50
Netherlands Indies: Co-Prosperity Sphere and, 57, 80–81, 85, 155, 193; Dutch trade with, 18t; economic talks with Japan, 55–58; German view of, 42; Japanese interests in, 19, 29–35, 38, 48, 57–58, 70; Konoe on, 56; Ribbentrop on, 224n17
New China Policy, 145–46
New Greater East Asia Policy, 145
New Zealand, 49, 55–56, 64, 220n12
Nogi Harumichi, 101–2
Nomonhan Incident (1939), 28, 49
Nomura Kichisaburō, 59–60, 62–64, 69, 74, 75, 229n54
Nu, Thakin, U, 125, 129, 134; as foreign minister, 174t, 176, 194–95, 199, 203

Obata Nobuyoshi, 79
Ogikubo conference (1940), 34–35
Oikawa Koshirō, 41–42, 52
Ōiwa Makoto, 83
Ōkawa Shūmei, 29, 158, 209
Ōkawachi Denshichi, 175
Okinawa, 212
Ōkōchi Kazuo, 82
Open Door policy, 17, 58–59, 74, 77–78, 96–98, 161, 231n88
Operation Barbarossa, 65–66
Operation Sea Lion, 39
Ōshima Hiroshi, 27, 38
Osias, Camilo, 194
Osmeña, Sergio, 107–9, 117, 123–24
Osmeña, Sergio, Jr., 201
Ōtani Kōzui, 79
Ōtsuki Akira, 98–99
Ott, Eugen, 34, 37–38, 41
Ottoman empire, 12

Studies of the Weatherhead East Asian Institute
Columbia University

Selected Titles

(Complete list at: http://weai.columbia.edu/publications/studies-weai/)

The Invention of Madness: State, Society, and the Insane in Modern China, by Emily Baum. University of Chicago Press, 2018.

Idly Scribbling Rhymers: Poetry, Print, and Community in Nineteenth Century Japan, by Robert Tuck. Columbia University Press, 2018.

Forging the Golden Urn: The Qing Empire and the Politics of Reincarnation in Tibet, by Max Oidtmann. Columbia University Press, 2018.

The Battle for Fortune: State-Led Development, Personhood, and Power among Tibetans in China, by Charlene Makley. Cornell University Press, 2018.

Aesthetic Life: Beauty and Art in Modern Japan, by Miya Mizuta Lippit. Harvard University Asia Center, 2018.

China's War on Smuggling: Law, Economic Life, and the Making of the Modern State, 1842–1965, by Philip Thai. Columbia University Press, 2018.

Where the Party Rules: The Rank and File of China's Communist State, by Daniel Koss. Cambridge University Press, 2018.

Resurrecting Nagasaki: Reconstruction and the Formation of Atomic Narratives, by Chad R. Diehl. Cornell University Press, 2018.

China's Philological Turn: Scholars, Textualism, and the Dao in the Eighteenth Century, by Ori Sela. Columbia University Press, 2018.

Making Time: Astronomical Time Measurement in Tokugawa Japan, by Yulia Frumer. University of Chicago Press, 2018.

Mobilizing Without the Masses: Control and Contention in China, by Diana Fu. Cambridge University Press, 2018.

Post-Fascist Japan: Political Culture in Kamakura after the Second World War, by Laura Hein. Bloomsbury, 2018.

China's Conservative Revolution: The Quest for a New Order, 1927–1949, by Brian Tsui. Cambridge University Press, 2018.

Promiscuous Media: Film and Visual Culture in Imperial Japan, 1926–1945, by Hikari Hori. Cornell University Press, 2018.

The End of Japanese Cinema: Industrial Genres, National Times, and Media Ecologies, by Alexander Zahlten. Duke University Press, 2017.

The Chinese Typewriter: A History, by Thomas S. Mullaney. The MIT Press, 2017.

Forgotten Disease: Illnesses Transformed in Chinese Medicine, by Hilary A. Smith. Stanford University Press, 2017.

Borrowing Together: Microfinance and Cultivating Social Ties, by Becky Yang Hsu. Cambridge University Press, 2017.

Food of Sinful Demons: Meat, Vegetarianism, and the Limits of Buddhism in Tibet, by Geoffrey Barstow. Columbia University Press, 2017.

Youth For Nation: Culture and Protest in Cold War South Korea, by Charles R. Kim. University of Hawaii Press, 2017.

Socialist Cosmopolitanism: The Chinese Literary Universe, 1945–1965, by Nicolai Volland. Columbia University Press, 2017.

Yokohama and the Silk Trade: How Eastern Japan Became the Primary Economic Region of Japan, 1843–1893, by Yasuhiro Makimura. Lexington Books, 2017.

The Social Life of Inkstones: Artisans and Scholars in Early Qing China, by Dorothy Ko. University of Washington Press, 2017.

Darwin, Dharma, and the Divine: Evolutionary Theory and Religion in Modern Japan, by G. Clinton Godart. University of Hawaii Press, 2017.

Dictators and Their Secret Police: Coercive Institutions and State Violence, by Sheena Chestnut Greitens. Cambridge University Press, 2016.

The Cultural Revolution on Trial: Mao and the Gang of Four, by Alexander C. Cook. Cambridge University Press, 2016.

Inheritance of Loss: China, Japan, and the Political Economy of Redemption After Empire, by Yukiko Koga. University of Chicago Press, 2016.

Homecomings: The Belated Return of Japan's Lost Soldiers, by Yoshikuni Igarashi. Columbia University Press, 2016.

Samurai to Soldier: Remaking Military Service in Nineteenth-Century Japan, by D. Colin Jaundrill. Cornell University Press, 2016.

The Red Guard Generation and Political Activism in China, by Guobin Yang. Columbia University Press, 2016.

Accidental Activists: Victim Movements and Government Accountability in Japan and South Korea, by Celeste L. Arrington. Cornell University Press, 2016.

Ming China and Vietnam: Negotiating Borders in Early Modern Asia, by Kathlene Baldanza. Cambridge University Press, 2016.

Ethnic Conflict and Protest in Tibet and Xinjiang: Unrest in China's West, coedited by Ben Hillman and Gray Tuttle. Columbia University Press, 2016.

One Hundred Million Philosophers: Science of Thought and the Culture of Democracy in Postwar Japan, by Adam Bronson. University of Hawaii Press, 2016.

Conflict and Commerce in Maritime East Asia: The Zheng Family and the Shaping of the Modern World, c. 1620–1720, by Xing Hang. Cambridge University Press, 2016.

Chinese Law in Imperial Eyes: Sovereignty, Justice, and Transcultural Politics, by Li Chen. Columbia University Press, 2016.

Imperial Genus: The Formation and Limits of the Human in Modern Korea and Japan, by Travis Workman. University of California Press, 2015.

Yasukuni Shrine: History, Memory, and Japan's Unending Postwar, by Akiko Takenaka. University of Hawaii Press, 2015.

The Age of Irreverence: A New History of Laughter in China, by Christopher Rea. University of California Press, 2015.

The Knowledge of Nature and the Nature of Knowledge in Early Modern Japan, by Federico Marcon. University of Chicago Press, 2015.

The Fascist Effect: Japan and Italy, 1915–1952, by Reto Hofmann. Cornell University Press, 2015.

Empires of Coal: Fueling China's Entry into the Modern World Order, 1860–1920, by Shellen Xiao Wu. Stanford University Press, 2015.

CPSIA information can be obtained
at www.ICGtesting.com
Printed in the USA
LVHW040652240123
737769LV00003B/354